# Finding Forgotten Cities

**HEDGEHOG AND FOX**

HISTORY AND POLITICS SERIES

*"The fox knows many things,*
*but the hedgehog knows one big thing"*

**General Editor**

**RUDRANGSHU MUKHERJEE**

# Finding Forgotten Cities

## How the Indus Civilization was Discovered

Nayanjot Lahiri

*New Centenary Edition 2024*

*and*

*Published by*
PERMANENT BLACK
'Himalayana', Mall Road, Ranikhet Cantt,
Ranikhet 263645
perblack@gmail.com
*and*

*Distributed by*
ORIENT BLACKSWAN PRIVATE LTD
Bangalore Bhopal Bhubaneshwar Chandigarh Chennai
Ernakulam Guwahati Hyderabad Jaipur Kolkata
Lucknow Mumbai New Delhi Patna
www.orientblackswan.com



ISBN 978-81-7824-691-8

This Centenary Edition contains a new Afterword
written for the centenary of the discovery of the
Indus Civilisation

Printed and bound by Manipal Technologies Limited, Manipal

To

The Archaeological Survey of India

which made possible this story

# CONTENTS

# ILLUSTRATIONS

# PREFACE AND ACKNOWLEDGEMENTS

THIRTY-FIVE YEARS AGO, AS A GIRL OF TEN, I read Mulk Raj Anand's tale of the Indus world, *A Day in the Life of Maya of Mohenjo-Daro*. I still remember that story's beguiling beginning ('It was five thousand years ago . . .'), and how much I identified with little Maya as she coveted her mother's tree-bark to redden her lips, or went on real and imaginary wanderings in the marketplace at Mohenjodaro, or to distant Harappa whose great granary she longed to see, also sharing her love of *khichri* (a gruel of rice and lentils) and her distaste of milk with *malai* (cream) floating on top of it. As far as I can remember, my curiosity about things Harappan began with that book.

The present book did not begin as a narrative about the Indus civilization. It began as an accident of research in 1996, when I came by some unknown documents connected with the archaeologist John Marshall while rummaging through references at the India Office Library in London. In those documents—as in my book now—Marshall is among the central characters, the man who, in 1924, finally pieced together the puzzle of the Indus cities and famously announced that a new civilization, 'the Civilization of the Indus Valley', had been discovered.

This remarkable figure remains something of an enigma to me even now. He never wrote his autobiography, nor has anyone cared to write his biography. Some of the shadows surrounding him I chased away that summer, when I found papers pertaining to his selection, in 1901, at the age of twenty-five, to the post of director general of the Archaeological Survey of India. That led me to begin scanning the files of the Archaeological Survey of India in the National Archives at New Delhi, specially those pertaining to Marshall's long archaeological career in India (1902–34). As far as I could see, the story that was beginning to form in my mind's eye related quite widely to Marshall's life and times in those decades: I thought then that my book might grow into an intellectual biography within the 'life and times' genre.

But the story has turned out drastically different from the way it was originally conceived. This has to do with some other chance events. Around 1999 Charles Lewis, whom I knew as the author of *Delhi's Historic Villages*, guided me to the head office of the Archaeological Survey of India at Delhi. In the spirit of a true fellow researcher, he went to a great deal of trouble to seek me out in order to draw my attention to archival material that I was not aware of. A treasure trove of files on all kinds of subjects and sites lay buried in the file room of the Survey.

Over the next couple of years, it was in those bundles of reports, letters, and notes that I came upon much that was unknown about the Survey and its officers. Through those documents I learnt about the little-known saga of how the Indus civilization was unearthed, and so resolved to write about it. Contrary to what I had thought, clues about an unknown yet distinctive culture had long been available from what would later become famous Indus cities. I came face to face with the ideas and work of men like Daya Ram Sahni and Rakhaldas Banerji as they grappled with what was emerging from the ruins of those ancient cities. The names of lesser known individuals, whose lives were linked in some way or other to the discovery of the civilization, also emerged from the files to which they had been relegated.

The most important of them, and the one who made the deepest impression on me, was the Italian explorer Luigi Pio Tessitori, whose unpublished work, and perhaps foreign nationality (i.e. neither British nor Indian), made him the least known. I had seen Tessitori's archaeological collection at the Ganga Golden Jubilee Museum at Bikaner in the winter of 2000. Unknown to me, my interest in Tessitori was communicated to an elderly Kanpur businessman, Sri Hazarimal Banthia. I later learnt that, ever since his youth, when he had found Tessitori's forgotten tomb in Bikaner and renovated it, Sri Banthia had done much to keep the memory of Tessitori alive. He firmly put me on the trail of that linguist-turned-archaeologist, which brought me back to Bikaner. In the Rajasthan State Archives at Bikaner I found precious correspondence pertaining to Tessitori's Rajasthan sojourns. I now realized that there was a great deal of material on Tessitori and his all-too-fleeting affair with an Indus city buried in the Bikaner region.

If my research for this book has been shaped by the unexpected intervention of enormously ungrudging individuals, it could never have been told in its present strongly narrative form without the advice of my editor and old friend Rukun Advani. To tell this story in a way that would make it accessible not only to fellow archaeologists but to a wider public was an idea which Rukun nurtured in me. Having earlier written primarily for academics, I first found this an enormously difficult task. I must emphasize that there is still a lot of detail in the present book which will centrally interest specialists; but if—as I hope—I have managed to write an archivally researched work in a form attractive to general readers of history, some of the credit should go to my editor. I am truly grateful to him for his belief that I could craft a tale in which a clear narrative path could cut through the jungle of archaeological fact and detail.

There are also a few other individuals that I should mention: Ramachandra Guha, who first pointed out the possibility of focusing my work around the main characters who figure in it; Stephen Shennan, who constantly reminded me through long years spent writing the book that this was as important as any academic paper I'd written or any volume I'd edited. His words certainly helped keep me on track; Dilip Chakrabarti, who read some of the chapters with a discerning eye and offered valuable comments and criticism; Upinder Singh, who constantly provided me with insights from her own considerable work on the history of Indian archaeology in the nineteenth century; Gregory Possehl, an enthusiastic supporter of my research which has carried forward his own work on the discovery of Indus cities; Malise Wagstaff, who provided me with a number of photographs and insights into Marshall's personality; Sanjukta Datta, who read the entire manuscript and reassured me about its contents; Raymond and Bridget Allchin of the Ancient India and Iran Trust (Cambridge), who invited me to take up their Charles Wallace visiting fellowship over February–May 1996, which marked the beginning of the research culminating in this book; and Carla Sinopoli, whose invitation to me in 2004 to be the Hughes Endowment Visiting Scholar at the Center for South Asian Studies at the University of Michigan, Ann Arbor, allowed me to make final revisions to the manuscript. My deepest gratitude to all of them.

The staff at the institutions where I researched have been enormously helpful, especially at the Oriental and India Office Collection of the British Library (London), the National Archives of India (New Delhi), and the Rajasthan State Archives (Bikaner). I would like specially to thank the Archaeological Survey of India for giving me access to its archives. The daily assistance of Mohar Singh, who unfailingly brought out file bundles, was invaluable. I read those files in the photographic library of the Survey. I will always remember how the staff there treated me as one of their own, tracking down unpublished photographs in the albums of the library and plying me with innumerable cups of tea. For the preparation of the manuscript I am very indebted to Kalika Prasad Shukla and Rajiv Rekhi, who have constantly helped with endless photocopying and printing.

My friends and family have shared in the angst and adventure involved in writing this book. The indulgence of Shivani and Ashwath Khanna has been as important as their wonderful hospitality. I also remember the warm enthusiasm of my late brother-in-law, Amar, and it will always be my regret that he passed away before this book was finished.

Finally, there are the two marvellous men in my life, my husband Kishore and our son Karan. From that wet morning in the summer of 1997 when the three of us spent long hours trudging across the hills of Chota Simla, locating the houses where Marshall had resided, our shared experiences have animated my research in so many different ways. A heartfelt thanks to them for having cheerfully lived with all the characters in this book, and for their constant love and support, which has been the single most important source of stability in my life.

## ACKNOWLEDGEMENTS AND SOURCES FOR THE ILLUSTRATIONS

The illustrations are reproduced with thanks by permission (where required) from the following sources: Plates 2, 4, and 5 are from Cunningham (1875); Plates 3, 16, 17, 18, 22, 23, 24, 28 to 32, and 34 to 46 are from the albums and files of the Archaeological Survey of India (the albums are in the Survey's headquarters at New Delhi); Plate 11 is from the *Annual Report of the Archaeological Survey of India 1904–5*; Plate 12 is from Mockler (1877); Plates 7 to 9 and Plates 13 to 15 were given to me by Malise Wagstaff; Plate 10 is based on illustrations in *Indian Archaeology* (1899–1905) in the Oriental and India Office

Collection (OIOC, London) and from a file in the National Archives of India (New Delhi); Plates 19 to 21 and 25 and 26 are from the Ganga Golden Jubilee Museum (Bikaner); Plate 27 is from Banthia (1989); Plate 33 is from Rupendra Kumar Chattopadhyay, Head, Department of Archaeology, University of Calcutta; Plate 6 is from Gregory Possehl. I am also grateful to Dr Possehl for drawing my attention to a photograph of Madho Sarup Vats (Plate 38), which I subsequently traced in the Archaeological Survey of India; Plates 47 and 48 are from Gadd and Smith (1924).

'Not often has it been given to archaeologists, as it was given to Schliemann at Tiryns and Mycenae, or to Stein in the desert of Turkestan, to light upon the remains of a long forgotten civilization. It looks, however, at this moment, as if we were on the threshold of such a discovery in the plains of the Indus.'—**John Marshall, announcing the discovery of the Indus civilization in 1924**

'The beauty of the dilapidated buildings and of articles discovered speaks volumes for ancient India and proves the truth of the historical statement, that in ancient times India was a great and powerful country and was not helpless as she is now. In view of this evidence of India's ancient greatness, Britain should treat her, if not as a superior, at least as an equal and respect her and set her free immediately.'—**Extract from the *Larkana Gazette* on Mohenjodaro in 1926**

# 1

# A RUINED CITY IN PUNJAB AND ITS FIRST EXPLORERS

THE EARLIEST KNOWN REFERENCE TO THE LEGEND of Harappa by an archaeologist is contained, almost certainly, in an 1872–3 report of Alexander Cunningham, the man who first excavated what is now recognized as one of the largest cities of the Indus civilization. After speaking to local inhabitants while he dug around its enormous ruins, Cunningham wrote:

> The people refer the ruin of Harapa to the wickedness of a Raja named Har Pal, or Hara Pala, who was in the habit of claiming the sovereign's rights at every bridal. At last, in the exercise of this royal privilege, he committed incest with a near relative. Some say his own sister, others his wife's sister, or his wife's sister's daughter. The girl prayed to heaven for vengeance, and then the city of Harapa was instantly destroyed. Some say it was by fire, and some by an earthquake; others say that an invader suddenly appeared, and that the city was taken by storm, and the Raja killed. The period of its destruction is vaguely said to be 1,200 or 1,300 years ago. If the date is correct, the city of Harapa must have been destroyed by Muhammad-bin-Kasim in AD 713, just 1,260 years ago. I am inclined to put some faith in this belief of the people, as they tell the same story of all the ruined cities in the plains of Panjab, as if they had

> all suffered at the same time from some common catastrophe, such as the overwhelming invasion of the Arabs under Muhammad-bin-Kasim.[1]

Cunningham had dug out a story. Fifty years later, one of his fellow countrymen announced that a whole civilization had been unearthed. The man who made that announcement and who presided over that monumental discovery was an archaeologist called John Marshall. In 1924, the year in which he made his astonishing announcement—a proclamation on the same scale as those made by Heinrich Schliemann (who discovered the treasures of Troy) and Arthur Evans (who unearthed the Minoan civilization)—this is what Indians, and the world at large, learnt from Marshall:

> Indians have always been justly proud of their age-old civilisation, and believing that this civilisation was as ancient as any in Asia, they have long been hoping that Archaeology would discover definite monumental evidence to justify their belief. This hope has now been fulfilled . . . The fact that at Harappa and at Mohenjo-daro where the present materials were discovered, seals of Sumerian type were found to be near the surface in city sites covering very large areas widely separated and remote from the sea, with clear evidence of multiple strata lower down, proves that, whatever the history of the Sumerians in Mesopotamia may have been, a culture closely akin to theirs must have been widely disseminated in the Valley of the Indus, and have undergone a development reaching back incalculable centuries on Indian soil.[2]

These early accounts by Cunningham and Marshall, when read together, remind us of the dramatic transformation that had taken place over the half century that separated them. This transformation had largely to do with the ways in which the remnants of ancient Harappa were visualized. Cunningham's account of the legend—of a medieval destruction through incest and conquest—had given way in 1924 to the knowledge of a third millennium BC world that extended from the upper tract of the Indus river in Punjab, where Harappa stood, to Mohenjodaro on the plains of Sindh. A ruin described in 1875 as evidence of a trail of destruction left by an Arab invader was now a symbol and proof of the antiquity of India's culture, going back many millennia, to an age that lay far beyond the time of Muhammad bin Qasim.

Ever since Marshall's pronouncement on 'the civilization of the Indus valley' (now more commonly described as either the 'Indus' or the 'Harappan' civilization), this city culture has become an integral part of popular perceptions of India's ancient past. Images of burnt brick drains, of a 'great bath', of a 'priest-king' and a 'dancing girl'—these are now as familiar to Indians as the names of the cities that housed them all—Harappa and Mohenjodaro. Yet the fascinating and complex story of how these and other Indus cities came to be discovered, and of how the great mystery of their antiquity came to be solved, is less well known, for it has never really been well pieced together from start to finish.

Our story begins in the nineteenth century, when Harappa was first visited, and its ancient ruins described by British explorers and archaeologists. The interest in Harappa among such early enthusiasts of antiquity is not a mere coincidence, for it was in the nineteenth century that a systematic curiosity over the material remains of India's past first came to be articulated. This quest, and the publication of accounts and findings resulting from it, is connected in turn with the needs of British rule in India—the empire's need to gather and order information on its newly acquired territories. Self-conscious and planned surveys, in the course of which numerous sites and antiquities were documented, became part of the East India Company's very system of governance under Governor General Wellesley (1798–1805) and gained in momentum after the capture by Wellesley of Tipu Sultan's island fortress of Sri Rangapattana in 1799, which practically completed the British conquest of India south of the Vindhya mountains. It was this political situation, then, that enabled all kinds of explorers to extensively survey Indian monuments and places of archaeological importance, and to treat them as a sort of happy hunting ground for their collections of antiquities.

British military men with an intellectual interest in Indian antiquities were particularly indefatigable. The best known among them, Colonel Colin Mackenzie (1753–1821), is said to have visited nearly every place of archaeological interest south of the Krishna river.[3] As he moved from place to place, he made detailed illustrations of what he saw. He saw a great deal. With the help of his Indian assistants, he produced about 2000 drawings of antiquities and copied around 8000 inscriptions. Another army antiquarian, James Tod (1782–1835), political agent to the Western Rajput states, enthusiastically documented the antiquities of Rajasthan. His parallel passion was collecting old coins, and in the rainy season he 'had a person employed at Mathura and other old cities to collect all that were brought to light by the action of the water while tearing up old foundations, and levelling mouldering walls.'[4] In this manner, he tells us, he accumulated about 20,000 coins of various denominations from there. Many such collections found their way to Great Britain, and such memorabilia even included sections and parts of old buildings. A prayer niche at the Elgin Museum in north-east Scotland is one such disembodied structural element. Originally it formed the central mihrab in the Sona mosque at Firozpur in Gaur (Bengal). It was 'removed'—a standard colonial euphemism for 'purloined'—from there by an official of the Bengal Civil Service and subsequently presented to the museum of his native place.[5] The modern study of the material paraphernalia of

India's past was accompanied by the acquisition and removal of vast numbers of such antiquities, most often by the very men who wished to understand and document them.

Around the time that Tod's account of his coin-collecting activity was penned, military men with antiquarian leanings similar to his had begun training their sights on the Punjab plains. In 1829, that considerable expanse was traversed by one Charles Masson, and, very soon after, in 1831, by the explorer Alexander Burnes.

Masson claimed to be an American from Kentucky, but he was actually a man named James Lewis; evidently, he had changed his identity because, having enlisted in his late twenties as a private soldier in the Bengal European Artillery, he seems to have deserted his regiment around 1826, while it was stationed in the vicinity of Bharatpur (or perhaps Delhi).[6] Along with a fellow deserter, Richard Potter, he made his way across the tracts of Bikaner and Bahawalpur into the Punjab, travelling as far north as Dera Ismail Khan. Somewhere along the way both travellers assumed American identities—this being common practice among deserters from the Company's regiments. While Potter became John Brown and entered the Sikh military service, Lewis took on the name Charles Masson. And this was the name he used when he wrote about his travels across north-west India and Afghanistan.[7]

Like Masson, Alexander Burnes was an officer in the Company's army. Fluent in Persian, Arabic, and Hindi, Burnes is well known for his assiduous geographical traverses which, in many cases, were journeys over which he gathered crucial political information for his British masters. For instance, his clandestine survey of the river Indus, when he sailed from Kutch to Sindh and then up till Lahore, was conducted under the pretence of escorting a gift of English dray horses from the British sovereign William IV to Maharaja Ranjit Singh.[8]

Other explorers had of course also travelled across this part of

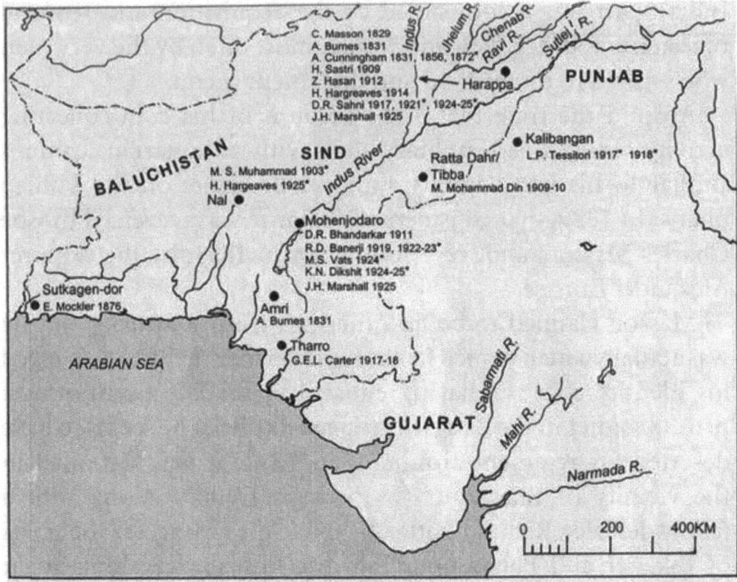


Fig. 1. Northwest India with sites mentioned in the book and those who visited/excavated them (*marks out the years when they were excavated)

north-west India, but among these early intrepid wanderers Masson and Burnes are distinguished for making it their business to visit scores of old mounds and record their observations on them. Created out of the accumulated debris generated by human activity over the same approximate spots over hundreds and sometimes thousands of years, such mounds ranged from minor elevations to high hills and ridges that could dominate the surrounding landscape. They were especially common in large parts of North India, where villages were frequently located on top of them. The resulting juxtaposition, of the dead past and the living present, was thus described by one insightful observer:

> The mass of thickly crowded dwellings, moulded from the earth of the plain in which they stand, and threaded by narrow and tortuous

> lanes, is indeed, strangely suggestive of an ant-heap. The suggestion is enhanced by the fact that the village is usually superimposed on a mound, which the casual traveller is apt to suppose to be some natural hillock, chosen by the villagers for the purpose of better drainage or defence. In this, however, he is usually mistaken, for the mound is commonly composed from the debris of dwellings, many of which had crumbled to dust before the art of writing was known or history had dawned. When wolves still howled where Notre Dame and St. Paul now stand, and the very name of Athens or Rome were unheard of, there lived and toiled on these sites the remote ancestors of the villagers who tenant them today. It is with some feeling of reverence then [that] the western parvenu should view these populous mounds and know himself to be but a creature of yesterday.[9]

As this description makes evident, entombed in mounds were the physical traces of bygone cultures; and British explorers, as we saw, were especially interested in the coins and sculpture that emerged from such ruins. More abundant was old pottery—broken, used, or discarded—measurable in tonnes rather than kilos; chewed animal bones, charred seeds, remains of structures, especially those of brick; clay figurines, terracotta beads, necklaces of gold and rare stones, and even the skeletons of a few ancient inhabitants—some of whom were buried wearing such exotic ornaments. All these emerged from the debris and were documented.

The interest that Masson and Burnes showed in old mounds and their paraphernalia of riches is important to this story most of all because both came specifically to Harappa. When these two explorers visited it, Harappa was a small, unremarkable town in the territory of Maharaja Ranjit Singh of Punjab (Fig. 2). The name of this town was later deployed as a shorthand to denote the third millennium BC city whose ruins were recognized by the mounds that dominate its vicinity.[10] In fact the city culture

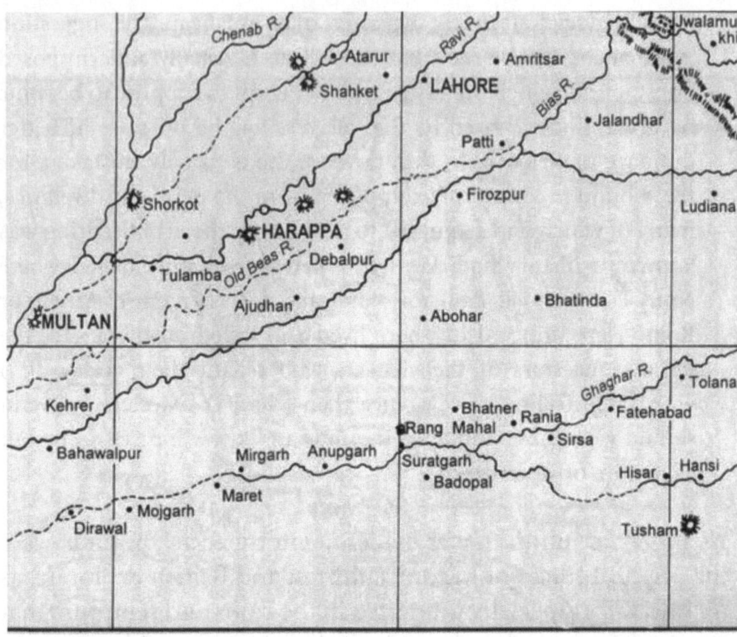


Fig. 2. Punjab showing positions of Lahore (from where Charles Masson came) and Tulamba (where Alexander Burnes disembarked) in relation to Harappa

of the Indus, more broadly, is today known after this very same Harappa—as the sobriquet 'Harappan civilization' suggests.

Situated between the Ravi and an old river bed of the Beas, the general area where Harappa stood was known as the Bari *doab*. 'Doab' means, literally, 'two waters', and this nomenclature we owe to Akbar, who coined it by combining the letters of the names of the two rivers between which it lay. Unlike many other parts of the Punjab, this tract, the Bari doab, was not agriculturally prosperous. Large parts of it resembled salt-encrusted desert wastes. The immediate landscape around Harappa, though, was marked by two very prominent features—an old river course, and a stretch of ancient ruins, the latter being those that were marked by massive mounds. The dead river was the main branch of the old Ravi river, and its presence suggested that the land was earlier more fertile than it appeared to be in the nineteenth century. By then, the peripatetic Ravi had moved twelve kilometres or so towards the north of Harappa. The ruins too were 'dead' in the sense that their antiquity was unknown to the nineteenth-century inhabitants who lived in their vicinity. With a circuit of more than two miles, these ruins appeared as a continuous line of colossal mounds, in places as high as sixty feet. They were all over the place, towards the north, south, and west of the settlement, and thickly littered the area with potsherds and old bricks.

Travellers passing through the Bari doab naturally came to Harappa. They came and saw the ancient ruins there—ruins of monumental proportion which could be seen on the horizon for miles. Masson and Burnes remarked at length upon them. In fact, of the various places that Charles Masson passed over his journey on horseback—from Lahore in Punjab to Larkana in Sindh—Harappa is one of the few to be vividly described.

> A long march preceded our arrival at Haripah, through jangal of the closest description. East of the village was an abundance of luxuriant grass, where, along with many others, I went to allow my nag to graze. When I joined the camp I found it in front of the village and ruinous brick castle. Behind us was a large circular mound, or eminence, and to the west was an irregular rocky height, crowned with remains of buildings, fragments of walls with niches, after the eastern manner. The latter elevation was undoubtedly a natural object; the former being of earth only, was obviously, an artificial one. I examined the remains on the height, and found two circular perforated stones, affirmed to have been used as bangles, or arm rings, by a faqir of renown. He has also credit for having subsisted on earth, and other unusual substances, and his depraved appetite is instanced in testimony of his sanctity. The entire neighbourhood is embellished with numerous pipal trees, some of them in the last

> stages of lingering existence; bespeaking a great antiquity, when we remember their longevity. The walls and towers of the castle are remarkably high, though, from having being long deserted, they exhibit in some parts the ravages of time and decay. Between our camp and it extended a deep trench, now overgrown with grass and plant. Tradition affirms the existence of a city, so considerable that it extended to Chicha Watni, thirteen cosses distant, and that it was destroyed by the lust and crimes of the sovereign.[11]

This is the first modern description of Harappa's mounds (Fig. 16). Though Masson erred in imagining that the western elevation (now known as Mound AB) was a natural rock formation, its majestic expanse is conveyed by his description. The summit of one of those mounds seems to have had enough room for setting up a camp which could house the entire group that Masson was travelling with, along with their horses. Masson's group was a fairly large one: a party of Sikhs on their way to Multan that he had joined a little beyond Lahore. Their retinue included a band of musicians, falconers, *munshis* (clerks), 150 horsemen, and even a brahmin for performing the daily rites.

It is a tendency among travellers to exaggerate the dimensions of what they see, and often to provide what they have seen with a respectable antiquity. Masson did not stint in this respect when he beheld such impressive ruins. He sought their history out from the texts which were then regarded as the foremost source of Western knowledge about India—classical accounts of the invasion of north-west India by Alexander the Great.

In the spring of 326 BC Alexander, with his Macedonian army, crossed the Indus river near Attock. Sacrifices to Greek gods, games, and horse races had been performed on the river bank. Invaders before Alexander had also approached India from the north-west, but unique to Alexander was the fact that he headed the greatest expedition ever to have embarked from Greek shores. The expedition combined a series of highly successful conquests. Alexander managed to reach as far as the present border between India and Pakistan in the north-west. The carnage and killing by his army was on an enormous scale.[12] The expeditions were recorded in vivid detail by Alexander's companions. In the case of his Indian campaign, one such companion was Nearchus, whom Alexander had put in command of a fleet which explored the coast between the Indus and the Persian Gulf. Another was Onesicritus, who piloted the royal vessel down the Indus. A third companion, Aristobulus, was constantly with Alexander as he made his way through north-west India. Books deriving from the accounts of these men were subsequently written, and what is most striking about this literature is the journalistic detail with which all kinds of information is flavoured.[13]

There are, for example, descriptions of the oxen and sheep that Ambhi, the king of Taxila (near present-day Rawalpindi) fed to Alexander's troops, along with an account of the manner in which he aided Alexander in the latter's famous fight against the prince of the Paurava house, Porus, who ruled on the other side of the Hydaspes (or Jhelum river).[14] There are also details about the movements of Alexander's army as it sailed down rivers and marched across the plains of Punjab. Masson was familiar with these classical accounts. Possibly, he also knew that many of the place-names mentioned in them had not been satisfactorily located on the ground. So, as he travelled around, he tried to identify the mounds that he encountered with the strongholds that Alexander was supposed to have stormed. In fact, he convinced himself, almost before he started, that all he saw must be traced back to Alexander the Great.

In relation to Harappa, Masson believed that its remnants strongly resembled the fortress of Sangala, inhabited by the Kathi tribe, described in an account by the historian Arrian:

> It was impossible to survey the scene before us, and to look upon the ground on which we stood, without perceiving that every condition of Arrian's Sangala was here fulfilled—the brick fortress, with a lake,

> or rather a swamp, at the north-eastern angle; the mound, protected by a triple row of chariots and defended by the Kathi before they suffered themselves to be shut up within their walls; and the trench between the mud and fortress, by which the circumvallation of the place was completed and whence engines were directed against it. The data of Arrian are very minute, and can scarcely be misapplied to Haripah the position of which almost perfectly coincides with what, from inference, we must assign to Sangala . . .[15]

A Greek historian and philosopher (*c.* AD 96–180), Arrian had written about the life of Alexander in his work entitled *Annabasis of Alexander*, basing his account on information derived from the writings of Alexander's fellow traveller Aristobulus. Arrian's description of Sangala occurs during his account of the city under siege, Alexander having encircled it:

> he advanced on the third day to where the Cathaeans and other neighbouring tribes had assembled and marshalled themselves in front of the city upon a hill which was not precipitous on all sides . . . During that day Alexander and his infantry encamped around the city, as much of it, at least, as his phalanx could surround; for he could not with his camp completely encircle the wall, so extensive was it. Opposite the part unenclosed by his camp, near which also was a lake, he posted the cavalry, placing them all round the lake, which he discovered to be shallow . . .[16]

Arrian's account is straightforward enough. There is nothing within it which specifically compels a comparison with the ruins of Harappa. Perceptions of the historical record, however, vary with the preconceptions that are brought to bear on it, and Masson's mind was rather too full of Alexander the Great. Some months before he came to Harappa, Masson had traversed this tract in order to reach Lahore. From the time that he entered it, he tells us, he was filled with a sense that he 'was now in a part of the country which, there can be no doubt, had been the scene of some of Alexander the Great's exploits',[17] and this image remained with him as he made his way back and forth through it. The town of Tulamba, he tells us, was the ancient capital of the Malli tribe mentioned by Alexander's historians. An old mud fortress near it was what remained of the ancient stronghold held by the brahmins during a fateful siege against Alexander's troops. Even certain pastoralists who lived between Chicha Watni and Multan were visualized as descendants of Alexander's most determined opponents, the Kathi tribe! Masson had, consciously or subconsciously, positioned Alexander's exploits as a pair of spectacles through which all that he surveyed, including the monumental site of Harappa, was understood and (mis)classified.

Harappa's own inhabitants, like their *firanghi* (European) visitor, viewed the mounds as relics of an ancient city. Like Masson, they perceived the traces of ancient occupation in their vicinity around a grid of ideas and beliefs which was familiar to them. However, in place of the legend of the Greek conqueror, their filtering spectacles were a local tradition. This tradition affirmed that the city had been destroyed because of the 'lusts and crimes of its sovereign'.[18] This sovereign was that king named Hara Pala—the very man mentioned by Cunningham—who had committed incest with a very close family member. We do not know her precise kinship with Hara Pala, but her prayers for revenge apparently resulted in the destruction of the city.[19] Ancient artefacts that frequently emerged from Harappa's ruins were explained in relation to another local notable, a 'faqir of renown'.[20] At the tomb of this putative faqir, which graced one of the mounds, lay large circular perforated stones which are today recognized as a specific class of chalcolithic ringstones of Indus vintage (Fig. 17, p. 142). However, they were described by the residents sometimes as the bangles of the faqir, on other occasions as his thumb-rings.[21]

This is not an unusual practice; in fact ethnographic literature is filled with references which suggest the wide prevalence of such practices. People look at the past in the way they like to, in ways that make sense to them. To this day, it is common to see elements of the archaeological past being redefined in India's villages. An instance in point is the district of Faridabad, which borders New Delhi on the south, where miraculous cures continue to be expected from archaeological iron slag—the waste that was left behind by past inhabitants when they converted ore into metal—from a mound in the settlement of Sihi. Similarly, a domed, medieval structure at a village called Dhauj is still considered locally to be the overnight handiwork of a djinn, a class of spirits regarded as belonging to the malevolent dead.[22] Such structural ruins and artefacts are not built or produced during the lifetime of the communities presently living in their vicinity, nor is their antiquity precisely understood by them. Yet these communities manage to assimilate these relics of a very ancient past and their remains within a more recent universe of local myths and beliefs—a tradition of assimilation that goes back at least to the nineteenth century, and probably well beyond.

But coming back to Harappa: we might well wonder how such large stones could be seen to serve as the bangles of a mere mortal, however renowned. The answer can be learnt from the observations of Alexander Burnes, the traveller-explorer who visited it a few years later, in the summer of 1831. The fabulous faqir, according to the legend, was of giant proportions. Burnes tells us that his tomb was eighteen feet in length, 'the assigned, but fabulous, stature of the deceased.'[23] Actually, later accounts suggest that the tomb was much larger—46 feet long and 3 ½ feet broad. The same account tells us that the faqir buried there was a Naogaza, or Naogaja, called Nur Shah.[24] *Gaja* (or *gaza*) is a measure of distance and the word Naogaja means 'nine yards', which was presumably the height of the buried saint.

This myth of the Naogaza Pir was actually not limited to Harappa. It was a widespread legend in nineteenth-century Punjab and this appellation 'Naogaza' was applied to several tombs varying in length from 10 feet to 50 feet. These were believed to be the tombs of the original Muslim invaders of India who fell 'in action against the Hindus'.[25] Every one of them was venerated as a Ghazi or Shahid (warrior and martyr for the faith) and all were supposed to be gigantic. Moreover, Harappa was not the only place where curious stones graced these tombs. Towards the west, at Multan, at the tomb of Pir Gor Sultan, there was kept a large circular stone with a hole in the middle, called a *manka*. This too was believed to be a martyr's thumb-ring. Naogaza tombs existed at many spots that had an ancient association. Near the old mounds of Sabz-pind, close to the Jhelum, there were as many as six such tombs, measuring between 29 and 38 feet in length. Close to Harappa, on an ancient mound at Bavanni or Barvani, there existed the tomb of a nine-yarder named Muhammad Shah. Again, hundreds of kilometres to the east, a Naogaza grave adorned Topra near the Yamuna river, a place where the Mauryan emperor Ashoka had inscribed his message of *dhamma*.[26]

Alexander Burnes commented on other aspects of Harappa as well. There are details about the size of its brick ruins and the location of the highest mound: 'The remains are extensive, and the place, which had been built of brick, is about three miles in circumference. There is a ruined citadel on the river side of the town.'[27] He further noted that the remains provided building material for the modern settlement there, which was resulting in their widespread dispersal: 'Harappa is in perfect chaos and has not an entire building; the bricks have been removed to build a small place of the old name near by.'[28] Incidentally, before coming to Harappa, Burnes had also visited Amri in the province of Sindh and seems to have been the first European to have documented a mound of some magnitude there: 'a mound of earth, some 40 feet high, which the traditions of the country point out as the halting-place of a king, who ordered the dung of his cavalry to be gathered together, and hence the mound Amree!'[29]

Later, in the twentieth century, Amri came to be acknowledged as a reputed site of the Indus culture.

But what brought Masson and Burnes to Harappa? Masson, as we saw, was a British army deserter masquerading as an American. At the point where we left him, he had reached Dera Ismail Khan with that other army deserter we met, called Richard Potter. While his companion stayed behind, Masson travelled across the north-west borders, through Peshawar and Jalalabad, to Kabul in Afghanistan. In January 1829 he returned to north-west India and spent the next one and a half years moving across Sindh, Baluchistan, and Punjab. It was during 1829, after spending the rainy season at Lahore, that he passed through Harappa. Eventually, Masson went back to Afghanistan, where he is known to have settled in 1833. From that time on, for a number of years, he received a retainer from the East India Company for collecting ancient artefacts and antiquities. Shortly thereafter he was also paid a regular annual stipend as the Company's accredited intelligence agent in Kabul.

Such intelligence-gathering was directly relevant to the frontier drama of dangerous adventure and diplomacy, popularly known as the 'Great Game', that was fast unfolding in the early part of the nineteenth century.[30] A phrase made famous by Rudyard Kipling, who used it in his novel *Kim*, the Great Game was a struggle for political ascendancy between Russia and Great Britain and was 'played' across the mountainous tracts of High Asia. In fact, the diplomatic manoeuvres, the covert moves and counter-moves that marked this century-long drama, started well before the time of Charles Masson.

The beginnings of the Great Game go back to the spring of 1810, when two British officers, Henry Pottinger and Charles Christie, undertook a secret reconnaissance to gather crucial political information and document uncharted territory in Afghanistan and Baluchistan. Assuming disguises that ranged from those of a Tartar horse-dealer to a pious *haji* (Muslim pilgrim),

Christie travelled through rugged Baluchi terrain to the Afghan city of Herat, while Pottinger, after parting company with his brother officer at Nushki, used the desert route to reach Persia. Breathtaking geographical traverses, armed skirmishes, and violent deaths were to mark the struggle between the Russian and British empires as their rivalry over this region unfolded through the nineteenth century. It was not until August 1907 that this war game was to end—when the two rival powers signed the Anglo-Russian Convention in St Petersburg, by which they agreed to resolve their differences in Tibet, Afghanistan, and Persia.

In the summer of 1833, however, when Masson came to Kabul, the Afghan capital was recovering from internal strife arising out of the struggle for the throne of Kabul. The ruling king, Shah Shujah, had been exiled to Ludhiana in Punjab. An Afghan prince, Dost Mohammad, had finally won Kabul by 1826, after having outmanoeuvred his older brothers. Dost Mohammad was frequently courted by diplomatic missions of the two rival empires. His capital city teemed with intelligence agents of various kinds, financed by the British East India Company on the one hand, and by Russia on the other. In the spring of the previous year, coincidentally, Kabul had been visited by Burnes—the other British army man who had travelled to Harappa.

One of the most promising officers of the Company's army, Burnes, like Masson, could also be described as a player in the Great Game. He had sailed up the Indus and assessed its viability for future movements of the Company's army, and it was in the course of that navigation that he visited Harappa in 1831, after disembarking at Tulamba and travelling four miles inland (Fig. 2). In 1832, Burnes was to come to the Punjab again, this time on a more risky adventure. He was on his way to Kabul and Central Asia in order to acquire political information about the countries bordering the Oxus. It was in Kabul that he died in 1841, at the hands of a violent mob. By then, many Afghans blamed Burnes for the diplomatic manoeuvres which had resulted in the British advance into Kabul in 1838. This advance Kabulwards was a hugely unpopular move, especially because it coincided with the installation of a puppet, Shah Shujah, as the ruler of the realm—the same Shah Shujah who had been removed by Dost Mohammad.

Clearly, both Masson and Burnes were remarkable individuals. But neither can be described as archaeologists. Of course, archaeology, at this point of time, was hardly an established method of studying the human past. Even in England, while there were individuals with 'a back-looking curiositie' who gave full descriptions of ancient monuments like Stonehenge and Avebury, and who hoped to base their accounts on facts and observations, the country's past was still largely a matter of guesswork. It was legendary people mentioned in the Bible, and by classical writers, that were thought by many to inhabit Great Britain's ancient and remarkable monuments.[31]

What is worth remembering, though, is that in the social milieu of early-nineteenth-century India many Europeans who displayed a keen interest in things archaeological did this more as an enjoyable pastime while pursuing their main vocations in India, as either doctors or irrigation engineers, army men or administrative officials. Consequently, their surveys of ancient sites and monuments were primarily geared towards uncovering as many antiquities as possible, rather than understanding their associational significance or the sequence in which they were found. Stupa-hunting, for instance, was very common in the north-west, as far as Afghanistan, where the motive was to acquire coins and sculpture rather than study Buddhist architecture. Most stupa robbers in these early years were not even aware that stupas were connected with things Buddhist, and tended to describe them as pyramids or as the sepulchres of ancient Indian kings.[32] At stupas and mounds that yielded artefacts—coins, sculpture, intaglios, etc.—collections of curiosities were speedily made, while at others, which did not yield such portable relics, descriptions of what was seen were usually recorded. The first English visitors to Harappa, Masson and Burnes, were thus very much within this mould. Harappa did not yield any treasures, but Masson is known to have made a collection of about 80,000 coins and antiquities from the famous ancient site of Begram near Kabul.

Twenty-two years were to elapse before an archaeologist visited the ruins of Harappa. This was in 1853 and the man was Alexander Cunningham (1814–93; Fig. 3).

Fig. 3. Alexander Cunningham

By this time, the mid-nineteenth century, India's archaeological past was becoming better understood.[33] For one thing, many more sites and relics were known. Buddhist monuments had been found and recognized as being related to the religion that Gautama Buddha founded in the sixth century BC. These ranged from the Manikiyala stupa in Punjab, to those in and around Sanchi in Central India. Indo-Greek coins and sculpture had been unearthed in the north-west. Megaliths had been uncovered in the southern peninsula. Historical sites like Brahminabad in Sindh and Behat in the Ganga–Yamuna doab were among the important and large discoveries of this period. These twenty-odd years, between 1830 and 1850, also saw the decipherment of early Indian scripts which had fallen into disuse and oblivion: scripts like the Brahmi and the Kharoshthi. Consequently, accurate readings of hundreds of ancient inscriptions had recently become possible. These, in turn, provided a reliable historical framework within which India's antiquities and sites could be contextualized. Cunningham himself had been one of the pioneers of Indian archaeology in this regard, and, interestingly enough, his working career spanned 'the whole period between the virtual inception of Indian epigraphic, numismatic and field archaeological studies in the 1830s to the penultimate decade of the nineteenth century when the study of ancient India was an acknowledged academic discipline.'[34]

Alexander Cunningham came to India in 1833 as a young lad of nineteen and began his career as a second lieutenant in the Bengal Engineers.[35] In short, he too came to archaeology via the army. He spent part of his early years in Calcutta, after he was appointed (in 1836) as one of the aides-de-camp of the governor general, Lord Auckland. It was in Calcutta that his interest in India's history began because of his close association with James Prinsep (1799–1840). Prinsep was then assay master of the Calcutta Mint and secretary to the Asiatic Society of Bengal.

Prinsep is remembered for many things.[36] His most famous accomplishment was the decipherment of the Brahmi script, which allowed him to read the epigraphs of the emperor Ashoka. He is also renowned for his numismatic scholarship, which, combined with his mastery of inscriptions, resulted in numerous important dynasties of ancient India being made known. Above all, Prinsep inspired a number of British officers, including the young Cunningham, to explore the subcontinent's archaeological sites and relics. Under Prinsep's tutelage Cunningham picked up the essential elements of Indian archaeology, and soon he was using his skills in many ways. He assisted in deciphering the Kharoshthi script—the script that had been in vogue in the north-western part of the subcontinent in early times. He helped discover the name of Skanda Gupta, this being a new name of one of the kings of the Gupta dynasty. This scholarship soon combined in Cunningham with an enthusiasm for discovering such data from the field. Unlike Prinsep, who remained largely in Calcutta—where he deciphered the coins and facsimiles of inscriptions showered on him by his collaborators—Cunningham became an ardent fieldworker. In that role, Prinsep pointed out, he brought so many facts and antiquities to light as to 'make me blush for my own inactive residence there'.[37]

Shortly after his Calcutta sojourn, Cunningham was deputed on geographical missions to various parts of the Himalayas, such as Kashmir, Ladakh, and Tibet. He combined his duties with a thorough and original documentation of ruined monuments and sites at these places. Indian archaeology gained a great deal from his official postings: for instance, while he worked as executive engineer for the king of Oudh, he located the ancient city of Sankisa (a city mentioned by the ancient Chinese pilgrim Fa-Hian) near Farrukhabad in present-day Uttar Pradesh (UP). Similarly, the Buddhist sites of Central India were mapped during the time that he worked in Gwalior as that princely state's executive engineer.

Cunningham visited Harappa while serving in Punjab. That was in 1853. By then, Punjab had ceased to be an independent state and was part of British-occupied India. Just before being deputed there, Cunningham was in Central India, in the late 1840s, where, as was just pointed out, he seems to have been busily investigating Buddhist structures and sculpture. But now archaeology took a back seat in his life for he was recalled to actively serve in the British army. He was present at battles fought against the Sikhs at Chilianwala and Gujrat (both in Punjab) in 1849 and finds mention in army dispatches. The battle at Gujrat turned out to be the decisive assault and left the Sikhs totally defeated, resulting in the formal annexation of their territory. Cunningham then returned to Gwalior, but within a few years (in 1853) was transferred back to Punjab.

He was now posted at Multan, where he was given the responsibility of dismantling the city's defences to prevent future rebellion. Multan lies in the same tract as Harappa. Naturally, Cunningham lost no time visiting it: in fact he went off to see it in the very year that he was transferred to Multan. Harappa's city ruins must have impressed him enough to ensure that, within three years, he returned to them once more. Unfortunately, these seem to have been brief sojourns, conspicuously unmomentous. A more complete examination of Harappa, by digging into its belly, had to wait another sixteen years, till 1872.

The year that Cunningham first saw Harappa also marks the beginning of India's railway system. Financed by British metropolitan capital, the railways are naturally remembered for the ways in which they linked different parts of the Indian subcontinent. They also radically altered the character of many of India's mounds and monuments. The search for ballast, essential for railway construction, resulted in the plundering of bricks and statues from ancient sites, one of the most devastating instances being the destruction of thirty-six temples at Tigowa (in the Jabalpur region) by a railway contractor who took away two hundred carts of stone from there. Harappa suffered a similar fate. Between the time of Cunningham's first visit to the site and 1872, when he began his excavations there, old brick structures had been dismantled at an alarming pace. This was because, as Cunningham pointed out, about a hundred miles of the railway line connecting Lahore and Multan had been furnished with brick ballast from Harappa. In fact, during his earlier visits Cunningham had seen the massive walls of (what he imagined to be) a Buddhist monastery on the southern mound of the site; only bare traces of it could now be found. When he came to excavate there, he tells us, 'the whole has now been removed to form ballast for the Railway.'[38]

In the 1853–72 interregnum, great changes had also taken place in the political destiny of India and in Cunningham's personal fortunes. For one thing, the administration of India was now directly under the British crown, following the famous rebellions of 1857. The 1857 rebellions were, however, rather far from the mental and physical horizons of Alexander Cunningham. He had spent most of those turbulent years in Burma, busily setting up a public works department. Shortly after, he became a major general, and in 1861 he retired from the army. All this notwithstanding, he was still relatively young: in his forty-eighth year he did not visualize this as being the end of his working life. His retirement from the military, in fact, marked the beginning of a new career in archaeology. Cunningham now became the investigator of India's monuments, sites, and antiquities under a government-sponsored archaeological survey.

Cunningham's archaeological interest and investigations were well known in government circles and were surely an important factor in his recruitment. His appeals for a government-sponsored archaeological survey were also common knowledge. These had been directed at the East India Company and had appeared in his writings from 1843 on. Initially, though, Cunningham underlined the desirability of an archaeological survey not in terms of its potential contribution towards an understanding of India's past but because he thought it would be politically useful:

> an undertaking of vast importance to the Indian government politically, and to the British public religiously. To the first body it

> would show that India had generally been divided into numerous petty chiefships, which had invariably been the case upon every successful invasion; while, whenever she had been under one ruler, she had always repelled foreign conquest with determined resolution. To the other body it would show that Brahmanism, instead of being an unchanged and unchangeable religion which had subsisted for ages, was of comparatively modern origin, and had been *constantly* receiving additions and alterations; facts which prove that the establishment of the Christian religion in India must ultimately succeed.[39]

Cunningham's conclusion seems a non sequitur, but in colonial times such justifications were needed to generate funds.[40]

Some years later, when Cunningham reiterated his idea of such a survey, the need to learn about that part of India's material past which was connected with Buddhism was still paramount. But the emphasis now was on its usefulness for the illustration of India's history by contrast with literary scholarship (such as 'the rubbish contained in the Puranas')—which had been the main preoccupation of Indological scholarship.[41] Again, in 1854, Cunningham's plea to the Court of Directors of the East India Company was to employ a competent officer to excavate and report on Buddhist remains. He expressed the hope that they would recognize how much a 'work of this kind would be of real value for the ancient history of India (the territory of the Great Company) than the most critical and elaborate edition of the eighteen Puranas.'[42]

But why were these suggestions accepted only after the rebellions of 1857? Crucial, perhaps, was a new sensibility among India's British rulers that government-sponsored archaeology was the duty and responsibility of 'an enlightened ruling power'. As the British crown began to directly administer its Indian empire, an idea increasingly gaining ground was that public works, education, and law ought to be part of Great Britain's 'civilizing mission', supposedly undertaken on India's behalf. In the context of such sentiments, it was natural that Lord Canning, India's first post-1857 viceroy, would be dismayed at the neglect of old architectural remains in those areas that were now designated 'British territories', and through which he travelled in 1861.[43] Consequently, investigating and recording the principal antiquarian sites of British India became integral to his vision of Great Britain's responsibilities towards her dependency:

> It will not be to our credit, as an enlightened ruling power, if we continue to allow such fields of investigation, as the remains of the old Buddhist capital in Behar, the vast ruins of Kanouj, the plains around Delhi, studded with ruins more thickly than even the Campagna of Rome, and many others, to remain without more examination than they have hitherto received. Everything that has hitherto been done in this way has been done by private persons, imperfectly and without system. It is impossible not to feel that there are European governments which, if they had held our rule in India, would not have allowed this to be said.

How such an investigation could be undertaken was outlined in an ambitious memorandum that Cunningham submitted to the viceroy. Cunningham had met the viceroy at Allahabad, where he was serving as chief engineer of the North-Western Provinces.[44] The investigation outlined in Cunningham's memorandum was to be based on the Chinese traveller Hsuan Tsang's itinerary, which covered Buddhist monuments from the northwest to Orissa, and 'brahmanical' remains in so far as they were related to Buddhist places. That itinerary, with fulsome details about the places he had visited, and his observations on them, had been made available to Western scholarship by a French translation published in the late 1850s.

Of all the Chinese Buddhists who came to India, Hsuan Tsang travelled the longest. He had left his native land in AD 629, and he did not return to it until the spring of AD 645. Over this considerable interval he visited Punjab and Kashmir as well as Bihar, Assam, and peninsular India. Wherever he went, he recorded his observations on monasteries, ruined cities, stupas, and a great deal else. Now, twelve hundred years later, Cunningham proposed to survey those places, Hsuan Tsang's journal in hand. At each place revisited, an attempt would be made to show 'the positions of all the existing remains, with a round plan of every building or ruin of special note, accompanied by drawings and sections of all objects of interest.' The time-schedule that Cunningham visualized for the survey was two field seasons.[45]

Cunningham's imaginative hobbyhorse was sanctioned in January 1862, and the retired general now formally became a government-appointed archaeological surveyor. Cunningham, in the words of the governor general, 'more than any other officer, had made the antiquities of India his area of study.' And so it was fitting that he be appointed to head a survey, initially for two years. Eventually, a government department of archaeology, better known as the Archaeological Survey of India, was created in 1871, with Cunningham as its director general; of this institution he remained in charge until 1885. In other words, Indian archaeology was to be under his charge for nearly twenty years. In fact, although 'he did not know it then, he would continue to be in the field in every cold season, writing up and preparing the reports in the succeeding summer and monsoon months till 1885 with four years' break in 1866–70. This is the longest record of archaeological peregrination by any individual in India.'[46]

These were years of extraordinary discoveries in a large swathe of territory that Cunningham traversed with enormous vitality, extending from the ruins of Taxila in the Punjab to the historic fortified city of Mahasthangarh in Bengal. The scale of the Cunningham surveys, in fact, has been compared to those of the Trigonometrical Survey: 'this work did for Indian archaeology what the great Trigonometrical Survey achieved for the

Indian land mass. Things were mapped out on a grand scale in both cases.'[47] What makes Cunningham's work even more extraordinary is the sheer amount of travelling that was done, frequently through forested tracts, by bullock cart, on horses, elephants, and camels, and in some areas even on foot. Cunningham and his assistants were in the field every year from November–December to March–April. During those months, scores of sites were visited, documented, and in many cases excavated.

Cunningham's agenda, however, was not to painstakingly document every structure and artefact. Instead, he demarcated the archaeological landscape in broad brushstrokes and with great speed. An account of Cunningham's career and work tells us how this was achieved:

> Usually he stopped from three to six days on a site, but for an exceptionally long operation he might stay for about a fortnight. During his visit to Sravasti in the season of 1875–76 he halted for eleven days, in the course of which he 'made excavations in twenty distinct mounds . . .' in the Jetavana area!
>
> Sometimes his explorations would degenerate into mere object-hunting expeditions; he would visit the site, clear the jungle around and employ a gang of labourers to search for coins, inscriptions, and sculptures, often offering rewards 'for even a single letter.' Then he would himself scour the countryside, gardens, bushes and the houses of the people. He collected a large number of inscriptions and sculptures by this means, particularly in Bharhut, Kosambi and Mathura. At Kosambi, he declared, his 'chief discoveries' had been made 'in the people's houses.'[48]

Today, the rapidity of Cunningham's surveys appears to be very strange, but plenty of excavation work in the nineteenth century was done in this way. In England, as the archaeologist Glyn Daniel points out, antiquarians 'would think nothing of excavating half a dozen round barrows in a day; whereas today the proper excavation of a round barrow can take anything from four to six weeks.'[49] In Egypt and the Near East, it was the same story. Sir Austen Henry Layard (1817–94), for instance, is known to have boasted that the cause of his excavations at Nimrud in Iraq was to obtain the largest number of works of art with the least possible outlay of time and money.

Still, in spite of the speed with which Cunningham worked, what remained constant was the rough blueprint he worked with. This was a Buddhist-centred archaeological survey, with pride of place being endowed to the accounts of Chinese pilgrim-travellers. At the sites, a thorough ground survey of the mounds and surviving monuments, with details about their dimensions, was made. The presence of antiquities such as coins and images was noted. Finally, Cunningham attempted in most cases to correlate the ancient literary descriptions, especially those contained in the Chinese accounts, with the surviving archaeological features that he observed on the ground.

The survey of Harappa is marked by these very same features. Cunningham gave a precise description of the mounds along with his assessment of earlier accounts:

> The ruins of Harapa are the most extensive of all the old sites along the banks of the Ravi. On the north, the west, and the south, there is a continuous line of mounds about 3,500 feet in length; but on the east side, which is only 2,000 feet in length, there is a complete gap of 800 feet, for which I am unable to account. The whole circuit of the ruins is therefore about 12,500 feet, or nearly 2 ½ miles. The highest mound is that to the north-west, which is 60 feet above the fields. On the south-west and the south the mounds range from 40 to 50 feet in height, and on the north side towards the old bed of the Ravi, from 25 to 30 feet. Burnes speaks of '*a ruined citadel* on the river side of the town', by which I suppose he means the *western* side, which is the most commanding portion of the ruins. Masson calls it 'a ruinous brick castle', and distinctly states that it was situated

> to the west, on what he erroneously supposed to be a natural rocky height but which is only an accumulation of masses of brick walls and broken bricks. He describes 'the walls and towers of the castle' as being 'remarkably high, though, from having been long deserted, they exhibit in some parts the ravages of time and decay.' I believe that Masson's visit was made in 1826; and just five years later, when Burnes was on his way to Lahor, the brick castle was already 'ruinous'. In 1853 I was informed that Mer Singh, a Sikh, had built a fort at Harapa, some 70 years later, or about AD 1780. Perhaps this was the castle seen by Masson and Burnes.[50]

Cunningham also provided a site plan of Harappa which graphically illustrates the alignment of the mounds and their location in relation to the old bed of the Ravi river (Fig. 4). His designation of the mounds—A–B, C, D, and E—remains what we continue to use today. Most important, in his work lie the first visual details of objects that we now commonly recognize as Harappan artefacts, including some that are 'type fossils' or archetypal objects of the civilization—an inscribed, rectangular stone seal, and flint implements (Fig. 5):

> My chief discovery consisted of a number of stone implements for scraping wood or leather. Several specimens of these are given in the accompanying plate. Most of them have one edge more obtuse than the other, with a flat surface between; but a few have the two edges alike, with a single ridge between them. They are nearly all made of a dull cream coloured stone, but a few of these are nearly black in colour.
>
> . . . The most curious object discovered at Harapa is a seal, belonging to Major Clark, which was found along with two small objects like chess pawns, made of dark brown jasper. All these are shown in the accompanying plate. The seal is a smooth black stone without polish. On it is engraved very deeply a bull, without a hump, looking to the right, with two stars under the neck. Above the bull there is an inscription in six characters, which are quite

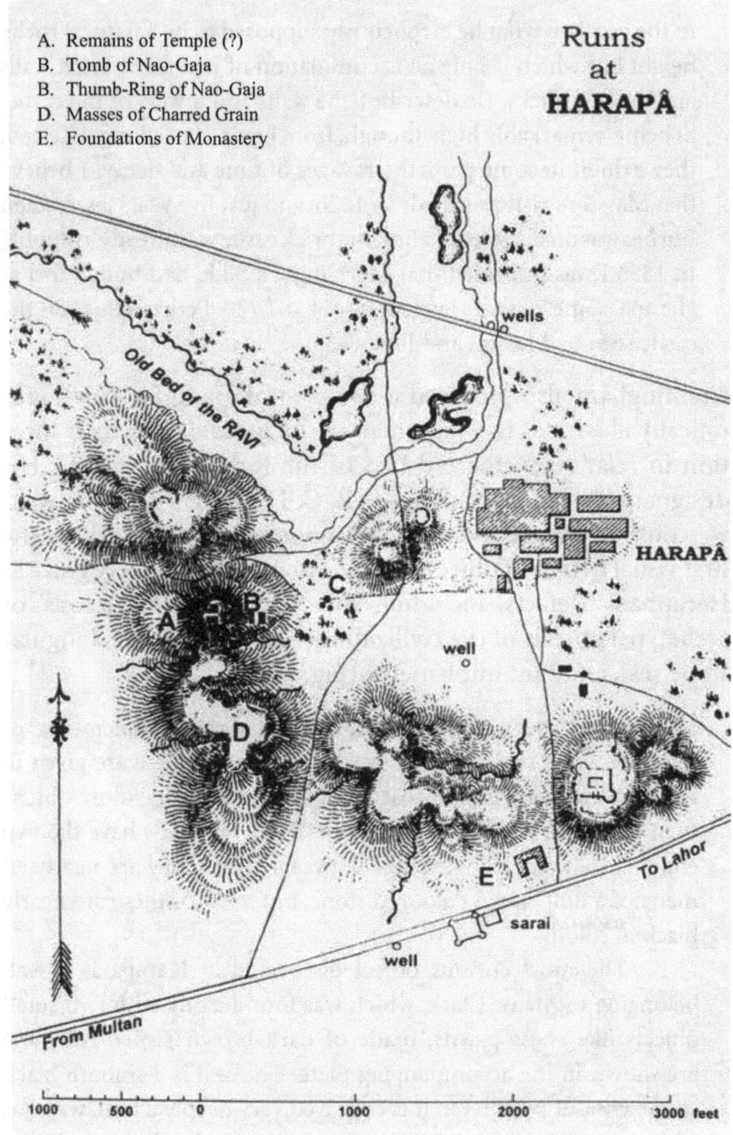


Fig. 4. Cunningham's site plan of Harappa

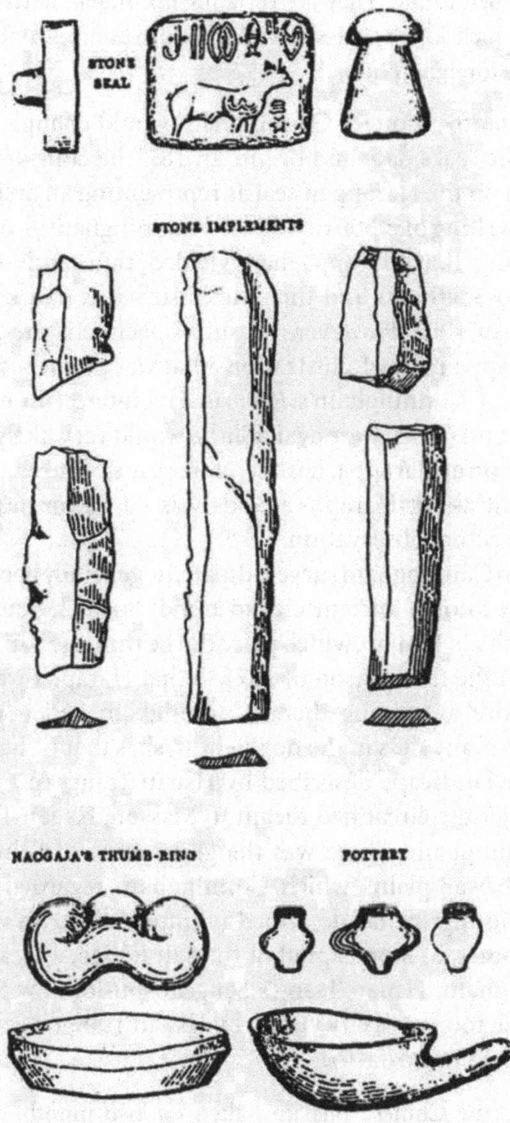


Fig. 5. Cunningham's caché from Harappa

> unknown to me. They are certainly not Indian letters; and as the bull which accompanies them is without a hump, I conclude that the seal is foreign to India.[51]

Subsequently, though, Cunningham would change his opinion about the seal's date and origin. In 1877 he considered the inscription on the Harappan seal as representing an archaic kind of Indian writing of *c.* 500 or 400 BC.[52] Cunningham also mentioned in passing that Harappa had yielded thousands of coins of the Indo-Scythians and their successors (i.e. dating to roughly 100 BC–AD 100). However, no such specimens are sketched in the Harappa plate of illustrations that was published in the fifth volume of Cunningham's *Reports.* His interest in coins is well known, and if they were available he would very likely have made a collection at Harappa. It is therefore plausible to assume that his statement about Harappa's coins was based on hearsay rather than on actual observation.

When Cunningham surveyed a site, he generally had a particular textually known ancient city in mind. So, as he excavated this ruined city in Punjab, which place did he think he had discovered? It was in the field season of 1872–3 that Harappa was surveyed, but before excavating there, Cunningham had made his way through many sites in the north-west, sites that he had identified with the landscape described by Hsuan Tsang. In a sense, what Alexander the Great had meant to Masson, Hsuan Tsang meant to Cunningham. There was the great stupa of Sahri Bahlol in the Peshawar plains which Cunningham regarded as the one which the pilgrim had described as Emperor Ashoka's handiwork. Further east, Mallot, capital of the Salt Range, was, according to Cunningham, Hsuan Tsang's Seng-ho-pu-lo, now Singhapura. Harappa, too, was a city visited by Hsuan Tsang: it was the city of Po-fa-to-lo or Po-fa-to

> where the Chinese pilgrim halted for two months to study the principles of the sect of *Sammitiyas* . . . the size of 20 *li*, or upwards

of three miles in circuit . . . the pilgrim assigns to *Po-fa-to*, or *Po-fa-to-lo* . . . the size agrees almost exactly with that of Harapa, and as the position otherwise corresponds, I believe that Harapa must be the very city visited by the Chinese pilgrim. He describes the population as very dense. There were four stupas and twelve monasteries counting about 1,000 monks, besides twenty Brahmanical temples. Near the town there was a large ruined monastery which had been destroyed by lightning.[53]

The remains of what he imagined was a Hindu temple on the high north-west mound of Harappa, and the traces of a Buddhist monastery in the large square building on its southern mound, must also have strengthened Cunningham's identification of Harappa with Po-fa-to-lo. Harappa, in fact, remained lodged in his mind long after the excavation. About a decade later, in the field season of 1883–4 (this is little known) he directed his assistant, H.B.W. Garrick, back to Harappa. Garrick also dug there and found bracelets, rings, a spinning weight, 'catapelt balls', and 10 to 12 pounds of charred wheat.[54]

The association that was suggested by Cunningham between Harappa's mysterious ruins and Buddhism, especially in relation to devout Buddhist pilgrims from China, was shortly taken up and developed by others.[55] For the French scholar Terrien de la Couperie, the writing on the Harappa seal was of Chinese origin. He was to describe it as 'the stone seal of Setchuen or Shuh writing which was found a few years ago in the ruins of Harappa, near Lahor.'[56] This scholar imagined that the seal was brought to India in the course of trade through Bactria, and possibly belonged to Buddhist pilgrims who must have visited Harappa.

Not everyone agreed with this interpretation. Mansel Longworth Dames, who himself drew the attention of the English-speaking world to Couperie's observations, pointed out that seals in what appeared to be an unknown language were unlikely to have been articles of trade.[57] Dames was an Indian Civil Service officer with some knowledge of the north-west, where he had served a number of years. Apart from what he wrote on Harappa, he is generally remembered for his painstaking documentation of a large body of verse that circulated orally among Baluchi folk in the hill country that lay west of the Punjab.[58]

The nineteenth century, thus, did see Harappa 'discovered', in the sense that it came to be recognized as an archaeological site, as a place where an ancient city lay buried. In this sense, the basic site of Harappa was discovered well before John Marshall's momentous announcement of 1924. In fact, what seems striking about the early reports are hints which show that their authors understood that they had encountered archaeological features unlike those usually seen at Indian sites. By 1872 Cunningham was a veteran archaeologist with field experience of over thirty years in scores of places. He was also an enthusiastic collector of Buddhist sculptures, very commonly found at sites in Punjab and the north-west. Yet neither Cunningham nor his assistant Garrick seem to have reaped the usual harvest of riches at Harappa that excavations at other places had yielded. Instead, they had only noted a few unique features. Cunningham recognized that the engraved seal of Harappa was in a script he had not seen anywhere else in India. That humble Harappan pottery and flint implements were illustrated by him is also interesting, and, in terms of the general character of his reports, an aberration. Certainly, the Cunningham volumes contain plates of drawings—of sculpture, sites, buildings, and inscriptions—but only in rare instances of ceramics and stone tools. At the very least, this indicates that Harappa intrigued him. Similarly, Garrick was struck by the singular absence of sculpture at Harappa, so commonly found at other subcontinental sites.

Why did these pioneer explorers fail to understand the significance of such absences? Perhaps the most important reason was that Cunningham surveyed Harappa through a predominantly Buddhist grid, just as Masson had viewed it through a Greek grid.

But this was a city of one of the first civilizations, a city that existed before those of the ancient world of written history. Its antiquity was unlikely to be discovered by archaeologists who were always in the company of the Buddhist pilgrims from China and Macedonian soldiers accompanying Alexander. Harappa had, after all, flourished in an age which lay far, far beyond such textual traditions and boundaries.

It was a half-glimpsed world, lying in wait.

# 2
# FROM SEALS TO A SPECIALIST

AROUND THE TIME THAT ALEXANDER CUNNINGHAM began winding up his archaeological trail across North India, the first known seal of the Indus civilization was carried away by its finder. This mysterious memento then travelled across the Indian Ocean to the shores of England and, by 1886, it had joined the collection of Oriental antiquities at the British Museum in London.

This seal, the same that had so intrigued Cunningham, was, as we saw, discovered by a Major Clark. The circumstances of its discovery are hazy. Hardly anything can be gleaned about Clark or his career in the army, other than that he had procured the Harappa seal before 1872–3, and that he was Major General Clark by the time he presented it to the premier museum of his native land.

About the same time, two more seals from Harappa, following the trajectory of the first, reached England. Before Clark had gifted his find to the museum, a farmer of Harappa who had found a similar specimen, rectangular shaped—'a drab-coloured smooth stone, perfectly flat on the engraved side and rounded at the back'—and etched with the same kind of writing, decided to hawk it to a British official.[1] The buyer was J. Harvey, a member of the Indian Educational Service based at Multan. He must have chanced upon it in November 1884 as he travelled to inspect the local school at Harappa. When Harvey returned to England, he too presented his souvenir to the British Museum. This was in December 1885, six months or so before a third specimen reached the same museum. This time it was because the district police superintendent of the area, T.A. O'Connor, had dug up an Indus seal from Harappa's ruins, apparently around August 1886.[2]

Practically nothing else is known about these officials, or about the archaeological paraphernalia they may have carried back as mementoes of their Indian experience. All we know is that, by an interesting coincidence, three specimens of the same type, each separately procured from Harappa, reached the same institution within a few months of each other (Fig. 6).

By the time the British Museum had added the Harappa seals to its cabinets of curiosities, it was one of the greatest museums of the nineteenth century. It had begun, though, as the private museum of one man, a London physician called Sir Hans Sloane (1660–1753). Along with studying medicine and seeing patients, Sloane developed an early interest in natural history and began to collect all kinds of 'natural curiosities'. By the time of his death in 1753, the 80,000 objects that he had diligently hoarded swamped his two houses in Bloomsbury Place and overflowed into his country manor in Chelsea.[3] There were diverse and numerous specimens of dried plants and bird feathers, corals and crystals, as also metals and mineral ores. 'Artificial curiosities', too, formed part of Sloane's collection: these comprising artefacts such as coins, medals, mathematical instruments, cameos, intaglios and semi-precious stone receptacles.

This private repository came to be transformed into a public museum as a consequence of Sloane's will, wherein he wrote that his collection should, if possible, be kept and preserved together. So, when he died, his appointed trustees offered it to the British government for a sum of 20,000 pounds. Although King George II is known to have remarked that he did not think

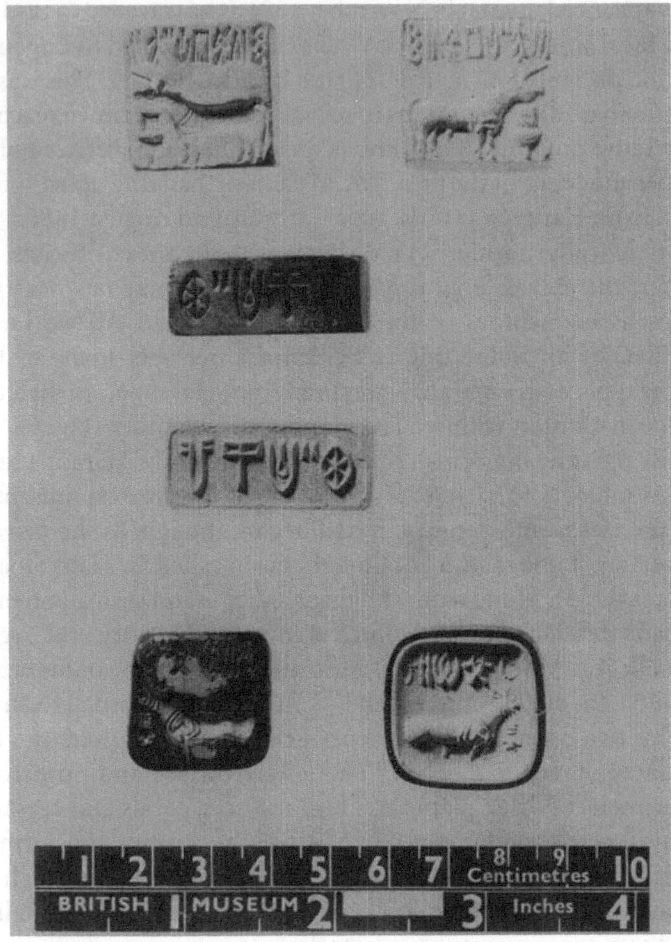


Fig. 6. Harappa seals in the British Museum

there were 20,000 pounds in the treasury, the money was found and, within a few months of Sloane's death, a parliamentary bill was passed into law for the purchase. By 1755, a home was located for Sloane's great collection. The trustees had wanted to purchase Buckingham House (now Buckingham Palace), but found it far too expensive. Instead, Montague House was bought—for 10,250 pounds. Located in Bloomsbury, which was then a kind of semi-rural locality, this decaying late-seventeenth-century nobleman's mansion stood upon a seven-acre estate. The site was once known as Bakers Field but had been sold in 1675 to a Ralph Montague (hence Montague House). Facing Russell Street, it was not far from the houses that Sloane himself had occupied. Even today, the British Museum stands on the same land, although virtually all of Montague House has disappeared.

The museum grew over the next hundred and fifty years, in circumstances both curious and diverse. A few collections came into it as war booty. For example, the capitulation of the troops of Napoleon to the British command in Egypt in 1801 included, as one of the terms of surrender, the condition that the French hand over antiquities that had been 'collected' by them and by scholars who had accompanied the French army in Egypt. King George III then gave over the spoils to the British Museum, and among these was what is now one of its prized possessions—the black basalt block known as the Rosetta Stone (so named because it was found near the Rosetta mouth of the Nile). It was the inscriptions on the Rosetta Stone, in three scripts—hieroglyphic, demotic, and Greek—which subsequently provided the key to understanding Egyptian hieroglyphic writing.[4]

Many more Egyptian antiquities were to enter the museum's portals in the following decades, frequently through diplomatic channels. These included fragments such as the two feet by three feet segment of the plaited beard of the 4000-year-old Giant Sphinx which stands as a guardian to the pyramids of Gizeh.[5] There were also colossal monoliths, like the bust of Rameses II, of the Nineteenth Dynasty of Egypt. This bust weighed several tonnes and had been taken out of the temple complex near Thebes with the help of levers and rollers by Giovanni Battista Belzoni, an Italian hydraulic engineer who made a great deal of money by robbing old graves and sites. In this case, he had collaborated with Henry Salt, the British consul general at Alexandria from 1815 to 1827, who had been instructed to look out for antiquities to add to the British Museum.

The British victory against Napoleon altered the balance of power in the Mediterranean and brought Great Britain close to Turkey. The changed diplomatic scenario contributed to the removal of a famed sculptural frieze, which adorned the Parthenon at Athens, to England. This fourth-century BC frieze was devoted to a single subject: the Panathenaic procession, an ancient festival held in honour of the goddess Athena. However, Thomas Bruce, Seventh Earl of Elgin, who in 1799 had been appointed as the British ambassador to Constantinople, pulled down a large part (as much as 247 feet in length) of the great jostling procession of horsemen, charioteers, gods, and sacrificial animals from their place on the Acropolis. These too, eventually, reached the British Museum.[6]

Elgin consistently maintained that his initial intention was only to get drawings and casts made, but that he had reviewed his plans when confronted by the continued destruction of sculptures by local people. However, there is little doubt that their removal was made possible by the special nature of Elgin's office, and because Greece, at that point of time, was part of the Turkish empire. Constantinople, in fact, had issued the *firman* (official order) to the governor of Athens that permitted Elgin to remove the marble panels. Notwithstanding the 'legality' of the Turkish firman, so gross was the manner and scale of this removal that 'Elginism' has since become a general metaphor for the plunder of cultural treasures.[7]

As Great Britain's trading empire and colonial stranglehold grew in strength and grasp, the same story—of British officials 'acquiring' archaeological artefacts and art treasures and the 'migration' of these objects to England—was repeated in many African and Asian nations. The main beneficiary, inevitably, was the British Museum. From India, this is how small curios like the Harappa seals reached the museum, as did large limestone remains from the Buddhist stupa at Amaravati. Elginism was at work here too: the destructiveness of 'natives' was used as a justification for dismembering the stupa and removing several hundred sculptural pieces from there. These were acquired by the museum around 1880.[8]

There are other interesting stories of colonial loot and archaeological rapine. Some years before the Amaravati reliefs became the finest single group of Indian sculpture in the museum's collection, and probably in the very year that Alexander Cunningham chanced upon the first known seal from Harappa, another Indian assemblage of images had been presented to the museum by the three daughters of an Englishman called George Bridge. Several of the most remarkable specimens of this group now decorate the British Museum—Marici, the Buddhist goddess of dawn, with her three grimacing faces; the equally sinister Chamunda wearing a necklace of skulls; and the more benign pot-bellied elephant-headed Ganesha.[9] These and many others were originally in East India and had been acquired from there by Charles Stuart (1758–1828), a collector and British military officer. This Englishman was known as 'Hindoo' Stuart because of his intimacy with the country's customs, and presumably because he is said to have bathed daily in the Ganga river. (Apparently, when he died in 1828, a miniature Hindu temple was built over his last resting place in a Christian graveyard in Calcutta.)

Stuart's love for Hinduism, though, did not prevent him from 'stealing our gods'—as a brahmin priest, whose idol he had forcibly taken away, is known to have lamented.[10] Many more images were undoubtedly acquired by such means during 'Hindoo' Stuart's long service in India. These were kept in his house in Calcutta and shown to interested visitors. When Stuart died, his hoard of sculpture was shipped to England for the benefit of his estate. There it was auctioned at Christie's and bought by the Bridge family, with whom it remained till the death of George Bridge in 1872. Then it was auctioned again, when, strangely enough, the only bidder was a trustee of the British Museum,

A.W. Franks. Although the auctioneer is said to have objected, the collection was 'knocked down for a nominal sum said to be five pounds.'[11] (Even this was not paid to Bridge's daughters because Franks persuaded them that instead of accepting such a paltry sum they may as well 'benefit from the glory of making a presentation' to the British Museum!)

Such were the ways in which works of art and antiquity reached the British Museum—through the sword, through avarice masquerading as diplomacy, and sometimes through sheer swindling. But of all the rare and precious objects in its collection, it is the Indus seals of the museum which are most relevant to our tale.

This is not merely because these seals were from what would later be shown to be one of India's oldest cities, Harappa. More importantly, they were among the first Indian objects seen by John Marshall (1876–1958). John Marshall is the name which has remained indelibly associated with the discovery of the Indus civilization (Figs 7–9); he of the apocalyptic 1924 announcement. In the winter of 1901, the twenty-five-year-old Marshall, who had just been appointed Director General of Archaeology in India, was spending some days examining artefacts of Indian origin in the British Museum in preparation for his departure to India.[12] This is when he first saw the seals. We do not know Marshall's immediate impressions of them: he remembered later that they had interested him.[13]

Fig. 7. John Marshall in 1902

Admittedly, 1901 is more than twenty years away from the momentous 1924.[14] But, as we shall see, this discovery was made possible by solving the mystery of the antiquity of the Indus seals—the sorts of seals that Marshall

Fig. 8. John Marshall with his wife, Florence (who he married on 11th January 1902)

Fig. 9. Marshall with Lord Reading (in 1925–6)

had first examined in 1901. So, as we explore the circumstances and situations which led to that dramatic announcement of 1924, his first glimpse of such seals in the British Museum can be seen in retrospect as the beginning of John Marshall's interaction with things Harappan.

The year 1901 was also the one in which Marshall first came to grips with the Indian past. Before this, his education and archaeological training had not taken him beyond the Mediterranean.

Born on 18 March 1876 at Chester in Cheshire, John Hubert Marshall spent a large part of his childhood and adolescence in Dulwich, on the outskirts of London. Dulwich is the place from where his father operated while working on the legal circuit. His father, Frederick Marshall, came up from very humble beginnings and had to go out to work at the age of fourteen. However, along with earning a meagre living in a printing firm, he studied law in his spare time, and eventually rose to become a judge. Frederick married a young widow whose name we do not know but who already had two or three children. She was to bear him many more children, taking the number up to as many as fifteen. As John Marshall's daughter, Margaret, later put it, this was 'a large total even for those Victorian days'.[15] Her father was the youngest in this brood.

During his early years, the family moved to Dulwich, and there the young John was first sent to a small 'Dame school'. At age twelve he became a day boy in Dulwich College, where he remained till 1895.[16] This was a well-known public school of South London which had been established in its modern form in 1857, but which traced its origin back to 1619. Marshall's fascination with things classical developed there, nurtured under the influence of the headmaster, a Mr Gilkes. In fact, a passionate love for the ancient civilization of Greece that Gilkes inculcated in him ensured that when Marshall moved with a scholarship to King's College at Cambridge, he studied for the Classical Tripos, in which he obtained a first class.[17]

Following his passion, Marshall decided to go to Greece and study Greek archaeology there. He was fortunate in that he went at a point in time when there was already a British institute that provided institutional backing in Greece for students like him. This was the British School at Athens, which had been set up in 1886. By the late nineteenth century, several such European bodies and funds were already in existence. The Egyptian Exploration Fund, for instance, had been founded in 1882 by Amelia Edwards, an English travel writer and author of a best-seller called *A Thousand Miles up the Nile* (first published in 1876).[18] She, along with Reginald Stuart Poole who worked at the Department of Coins and Medals at the British Museum, set up the fund for the purpose of conducting excavations in the Egyptian Nile delta.

The idea of setting up the British School at Athens was the brainchild of Sir Richard Jebb, who is generally remembered as Regius Professor of Greek at Cambridge. But before that, in 1876, when he was at Glasgow (also as Professor of Greek), he had proposed the creation of a British institute for classical scholars on the lines of French and German institutes which were already established at Athens and which had greatly impressed him. All these were primarily geared to provide the institutional and logistical support that their countrymen required to pursue research in foreign lands. 'Pure' research was also combined at such institutes with antiquarian collecting of archaeological and art objects. Many scholars who came to Greece, following the example of army men and administrative officials in British colonies, carried back artefacts for the museums of their countries. The Fitzwilliam Museum at Cambridge, for instance, acquired several Cretan antiquities, including a marble human figurine from Chersoneos, beads and a classical bronze ring from a tomb at Anavlochos, a seal from around the Gulf of Mirabello, and several metal objects from Praisos—all through John Marshall in 1901.[19]

The British School had, to begin with, only very modest means at its disposal. But by the time Marshall came to Athens, it had received its first government grant from England. Alongside, in 1899, the Cretan Exploration Fund had also been formed, this being a joint venture between two well-known English archaeologists, Arthur Evans and David Hogarth.[20] Evans was an Englishman of education and means with a passion inherited from his father and grandfather for old coins and antiquities. He became Keeper of the Ashmolean Museum at Oxford and is known to have devoted a large part of his working life to the Mediterranean.[21] It was Evans who, at the start of the twentieth century, made the dramatic discovery of a prehistoric civilization at Crete. Hogarth, at the time when the Cretan Exploration Fund came to be formed, was director of the British School. He excavated many important archaeological sites, including Knossos, where he assisted Evans. Like Evans, he came to be associated with the Ashmolean Museum as its director from 1909 on, although in his later years he became more of a diplomat than an archaeologist. (Among other things, in 1915 he was sent—shades of Lawrence of Arabia here—by the British government to Cairo, to organize a revolt against Turkish rule.)

But at this point of time Hogarth was actively involved in the British School at Athens, under whose aegis he was training young scholars like Marshall. This Cambridge student seems to have impressed him specially, and later, while he was job-hunting, Hogarth gave Marshall a flaming testimonial. There he wrote that Marshall, during his stint at the school, 'showed great sympathy with, and grasp of, Greek Archaeology on all its sides. Indeed his promise there was superior to that of any other student of the year, and fully prepared me for his subsequent brilliant career at Cambridge.'[22] Hogarth was obviously referring to the fact that when Marshall returned to England, he obtained a first once again, this time in Part II of the Archaeological segment of the Classical Tripos at Cambridge.

November 1900 saw Hogarth's student back in Greece, helped by the award of a Pendergast Travelling Studentship. But this was to be the beginning of the end of Marshall's professional association with the Mediterranean. In less than a year, he was quite literally plucked out of Greece and installed in the world of Indian archaeology. These developments must have been as much a surprise to Marshall as to everyone around him.

The year 1901 began in an uneventful way. Marshall spent the winter months at Athens and Crete, working out a comparison of the Mycenaean remains in Crete with those on the Greek mainland. In the following summer he joined an excavation team from the British School that was moving to Praisos in the mountains to the south of Sitia in Crete.[23] The Praisos excavation was directed by R. Carr Bosanquet, who had succeeded Hogarth as director of the British School at Athens.[24]

Praisos was one of the two sites selected by the Cretan Exploration Fund, and there excavations would lead to the investigation of both the Minoan and later civilizational remains. The other was Kato Zakro on the coast, to the east of Praisos, which turned out to be a Minoan palace site. Digging at Praisos continued until July, and during this time Marshall was also responsible for the excavation of some tombs west of the road from Vavelli. Now called Nea Praisos, Vavelli was once described as the richest and loveliest village of eastern Crete. But by this time, it had become a mass of ruins. At some point Marshall joined Hogarth, who was excavating at Kato Zakro. Marshall was supposed to work out the classification of the pottery of Kato Zakro, but he suffered an attack of fever and left early.[25]

Alongside digging and classifying ceramic sherds, Marshall was looking around for a professional opening in the world of Greek scholarship. We do know that he had some testimonials written for himself, and that he had been seriously contemplating putting in an application for a professorship of Greek at Sydney University.[26] However, in the summer of 1901, unknown to him, the India Office in London, in search of a suitable archaeologist, had been in touch with the British Museum. They were looking for a man for the post of director of archaeology in India. As we shall see, it did not take more than a couple of months for Sir Edward Maunde Thompson, director of the British Museum, to hunt out Marshall and get the India Office to offer him the top job in Indian archaeology. Shortly afterwards, in November 1901, an agreement 'for service in India as Director of Archaeology' between 'John Hubert Marshall of the Oaks, Alleyn Park West Dulwich London S.E.' and 'the Secretary of State for India in Council' was signed.[27]

It became imperative now for Marshall to familiarize himself with the world of Indian archaeology.[28] That is why, in late 1901, he was groping his way through the Oriental antiquities holdings in the British Museum, where he first saw the Harappa seals.

A question may be posed at this juncture: How did this young archaeologist, actively exploring the possibility of a professorship of Greek at Sydney University, come to head a subcontinent's Archaeological Survey? To put it another way, from the point of view of the Indian government, what made a man trained in the classics and Greece suitable for the top post in Indian archaeology? At twenty-five, Marshall was much younger than many of the officers who would serve under him. He was also without any India connections, and, despite his excellent academic credentials, he had no training or background in Indian studies. With hindsight, one realizes that the India Office had chosen the best man for the job. But in 1901 his selection must have seemed to many a very strange choice.[29]

Marshall's appointment was made possible by two main events that intermeshed: George Nathaniel Curzon's appointment as Viceroy of India in 1898, and the revival of the post in India of director general of archaeology in 1901.[30] The latter event, in turn, was the unexpected outcome of a tortuous series of developments in government handling of archaeology that can be followed back to the retirement of Alexander Cunningham in 1885.

The Archaeological Survey of India, we may recall, had been set up more than a decade after India became a direct British dependency, following the suppression of the revolts that broke out in 1857. With Cunningham at the helm, the achievements of this organization were considerable; above all, in systematically giving the landscape of ancient India, as reflected in literary sources, its topographical bearings. Scholars who have written the history of Indian archaeology have generally focused on this, especially on the grand scale of the Cunningham surveys, and on the work of his successor, James Burgess, in the field of architectural scholarship. They have been less attentive to the severe tribulations that this organization had to undergo, especially after Cunningham's exit. The details relating to these tribulations are many, but if we must isolate a single recurrent imperative in government policy with regard to monuments and archaeological research, it was the urgency to scale down expenditure.

The Archaeological Survey, as we know, was an arm of the British Raj. All its establishment charges came out of the coffers of the government. This, of course, was true for other departments as well. But some of them, in turn, generated money for the government or were vital for the military and commercial stability of the British empire. The tasks of the Survey, which involved documenting and surveying archaeological sites and monuments, were qualitatively different. Such work earned accolades in scholarly circles and had proved of vital significance for the reconstruction of India's historical past. In government corridors, however, plenty of penny-pinching bureaucrats were sceptical about the 'usefulness' of this work. These men, especially the ones who balanced the government's books of accounts, wondered why a department that was neither revenue-earning nor one that contributed to the security of British India should be indefinitely supported. Practically speaking, what this meant was that during times of economic hardship the retrenchment axe first fell, as it always does, on knowledge-generating and supposedly inessential organizations.

The 1880s and 1890s were financially bleak and, for the Indian government, marked by large fiscal deficits—to the tune of about four million pounds in 1886, which rose to thirty-five million by 1894.[31] Such deficits were partly due to the massive increase in military expenditure that the government incurred because they decided to annex Burma, and also because of their anxiety about frontier defence, this being a consequence of the establishment of Russian power in Central Asia. A decline in opium revenues and expenditures incurred in servicing the interest obligation on loans taken for railway construction also added to the state's burgeoning deficit.

Measures to cut down spending on archaeology were related to this shortage. In 1886 itself, on the question of the archaeology outlay, the finance committee expressed its 'conviction that most of this expenditure is of a kind which might, and in time of financial emergency perhaps ought to be retrenched . . . we are far from denying the interest and value of such work as this but we venture to think that much of it has already been done sufficiently well, and that what remains to be done might be left to private enterprise, which is becoming increasingly active and intelligent in this direction; or if that should fail, might be postponed to more prosperous times.'[32]

So, the Archaeological Survey's budget was steadily reduced. In 1888 it was about a hundred thousand rupees, but by 1895 the total annual cost of running the Survey was slashed to just over sixty thousand rupees and continued to remain at that paltry figure for several years.[33] The other method by which financial stringency came to be exercised was by curtailing the organization's work. When Burgess retired as director general in 1889, the archaeological surveyors of Bengal and Punjab were directed to close their field operations and only complete their reports on past work. The Archaeological Survey was divided into a number of circles, or administrative zones, of which two out of the three circles in North India were those of Punjab (to which Sindh and Rajputana were attached) and Bengal (which also included Bihar, Orissa, Assam, and Chota Nagpur). In effect, such curtailment resulted in the reduction of staff to a bare minimum and a dramatic shrinking of archaeological operations.

Other crucial archaeological posts were also allowed to lapse. The Survey had a small staff of half a dozen officers, but by 1892 the post of the superintending officer in charge of archaeology in the North-Western Provinces was abolished. The government even decided that the Survey did not require a director general! So, from 1889, while an impoverished and shrivelled Archaeological Survey somehow managed to survive, it became a body without a head. This remained the state of affairs until Curzon personally ensured that the post of director of the Survey was revived in 1901.

In fact, at times in the years before Curzon was appointed, there had seemed every likelihood that government commitment to archaeology would be so drastically diluted that it might virtually cease to exist. The viceroy of British India over 1894–9 was Lord Elgin, who, interestingly enough, was the grandson of the infamous Thomas Bruce, the Seventh Earl of Elgin (also known as 'Lord Elgin'), the same who had notoriously removed marble sculptures from the Parthenon in Athens. The grandson, unlike the grandfather (who had got the British government to spend money on buying that collection), was anxious to reduce state expenditure. He suggested to C.J. Lyall, president of the Asiatic Society of Bengal, that most of the work done by the Archaeological Survey be taken over by that society. The Asiatic Society firmly declined the offer. Apprehending, however, that the government wished to sever its connection with archaeological research and conservation, the president and council of the society warned:

> Nothing could be more erroneous than the belief that this work could be left in India to private enterprise. Excavations and explorations of ancient sites made by private explorers without archaeological or scientific knowledge are positively detrimental. The work is done recklessly and selfishly. Valuable memorials of the past are in this way mutilated, destroyed, or abstracted from the country . . . There can, in the opinion of the Asiatic Society, be no doubt that in India funds ought to be provided by the State for this class of operations, and that the work itself should be supervised by the Government.[34]

As this question and the future of the Archaeological Survey came to be widely debated, strong and similar sentiments were expressed by others. Georg Buhler (1837–98), a German Indologist, penned a representation which argued that 'even the possibility of such a prospect naturally causes deep concern and regret to all those engaged or interested in Indian research, as the stoppage of Government assistance would seriously impede, perhaps make impossible, the further reconstruction of the political, religious and literary history of India.'[35]

So, in 1898, Viceroy Elgin and his council reluctantly recommended the continuation of government spending on archaeology. This was partly related to the pressure exerted by such individuals and societies: 'We are forced to the conclusion that there is still work which should be done by Government and may rightly be included amongst its responsibilities, and that moreover to withdraw from Archaeological research would lay the Government open to general condemnation in scientific circles.'[36] The government was, however, still willing to consider the possibility of private societies conducting archaeological research in India. An international Indian Exploration Fund, on the lines of the Cretan Exploration Fund and other such societies, was mooted around this time and the suggestion was warmly welcomed by Elgin.

Despite Elgin's enthusiasm, nothing came out of these proposals 'to send a motley crew of international archaeologists rampaging about India'—as Curzon put it.[37] Unlike his predecessors, this new viceroy assessed the problems and requirements of Indian archaeology with a new and radically fresh sense of urgency. In his scheme of things, these could be solved not through motley associations and funds but by vigorous governmental initiative. He wasted no time and minced no words in expressing his dismay at the existing chaotic system, under which the central and provincial governments (mis)managed archaeology, the absence of any central advisory authority, and the crumbling decay and disrepair into which important buildings had fallen. 'The continuance of this state of affairs' seemed to him to be 'little short of a scandal'.[38]

Curzon had long been interested in matters pertaining to monuments. Even before he came to India, their conservation and care was a high priority in his vision of life. As early as 1890, following a visit to Greece, he had publicly advocated and tried to persuade Gladstone to return the Parthenon marbles in the British Museum to their original site on the Acropolis of Athens.[39] In India, one of the first and perhaps most significant archaeology-related decisions that he took was to revive a post—that of the director of the Archaeological Survey—which would shortly result in pulling Marshall into India.

Because reviving this post meant that the government would now have to fork out more money, this could only be done with the consent of the India Office in London. Its consent in turn partly depended on the pressures that could be brought to bear upon it. In order to do this, Curzon followed a dual policy. On the one hand he chose to consistently reiterate in public speeches the necessity of discharging the imperial government's obligations towards the conservation of 'the most beautiful and perfect collection of monuments in the world.' His address on 7 February

1900, at the annual meeting of the Asiatic Society of Bengal, is just one example of many such fervent pledges: 'I hope to assert more definitely during my time the Imperial responsibility of Government in respect of Indian antiquities, to inaugurate or to persuade a more liberal attitude on the part of those with whom it rests to provide the means, and to be a faithful guardian of the priceless treasure-house of art and learning that has, for a few years at any rate, been committed to my charge.'[40]

At a second level, he used his influential position to lobby for more money and posts within the Archaeological Survey as a means of carrying out his pledge. Curzon was fortunate here in having, as secretary of state for India, George Hamilton, 'a man easy-going, tired and content to support the Viceroy'.[41] In this relationship, it was the viceroy who took policy decisions while the secretary of state tamely acceded to his requests. Within a few months of his arrival in India, in May 1899, Curzon got Hamilton to approve a nearly 30 per cent increase in the annual budget for archaeology.[42] This was followed, at the end of 1900, by a series of comprehensive proposals to the secretary of state for the reorganization of the Survey. Here, the viceroy requested that the direct responsibility of Indian monuments be assumed by the imperial government. Additionally, he asked for a lakh of rupees to be annually spent on archaeological work of special importance. And most significantly, he now stated the urgent need for a director of archaeology:

> The question of providing in a more satisfactory manner than is the case at present for the conservation of ancient remains of archaeological or historical interest has occupied our attention for some time past. We have come to the conclusion that this object can only be attained by the exercise of a larger measure of control on the part of the Supreme Government than has for some years been the case; and that for this purpose it will be necessary to appoint a highly qualified officer for a term of years to advise us as to the state of these monuments of antiquity, and as to the measures to be

adopted for their conservation, and generally to direct and control the working of the Archaeological Department in all its branches.[43]

Curzon also used the dispatch to remind Hamilton about the attacks of continental scholars like Buhler, who had published sharp criticisms of the government's presumed apathy and of the sentiment being articulated in the Indian press for a more liberal policy towards Indian monuments. As expected, Hamilton gave his sanction, and by May 1901 the viceroy had succeeded in reviving the post of director general of archaeology in India.

But how did he now propose to find a suitable man?

Even before Curzon could begin looking for a suitable director, the Home Office, in the very telegram communicating George Hamilton's sanction for the director's post, suggested an aspirant who they considered suitable—Vincent Smith.[44]

To understand how this suggestion came to be made, let us look at the manner in which the India Office operated. From the records of the revenue and statistics department, it seems that Hamilton, on receiving the proposals from Curzon and his council in December 1900, almost immediately decided to go along with the viceroy's proposal. But before communicating his sanction he thought it desirable to also look for a suitable man for the post. Opinions were sought from old India hands and experts in England. One of them, George Birdwood, best known for his study of *The Industrial Arts of India*, did not think much of the viceroy's proposal. Very much in the mould of the 'abolitionist' school, Birdwood maintained that the proposed director was not required, and that not even provincial archaeological surveyors were necessary. However, if a director *had* to be appointed, he believed one or other among the British archaeologists working in the Mediterranean and Egypt would be most suitable.[45] Charles Lyall, an India Office man, on the other hand, impressed upon the secretary of state the necessity of getting a person well versed in ancient India's languages, epigraphy, and archaeology. Evidently, he was lobbying for a person he thought eminently suitable—Vincent Smith. As early as March 1901, much before the sanction for the post of a director was formally communicated to Curzon, Lyall had sent a long note to Hamilton strongly recommending Smith's candidature.[46]

Smith's qualifications were several. At fifty-two, having retired after nearly thirty years in the Indian Civil Service, he was an old India hand. He had a great deal of administrative experience, having held various important posts in the North-Western Provinces and Oudh as district officer, settlement officer, judge and secretary to the government. Furthermore, he had published a fair amount on subjects pertaining to Indian history and archaeology. Smith also had the advantage of being supported by Hamilton, who thought he 'is as good a man as we are likely to get.'[47]

But Smith's limitations, as it appears, proved to be the more serious. Curzon articulated these with his customary bluntness: 'My impression is that he is deficient both in expert and artistic knowledge and in energy.'[48] Being only forty when he took over as viceroy in January 1899, Curzon's predilections for a younger, more energetic man, someone in the viceroy's own mould, are obvious. He himself had an astounding capacity for work, about which his most recent biographer, David Gilmour, has this to say: 'Anyone who studies Curzon's outpourings over a particular period—the despatches, the resolutions, the letters to Hamilton and Godley, the minutes, the telegrams, the epistles to friends, the speeches, the admonitions, the communications to all parts of India—is likely to feel that they took less time for the Viceroy to produce than they do for the reader to study. Although he told Hamilton that he had worked at least ten hours each day during August and September 1901, it is difficult to understand how the quantity of work could have been accomplished in less than twenty.'[49]

Possibly, Curzon was also aware of Smith's memo on the terms that he expected if he was appointed. These included 'permission to come home in the summer of 1903 and 1905, for not less than four months or more than six months in each of those years.'[50] It is unlikely that Smith's terms would have found favour with a workaholic viceroy.

Finally, on the subject of monument policy and archaeology, which were so close to his own heart, Curzon may have felt that an older man who had worked for several decades in India would not be content to follow the new paths that a new viceroy might chart. To this may be added the dim view that Curzon may have taken of Smith's brand of scholarship, for this was the kind of colonial scholarship in which every noteworthy aspect of India's architectural, pictorial, and numismatic art was seen as being of Western origin. The damage done to the study of archaeology by such scholarship had been expressed to Curzon by some of the old guard of the Survey, such as J.B. Keith, who had retired as surveyor of the North-Western Circle in the 1880s. In a letter to Curzon from Lausanne, he had said: 'For years the necessities of Indian Archaeology have fallen into the hands of philologists who have made a preserve in pressing home the exploded theories of Professor Max Müller, largely responsible for the exaggerations of Western Civilization.'[51]

So, a polite but firm refusal of Smith's candidature was dispatched: 'Your telegram May 14th. Director General, Archaeology. From careful enquiries we are clear that Vincent Smith is not suitable. He is a mere amateur in archaeology, and has neither expert knowledge nor energy we require.'[52]

Curzon's estimate of Smith's fitness for the post sent clear signals to the Home Office about the kind of man the viceroy wanted:

> the Government of India want a younger man, and that they do not consider oriental scholarship essential . . . their idea is that a comparatively young man who has distinguished himself as a scholar at one of the English Universities and who has since devoted himself to archaeological work in Greece or Egypt or Asia Minor, and who has the capacity and energy and power of work would

> be fitted for the post. He might or might not grow into an oriental scholar but his training would enable him to appreciate and utilise the work of oriental specialists.[53]

Looking back, the extraordinary congruence between the viceroy's requirements and the qualifications of the man who would become director of the Survey is striking. Clearly, the young John Marshall, with his brilliant Cambridge career and his classical archaeology training, was tailormade for the post.

As Curzon was not specially keen on an Indologist, the India Office decided to approach the trustees of the British Museum. It was felt that the authorities there, being in close touch with the archaeological work of the societies working in Greece and other Mediterranean lands, might be able to suggest a suitable man. The director of the British Museum, Sir Edward Maunde Thompson, seems in fact, to have quickly mobilized his university friends. By September 1901 he wrote to Arthur Godley, the under secretary of state for India, that he had found

> the very man for Your Archaeological Inspector. J.H. Marshall of King's Coll. Camb. His age is 25 and his University record of the highest. . . . Personally he seems a very pleasant fellow—and, though young, impressed one as an older man. Of course he had no Indian knowledge but with his university career and his experience at the School of Athens, he will soon adapt. Our archaeologists have a high opinion of him. I have told him that you wish to see him and so hold himself prepared.[54]

Marshall made an excellent impression on those who interviewed him. By the middle of October 1901, the job was offered to him. The search for a director of archaeology in India was thus finally concluded.

But for John Marshall, of course, the most extraordinary part of this saga was now about to begin.

# 3

# JOHN MARSHALL'S EARLY YEARS IN INDIA

MARSHALL LEFT FOR BOMBAY ON 6 FEBRUARY 1902, arriving there two and a half weeks after the *S.S. Massilia* had sailed from Marseilles. His limited knowledge of India may not have prepared him for the magnificent geographical scale of the subcontinent, which was at least twenty times larger than his previous field area. His travels over the next couple of months almost certainly underscored the difference in the dimensions now confronting him—from Bombay on the western shores to Calcutta and then towards the end of March across the heart of Gangetic India to the north-western Himalayas and finally to Simla, the summer capital of the government.[1] Almost immediately, Simla became his permanent headquarters. Marshall had taken up charge as director of archaeology in India for a period of five years, but in fact, although at this stage he had no thought of growing old in the tropics (in fact he left India aged fifty-seven), the subcontinent's sites and monuments were to become his lifelong work.

When Marshall first came to India, he hoped to introduce there what he had learnt in Greece. He came with the idea of changing what used to be called the idol-digger method of archaeological excavation. This predatory practice of excavation was vigorously pursued in nineteenth-century India, where sites were treated more as sources of sculpture than as the means for understanding civilizational evolution and an area's history. David Hogarth too had expressed a desire to dig in the north-west frontier region, and Marshall may well have been looking forward to finding a practicable way of bringing his mentor out to India.[2] Almost certainly, he will have imagined himself making great discoveries in that area as well. The north-west frontier and its buried cities, through which Achaemenid and Hellenic conquerors had passed on their way to the land of the Indus, had as we saw been frequently described in classical scholarship. This was a world with which Marshall, fresh from archaeological excavations in Greece, was utterly familiar. It seems more than conceivable that he contemplated following the trail of the British Museum seals back to Harappa, about which he now had a better idea from Alexander Cunningham's survey report.

But five years or so were to pass before Harappa and its intriguing seals reappeared in Marshall's new life.

This is because, from the outset, Marshall was firmly taken under his wing by Curzon who had very definite ideas about how the Archaeological Survey should be revived. For one thing, the viceroy's main focus was not field research upon promising mounds like Harappa. The fact that only Rs 5000 was spent on the excavation of archaeological sites during Marshall's first year in India—a mere 5 per cent of the archaeological budget—reflects this. Instead, the repair and restoration of monuments, from the Arhai-di-ka Jhompra mosque in Ajmer to the Gol Gumbaz in Bijapur and from the Jamalgarhi ruins of the North-West Frontier Province to the Mandalay palace of Burma, was given precedence over everything else. Later, Marshall would generously acknowledge Curzon's role in guiding and moulding him in his early years: 'had he been my *guru* and I his pupil, he could not have taken more trouble or been more patient and enthusiastic.'[3] In sum, Curzon set the agenda for the organization that Marshall headed. The young director general, in fact, barely had the time or space to follow up or implement his own ideas.

Curzon's conception of what his protégé had to do was all-embracing, ranging from his training, to the organization of his office and work, to the tenor of his writings. Marshall's grooming began from the moment of their first meeting, a memory of which the viceroy preserved. This was when Marshall travelled to Calcutta, soon after arriving in Bombay. Curzon had just returned from a tour of north Bengal, where he had inspected the ruins of Pandua, and was soon to leave for Hyderabad on his way to becoming the first viceroy to have seen the exquisite frescoes of Ajanta.[4] Curzon later wrote to the secretary of state about the Ajanta caves, and it is in that letter that he also penned his first impressions of the man Hamilton had sent to India: 'I made his acquaintance before leaving Calcutta, and thought him rather distinguished in appearance and quite becomingly keen. I told him that he must learn Sanskrit at once, in order to be able to deal with inscriptions, one of the most important branches of Indian Archaeology.'[5] In the prolonged interaction that followed at Simla, important innovations in the director general's establishment were suggested by Curzon. The viceroy, for instance, urged Marshall to set up an archaeological library attached to his office, one whose primary function would be to aid the officers of the archaeological department. Almost immediately, the proposal was formalized and a few thousand rupees were provided for the purchase of books. The library seems not to have got into working order till 1904, but over the years its nucleus of books steadily expanded. Eventually, it went on to become the most famed archaeological library of India.

Another innovation, also viceregally inspired, was the publication of an archaeological annual. This was to contain the latest results of the work of the Archaeological Survey and whet the public interest in fresh discoveries. Curzon's guidance is writ large not merely in what the journal was expected to contain but also in how it ought to look. He did not, for instance, approve the original draft that Marshall had written for the inaugural issue: 'It is too long, it contains unimportant details, there is too much of the first person singular and the information communicated is given in a strictly official style, which will excite little or no interest.'[6] Even its binding caught the viceroy's eagle eye; he noted a mismatch between that and the contents: 'If these are worthy of the rather pretentious cover it might stand. If they are not, something more modest might be substituted.'[7] The volume was redrafted and rebound, naturally. The inaugural annual report finally appeared, looking suitably worthy. It was a large, handsome volume, bound in green cloth.

Above all, in those early years, Marshall was largely involved in overseeing architectural conservation and restoration initiated by the viceroy. Because discharging Curzon's ambitious programme of conservation provides the frame for most of Marshall's early archaeological work, it is first necessary to understand it; one can then appreciate what was involved in the preservation of some of the subcontinent's most important monuments, with Marshall serving as Curzon's right-hand man.

The natural and human factors involved in the despoliation of Indian monuments were several: exuberant vegetation, illegal excavation, indigenous as also British destruction through conversion of old structures into offices or residences, and a complete lack of financial and supervisory responsibility at all levels. The long era of vandalism inaugurated by the early phase of British rule in India was, however, singled out by Curzon as being the most recent context of such despoliation. In Lahore alone, without any apparent sense of incongruity, the Diwan-i-Am was serving as a summer dormitory for British soldiers; the Moti

Masjid was a currency reserve treasury; the Choti Khwabgah a church; Anarkali's tomb the civil secretariat record room and library; and the Dai Anga Masjid (also called 'Railway Mosque') the railway traffic superintendent's office. In Delhi, the Red Fort had been adapted to the needs of a European garrison. Two-storeyed barracks were built within the fort walls, while the rooms over the fort's 'Lahore' and 'Delhi' gates were occupied by officers of the garrison.[8] British occupation of Indian monuments had become especially widespread in the wake of the revolts of 1857, these having functioned as the strongholds of rebellious Indian rulers, soldiers, and citizens. Since they were perceived as symbols of Indian resistance they were inevitably brutally metamorphosed.[9]

To Curzon the plight of these historic buildings, which he encountered across much of India, proved an embarrassing reminder of, as he put it, 'a century of British vandalism and crime'.[10] This must have been especially embarrassing because their state of dilapidation or misuse went against the grain of his attempt to make the British administration of India appear evenhanded and enlightened. He considered this necessary because on India, he was convinced, the position of the British empire somehow depended: 'As long as we rule India we are the greatest Power in the world. If we lose it, we shall drop straightaway to a third-rate power.'[11] Within this large imperial vision it seemed urgent to promote a more cultured administration which gave priority to the restoration of India's architectural heritage. This was to be an enterprise in which the initiative was to come from the imperial government: 'The Government of India and not the Provincial Governments, will always be responsible for maintaining intact this great inheritance.'[12] Its sustenance also could not be provided by the alternative that Curzon's predecessor, Elgin, had warmly welcomed: a European association overseeing an Indian Exploration Fund for subcontinental archaeology.

Curzon's distinct lack of enthusiasm for the Elginian view of conservation was because of his belief that continental scholars and travellers would, as in the past, loot Indian antiquities and enrich the collections at the Louvre in Paris and the Royal Museum for Ethnography at Berlin. This was a widely shared sentiment. In a confidential letter, James Burgess complained to the secretary of state about French vandalism in the north-west. He was outraged at the fact that while the British Museum hardly possessed Gandhara sculptures—and those it had were mostly presented by private individuals—in Paris apparently a hundred pieces representative of early Buddhist art from Swat and Yusufzai were about to be exhibited.[13] These had, it seems, all been lately brought home by a French traveller. Burgess also used this letter to draw attention to a case of what he described as German banditry in Burma, where a well-known antiquity looter called Thomann Gillis had removed, slab by slab, the fresco paintings of the Theinmazi Pagoda and had tried to sell them to the Ethnological Museum at Berlin. The British ambassador to Berlin had taken up the case, whereupon the German government admitted they had indeed been offered a collection of objects from Burma, including the frescoes mentioned by Burgess, but the price asked for being exorbitant, they had not accepted the offer.[14]

For all these reasons, in Curzon's scheme of things archaeological work in India was a British responsibility, to be discharged by the imperial government, with no space for other European nationals. To these ideas he added another perspective. While British interest *vis-à-vis* Indian archaeology was to be jealously safeguarded, this would not give Britons automatic right to cart away antiquities and sculpture to England. Instead, relics of archaeological and historical value were to be conserved in British India, and the earlier cultural plunder might, in some cases, even be returned to India by England. At the viceroy's initiative the *pietra dura* panels, which today form the backdrop to Shah Jahan's throne in the Diwan-i-Am of the Red Fort at

Delhi, were brought back from the Victoria and Albert Museum in London and successfully restored in their original place. Their repatriation to India coincided with a special occasion, the 1903 Delhi coronation of Edward VII. As Curzon shrewdly argued: 'the background of the throne should represent to assembled spectators, by a careful restoration to its original condition, not the vandalism of an earlier generation, but the generous enlightenment of a later and more cultured age.'[15]

These then, very broadly, are the ways in which Curzon visualized his conservationist mission. But how was this project actually discharged? Curzon himself visited and inspected an astoundingly large number of monuments. Here, 'detailed instructions were left on his departure extending to such items as cracked plaster and cobwebs on a staircase; at Ajanta he ordered the bats to be driven out of the caves and the insect nests scraped away.'[16] In relation to a mosque at Fatehpur Sikri, he even left instructions on the devices that needed to be installed to prevent colonization by birds and bats. These consisted of a thorn bush that he wanted hung in the centre of the building and some fine steel wires which were to be stretched across the dome from side to side.[17] Detailed sketches made by the viceroy sometimes accompanied many of these instructions, graphically illustrating exactly what needed to be done (Fig. 10).

Naturally, as the viceroy's right-hand man, it was Marshall's responsibility to see that his instructions were followed. Most of Marshall's early tours were, in fact, related only to overseeing and supervising architectural conservation. In his first year, from the time that he reached Simla till the spring of 1903, over eight months were spent in such surveys, covering historic sites in very scattered parts of India—Mathura, Lahore, Gwalior, Ahmedabad, Bijapur, Tanjore, Mount Abu, and Mandu being some of these.[18] On at least two occasions he accompanied Curzon when inspecting monuments at Delhi and Agra. In those early years, Curzon took it upon himself to draw Marshall's attention to historic

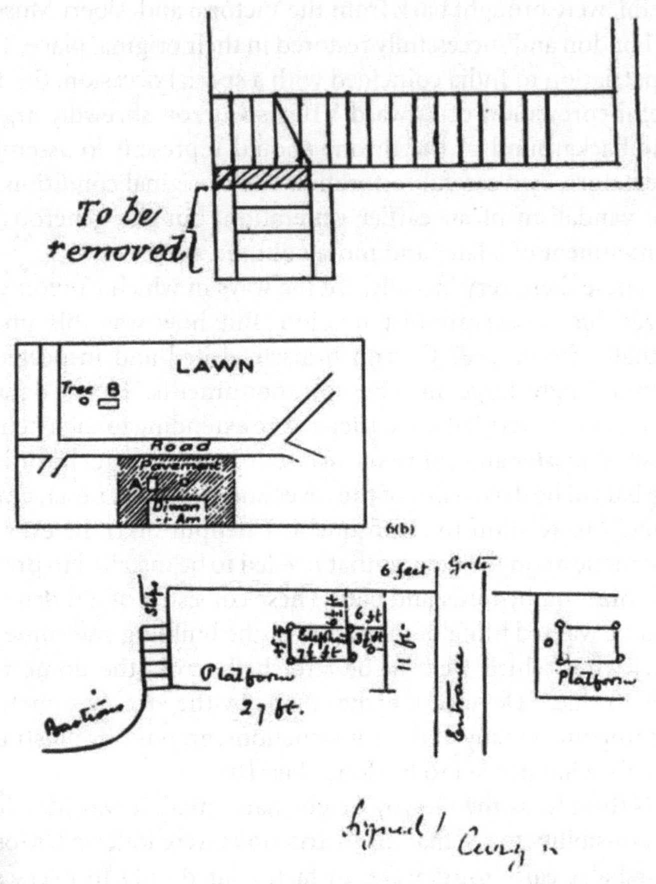


Fig. 10. Sketches that accompanied some of Lord Curzon's communications: (i) pertains to the Taj complex (Saheli Burj No. 2) (ii) relates to the Diwan-i-Am in Agra fort (iii) is a sketch of the Hatipol or Elephant Gateway at Mandu

places, to their beauty, and to the kind of repairs that he imagined they required.

Take the case of Mandu. Curzon visited it in 1902 and was soon writing to Captain Ernest Barnes, political agent of the

Bhopawar Agency, about how impressed he was with both its archaeology and natural grandeur. He also proposed 'to direct the eye and the footsteps of the Director General of Archaeology towards it . . . Indeed an Archaeologist has merely to come to Mandu to find almost every sentiment gratified to which he is prone—the delight of seeing magnificent buildings, of realising that in some cases they are not beyond repair, and of acknowledging that nothing except the want of money stands in the way of restoration.'[19] Promptly, Marshall was dispatched to Mandu and was equally enthusiastic. He found Dhar a delightful state and the magnificent Jama Masjid at Mandu reminded him, he said, 'of the Doge Palace at Venice; indeed its natural tints are finer.'[20] In the years that followed Marshall revisited Mandu on many occasions, coordinating debris clearance and the removal of unaesthetic accretions, and thus ensuring proper conservation activity in the Jama Masjid, at Hoshang Shah's tomb, and in the mosque of Dilawar Khan.

The problems with several other monuments, though, were more complicated. Before conservation work could begin, the task of evicting various government offices and establishments from their precincts had to delicately proceed. How this was done was generally planned by Curzon and followed up by Marshall. The stipulated procedure required that the proposed evacuation of the military from monuments in Lahore and Delhi be routed through the local governments. But, as Curzon put it:

> In practice, I know, *alas*, what this means. The Punjab Government were to consult the local/military authorities about evacuating the Moti Masjid and the Choti Khwabgah in the Lahore Fort as far back as April 1899. But 3½ years have elapsed and we are scarcely any forwarder. They were similarly to consult the Railway authorities about the Railway Mosque; three years have elapsed and it is not yet evacuated.
>
> I have never been able to get a thing done by the Military authorities through the Local Government without inordinate delay. If

ever anything has been done, it has been by going to the Military Department straight and getting them to issue orders.[21]

So, Marshall spent a great deal of time coordinating with military authorities on the best procedure for clearing the forts of Delhi, Lahore, and Agra. The technicalities of overseeing the actual work, once it got started, was equally time-consuming. In Delhi he oversaw all details, ranging from stone work to the excavation of old foundations. In the Moti Masjid, for instance, the renovation of its flooring was carefully scrutinized, and while Marshall found the inlay of black marble in the quadrangle flooring to be satisfactory, the repairs in the paving of white marble were very clumsy and instructions came to be given for it to be redone.[22] As for the marble screens that were being carved, he found the patterns and the manner of execution so full of fault that he personally met the contractor, Nathu Ram & Sons, at Agra, and 'pointed out to him that unless there are more satisfactory results to show when I revisit Delhi, the contract will have to be withdrawn and placed with some other firm.' The *pietra dura* plaques brought back from the Victoria and Albert Museum in London had to be put back where they belonged, and the restoration of these to their original position in the Diwan-i-Am was supervised by Marshall as well.

Supervisory tours soon took Marshall to Lahore. Several of its magnificent monuments had been spasmodically mutilated by various rulers—by the Durranis, by Maharaja Ranjit Singh, and by the British (who had also converted most of the important ones into offices, domestic spaces, and churches). The process of repair and restoration at Lahore took several years and the director general frequently journeyed there to inspect monuments, prepare detailed notes, and suggest measures for their preservation. Lahore is less than two hundred kilometres to the north-east of Harappa. Nothing prevented Marshall, while he toured this part of Punjab, from visiting the ruins from where the seals he had seen emanated. Harappa now was a well-known site and British officials, notably Masson and Cunningham, had as we saw reported on its possible significance.

But Marshall did not go to Harappa. Just why he did not venture to visit it cannot be satisfactorily explained. It is possible that, although its seals had interested him, they had not inspired him sufficiently. Perhaps also, unlike many of his predecessors, he was a cautious man who was unlikely to follow up intriguing clues from unknown mounds on impulse, especially when practically all his energies had to be devoted to the viceroy's conservation programme.

While the viceroy's wishes were Marshall's overriding concern and the Archaeological Survey's primary preoccupation at the beginning of his tenure, it is not as if the only archaeological work undertaken in British India at this time was conservation. On the contrary, field excavations and explorations, even if only a few were undertaken either directly by the Survey's officers or by others in related departments.

When Marshall arrived in India, the Survey was a very small organization, with just six officers. Five of them—Henry Cousens, Alexander Rea, Theodore Bloch, J. Ph. Vogel, and Taw Sein Kho—worked as archaeological superintendents of Survey circles, these being provincial divisions of the archaeological department—namely, Bombay (with Sindh and Berar), Madras (with Coorg), Bengal (with Assam), the Punjab (with Baluchistan and Ajmer), and Burma. Eugen Hultzsch was the government epigraphist, while the United Provinces Circle was then without a superintendent (because the incumbent, E.W. Smith, had recently died). Each circle also had a few assistants attached to it: draftsmen, clerks, and photographers.

Taken together, these men were expected to oversee exploration, excavation, documentation, conservation, and epigraphy. The pressure of work was tremendous, but almost all the surveyors managed some field research. Alexander Rea, for instance, excavated Amaravati in the Madras Presidency. Theodore Bloch opened up parts of the ancient city of Vaisali, which was buried in the mounds at Basarh in Bihar. J. Ph. Vogel undertook excavations at Charsada in the North-West Frontier Province and subsequently at Kasia in the United Provinces.

All these places—Charsada, Kasia, Amaravati, and Basarh—were located in widely different parts of the subcontinent. What was common to them was the presence of old mounds, and the remains of structures that either had Buddhist associations or revealed sculptural relics intimately connected with the life and times of the Buddha. Were the circles of the Archaeological Survey, therefore, working in harmony, and according to a preconceived plan?

Marshall's retrospective assessments do suggest that such an overall plan existed. In a widely quoted passage from an assessment made by him in 1915 as part of the quinquennial review of the Archaeological Survey, Marshall described its early research aims:

> From the time of its re-organisation in 1902, it has been the design of the Department to take in hand the excavation of the great buried cities of antiquity; but before this design could be carried out, it was deemed advisable to re-examine some of the Buddhist sites which had already been partially uncovered, in order to coordinate the results obtained by earlier excavators and to check the often unreliable conclusions which they had drawn.[23]

Later, on several occasions, Marshall presented the excavations undertaken at the outset of his tenure as forming part of a conscious strategy connected with Buddhist sites. Such places, we may recall, had been the early focus of British interest, at least since the time of Cunningham, who, as we saw, Chinese Buddhist pilgrims' travelogues in hand, had successfully mapped and identified many of them. But Cunningham's excavations had also removed images and objects with impunity, without even an elementary recording of their locations within the areas excavated. It was with a view to changing all this that Marshall now approached Buddhist sites. He was expected to introduce 'the scientific methods of digging which had yielded such brilliant results in Greece and Crete', and which apparently formed one of the reasons for his Indian appointment.[24]

Being overwhelmed with conservation work, Marshall had at this point time only for issuing instructions; the excavations were generally conducted by his officers. But far from being capable of introducing 'scientific methods of digging', some of these officers were not even trained to conduct excavations. In this respect, the case of Charsada in the Peshawar valley of north-west India is instructive. The need to undertake an excavation at Charsada had been spelt out by J. Ph. Vogel in May 1902. Charsada was rich in all kinds of literary association and was identified with ancient Pushkalavati, an important city of the north-west during the late centuries BC. Apparently, it had been invaded by the troops of Alexander the Great, who possibly established a Macedonian garrison there. In the classical sources which chronicle Alexander's exploits, the city was known as Peucelaotis and Proclais. Legend suggested that, during the time of the Mauryan emperor Ashoka, several Buddhist monuments were constructed here, some apparently by the king himself. The legend of the Buddha having made a gift of his eyes at Pushkalavati, because of which the great stupa of the 'eye-gift' was constructed, added to its importance, at least in the eyes of two well-known Chinese pilgrims, Fa Xian (AD 404–14) and Hsuan Tsang: both visited it. After Hsuan Tsang's time, the city appears to have sunk into complete oblivion.[25]

Excavations began there towards the end of February 1903

under the supervision of Vogel, who was undertaking such a task for the first time in his career. Marshall could not be present because he was touring western India and received several jittery letters from Vogel, who was obviously very nervous about his maiden project. 'I must tell you that you are seriously wanted here. I have never done any excavation before and am simply going on digging in my own stupid way.' Vogel's description of his first two weeks at Charsada makes irresistible reading:

> You will be anxious to hear how the excavations are going on. Great discoveries have not been made yet but a certain number of small objects come to light regularly such as terracottas, lamps, pottery and beads. Yesterday a piece of Gandhara sculpture was found, which would point to the existence of a temple or *stupa* inside the Fort, and two coins one Hindu and one Muhammadan. We have started now digging pits of 12 x 8 yards and about 6 feet deep from three corners of the Hisar and continue so along the edges. Each of the parties will have to make a dozen of such pits in order to finish the whole outline of the Fort. Here and there walls have been found which have been preserved for your inspection.
>
> There are three gangs each of thirty men under a jamadar at work now, at a pay of Rs 2—each a week (the jamadar gets Rs 3). This is considered a very good pay and there is no difficulty in procuring as many men as we want.
>
> They work with real enthusiasm encouraged by their jamadars with the war cry 'Shabash Imandars!' as if the object was a religious one instead of revealing the remnants of despised idolators.
>
> At the same time they work far more carefully than I had anticipated as appears from the fact that many objects like beads do not escape their notice. This is undoubtedly due to the reward system, which is very popular with them. One wonders how much material must have been lost at previous excavations when no rewards were given and consequently any small objects were thrown away . . .[26]

Vogel's assistants, too, were only partially equipped to handle the excavation. Neither of his two draftsmen knew how to prepare site maps, and so the services of the director's draftsman, Bhairon Baksh, had been requisitioned. Marshall joined the excavations only towards the end of March and remained a month.

During these weeks, from late March to April, four mounds were opened and a few structural features relating to them came to be better understood. For instance, Bala Hissar was shown to be a fortified citadel, while at Mir Ziyarat the remains of dwelling structures were unearthed. Palatu Dheri yielded a *vihara* or monastery which originally had a superstructure of wood, while Ghaz Dheri contained a relic-bearing stupa base. Various types of antiquities were excavated—inscriptions, sculpture, beads, coins, and metal objects—but were not described in relation to the trenches from which they emerged. In classifying the structural remains and minor finds at Bala Hissar, a curious twofold division was adopted: 'Muhammadan' and 'pre-Muhammadan'. With the exception of coins, 'Muhammadan' artefacts were not described.

Whatever may have been Marshall's own training and the expectations of those who had appointed him, excavations such as the one conducted at Charsada can hardly be considered textbook examples of 'scientific digging'.

But what of the Indian archaeological arena outside the world of these Buddhist sites? Was there any sense of a past that extended beyond the world of Buddhist complexes? And how was anyone going to find out? Had any new clues turned up? Such questions are important to the story of the Indus civilization because its discovery, many years later, was to hugely push back the frontiers of the Indian past. Before such a discovery could be made, there had to be men who believed that such a past existed, and that it could be archaeologically explored.

First, though, we must understand exactly how 'early' the early Indian past was believed to be at this point of time. Generally speaking, the literary history of India, within which its various aspects could be assigned with confidence to specific time periods and geographical areas, was seen to begin around the fourth century BC, with the invasion of Alexander the Great. Before the arrival of these Greeks, the general pattern of historical developments had only been reconstructed on the basis of a variety of religious texts frequently visualized through the prism of racial migrations. The writings of William Jones, founder of the Asiatic Society of Bengal, are an example of this. Jones's discourses focused, to an important extent, around Sanskrit texts, and, among other things, on the affinities between Sanskrit on the one hand and Asian and European languages on the other. Sanskrit was seen as being closely connected to the language of Persia, to Greek and Latin, as also to the languages of the Celts, Germans, and Slavs. The speakers of these tongues were all placed within a framework which saw the dispersal of various groups from an original common stock. Generally speaking, though, early Sanskrit texts were poorly dated, and their cultural details had not been corroborated by archaeology. In fact, as the first volume of *The Cambridge History of India* put it many decades later, the light thrown by sources like the hymns of the *Rigveda* on the material conditions of life in ancient India was disappointingly meagre.[27] What had been suggested by archaeology represented, at this point, only faint glimmerings. Marshall himself admitted that 'almost the only remains of those early times that have come down to us have been rough implements of the Stone and Copper Ages, groups of prehistoric graves in the south of the peninsula, and some rude cyclopean walls at Rajagriha in Bihar.'[28]

What is important, though, is that Marshall, even at the very start of his career in India, does not seem to have been intimidated by this lack of really ancient evidence. In fact, he had visualized an archaeological canvas, waiting to be found, which preceded what was then considered to be the beginning of the subcontinent's historical past.

This vision is evident, for example, from the work that Marshall deputed Hirananda Sastri to undertake in 1903. In this context, it seems important for us to note the activities of such subordinates and assistants, for very often these were the people without whom Marshall and the Survey would not have discovered all that they did. Hirananda was one of these assistants. He was the 'Pundit in charge' at the archaeological office of Punjab. Virtually all the European officers of the Survey required the assistance of traditional scholars—called Pundits and Maulvis—to comprehend and translate inscriptions and relevant manuscripts in Indic languages and scripts. However, since there was always more work than men on hand, such assistants also helped out in a number of other ways. In this case, Hirananda was sent to survey a particular genre of archaeological sites in the Ganga–Yamuna doab.[29]

These were settlements—those of Rajpur Parasu, Bithur, and Pariar—that had yielded copper objects in the form of hoards. Their description as hoard objects is related to the manner in which they occurred, buried together as caches. They had been found by chance rather than in controlled excavations. From Rajpur Parasu, in June of 1896, a hoard made of axes, an axe-ingot, a bar, and harpoons had been acquired by the Lucknow Museum. Bithur, situated on the south bank of the Ganga, about nineteen kilometres north-west of Kanpur, was also a provenance spot for such objects, while Pariar, opposite Bithur, to the east of the Ganga had yielded axes and a sword fragment.

Evidently, Hirananda was asked to visit these sites because Marshall considered the copper hoard objects that they had yielded as belonging to an age of bronze. Such information about a 'Bronze Age' could, Marshall believed, be correlated with the early 'Vedic Age'. In a letter written much before the survey began, he had expressed concern at the lack of information on the provenance of such objects in the rich holdings of the various Indian museums:

> I have, I believe, collected sufficient literary and philological evidence to prove that the early Vedic Age was of bronze and not of iron, as has hitherto been supposed. It is of some importance, having backed up my conclusions by the evidence of existing antiquities, to correct the impossible anachronisms perpetrated in previous translations of the Rig Veda, and of still more importance to know that—assuming the existence of a bronze age at that period in India—the recovery of its monuments will present no insuperable difficulties. I have naturally been on the look out for implements belonging to an age of bronze and have succeeded in finding specimens in several museums, but without, unfortunately, a single note on the circumstances of their discovery or place of provenance![30]

What did Hirananda discover in the couple of weeks that he spent in the United Provinces during December 1903? Apart from some general descriptions about the find-spots, there is not very much in his report. At Rajpur Parasu (in present-day Bijnor district), he discovered that copper implements had been found quite accidentally about eight years earlier, at a depth of a couple of feet, while digging a well. There was a small mound called 'Kheda' (which is what mounds are locally called in large parts of North India) adjacent to this spot, from where he also collected some pottery. As for the other two find spots, in Bithur he noted that a part of the bed of the Ganga river formed the find spot, while in Pariar the implements had been found along the road going to Lucknow, and in a lake surrounding the village. Hirananda further noted that some of these were being actively worshipped as emblems of a battle that figured in the *Ramayana*: 'four persons in these villages have got some implements which are used as objects of worship and considered as relics of a fight between "Rama's hosts and sons!" '[31] Evidently, the reverence we earlier observed around ancient artefacts at Harappa—where what are now recognized as chalcolithic ringstones, were described as the bangles and ring of the town's legendary faqir—extended to other kinds of objects in areas much beyond the Punjab. Later, these copper hoard objects too would be recognized as belonging to a period almost as old as the city of Harappa.

At that point of time, though, from the details that Hirananda provided, Marshall was unable to substantiate the connection that he had thought might exist between copper objects and the 'Vedic Age'. Eventually, only some decades later, through the discovery of the Indus civilization in 1924, was the reality of a 'Bronze Age' (albeit an age much richer than that described in the Vedas) firmly established. But what is important here is that, as early as 1903, the prism through which Marshall viewed the Indian past was one which accommodated such a notion.

In the same year that Hirananda explored copper hoard sites, other clues of an unknown yet equally early segment of subcontinental history were unearthed from Baluchistan. The man who chanced upon these clues was an intrepid explorer called Hughes Buller, and the clues he discovered were in a village called Nal in the Las Bela region, on the main route from the Makran coast towards the north. Before we scrutinize the Nal finds, the explorer himself needs some introduction, for he was not an Archaeological Survey officer, nor even an archaeologist by training.

While we have, thus far, been in the main concerned with the work of the Survey and the renewed vigour with which it was reorganized under Curzon's viceroyalty, it is equally necessary to emphasize that, even in the first decade of the twentieth century, the archaeological research arena in India was not always synonymous with the work of the Survey. There were, as in the past, sundry characters exploring and excavating all kinds of sites and antiquities. Some were travellers with archaeological predilections. Kazui Otani, a Japanese savant, had travelled from England to India via Central Asia and the Kilik Pass and came in search of Buddhist sites. Having riffled treasures along the Silk Route, he was evidently looking out for similar treasure in India. Armed with a letter from the private secretary to Curzon, he obtained permission to explore Rajagriha and surrounding areas in Bihar.[32] More common, though, were officials who, in the course of their duties, found and collected all kinds of ancient paraphernalia. Hughes Buller was one of these. He is best remembered as the compiler of the district gazetteers of Baluchistan, although he seems to have enjoyed his 'archaeological' forays, made in the course of his tours, as much as his duties as 'Superintendent of the Imperial Gazetteer'.

Baluchistan is an oblong mountainous stretch of country in the north-western corner of the Indian subcontinent. At the beginning of the twentieth century it had a practically unexplored archaeological landscape. The only man who had interested himself in that area's ancient mounds was a Major E. Mockler, who, more than twenty-five years before Buller, had excavated a site which we know today as being Harappan.[33] Situated in the Dasht valley of Makran, this was Sutkagendor, from where Mockler recovered charcoal, fish bones, pottery, stone knives, and pieces of copper, as also a 'burnt brick' house. Sketches of some of the artefacts and Sutkagendor's mounds were also provided (Fig. 11), even though their age remained unknown to Mockler.

Buller's description of the Baluchistan landscape was more wide-ranging than Mockler's. Its relics, according to him, ranged from embankments or dams called *gabarbands* to crumbling *tumuli* containing centuries of past human debris—pottery, coins, statues, and terracottas.[34] Part of Buller's task in compiling the gazetteers was to write the history and archaeology of the different districts of Baluchistan. Therefore, as he travelled around,

Fig. 11. Mockler's 1877 sketches of Sutkagendor

he made it his business to visit and make collections from as many of its old mounds (or *dambs*, as they were locally called) as possible, and, on occasion, he also organized excavations there.

The sites themselves were spread over hundreds of kilometres and yielded diverse finds. At Tiz near Chahbar on the Persian border, pottery, beads of amber, glass, shell, and terracotta were found. Pottery and beads were also picked up at Hissar in the Jhalawan country, while a mound at Chalgari in Kachi yielded two terracottas: one of the designs seemed to be that of a tiger, and the other a man holding a drum. Then, at Gazg, high up in the mountains to the east of Kalat in central Baluchistan, Buller found animal figurines, as also gabarbands: 'Gazg is full of Gabarbands and that on excavating we found charcoal and lime, things which the people nowadays never think of using. We also found a cemented water channel . . .'

Buller regarded himself as too much of a novice in matters archaeological to be able to ascertain either the precise historical nature or the time period to which his finds belonged. And so, in his search for such information, he corresponded with various people in India and abroad. For instance, he sent the coins from Khozdar and Dabar Kot to the director of the British Museum, who identified the dynasties to which they belonged.[35] The raw materials of the objects from Tiz were recognized by J.H. Burkitt in the industrial section of the Indian Museum in Calcutta, while the prehistoric, 'pre-Hindu' antiquity of the pottery was tentatively suggested by Theodore Bloch, the archaeological superintendent of the Eastern Circle.[36] Another archaeologist that Buller began to write to for clarification was John Marshall, and by 1903 a lively correspondence developed between them. In October that year, Buller wrote to Marshall about some pottery from the mound at Nal, locally called Sohr Damb.[37] Nal was a fairly remote and inaccessible village in the Jhalawan area, in whose vicinity Sohr Damb was located. This was the largest and highest mound for miles. Because the southern end of this site had been subject to great heat, the earth had been baked to a red colour: hence its local name, Sohr Damb, which translates as Red Mound.

Buller had not himself visited Nal, but a member of his gazetteer staff, Mirza Sher Muhammad, had. In fact, with the permission of the headman of the place (who happened to be the chief of the Bizanjo tribe), he had part of the Sohr Damb dug up in a couple of days, which resulted in the discovery of pottery.[38] He carried a set of fifty-nine bowls from there to Buller. Having got the most interesting of these photographed, Buller informed Marshall that they were painted with polychrome designs and that some could have been cinerary urns: 'the designs are in red, black and yellow. As far as I can judge, it is much more delicate than anything that is made in Sind even at the present time . . . Some of the pots contain earth and bones.'[39]

When photographs of the Nal pottery (Fig. 12) reached Marshall, he immediately declared them the most interesting and finest yet procured in India and urgently asked Buller for more information:

> Could you find anything at all in the way of implements or other things which would give a possible clue? The trenches from which they come must be of supreme interest. Will you ask your agent to procure every single specimen he can on this pottery? I am quite willing to pay anything upto 25/- a piece; and that ought to tempt them; but I don't like the idea of any unorganized digging. There may be so much evidence to be obtained if it is done under skilled supervision—evidence which would otherwise be lost. Is the country, where the mound is situate, such that we could dig there ourselves? The sight of this pottery has made me intensely keen. I cannot be rash enough to commit writing my own yet vague ideas about it, but I believe if other objects could be discovered we may show that *we have got back to a date as yet unrepresented in the region by any antiquities.*[40] (Emphasis added)

A few months later, Marshall felt confident enough to state that they were closely allied to a type 'found in Cyprus, Phenicia etc. about the eighth century BC, which show a decadent Mycenaean technique and design combined with more purely Asiatic influences.' He was quite categorical about that fact that he

Fig. 12. Pottery from Nal

knew of no other wares that were anything like these from Baluchistan, and he thought it highly improbable that such wares could have been invented independently. Because of this, he was very keen to get Nal opened: 'I want very much to have some more excavations done in the mound at Nal. I believe that we shall probably get most important results from it, perhaps some of the most important that have ever been obtained in this country.'[41]

Retrospectively, these appear to be very interesting observations, on at least two counts. First, Marshall's instinctive reaction was to link Nal with the eastern Mediterranean. This is understandable in the light of his training. Like Charles Masson and Alexander Cunningham before him, Marshall was viewing an unknown culture in relation to what he knew best. If Masson's point of reference was Alexander the Great and Cunningham's was Buddhist pilgrims from China, for Marshall it was the Mediterranean regions upon which he had received his field training. Second, his intuition that the date of the ceramics from Nal could push back the existing chronology of Baluchistan proved to be correct. Nal is today recognized as part of a culture that forms the general background to the birth of Mohenjodaro and Harappa. Indeed, after the discovery of the Indus civilization in 1924, Marshall himself was to depute one of his officers to excavate it in order to understand how it synchronized with the 'civilization of the Indus valley'. He must certainly have taken the later decision to get Nal opened because of the glimpse that he had been given of its pottery more than twenty years earlier, via Buller, in the autumn of 1904.

But what about the excavations that Marshall was so keen to get going at Nal in 1904? In this year, he asked Aurel Stein to conduct a small dig there. Marc Aurel Stein (1862–1943) is one of the most famous names in the archaeology of Central Asia and north-west India. He discovered scores of buried cities and sites along the alignment of the famous Silk Route, in Baluchistan and the frontier areas. A large part of this work, incidentally, was done by him while he was formally attached to India's Archaeological Survey. In 1904 he held the post of archaeological surveyor of the North-Western Frontier Province and Baluchistan and this was the reason why Marshall wanted him, rather than anybody else, to excavate Nal. Aurel Stein, however, was not at all enthusiastic about performing his 'official' duties. Instead, he wished to concentrate on preparations for his tour of Chinese Turkestan. This tour would become difficult, he claimed, if he were to engage during the ensuing season in excavation enterprises which he would have neither the time to complete on systematic lines, nor properly describe.[42]

Stein's negative must have deeply disappointed Marshall. He is known to have complained that 'Archaeology has been at a standstill in the Frontier Province.'[43] Therefore Nal was very much on his mind. During the winter of 1904–5, the possible links that Baluchistan may have had with the Mediterranean became, for Marshall, a very exciting possibility, and one that he himself resolved to explore. It was with a view to following up the 'definite traces of Phoenician influence in Baluchistan' and unearthing fresh links in the chain of connection between it and the Mediterranean that, in 1904, he seriously contemplated excavations at Bahrain. J.G. Lorrimer of the Foreign Office had aroused his curiosity about a huge necropolis there which had yielded objects identified by a British Museum man as being of Phoenician workmanship.[44] Marshall's communications reveal his excitement about undertaking work there, and also throw light on what he proposed to do. He first wanted to go to Bahrain to understand its Phoenician links: 'I am particularly desirous of being present in person at the proposed excavations, as I have made somewhat of a speciality of Phoenician civilisation in the Levant and Turkey, and the evidence hitherto obtained in Bahrein points to its antiquities being of Phoenician origin.'[45] From Bahrain he wanted to move north and excavate a Baluchistan site which presented features analogous to those in Bahrain. By January 1905, practical arrangements for undertaking fieldwork in Bahrain were under way. Marshall had been in touch with a firm of contractors in Karachi about his requirements of tackle, pickaxes, shovels, knives, stout rope, etc., and concerning the need for a 'native' overseer who could speak English as well as the native tongue of Bahrain.[46]

How is this proposed excavation, which Marshall was so keen to get under way in Bahrain, relevant to the story of the discovery of the Indus civilization? Located in the Persian Gulf, Bahrain was in ancient times an area actively involved in commercial interactions with Harappan cities—as also with Mesopotamian ones.[47] Its ancient name was Dilmun, which frequently occurs in Sumerian literary compositions. Of more positive significance from the Indus perspective is the presence there, at places like Ras al-Qala and the Barabar temple complex, of artefacts of Indus provenance and/or inspiration, including seals with Indus designs, apart from the occasional inscription. Therefore, hypothetically, it was plausible that a field expedition to Bahrain might lead to the discovery of links between that region and Punjab via Harappan material. Marshall may have found a seal in Bahrain with characters similar to those that he had seen on the specimens from Harappa.

But, we will never know whether a field expedition to Bahrain may have hastened Marshall's understanding of the traces of a 'Bronze Age' that he had inadvertently chanced upon in his early years in India. This is because the excavation that he was meticulously planning for in the Persian Gulf never took place. At the last moment, the expedition was pre-empted by the viceroy's veto.

Curzon had apparently been unaware of Marshall's plans, until a proposal to get W.H. Nicholls (recently appointed archaeological surveyor in the United Provinces and Punjab) to accompany Marshall to Bahrain, reached the foreign department. When this was brought to Curzon's notice, his instructions were unambiguous. Sanction to take Nicholls was, of course, refused—'I think it is clear that Bahrein must be completely outside the legitimate boundaries either of the United Provinces or the

Punjab.' Curzon's annoyance at Marshall's proposed tour was even more categorical:

> I wish I had seen this case earlier. For greatly as I admire Mr Marshall's energy and glad as I shall be to see the *tumuli* at Bahrein systematically excavated, I should yet have felt compelled to raise a serious doubt as to whether the Director-General of Archaeology in India—paid out of Indian revenues, and surrounded by a field of work, which we are simultaneously assuring the Secretary of State will occupy his undivided energies for many years to come—has any business to go outside of India at all. If to Bahrein, on the ground that we have a Political officer there, why not to Baghdad and incidentally Babylon? If on the ground that Bahrein is under a British protectorate, then why not to Ceylon, on the ground that it is a British possession?[48]

So the tour was cancelled, leaving Marshall resentful and disappointed. A note to P.Z. Cox, the political resident at Bushire, about his inability to get there followed:

> I much regret to tell you that at the last moment our Archaeological Expedition to Bahrein has had to be abandoned owing to difficulties raised by the Government of India. It was very kind of you to send me so much useful information, and I shall hope to turn it to good account at some future time when I may be able to go to Bahrein on privilege leave. The antiquities there are particularly interesting to me and my disappointment is therefore the greater that I am not able to explore them under the auspices of the Government.[49]

As it so happened, there was political trouble in Bahrain at this point of time, and, quite independently of Marshall's communications, a telegram from Bushire arrived on 23 January asking if Marshall's visit could be postponed because of the unsatisfactory state of affairs there.

Marshall's teething years had, in sum, coincided with the discovery of artefacts on the subcontinent which were then unrepresented in existing narratives of ancient India. Such discoveries would keep on increasing with the passage of time. For the moment, though, the scent of all these clues could not be followed up. With Lord Curzon as a guru who also held him captive, Marshall's main brief remained the rescue of India's monuments from the ravages of vegetation and vandalism. It was only following Curzon's exit from India in 1905 that Marshall began to seriously train his eyes on some of these exciting clues and places.

Harappa was one of them.

# 4
# HARAPPA MAKES A FLEETING REAPPEARANCE

HARAPPA RESURFACED IN JOHN MARSHALL'S LIFE in much the same way that it had first appeared: in the portals of the British Museum in London as he rummaged through its vast collections.

This was in 1906, when Marshall returned to England for eight months or so. Some months before, his mentor, Lord Curzon, had gone back home after resigning his post as viceroy of India. The opposition he had to face in India because of his decision to partition the province of Bengal, his differences with the secretary of state on major and minor issues that ranged from appointments to his council to military administration, and above all the machinations of his own army commander-in-chief, Lord Kitchener—these various manipulations and pressures had forced Curzon to resign. But they need not concern us here.[1]

Marshall, though, must have felt the loss of his patron most acutely, as did many others in the Archaeological Survey. This is captured most tellingly in the tribute that one of them, Alexander Rea, archaeological surveyor of Madras, penned: 'I have been for the past 23 years engaged in this work, and I can confidently say, that his Excellency has done more towards archaeology, than any other that has occupied a position of authority during my period of service. Such friends of archaeology are badly needed, and are only too few.'[2] Unlike Marshall, who had been brought over by the viceroy and had enjoyed his unstinted support (except over the proposed trip to Bahrain), Rea was part of the old guard of the Survey who had worked in the bleak decade between the retirement of Burgess in 1889 and the arrival of Curzon in 1899. As we saw, those were years when the imperial government had viciously pared down the archaeological establishment's budget and manpower, even considering ending support to the Archaeological Survey altogether. In comparison, the short Curzon years had been a truly a 'golden age' when monuments had become a matter of priority even for those who were part of the highest echelons of the British Raj.

Fortunately the basic structure of archaeological policy laid down by Curzon was to remain in place for a long time to come. This was in large measure something that Curzon himself ensured almost as the last thing he ever did in India. Even as he made preparations for his return to Britain, India's monuments and its institutional guardian, the Archaeological Survey, were very much in Curzon's horizons. His final journey in India, from Simla to Bombay, from where he sailed in November 1905, was marked by sojourns at Lahore and Agra where he made it his business to take time out to examine the restoration work in progress. Crucially, just days before his departure, he drafted a dispatch to the secretary of state about the manner in which he had overseen the reorganization of the Archaeological Survey, and asking that this be now placed on a permanent footing.[3] It was as a consequence of this that, by early 1906, the India Office in London sanctioned the permanence of the archaeological department and that of the post of its director general.

For Marshall, this meant that when he left for England in April that year, he did so secure in the knowledge that his professional future was now tied to India. The last letter he wrote to Curzon before sailing for England captures rather well the sense of security in which Marshall now basked, the knowledge that he would spend the rest of his working life in India. It also captures the relationship that he had forged with Curzon during the time that the guru had closely watched and guided his young protégé. This bond was to outlast their official association:

> Dear Lord Curzon,
>
> I hope that you will forgive the delay, which has occurred in procuring a copy of Colonel Hodgson's plan of the Taj, for which Mr. Nathan asked some months since. I enclose it along with lithography of the large coloured map in the museum. Neither Nicholls nor myself has been able to trace any other plan of interest, but should we succeed in finding one, I will of course forward a copy.
>
> Your legacy of conservation work both here and elsewhere goes on very satisfactorily, despite the little interruptions of the Royal visit. General De Brath gave us most valuable assistance in the Committee on the Lahore buildings, and I have little doubt that we shall soon be in possession of those which we want. Several premutiny photos which we have just discovered show us the river front of the palace at Delhi in the old days, and will help us greatly in the restoration there. The rescue of the so-called 'Zenana' in the Allahabad Fort is nearly accomplished, and the renovation of the somewhat similar structure at Ajmer is finished.
>
> Our excavations also at Kasia, Rajgir and Amravati are proving very productive, and like our previous work at Sarnath and Basarh, quite dispel the idea that India does not offer as good a field to the explorer as most western countries do.
>
> The Secretary of state has now sanctioned the permanency of our Department and I am proposing to take a summer holiday in England before settling down to what will now become a lifelong work to me.[4]

What Marshall described in this letter to Curzon as a summer holiday in England was, actually, a forced leave of absence. In the four years or more that he had spent in India, Marshall had been plagued by chest infections, bouts of serious lung congestion, and pleurisy. The medical board that examined him recommended rest and 'a change of air'.[5] Consequently he sailed from Bombay for England on 14 April aboard the *S.S. Egypt*.

In England, even though he was on sick leave, Marshall spent some of it trying to pursue various kinds of leads in London's libraries and museums. The prehistoric culture of Baluchistan was one issue that he seems to have followed up, for he had carried about a dozen paintings of Nal pottery with him.[6] His main purpose was to try and find analogies for this in the ceramics of the eastern Mediterranean, of which there was a large collection in the British Museum. Such a correspondence was certainly required if Marshall's intuition, that there was a Mycenaean link with India, was to be archaeologically verified. As it happened, Marshall failed to locate any similarities between Nal and Mediterranean wares.

While he was looking at the British Museum's Greek ceramics, Marshall also re-examined its Harappa seals. Whether that re-examination led to any special revelations is not known. Yet those seals must have rekindled his curiosity, because we do know that after returning to India Marshall set in motion the process for beginning an excavation at the mounds of Harappa.

This process of excavation involved a number of things. First, the mounds themselves had to be 'protected'. What this really means is that, once an area was considered as being of historic interest and value, it was necessary to prevent it being tampered with or trowelled in a way that would disturb its character. For this purpose, the government had enacted a special legislation: the Ancient Monuments Preservation Act. Piloted by Curzon in 1904, through the operation of this act such areas were notified as 'protected'. The government, under the act, became the protector or guardian of all the remains there—of ancient buildings, tumulus, caves, inscriptions, antiquities—whether they were visible or buried. Generally, before excavations were conducted, it was the practice of the Archaeological Survey to bring the site within the ambit of this act so as to prevent it being disturbed.

In the case of Harappa, such protection was most necessary because practically the whole area was privately owned and its landowners had extended the devastation wrought by the railway contractors of the nineteenth century. They continued to remove old bricks in large quantities, thus destroying a great deal of the city's ancient structural remains. In fact, by the time Marshall's department began contemplating excavating at Harappa, the surface of the two principal mounds—marked E and D in Cunningham's plan—was pitted with local excavations which resembled newly opened graves.[7] Such excavations were made to rob bricks from the ruins and normally took the form of four foot square openings which went down to the point where a brick wall was reached. This was then destroyed by a process of continuous tunnelling, in which brick after brick was removed, and these were then used to construct modern buildings.

Notifying an area as 'protected' though, could be a fairly complicated and long-drawn process. A sense of how complicated this could be can be understood if we leave Harappa for a moment and move north of it to the valley where the ruins of ancient Taxila were situated.

Straddling two provinces, the North-West Frontier Province and the Rawalpindi division of Punjab, this historic area was dominated by multiple city sites and by the ruins of Buddhist stupas and monasteries within the valley and in the surrounding hills. Marshall had visited Taxila within a year of coming to India and had been instantly drawn to it. As he later recalled: 'I still remember the thrill I got from the sight of its buried cities. At that time I was a young man, fresh from archaeological excavations in Greece and filled with enthusiasm for anything Greek;

and in that far-off corner of the Panjab it seemed as if I had lighted of a sudden on a bit of Greece itself. . . . No wonder that I was all eagerness to get to work on such an alluring site and uncover with pick and spade whatever might be left of its ancient secrets.'[8]

But ten long years were to elapse from the time that Marshall first contemplated excavations there, in 1903, to when its ancient tracts came to be protected. A large part of the ruins were scattered over land under cultivation and many of the local zamindars were actively opposed to a protected status for that area. This, they argued, would subject them to petty prosecution, as they said, even 'for tilling their own lands'. What seems to be more probable, however, is that the zamindars presided over a lucrative business in antiquities from the Taxila ruins, which would certainly have been adversely affected by the proposed notification. An illegal antiquity trade in objects from the frontier region had been flourishing since the time of Alexander Cunningham and Marshall was aware of it. After all, he systematically built up several museum collections in India by purchasing artefacts—coins, sculpture, metal vessels, etc.—from such coin and antiquity dealers. Several of them were based at Rawalpindi, not far from where Taxila stood.[9] These dealers frequently obtained antiquities from historic sites, in all likelihood from people such as the local zamindars of Taxila.

Although Marshall pressed for a notification of the site in 1909, it was as elsewhere up to the local government and authorities to decide whether this was feasible. In this case, the deputy commissioner of Rawalpindi was more concerned about whether such a move would create an administrative problem for him *vis-à-vis* the local populace. Notwithstanding the pressure exerted by the Archaeological Survey, the notification did not come into effect. Eventually, in 1911, through the intervention of the lieutenant governor of the Punjab, tracts like Bhir Dargai, Hathial, and Babar Khana, which comprised the ancient site of Taxila, came to be declared as protected.[10] Excavations began there, finally, in the spring of 1913.

The modalities involved in protecting a site differed from area to area. At Taxila the lands where excavations were planned first came to be temporarily acquired, with compensation for any loss the zamindars would suffer because of the diggings. At Sirkap (a site in the Taxila valley), for instance, nearly four hundred rupees was paid by the Archaeological Survey to various villagers who had rights in the fifty-five *kanals* of land that were temporarily taken up by the Archaeological Survey.[11] Moreover, as antiquities began to emerge, local people frequently claimed their share under the provisions of the Treasure Trove Act. In one such instance, where jewels and pearls had been found near the Archaeological Survey guest house in 1913, a quarter of their intrinsic value was paid by Marshall to the landholders.[12] Subsequently, as the remains of cities and shrines began to emerge with astonishing rapidity, the lands were permanently purchased by the Survey at the market rate.

In the case of Harappa, however, local enquiries made by the deputy commissioner of Montgomery in 1907–8 revealed that the government could not officially protect the mounds without outright purchase.[13] The owners were not inclined to allow a temporary occupation by the government. Nor were they willing to accept alternative land which had been offered to them in exchange for the mounds. Instead, they wanted the government to purchase the mounds. The price they demanded for them was a little more than four thousand rupees.

This was a substantial sum of money. It amounted to roughly one-fourth of what the government would spend that year on excavations in all the different parts of India. Naturally, before deciding on such a substantial purchase, the Archaeological Survey wanted to get Harappa vetted by their own man. Since Harappa was located in Punjab, which was the direct responsibility of the Northern Circle, Pandit Hirananda Sastri was deputed to survey it.

We first encountered Sastri just a year or more after Marshall came to India, when, in December 1903, Sastri probed several settlements that had yielded copper hoard objects in the Ganga–Yamuna doab. He was searching these sites on Marshall's instructions. Marshall had hoped they would yield archaeological clues that would corroborate what was then described as the early Vedic Age. The surveyed settlements yielded no such leads. But since then, Hirananda had rather more successfully explored antiquarian remains in the Kangra district. His documentation of more than a hundred such remains in its villages and towns ranged from inscriptions to medieval temples and Buddhist statues. In fact, around the time that he visited Harappa, Sastri was in the process of completing a list of ancient monuments in Kulu, Mandi, and Suket. As assistant to J. Ph. Vogel, he also surveyed other parts of the Punjab and United Provinces Circle. In early 1909, along with Harappa, his tour included visits to Saheth-Maheth and Shorkot. There too, his surveys were meant to ascertain whether certain sites in these places could be protected under the Ancient Monuments Act.[14]

In the case of Saheth-Maheth, we do know that Vogel had begun excavations there in 1907–8, and evidently further areas there were sought to be acquired for digs.[15] These twin mounds stood at an equal distance from Bahraich and Gonda in the United Provinces and were closely identified with the life of the Buddha. Maheth, the larger of the two, represented the ancient city of Sravasti, while Saheth is where Anathapindika, one of the richest disciples of the Buddha, constructed a monastery, called the Jetavana-vihara, for his residence.

As for Harappa, there is nothing to show that Vogel had any interest in it at all. It is likely that he instructed Sastri to survey it because of Marshall's interest in its seals.

The director general himself, at this point in time, had trained his sights away from the Punjab and towards the buried remnants of an ancient historical city elsewhere. This is important in as much as it makes clear that, for the moment, *no one* foresaw the existence of a buried civilization around Harappa, exonerating Cunningham's similar lack of perception earlier. Marshall was hoping to explore Besnagar. This is the modern town around which the ruins of ancient Vidisa were scattered, in Central India, and where in the spring of 1908 a unique inscription on a stone column had been discovered. The inscription recorded that the pillar was erected by Heliodorus, a Bhagavata (worshipper of Vishnu), who came from Taxila in the second century BC as an ambassador of the Indo-Greek king Antialkidas. The ancient city of Vidisa was itself also very impressive. It stretched across several miles; and Marshall, following the discovery of the inscribed pillar there, was very keen to excavate it himself. As he put it, there was enough work to allow a thousand men to dig there for fifty years and more.[16] As it so happened, the Gwalior Darbar, in whose principality this site was located, preferred to have the work done by their own state official. Unlike British India, the princely states could and did occasionally veto the colonial authorities in matters archaeological.

Disappointed, Marshall moved on. He moved, in the following year, to the Allahabad region, where he excavated Bhita (Fig. 13). In comparison with Besnagar, Bhita was relatively obscure. It is to Marshall's credit that his work there revealed, for the first time, the configuration of a small Indian town of the Christian era. The fortifications and streets, the houses with their well-defined plans, the occupants of houses (who could frequently be identified on the basis of the inscribed seals that were found there), all these and many other things emerged from Bhita.[17] What is evident, though, is that, as before, it was the historical canvas of early India rather than relatively unknown though promising sites, such as Harappa, that continued to be the main concern of the Archaeological Survey.

At the same time, it may be worth remembering that in many cases the interest of the Survey in a particular area or site depended upon the enterprise and enthusiasm displayed by the

Fig. 13. In camp in Bhita in 1910
(Marshall with Florence and their children, Margaret and John)

person who dealt with it at the local level. In the case of Besnagar, it was H. Lake, the state engineer of the Gwalior Darbar, who had first discerned lettering under the thick encrustation of *sindoor* (vermilion) which had been smeared on the Heliodorus column by pious pilgrims. Marshall's vigorous interest in Besnagar was spurred by this discovery.[18] Similarly, what became known about the sculpture and archaeology of Mathura in these years was not because the Survey initiated any large-scale exploration there; rather, some major discoveries were made by a local man, Pandit Radha Krishna. It was through his exertions that many important pieces of Mathura sculpture, which had over time been built into the walls and environs of houses in the city of Mathura and its neighbouring villages, were located and eventually deposited in the local museum there.[19] The manner in which the Pandit procured such sculpture and drew Vogel's attention to them is graphically described by Vogel in a letter to Marshall.

The object that Vogel describes here is part of an early historic gateway or *torana*:

> Yesterday evening at 7 P.M. Radha Krishna brought me the Torana architrave. He had great difficulty in obtaining the permission of the owner of the house, had to go twice to see him in his village and had a third long discussion with more than sixty persons who all somehow fancied to have a word to say in the matter. The Pandit's patience and endurance are really admirable.
>
> While the stone was being taken out of the wall, he remained almost all the time so that no damage should occur. He said to me: 'You see, it is just like the birth of a child; you cannot tell before hand the exact time when it will come!'
>
> But the stone is worth the trouble. I consider it one of the finest specimens of Mathura sculpture. It is moreover as far as I know the only complete specimen of a torana architrave found here. The reverse has in the centre the adoration of the bodhi treee shown behind (or inside?) a building with a large gate. On the sides two small panels: adoration of a *stupa* and of a *dharmachakra* placed on three lions exactly as on the Sarnath pillar. At both ends are beings half man half makara. The carving is wonderfully preserved.[20]

It therefore comes as no surprise that Marshall was willing to provide Radha Krishna with several hundred rupees to acquire such sculpture and antiquities. In fact, within a couple of years of such discoveries, two thousand rupees were earmarked for trial excavations at Ganeshra, Jaisinghpura, and Mora in the Mathura area. These were supervised by Radha Krishna on behalf of the Archaeological Survey. Subsequently, in the following winter, excavations were also carried out by him at the Katra mound, which revealed an early centuries AD Buddhist brick stupa below the foundations of the Keshab-Dev temple on whose ruins Aurangzeb's mosque was constructed.[21]

But to return once more to the Indus area: in the case of Harappa, was there anything in Hirananda Sastri's report that may have whetted the interest of his superiors? We will never know, because Sastri's original report is untraceable and presumably lost. What we do know is that, in his subsequent publications, Sastri never mentioned his visit to Harappa—not even when he discussed the Indus civilization. Many decades after his 1909 survey, he is known to have delivered a series of lectures on 'Archaeology and Ancient Indian History'. In these he dwelt upon various Indus sites, including Harappa.[22] But oddly he did not remember to touch upon his own association with it. This may have been because, like Cunningham, Sastri had misjudged Harappa's potential. From the few details that we have of his report from secondary sources, it seems that his first impression of Harappa was unenthusiastic. For instance, more than ten years after his visit, one of the premier excavators of Harappa, Daya Ram Sahni (about whom a great deal will be said later), remarked that the tenor of Sastri's report had not been very optimistic. This can only mean that either Sastri did not understand the archaeological potential of the mounds, or that he did not consider they contained buried evidence of the kind that warranted the expenditure of several thousand rupees.

Sastri's 'failure' with Harappa, if it can be called that at all, is not really surprising because, as we saw earlier, Harappa was not known to yield antiquities—sculpture, coins or inscriptions—of the kind that Sastri was familiar with. What is interesting and important, though, is that he noted the size of the ancient bricks that littered Harappa.[23] One type that he mentioned—measuring 12" x 6" x 3"—is especially significant because this is the first published reference to what is today recognized as a typical brick size of the Indus civilization, with proportions in the ratio of 1:2:4. Such bricks were practically unknown from the Buddhist complexes and early historic cities that Marshall's department had routinely surveyed and excavated. Sastri himself had visited many such ancient sites. And yet the discrepancy in the brick sizes that he observed at such places on the one hand,

and those that he saw at Harappa on the other, and the possible significance of this, seem to have escaped him.

Sastri is, in this sense, only a part of what amounts almost to a tradition of early archaeologists who failed to spot the gigantic dimensions of the city lying beneath their feet.

That Harappa vanished after making a fleeting reappearance from the arena of the Archaeological Survey was, of course, not merely because Hirananda Sastri had been lukewarm about its ancient ruins. For one thing, around the time that he visited Harappa, Sastri's immediate superior, Vogel, the superintendent of the Northern Circle to whom Sastri was to submit his report on Harappa, proceeded on almost a year's leave. So, even while he may have penned it in 1909 (at the very earliest), Sastri's report could only have been read in January 1910, when Vogel returned to India. But Vogel's return to his circle was short-lived. In the month of May that year Marshall went on leave, and Vogel was deputed to officiate for him. Vogel was to remain the Survey's officiating director general for almost two years, till about February 1912.

So Marshall, the man who was interested in solving the archaeological puzzle of Harappa, was away for a fairly long stretch of time. He had not planned on such an extended leave for himself. It had become extended because, during his absence, a chain of events was to unfold which not merely prevented his return but almost succeeded in making his post—director general of archaeology in India—a posthumous one.

Let us see what happened. In the summer of 1910, shortly after Marshall arrived in England, the appointment of a successor to the departing viceroy, Lord Minto, was announced. The new viceroy of India was Charles Hardinge. A career diplomat, Hardinge followed in the footsteps of his grandfather, Viscount

Henry Hardinge, who had served as governor general of India from 1844 to 1848. On the face of it, one would hardly have expected that this would adversely affect the archaeological department; on the contrary, since the new Hardinge was an old friend of Curzon's, his appointment was likely to have been beneficial for Marshall. Even before he left for India, Hardinge had regularly interacted with Curzon, who, among other things, assuaged his concerns over his likely financial situation. Curzon invited him to his country residence in Hampshire, where Hardinge was shown an enormous ledger which contained all the accounts of Curzon's viceroyalty, penned in his own hand![24] After Hardinge sailed for India, the former viceroy regularly sent him letters laced with recollections and advice. Some of this concerned Curzon's pet projects, such as the Victoria Memorial Hall at Calcutta, whose construction had been stalled by Hardinge's predecessor. Curzon is also known to have specifically urged Hardinge to devote attention to the Archaeological Survey which, as he put it, sighed 'for a little revival of viceregal patronage'.[25]

Yet old friend though he was, Hardinge did not heed Curzon's advice on many matters pertaining to India's governance. Just over a year into his viceroyalty, during the Royal Darbar of 1911, he had the partition of Bengal—one of the major changes of Curzon's rule—revoked. He also announced the transfer of India's capital from Calcutta to Delhi. Less spectacular, yet equally far-reaching, was the programme of administrative reorganization that Hardinge came to endorse in the summer of 1911. It was this scheme which, rather than reviving viceregal patronage to the Archaeological Survey, almost put an end to Marshall's career.

It is from the budget proceedings of March 1911 that one first gets a sense that major departmental reforms were being considered. The viceroy's closing speech on the debate in the Imperial Legislative Council, for instance, discussed not merely the need for caution and sobriety in public expenditure but equally how this could be achieved. It suggested a re-examination and restriction of military and civil expenditure. In this speech he also hinted at retrenchments as a means for achieving the desired financial ends.

For Hardinge's government, the main budgetary problem lay in the imminent loss of its opium revenue. Following the two 'Opium Wars' which resulted in the opening of China to British trade in the nineteenth century, opium had become among the most important items of Indian export. By the beginning of the twentieth century, its value was over a hundred million rupees. However, in 1907 and in 1911 the Indian government formally agreed to the Chinese request for a voluntary restriction of the export of this narcotic. Consequently, it was expecting significant revenue losses: at least that is how Hardinge presented his case. What he failed to mention, though, was that, anticipating some of these losses, the customs duties of a number of articles, such as tobacco, beer, and petroleum were raised. Consequently, in the financial year ending March 1911, when the viceroy was extolling the virtues of public economy to the legislative council, there was actually a budget surplus of nearly six million pounds.

What were the concrete measures that the government proposed for cutting down their spending? With regard to army expenditure, Hardinge wrote an official memorandum on the subject pointing out where reductions could be made without affecting the fighting strength of the army. This provoked a very long memorandum by the chief of the general staff and the army department, in which they fought hard against any reductions whatsoever, even for those regiments they regarded as worthless. As for civil expenditure, the scheme envisaged by Hardinge and his council was outlined in the form of a series of recommendations to the secretary of state in August 1911.[26] These ended the suspense about the retrenchments that the viceroy had indicated in his March speech. A number of posts that had originated in the Curzon era were now unambiguously sought to be abolished.

These posts were those held by various 'experts' that Curzon had either created or revived in order to raise the standard of work in government departments, and to bring them in touch with modern requirements. The functions of these experts were mainly consultative and advisory in relation to local governments; they had supplied the central government with technical knowledge and a personal standard of departmental competence. One of these experts facing the axe was the director general of archaeology in India.

It seems worth pointing out that when the council members framed their economy recommendations, they also went to great lengths to justify these as administratively desirable and in line with changing Indian conditions. What did they mean by this, and what were the Indian conditions they were talking about?

While under Curzon bureaucratic centralization had reached stratospheric heights, since 1907 a scheme for the devolution of power to local governments had also, ironically, been under active consideration: a Royal Commission of Decentralization had been appointed.[27] This measure was, in part, a response to the growing recognition of the political unrest unfolding in India and to the gradual acceptance, within British strategy, of the view that moderates within the ranks of the Indian National Congress and its sympathizers should be courted as suitable allies. The moderate Indian nationalists were among the strongest advocates of decentralization. So, in fact, the essence of the conclusions of the Decentralization Commission were in line with the recommendations of Gopal Krishna Gokhale, an Indian nationalist who was then a member of the Imperial Legislative Council.

At the same time, Hardinge's dispatch did not take up the bulk of what was contained in the report of the commission. Rather, the dispatch only concerned itself with decentralization inasmuch as the commission had called for limiting the functions of certain inspector generals to promote decentralization in the administration of some departments. Hardinge's council, however, argued for a more radical remedy than anything suggested by the commission: it called for the abolition of seven such posts.[28] These posts were thought dispensable, for expert advice could be obtained through conferences and meetings. These would ensure that the government secured the technical assistance they required 'through the concentrated experience of many minds' rather than in the form of 'the one-sided opinion of an isolated expert'.

Whether this view was justified in the case of the director general of archaeology is debatable, but the label 'isolated expert' hardly describes John Marshall. Much of his work required extensive travel and interaction with local authorities, which was evident even from Marshall's administrative reports, which he regularly submitted to the government. In his 1908–9 annual report, for instance, he described his tours over that year:

> My own tours took me to Ambala, Delhi, Muttra, Agra, Lucknow and Saheth-Maheth, where I was engaged for some weeks supervising the work of excavation. Thence I proceeded westward, visiting Cawnpore, Delhi, Gwalior, Jalgaon, Erandol, Ajanta, and Mandu, and afterwards made my way to Sanchi, Besnagar, Kajuraho and Agra and so back to Simla on February 2, 1909. On February 11, I again left Simla for Mandor in Jodhpur State to direct excavations in the Fort there, and subsequently visited Karachi, Sukkur, Bahawalpur, Multan, Sangla Hill, Sarai Kala, Peshawar and Lahore.[29]

At many of these places, he was supervising work related to archaeological conservation and restoration which required his close co-operation with local governments.

The Council members seem not to have seen this report because, among other things, their August dispatch to the secretary of state reprimands Marshall for not having produced an annual report after 1906–7. Their criticism was not confined to the director general but extended to his provincial superintendents, who were reproached for going 'their own way', while museums were said to be 'neglected'.[30] The local officers, the council argued, should be administratively independent and get scientific advice not from an expert like Marshall but from a central research institute. Marshall should be given notice, and if he could not be absorbed within sanctioned appointments, he should be given the compensation gratuity to which he was entitled under the rules.

Examining the extensive correspondence of 1911 on this issue, it seems clear that the proposed abolition of Marshall's post had less to do with both his alleged inefficiency and that of his officers. His exit had in fact been carefully thought out by the government for some time before it was formalized. The central research institute which Hardinge and his council mentioned to the secretary of state as an alternative advisory body for expert advice, in place of Marshall, had emerged out of the deliberations of a conference of Orientalists held in Simla in July 1911. The proposal was contained in a note circulated by Edward Denison Ross to the members of the conference with a view to assisting its deliberations.

This Ross is generally remembered as a scholar of Persian, for which he was awarded a doctorate from Strasbourg University in 1894, and also as the first director of the School of Oriental and African Studies in London, where he was appointed in 1916. In the interregnum he served a number of years in India. In 1901 he was principal of the Madrasah Muslim College at Calcutta, and in 1903, through Marshall's initiative, he became honorary epigraphist, in charge of 'Moslem' inscriptions, to the Government of India. In 1911, when Hardinge was presiding over the retrenchments issue, Ross was serving as assistant secretary in the department of education. It was very likely in this last capacity that he set out his note to the conference of Orientalists.

The main issue Ross set out to explore in this note was how the government might best offer facilities for 'the higher branches of Oriental study to both Indians and Europeans'.[31] The practical remedy that he suggested was the amalgamation of various resources in Calcutta—those available with the Indian Museum, the Calcutta University and the Asiatic Society of Bengal—for the creation of an Oriental Institute on the lines of the Ecole Française d'Extreme Orient at Hanoi and the Oriental Institute at Vladivostok. Within this scheme, Ross's proposed Oriental Institute does not appear to have been envisaged as an alternative to the Archaeological Survey. In fact, while Ross's scheme does talk about epigraphy, numismatics, and anthropology, along with comparative philology and languages, the one subject that does not figure in the list is archaeology. The regular staff proposed for the institute also does not contain any archaeologist. The director and assistant directors, in the manner that Ross visualized it, were all European Sanskrit scholars.

Proposals that would encourage the training of language specialists had been made on numerous previous occasions as well, frequently by those who wished to see such specialists appointed to posts in India and England. While in this case the idea had emanated from the education department of the Indian government, a few years before this, in 1905, certain Oxbridge Indologists had suggested a similar line of action to encourage such studies. Specifically, that proposal had come from the professors of Sanskrit and Arabic in England—including A.A. Macdonell, then Boden Professor of Sanskrit at Oxford; and E.J. Rapson, Professor of Sanskrit at Cambridge—and then, as now, while Marshall was away on furlough. The professorial representation, while complaining about the inadequacy of encouragement to Oriental studies, had suggested the establishment, at the cost to Indian revenues, of a system of teaching fellowships to be held in India by English Orientalists who would subsequently be qualified for educational work in India. The Indian government was additionally asked to comment on Macdonell's suggestion—made in his paper on 'the study of Sanskrit as an Imperial question' (and read before the Royal

Asiatic Society)—that Sanskrit be treated as a *sine qua non* when making appointments to the archaeological department.

Marshall was actively opposed in principle to the policy of appointing language experts in his department. He had previously advocated the filling up of vacancies with recruits from the ranks of architects rather than Sanskritists. However, as he was on leave, the matter was referred to Henry Cousens, then officiating as director general of the Survey. Cousens was in complete agreement with Marshall's line of thinking and was as forthright in expressing his views as Marshall would undoubtedly have been. His reply, in fact, sharply underlines the divide in this regard between the perception of the Archaeological Survey and Indologists: 'Epigraphists seem to come to India in order to prosecute their studies in Sanskrit with a view to getting the first vacant chair at some University at Home; they make the survey a means of support in the meantime . . . As Superintendent in the Survey we want a practical man with a more comprehensive knowledge; this an epigraphist rarely is.'[32]

In the conference of Orientalists that was held at Simla in July 1911, however, the deliberations did not revolve around ways to introduce language specialists into the Archaeological Survey, but rather on the feasibility of a new central institute which would include the study of languages and various other subjects. Not everyone who attended the conference was in favour of Ross's scheme. R.G. Bhandarkar was one of those who thought that the establishment of such an institution in Calcutta would result in provincialism and create jealousies. He was in favour of the development of existing institutions and of a central institute only if such development were impracticable.[33] Vogel, officiating for Marshall, supported the scheme but disagreed on several matters of detail.[34] The general sense among most of the members, on the whole, was in favour of its creation.

What appears astonishing, though, is the rapidity with which a scheme, basically visualized for the encouragement of Oriental studies and languages, was actually put forward by the viceroy's council as a substitute for the director general of archaeology in India. The precise details of what transpired in the three weeks that elapsed between the end of the conference in the middle of July and early August (when Hardinge's memorandum was dispatched) are hazy. So, at what stage the proposed institute came to be seen as the umbrella body which would take over some of the functions of Marshall's office remains unclear. What is certain is that, within a few days after the conference of Orientalists supported Ross's proposal, the finance and education departments had already begun exchanging memos on the abolition of the post of the director general, and the manner in which the administrative work of his office would subsequently devolve.

The first suggestion that the proposed Oriental Research Institute would actually take over some of Marshall's functions came from Harcourt Butler, education member of the viceroy's council. In a note written at the end of July, Butler discussed the disbanding and transfer of the director general's establishment.[35] He proposed the creation of a professorship of archaeology, first in the Indian Museum, and later in the research institute, once the latter had started functioning. The professor would be responsible for the archaeological section of the museum, for the publication of the reports that had been the responsibility of Marshall's office, and for the distribution of the grant of a lakh of rupees for archaeological work among the various local governments. Simultaneously, the various archaeological superintendents would, for all practical purposes, be placed under provincial governments. The archaeological library attached to the director general's office would, similarly, first be transferred to the museum and afterwards to the research institute.

Shortly afterwards, the education department that Butler headed became very busy calculating the thousands of rupees it believed would be saved through such measures. Various drafts were circulated in September and October, in which the general annual saving from the abolition of Marshall's post was calculated at Rs 20,000, and another 15,000 or so from his office expenses.[36] By then it also became crystal clear that archaeology would be the junior partner in the Oriental Institute, which would be dominated by specialists in textual sources.[37] Of the five professorships in the institute, only one would be in archaeology; the other four were to be in the Vedas and Vedic culture; post-Vedic literature and culture with special reference to Indian philosophy; Buddhism with Pali language and literature; and Arabic with history of Islam. Additionally, there were to be readers in Persian, as also Sanskrit poetry and rhetoric. Indians who joined this institute would, among other things, be 'given training for posts in the archaeological department'.[38] In other words, this would be an institute made up of language specialists who would impart training to archaeologists. For the first time, Indian archaeology seemed in danger of being swallowed up by textually trained scholars.

Vogel found little reason to feel enthusiastic about this new arrangement and expressed serious fears about the future of monument conservation in India. He offered an assessment of this scheme wherein he drew attention to architectural preservation being possibly the most important function of the director general. As we know, Marshall spent most of the winter season touring the subcontinent, inspecting buildings and advising local governments and provincial superintendents on preservation.[39] Vogel was hopeful that, as soon as the financial outlook seemed more favourable, better provision would be made for the preservation of ancient monuments. But with regard to Marshall's future he was very pessimistic and believed his exit imminent.

Consequently, in September, he took it upon himself to inform all officers and staff about the report made by the government to the secretary of state recommending the abolition of the director general's post and about the seriousness of the imminent loss: 'after having been reorganized only a few years ago and after having flourished under Mr. Marshall's able guidance, the Department could not suffer a severer loss than that of being deprived of its distinguished head.'[40] Vogel's letter was received with shock and dismay by officers of the Archaeological Department. Taw Sein Kho, archaeological superintendent in Burma, was 'staggered' by the news and believed that archaeological research in India would receive a major setback.[41] His genuine regard for Marshall also shines through: 'We shall miss his tact, sympathy, his varied gifts and his marvellous powers of coordination and organization.'[42] Alexander Rea from Madras denounced this 'retrograde step specially after the good work that had been done during Mr. Marshall's regime'.[43] And from Calcutta Rakhaldas Banerji, whom we will get to know later, expressed hope that Lords Curzon and Minto would 'succeed in keeping Mr. Marshall on'.[44]

Banerji must no doubt have known of the opposition that Hardinge's proposals had by then evoked. In relation to abolition of the post of Inspector General of Forests, we do know that one of the members of the viceroy's council, Sir Robert Carlyle, had given a note of dissent. Carlyle was member for the public works department and it is not fortuitous that he would later be described by Hardinge, in his reminiscences, as 'the most difficult member of my Council'.[45] In this case, because of Carlyle's opposition, the Government of India was asked by Lord Crewe, secretary of state, to reconsider its recommendation abolishing the post.

As for the post of director general of archaeology, the secretary of state made it absolutely clear that it was not to be abolished at all. Obviously, this decision Crewe had arrived at because of the outrage it had caused among numerous people and organizations in England. In fact, in the dispatch that he addressed to the Indian government, he appended various memorials he had received about the impending loss of Marshall.[46]

It appears that there had been an active campaign to save the director general, spearheaded by two former viceroys. In October, Curzon had addressed an extensive memorandum attacking the proposed abolition to Crewe. He also published his views in *The Times* which were publicly supported, in the same newspaper, by Lord Minto.[47] Such influential opposition must have been the reason why the secretary of state soon overruled Hardinge's advice. In fact, Crewe's prose in the dispatch, where he reminded the Indian government about the importance of continuing to support archaeological work, is reminiscent of the pronouncements of Curzon himself:[48]

> It is clear that in the past the ancient monuments of India have suffered from neglect and inexperience. Their proper conservation and the systematic prosecution of antiquarian research connected with them require continuous supervision and direction by a trained expert . . . In the past the Government of India have supplied most of the funds for archaeological work, in discharge of the responsibilities which in the judgment of the civilised world rest upon them in respect of the great historical monuments of India. For these reasons I have decided that the post of Director General of Archaeology shall be maintained.

Following this December dispatch, Marshall was asked to return within February 1912, to India and to his old job. Within some months, he also heard from Cambridge, his old university, that he had been conferred the degree of Doctor of Letters.[49]

In India, though, there is good reason to believe that, for some time after this, Marshall was treated, as he put it, 'like the naughty boy in the corner'.[50] He noted that for several months after his arrival, there was no contact at all between him and the viceroy. Evidently, this was unusual and he privately wrote to Lord Curzon about this lack of communication: 'I have not yet spoken to the viceroy; but that is not perhaps strange. He appears to keep aloof from most people and to maintain a sphinx-like attitude towards men and matters. Probably he is unaware that I am in India or indeed of my existence!'[51] There may be a touch of disingenuousness about the surprise Marshall expresses here: it was surely logical of Hardinge to avoid meeting a man who had succeeded in 'retaining' his job against the wishes of the viceroy himself.

For another thing, even after Marshall's return to his position, uncertainty about the exact nature of his duties continued for a while. Initially, he was told that, along with his position and status as director general of archaeology, he would be a professor at the research institute, which now was likely to be founded in the new capital, Delhi. A few months later, he was less sure about his future functions and the security of his post since apparently, as he was informed by Sir Harcourt Butler, in a few years' time someone else would be put in his place at the institute and only conservation would remain in his hands.

As it happened, none of these changes took place. Marshall's control over his domain remained pretty much intact and he continued, as before, to supervise all archaeological work in the country.

And, as for the institute that threatened to take over his functions, to Marshall's great relief it never got off ground.

# 5

# AMONG CITIES AND STUPAS

EVEN AS JOHN MARSHALL RETURNED TO INDIA IN February 1912, still anxious about whether he would 'profess' archaeology at the Oriental Institute or continue as director general at the Survey, his apprehensions were soon pushed into the background by momentous happenings.

In the autumn of that year there began a phase in Marshall's career dominated by field research at some of the great sites of antiquity. The many excavations he had conducted before would all now be eclipsed by the work that commenced at Sanchi, Taxila, and Pataliputra. These were known to be among the most renowned ancient sites in the Indian subcontinent, and at each of them the Archaeological Survey would undertake extensive, systematic campaigns of work spread over several years: in Taxila this extended over more than two decades. At each of these sites the Survey would reap a remarkable harvest of old antiquities and new insights. Harappa too, as we shall see, made a quiet comeback, and this time Marshall's interest in its ruins would remain uninterrupted. From 1912 onwards, Harappa would always be visible, albeit as a small thread on the fringes of the rich tapestry of historic city sites and stupas that were emerging.

That archaeological research began almost simultaneously at these sites was not intentional but because of a coincidence of circumstances. Take the case of Sanchi. Situated in the principality of Bhopal, its ancient stupas, *chaityas*, and *viharas* had first figured in a major way during Marshall's early years, when repairs had begun there, without his knowledge. Sanchi's monuments needed urgent and extensive repair because, even while they had been in a remarkably good state of preservation when they were rediscovered in 1818, as they came to be dug and documented by British treasure hunters and archaeologists they were substantially disfigured by the means and circumstances of work of these people.[1] The stupas were first opened up in 1822 by T.H. Maddock, the political agent at Bhopal, and his assistant, Captain Johnson.[2] In the general system of British suzerainty then, such political officers were to be found in several princely states. Theoretically, in the case of Bhopal, the political agent was supposed to advise and assist the ruler in various ways since he formed the sole channel of communication with the British governor general in India. But in fact political agents did a great deal more. For example, in the 1870s, H.C. Barstow undertook to translate, from Urdu into English, a history of Bhopal written by its ruler.[3] The actions of some of Barstow's predecessors, on the other hand, had destructive resonances. Maddock and Johnson are an instance in point for, in their search for hidden antiquities, they succeeded in destroying substantial parts of old monuments there, one of which was the main ('the great') stupa of Sanchi.

Another pioneering Sanchi explorer was Alexander Cunningham. Before he stuck his spade into Harappa, he, along with a fellow officer, Lieutenant F.C. Maisey, had excavated deep into Sanchi's stupas and at many other such monuments in that region. Done very rapidly, Cunningham's operations did not take more than a few hours; the stupa was shafted vertically from the top and down to the centre. This ensured that what was enshrined in the stupa, such as relic boxes, caskets, and fragments of the bones (presumably of monks), including those of the Buddha's foremost disciples, were recovered as quickly as possible.[4] In his techniques, Cunningham, like most excavators of his time, aimed to extract what he considered to be important finds and not to actually build up knowledge about more mundane matters such as building techniques, the changing character of monuments, and the common artefacts of daily existence.[5]

From the 1860s, some attempts were being made in Europe to conduct more careful and complete excavations than the somewhat hasty and haphazard digs of earlier times. Guiseppe Fiorelli, who took over the excavations of Pompeii, for example, repeatedly reiterated that his main purpose was not the discovery of works of art but a thorough knowledge of the 'life of bygone ages . . . not only of the houses of the wealthy but also of the dwellings of the poor.'[6] Between 1880 and 1900, careful adherence to what we would today consider the principles of scientific professional excavation techniques became more evident. In Cunningham's native land an army man like him, General Pitt-Rivers, conducted digs on a grand scale in his inherited Rivers estates. Insisting on total excavation, Pitt-Rivers carried forward the ideas of Fiorelli by highlighting the importance of common things. These, he is said to have written, 'are of more importance than particular things, because they are more prevalent'.[7] Equally, he stressed the centrality of stratigraphical observation, i.e. proceeding and recording strata by strata, and of the necessity of noting the position of everything found. Along with descriptions, detailed plans and drawings of the excavated sections and sites were made, all of this being conducted 'with the precision, thoroughness and discipline of a military operation.' But, generally speaking, a critical awareness of the need for such standards in archaeological technique was not universally felt in the middle of the nineteenth century, when Cunningham and Maisey excavated the stupas of Central India.

Nor was there an urgency to repair what had been excavated. In this, too, Cunningham was not ahead of his times but exemplified the spirit of his day. Great discoveries were combined with great damage, because, like Maddock and Johnson before them, Cunningham and his co-excavator did not think it necessary to repair the massive breaches that their shafting had created at the Sanchi monuments. The extent of damage must have been considerable because, even thirty years later, Lepel Griffin was to angrily remember that 'a thousand years of time and weather have not done so much injury to the invaluable Topes [i.e. stupas] at Sanchi as was caused by the action of Major-General Cunningham, the Director General of Archaeology, who years ago mined deep into the Topes in the vain search for coins or inscriptions, and never filled in his excavations.'[8]

Griffin was a senior member of the British Raj and was then serving as agent to the governor general in Central India. It was he who, in the early 1880s, persuaded the imperial government to spend several thousand rupees on repair work at Sanchi.[9] As a consequence of this, the enormous breach in the face of the great stupa was built up with dry masonry, and its two gateways, which had earlier collapsed, re-erected. The gateway of Stupa 3 was also re-erected, sculpture was cleaned, and the approach road on the northern side of the hill, along with the ancient causeway which led to Stupa 2, improved and restored. In subsequent years, although one does not hear of major conservation at Sanchi, some minor repair works did continue. The pace of work in the 1890s must have been very slow because, as we saw, the money allocated by the imperial government for archaeology had been severely slashed.

When monument restoration got a new lease of life under Curzon, Sanchi was thought among the most important and was visited by Curzon in the very first year of his viceroyalty. As at various other monuments that he visited, he left here a list of instructions on how repairs should be undertaken.[10] Following Curzon's visit, Henry Cousens, the archaeological superintendent of the Western Circle, drew the attention of the Bhopal state to other measures necessary for the protection of the gateways of the main stupa and the conservation of Stupa 2.

Repairs were started in 1904 by H.B. Cook, the state engineer of Bhopal, but his manner of execution proved alarmingly destructive. Officials charged with such work usually tried to conserve all the old relics in these ancient monuments—broken and half-decayed though they frequently were—because their value and authenticity depended upon the preservation of their ancient fabric. But the state engineer of Bhopal, instead of repairing the old structural elements, decided to remove them. Several old rails, coping stones, and pillars from the main stupa's balustrade were taken out by him and replaced with new stones. Marshall had been completely unaware that repairs of any kind were going on at Sanchi. He was to visit it shortly afterwards, by which time, he reported, it was too late to rectify Cook's 'restoration'. Not surprisingly, Curzon described Marshall's report as the 'consecration of a desecration'.[11]

Cook's faulty restoration had at least the virtue of becoming the occasion for a larger dialogue within the portals of the colonial government about ways of conserving Sanchi. Interestingly, while the poor restoration was explained away by Marshall as an aberration that had resulted because the state engineer had suffered personal injury, the religious affiliation of the chowkidars or caretakers came now to be blamed for the highly unsatisfactory state of the hundreds of sculptures lying around the Sanchi hill. For Marshall, Muslim chowkidars were inherently incapable of looking after Buddhist monuments.[12] These, he suggested, required to be tended by 'devoted hands', those of Buddhist chowkidars, whose services he believed could be arranged through the Maha Bodhi Society.

When making this suggestion the director general had evidently not bargained for the existence of the rather formidable ruler of Bhopal, Nawab Sultan Jahan Begum. The last in a dynasty of women rulers in this major princely state of Central India,

Sultan Jahan (1858–1930) is generally remembered for her pioneering work on education and women's emancipation. An ardent reformer, she is known to have publicly abandoned purdah a couple of years before her death. Apparently, she was also a hands-on begum and was known to personally examine all files, inspect the treasury, look through the registers, and even appoint every state employee herself.[13] Marshall's letter suggesting the replacement of Muslim chowkidars at Sanchi with Buddhist ones was referred to her. Almost immediately, she conveyed her distaste and opposition to his proposal.

Some of this opposition, it seems, stemmed from the well-known 'troublemaker' reputation of the Maha Bodhi Society's founder.[14] This was Anagarika Dharmapala, the scion of a wealthy Ceylonese family who, in 1891, had founded this society in Colombo. The timing of the society's founding was closely connected with Dharmapala's plan for an ancient shrine complex in North India, which he had then just visited. This plan involved the Mahabodhi temple at Bodh Gaya in Bihar, situated in proximity with the site of the Buddha's enlightenment. Over the centuries, this had developed into a religious place for a mass of both Buddhist and Hindu practices. Since 1727, legal proprietorship of the shrine had in fact vested with a Hindu (Saiva) *mahant* (priest). This had not created problems for the conduct of Buddhist worship, nor was this situation unique; it was just one of the many places in India attracting the worship of many faiths.[15] But in the latter part of the nineteenth century, certain purists had come to regard the multi-religious character of the shrine as evidence of its desecration. These were people influenced by a revivalist wave sweeping across large parts of Asia, which aimed to 'cleanse' Buddhism of such practices.

We need not go into the details of this revival, but, from Thailand to Ceylon, various Buddhist societies and wealthy patrons were attempting to re-establish a supposedly pure religion in consonance with orthodox practices and attitudes contained in Pali religious texts. Anagarika Dharmapala was the best representative of that movement in Ceylon. By the time he came to Bodh Gaya, he had preached over large parts of his country, raised funds for his faith, and propagated his agenda through pamphlets and periodicals. For a religious crusader of this mould, Mahabodhi, where both Hindu peasants and devout Buddhists worshipped at the same shrine, was abhorrent, as was the presence of a Hindu legal proprietor. Consequently, one of the main objects of the Maha Bodhi Society that he founded was to reclaim the Mahabodhi temple for Buddhists.

No legal proprietor, especially one whose preceptors had enjoyed the fruits of religious patronage there for a hundred and fifty years or so, was likely to give in to such demands without a serious fight. Consequently, a massive dispute came to develop around this shrine in the late nineteenth century, one that made national headlines and went on to become the subject of several legal cases. The Begum of Bhopal could hardly have failed to be aware of this and must also have been aware of the parallels between her situation and that of the Saiva proprietor of Mahabodhi. Her personal faith, like that of the mahant, was of course not Buddhist, so she probably anticipated that, if the help of the Maha Bodhi Society was sought for the superintendence of Buddhist monuments in her principality, Dharmapala could sooner or later make a claim for taking over Sanchi as well.

The Begum was also incensed by Marshall's suggestion because it cast doubt on her capacity to look after Bhopal's monuments. This seemed to her an undeserved slur on her administration. Marshall, on the other hand, (mis)understood her resistance to the appointment of a Buddhist watchman as a consequence of her Islamic faith, and this soon came to be represented by him as a disinclination to preserve Sanchi. So, he seriously mooted the idea of 'relieving' the Begum of Sanchi, by taking over its custody.[16] The endeavour here, as in the case of the chowkidars, was to exclude the local princely family from a monument within its own principality because of a hypothetical conflict of religious interests. Fortunately, this takeover was not to happen. But Marshall's interaction with Sanchi and the Begum of Bhopal had begun on a sour note.

Yet, many years later, their relationship would take an entirely different and altogether more propitious turn. This was in the summer of 1912, when Sultan Jahan Begum let it be known that she was anxious to procure some monographs on the Sanchi stupa. There is nothing in the official records to throw light on the timing of her request. We do, however, learn from her autobiography that Sanchi had figured in her public life on many occasions. Over the years, she had hosted viceroys, military commanders, and members of Indian princely families there. Even her son, Hamidullah Khan, and his child bride, were first brought there before being taken to Bhopal.[17] This had happened in 1905, when the bridal couple's wedding party were returning from Peshawar and were received by the Begum with pomp and presents at Sanchi's dak bungalow. But, it must have been her own latest visit to Sanchi that was still fresh in the Begum's memory. In November 1911, returning from Europe, Sultan Jahan stayed at Sanchi because of an outbreak of plague at Bhopal, and it was from there that she had proceeded to Delhi to attend the Darbar of George V. It is possible that this last sojourn rekindled in her a desire to glean more about the splendid Buddhist remains in whose vicinity she had so recently camped.

When Marshall heard that the Begum was trying to get hold of the available publications on Sanchi, he decided to take the initiative and offered her the relevant volumes in his library. Apparently, at some point in the not-too-distant past, she seems to have also acquainted Marshall of her interest in getting a monograph published on Sanchi. Marshall now used this as an opportunity to remind the Begum that the available monographs on Sanchi were outdated and inaccurate. They ought to be replaced, as he put it, by a publication more worthy of the famous monument with which they dealt, one financed by the Bhopal Darbar.[18]

To Marshall's delight and surprise the Begum responded generously and enthusiastically. Since the writing of such a monograph required that the director general stay at Sanchi, she offered him all the necessary logistical and financial support (Figs 14 and 15). A bungalow was reserved for his wife, children, and

Fig. 14. In camp in Sanchi (Marshall with his family accompanied by liveried attendants and elephants for transport)

their governess; cows were arranged for his camp; coolie labour was provided for the actual work of survey; and she even agreed to Marshall's suggestion that a handsome honorarium be paid to Alfred Foucher, a professor at the University of Paris, for his collaboration on the publication of the proposed Sanchi volume.[19] Foucher was a renowned French scholar, well recognized as an authority on Buddhist iconography. Evidently, his services were drafted by Marshall because Buddhist iconography would need to be a central theme in any proposed publication on the monuments of Sanchi.

Fig. 15. Marshall's daughter, Margaret, in front of a Sanchi gateway

Around this time, while such arrangements were being worked out between Marshall and the Bhopal Darbar, Harappa stepped back into the ambit of the Archaeological Survey. One of Marshall's assistants, Maulvi Zafar Hasan, had just visited it. Zafar

Hasan had joined the archaeological department three years earlier, when he was awarded its Arabic and Persian scholarship. Since 1903, when two archaeological scholarships—one in Arabic or Persian, the other in Sanskrit—had been instituted for training 'native' students in archaeological work, there had been a steady influx of very promising young Indian scholars into the Survey.

Zafar Hasan had been recommended by half a dozen people, such as the headmaster of the Mission High School at Moradabad, where Hasan had been at school, as well as by his teachers at the Mohammadan College at Aligarh, from where he had graduated. They all spoke highly of his abilities and some of them specifically mentioned that Zafar Hasan 'was of a good family, who have proved their loyalty to the Government.'[20] (Evidently, even fifty years after the 1857 revolts, which the British saw as a rebellion masterminded by disgruntled Muslims, it was thought politic to vouch for a Muslim's dependability if he was applying for a job in the British sarkar.)

Initially, the young man was attached to the office of the director general, and it is likely that he was sent to Harappa by Marshall himself. This can only mean that even though Hirananda Sastri had not sounded terribly enthusiastic about Harappa, Marshall's interest in the site, and especially its mysterious seals, remained. It also seems likely that a civil service man called Miles Irving, who was posted at Montgomery town, twelve miles from Harappa, was equally keen in getting the Survey to begin excavations there. Most historians of modern India have heard the name Irving—he was the deputy commissioner of Amritsar in 1919 who ordered his troops to fire on a large crowd gathered there at the height of the Gandhian anti-Rowlatt Act satyagraha. The snowballing effect of that firing had culminated in the sordid massacre of a large number of Indians at Jallianwala Bagh.

Before this, though, Irving had made his mark in less ignominious circumstances. He was interested in archaeology and a comprehensive list that he published in 1910—of inscriptions on

Christian tombs and structures in a large swathe of territory that stretched from Punjab to Afghanistan—still remains a most useful source for such epitaphs and epigraphs.[21] In 1912 he had corresponded with Marshall on Harappa, on the possibility of beginning work there. Irving had also expressed great enthusiasm about the ruins of what he imagined to be another ancient city, on the banks of the Ravi, four miles from Harappa, called Rajanpur. This was marked by a mound similar to Harappa's and yielded large-size bricks. Irving had not of course been able to say if it was 'as old as Harappa—it may be an offshoot from it founded on the bank of the river when it changed its course in which case of course it must be much more recent. But it is also possible that the river once flowed between them and that it is of the same age.'[22]

Having the local administrator interested in ancient mounds was always a help, and, as we saw in the case of Taxila, could frequently prove crucial to the Archaeological Survey's work. Among other things, it was on the advice of such people that notifications for the protection of sites were issued. Zafar Hasan may have been sent to survey the area for all these reasons. If planning for the forestalled yet long-planned excavation at Harappa was to begin, this was clearly a good time to start.

Hasan's visit is not an expedition that can be honestly described as historic. Yet it is worth mentioning for various reasons. For one thing, Hasan penned a note which no one seems to have remembered, not even those archaeologists who went on to excavate Harappa and who were his contemporaries.[23] In this note, he recorded his observations on the site, and some of these are relevant to the trail that we are trying to trace, one that will eventually lead to the discovery of the Indus civilization.[24] Hasan briefly described the small settlement at Harappa, with its 200 *pucca* (permanent) houses built from bricks that had been dug out of its ancient mounds. He mentioned, in this context, a low class of 'Mohamaddan converts' called Khojas whose profession it was to dig out such bricks. While they removed bricks, they also frequently found seals, stone ornaments, and antiquities which they generally presented to visiting 'European gentlemen'—officials and tourists. Hasan imagined that the ancient town was destroyed by fire since apparently burnt timbers, bricks, and grain were found within a mound there.

For another thing, Hasan bought several objects at Harappa. These included beads, earthen bowls, a piece of *sankh* (conch shell), an earthen ring, and terracottas. Most importantly, he managed to purchase two seals, evidently of the type kept in the cabinets of the British Museum.[25] These were seen by Marshall and perhaps remained in his head office for several years after. They must certainly have made him wonder, once again, about Harappa's secrets. After Zafar Hasan's report was submitted, Marshall was to write to Miles Irving saying he anticipated that 'the excavation of Harappa, when it can be arranged will be productive of most valuable results and open up quite a new chapter in Indian history.'[26] In retrospect, this suggests in Marshall an archaeological intuition verging on the ability to prophesy.

But at this point there still lay a vast abyss between the articulation of a prophecy and its fulfilment.

In the immediate context of 1912, shortly after his communication to Irving, Marshall made his way to Sanchi that winter, where he had decided to spend several weeks in camp. Harappa, for the moment, was simply filed away in the director general's office. The file's subject heading, though—'Proposed Excavations at Harappa in the Montgomery District, Punjab'—suggested that this relegation would not be for long.

Marshall had visualized his Sanchi work as only a prelude to the preparation of a monograph on the monuments. Soon after arriving there, he realized that before such a monograph could be produced the area would need to be extensively surveyed, excavated, and repaired.[27] This was an enterprise that would take much longer than the six or seven weeks he had originally planned for. The extract reproduced below is from a letter written by Marshall to the private secretary of the Begum in early 1913, drawing attention to the enormity of the operations there:

> My operations here fall under several main heads namely (1) The detailed survey of the whole site and its remains on a scale of one inch to fifty feet. This survey will engage the attention of a trained surveyor with 12 assistants for a period of about five weeks longer. (2) The clearance from debris of the more important buildings with the exception of the two main topes. On this work I have about 250 coolies working under the supervision of my own staff. (3) The survey and illustration in elevation and section of each individual building and of such details in them as are required for reproduction. (4) The photographing of such buildings and of their sculptural decorations as have not yet been photographed. Of these we are preparing about 400 additional illustrations. (5) The preparation of *papier mache* estampages of all inscriptions. These number about 1000. (6) The cutting out of jungle from the monuments and their structural repair in order to save them from further decay. On the latter work I have 20 masons engaged at the present moment. (7) The clearance of debris from the site so as to render the buildings accessible to visitors. (8) The examination of the site which is to be occupied by the museum and the cutting of trenches for the foundation of the same.[28]

So, from 1912 onwards, excavation and conservation had to be conducted on a massive scale and were spread over several years, till about 1919. Even today, Marshall's stamp is writ large over Sanchi: on its monuments, which he carefully uncovered and restored, among the *khirni* trees that he planted all around them, and even on the house where he frequently stayed (which is locally still referred to as 'Marshall House'). All this has obscured

Sultan Jahan Begum, Marshall's main benefactor there. The cost of that work, as also that of the construction of the Sanchi museum and the eventual publication of Marshall's definitive volumes on Sanchi (which he dedicated to her memory), was entirely financed by the Bhopal Darbar.

Most strikingly, in sharp contrast to what he had to say in 1905 about the unreliability of Muslims, including those that he employed in the Archaeological Survey, now in Sanchi a Muslim, Munshi Ghulam Qadir, was Marshall's excavation assistant and right-hand man. Marshall's preface to the Sanchi volumes acknowledges that Qadir 'did yeoman's service in the task of excavating and restoring its monuments' and devotes an entire paragraph to his contribution.[29] Incidentally, this same Ghulam Qadir was later also entrusted with the excavation of the Dharmarajika stupa, another Buddhist monument, at Taxila.

There will be occasion to discuss the director general's archaeological assistants subsequently, but for the present let us move on to Taxila where Marshall, as soon as he completed his winter sojourn at Sanchi in February 1913, began explorations. He had waited many years to begin work there; as we saw earlier, Taxila had captured Marshall's imagination shortly after he arrived in India. He regarded it as a peculiarly promising field for excavation owing to the fact that there were practically no medieval or modern remains to be removed before the ancient strata were reached. Plans for trial diggings were made in October 1910 and consequently, he had asked the local government to inform all the relevant landowners of the intended excavations, and to explain that they would be compensated in full for any temporary loss they might sustain.

However, when the notification declaring the site 'protected' was issued, there was a chorus of protest from the zamindars, the villagers around Taxila being loath to lose their steady income from the antiquities that the ruins yielded. As we saw, these were regularly sold to antiquity dealers and government officials.

What made matters worse, the deputy commissioner of Rawalpindi district, acting in haste, recalled the order, making Taxila the only site in the whole of India where notification of protected status had been withdrawn. More than a year was to pass before Taxila, through the intervention of the lieutenant governor, came to be formally protected.

This happened in September 1911. With all the official hurdles cleared, Marshall would no doubt have liked nothing better than to start his survey of Taxila's remains. Unfortunately, as we know, he was then in England, fighting a rearguard action against viceregal recommendations that pressed for his removal. Marshall thus arrived to begin his work at Taxila only in March 1913. At this time the snow had still not melted on the ranges to the north and east of the picturesque valley where Taxila stood.

That Marshall chose the season of spring to begin his work at Taxila is ironic. For it was in that very season, as we saw, that another and more famous Westerner had descended upon this great city: Alexander the Great in 326 BC had then, in his bid to assert claim to the provinces of the Achaemenid empire, crossed the Indus and conquered the Punjab. That remote spring had seen a flurry of activity at Taxila as its king surrendered his kingdom to the Greek conqueror and gifted him several riches, ranging from coined silver to animals such as elephants and bulls. Shortly after, Alexander had marched eastward to attack Porus, and then moved south along the Indus river and across the desert stretch of Baluchistan to go back to Persia. He had never returned to Taxila but had left a garrison of Macedonians and mercenaries under a commander. The mercenaries soon murdered their commander. But they too did not last long. In less than a decade, any Greek troops that remained in the Punjab were subjugated by another conqueror, this time from the east: this conqueror was Chandragupta, the founder king of the Mauryan dynasty, who came from Pataliputra (where we shall shortly proceed).

To return, however, to 1913: the Westerner who now arrived in Taxila would stay there rather longer than Alexander. Marshall summed this up in a monograph that he published on his work there, some years before his death: 'There can be few archaeologists now living who have devoted as many years to the excavation of a single site as I have devoted to Taxila. I started work here in the spring of 1913 and continued it almost every autumn and spring (the only seasons when digging is feasible) until 1934.'[30] Twenty-two years, by any standards, is a long time to devote to a single city site. It is something that Indian archaeology had not witnessed before, nor has since the Marshall era.

But, what ancient secrets did Marshall so patiently uncover in the course of those years?

The Taxila report, published long after the work began, brilliantly conjures up the archaeological dimensions of north-west India's political, religious, and social history.[31] The pots, weapons, tools, sculpture, and so much else that Marshall's long years of work unearthed there provided direct evidence of a prosperous city culture. Along with this were the rich structural remains—stupas, temples, and monasteries, as also fortifications, houses, shops, and streets—that spanned several centuries. More than anything else, the palpable shift in archaeological perspectives from the Cunningham era to the Marshall years is easily recognizable. The religious architecture of Taxila had been the primary focus of Cunningham's three field seasons (in 1863–4, 1872–3, and 1878–9) there. In Taxila's extensive ruins and those surrounding it, he is known to have traced as many as fifty-five stupas, twenty-eight monasteries, and nine temples.[32] There was, however, no interest in understanding either its changing urban character or the lives of its citizens. On the other hand, what we 'see' in the environs of Taxila, as evoked by Marshall, is a panorama of three city sites, each different from the other, along with a number of religious complexes situated within the cities, as also those sequestered from them. Above all, the care taken to slowly and systematically excavate sites, stratum by stratum, with an understanding of the exact locations of the artefacts and antiquities being unearthed, transformed Cunningham's image of Taxila as static and religious into a dynamic and vibrant urban location.

From the perspective of 1913, what is most striking is that even in that initial year a sense of this can be had from what was turning up in Marshall's first season of trial diggings. For one thing, there was already a clear understanding that there were three separate and successive cities covering a dozen square miles or more. Each was made up of several strata of remains, and together their history already appeared to span many centuries, from the Mauryan period to the Kushana epoch. The sites were also remarkably prolific in all kinds of antiquities. Marshall's first report talked of 'many hundreds' of coins, 'several hundred' Gandhara-style sculpture, scores of bronze vases, gold and silver jewellery, and 'a large number' of pearls, amethysts, garnets, corals, and other stones.[33] By the time he finished, the range and number of such objects would greatly expand. Also evident, right at the outset, were traces of what had been left behind by the Greeks. These ranged from coins and pottery to the 'spirit' of Syctho-Parthian architecture, which Marshall found to be Hellenistic in inspiration. For a man whose training was in classical archaeology, such elements must have been enormously alluring and worth exploring over a period of time. It is therefore not surprising that, in 1913 itself, Marshall predicted that 'the examination of such a vast site is likely to occupy a great many years'.[34]

No wonder then, that, before his departure in summer that year, he made it his business to ensure that the bungalow where he anticipated staying for a succession of seasons, was carefully looked after. The notes to his assistant, Natesan Aiyar, are full of instructions about how the durries and curtains were to be cleaned and kept with naphthalene balls between their folds, on the necessity of weekly oiling the bungalow furniture with linseed, and keeping out white ants by placing small earthenware pots with a little kerosene near the legs of all trestles and furniture.[35] There was also a detailed sketch on the manner in which the grass and shrubberies were to be laid out in the garden there; on the various creepers (quick-growing species like morning glory or railway creeper) that were to be planted to cover all visible walls in the garden; and as for vegetable seedlings, these had to be planted to be ready by the early part of November, when he returned! Clearly, this was an archaeologist who, both metaphorically and literally, left no stone unturned.

Uppermost in his mind, though, was the urgency of securing Taxila's remarkable antiquities and excavated areas from depredation. Natesan was told that on no account was 'anyone to be admitted to see any of the antiquities' in the godowns or in his bungalow.[36] Surprise checks were to be conducted at irregular intervals at Sirkap, Jandial, and Chir Tope so that the chowkidars there would not know when to expect such visits. Marshall had waited for many years to excavate Taxila and wanted no pilferers lurking behind his manicured hedges.

If Taxila and Sanchi received Marshall's personal attention, the ruins of Pataliputra, the other great city where excavations began in 1913, witnessed a qualitatively different pattern of work. Here, a private patron underwrote archaeological work, and on a scale that the Survey had not witnessed before. This patron was Sir Ratan Tata, the younger of the two sons of Jamsetji Tata, India's pioneering steel magnate. Unlike his father, he was not known for his industrial talents. Instead, it was another kind of work that brought him accolades—the philanthropic support he extended to a number of people and projects.[37] He was the benefactor of both Mohandas Karamchand Gandhi, then a relatively unknown lawyer in South Africa whose non-cooperation movement Ratan Tata supported, and Gopal Krishna Gokhale, whom he helped to set up the Servants of India Society. A house at Santiniketan in Bengal was also endowed by him for European research scholars coming to India to study Oriental literature and culture. Tata had a deep interest in collecting art and antiquities as well, and eventually the formidable collection that he built up was bequeathed by him to the Prince of Wales Museum in Bombay.

Ratan Tata travelled frequently to England, where he maintained a home at Twickenham. Apparently, during one of those visits, he met Marshall, who was then still in a state of limbo about his future, and discussed his keenness to fund archaeological work in India. Not very much could be done at that point of time, but back in India, towards the beginning of 1912, Vogel, who was officiating for Marshall, on the instructions of Sir Harcourt Butler, began preliminary discussions on the subject with Tata.[38] Shortly afterwards Marshall returned and wasted no time in arguing that the government should offer every encouragement to Tata's proposals. Apart from the fact that the funding that Tata could offer would allow the Survey to carry out excavations on a scale which, with their own limited resources, was then impossible, archaeology, he argued, needed such private support and interest.

It is not as if there were no precedents for private enterprise in archaeology. On the contrary, devout worshippers, for instance, had long provided support for the preservation of shrines with which the annals of their traditions were intermingled. In the first decade of the twentieth century, more than a lakh of rupees for repairing the Dilwara temples at Abu was raised entirely by the Jain community, who patronized it.[39] Again, a little after Ratan Tata made his offer, the Muslim community of Kashmir—by no means wealthy like the Jains—funded the repair of the Jami

Masjid at Srinagar, the chief ceremonial mosque of Kashmir.[40] While the Kashmir Darbar gave forty thousand rupees for the repairs that were undertaken under the guidance of the Archaeological Survey, ordinary Kashmiri Muslims in 1915 contributed between two and three lakhs of rupees.[41] The contribution of the Kashmir Darbar (despite all the religious biases it may have had) is worth remembering because British officials frequently labelled local princely rulers as vandals; Lord Curzon, for instance, is known to have remarked that 'vandalism was congenital' among them.[42] But in fact several princely rulers actively involved themselves in the conservation of monuments that had little do with their personal faith or religion. The Hindu Dhar Darbar of Central India had since the nineteenth century helped repair many old mosques in Dhar and Mandu, the most famous being the Lat Masjid and the Kamla Maula mosque.

On occasion, local royalty supported archaeological research as well. In 1910 the Varendra Research Society had been set up in Rajshahi in Bengal. This eventually became the most efficient private body of antiquarian scholars in India, funding fieldwork at ancient sites in Varendra or North Bengal, creating its own museum, and even publishing monographs (see chapter 9). The guiding spirit behind the society was none other than the brother of the local Raja of Dighapatiya, a man called Sarat Kumar Roy. Some years later, the Parsi community to which Tata belonged collected several thousand rupees for a proposed dig at Sanjan near Bombay, where their first settlement in India had apparently been located.[43] It is simply that, unlike these groups, Ratan Tata was perhaps the first patron who was willing to finance archaeological work unrelated to either the religion or the region to which he himself belonged.

At the same time, Tata's offer was not unconditional. One thing that the Parsi millionaire made clear was his preference for a proposed excavation at a 'Buddhist' site in the Peshawar district.

That a discerning collector should desire to spend his money on this type of site and area is entirely logical, given the rich sculpture usually found in the Frontier region. Again, the 'finds', according to the terms of agreement that he initially visualized, were to remain in his possession. Quite understandably, some in the Survey believed that his generous offer was merely spurred by a desire to augment his collection. As Aurel Stein—who Marshall had approached for the possibility of overseeing the proposed excavation of Ratan Tata—put it, he was unsure about whether this benefactor had been prompted by 'genuine interest in Indian history and antiquities or the rich collector's ambition to acquire art remains and the like, or perhaps only by the desire, not altogether common among rich Parsis, of making an impression by some "public service" of a novel kind.'[44] Stein himself was not willing to take up 'this very tempting offer' because he was once again preparing to move beyond the Indian borders, towards Afghan Turkestan.

In truth, Ratan Tata did not wish to amass archaeological finds for his private pleasure alone. But he did want that the material that his proposed excavation yielded should be eventually placed in the Prince of Wales Museum, then being built at Bombay, and that his name should remain attached to it. This was in fact to be the main hurdle with regard to financing work in the Frontier area. Although Taxila was soon to be excavated, and that city site was likely to yield antiquities in vast numbers and of the kind that Tata desired, the imperial government thought it most unlikely that these would be permitted by the local government to be carted away to the Prince of Wales Museum.

The other city site that the Survey was planning to simultaneously excavate was Pataliputra. Long and narrow in its dimensions—like Patna, which is built over it—this had been the capital of the Mauryan empire. Among other things its sheer size, 2000 hectares or so, underlined its status as the Mauryan metropolitan centre and made it larger than any other city of its time.[45] The main objective of the Survey, though, was not to understand its character or morphology but to unearth grand structural remains. Specifically, it was the palace of Emperor Ashoka which they wanted to dig out. This was supposed to have extended over an area of several acres and was said to have been in a state of reasonable preservation when the Chinese pilgrim Fa Xian visited Patna in the beginning of the fifth century AD. It was apparently 'a particularly magnificent structure of stone, so elaborately and wonderfully carved and covered with inscriptions that later generations attributed its building to "genu"'.[46] The person who was to be in charge of excavations there was D.B. Spooner, superintendent of the Eastern Circle of the Survey. And Spooner had ascertained there was no objection locally to accepting Sir Tata's plans.

So, instead of Taxila, the Archaeological Survey suggested that Ratan Tata finance the Pataliputra excavations. It would still be some time before the details of this arrangement were conclusively settled, but by October 1912 arrangements for the first large privately funded excavation were well under way.[47] While the government agreed to Tata retaining the finds, they attached certain conditions. The collection would be maintained intact in Bombay, and Tata would consider specially the case of any particular object which local reasons might render inexpedient to remove. Reasonable access would also be given for the scientific examination of the collection by students; and eventually, it was agreed, the whole would be bequeathed by him intact to the government.

But before the final round of negotiations between the government and Sir Ratan Tata were to take place, unusual and fortuitous circumstances intervened to hasten the beginning of work on Pataliputra. As most people who are familiar with Patna know, the stretch along the Ganga where it stands is fringed on one side by a lowland which is inundated during the monsoon; and on the other side it is backed by marshes created by the

Punpun river. In effect this means that, following the monsoons, the water-table in Patna is fairly high, which interferes with any deep digging that is done there in the winter season. However, that year the monsoons had partially failed, and owing to this the subsoil water was exceptionally low—the lowest that local people had witnessed in a long time. Wanting to take advantage of the opportunity afforded by this otherwise disastrous situation, Spooner proposed to Marshall that, instead of wasting the months during which the final arrangements with Tata were being negotiated, he could actually begin work at Pataliputra with his own office funds.

So, excavations began in January 1913 at the site of Kumrahar, the name of a village on the outskirts of Patna (also the name popularly given to a fairly wide stretch of country extending to a considerable distance to the west of the actual village). Much of this land was higher than the surrounding country and, in the late nineteenth century, fragments of polished sandstone which seemed to have been of Mauryan manufacture had been recovered there. These were found by Laurence Austin Waddell (1854–1938), a lieutenant colonel associated with the Indian Medical Service who had also served as Professor of Chemistry and Pathology at the Medical College in Calcutta. Equally, this medical man had a keen interest in the history of Buddhism, and in Patna he had tried to identify the fragments that he found with a particular Ashokan pillar, for which there was literary evidence in the work of an itinerant Buddhist pilgrim.[48]

Apparently, Hsuan Tsang, the Chinese Buddhist we encountered—the same who Alexander Cunningham believed had stayed at Harappa—had visited Pataliputra and mentioned two pillars set up by Ashoka there. One was the Jambudvipa column, which lay to the south; and the other was called the Nilli column, which Ashoka is said to have erected in the midst of his palace enclosure.[49] As Waddell had imagined that the Jambudvipa pillar was much further to the south, he surmised that what he found at Kumrahar must be portions of the more northerly Nilli pillar. So, Spooner decided to reopen Kumrahar to further explore Waddell's theory and, more importantly, if that was correct, he believed that the palace of Ashoka where that pillar apparently stood would also be unearthed.

Although no edict bearing fragments of the Ashokan pillar were found, within weeks Spooner unearthed the remnants of a pillared hall. The columns, of which about thirty specimens were located, were in a much shattered condition. Nevertheless, from the technique in evidence, he believed they could be assigned with certainty to the time of Ashoka. The discovery was truly exceptional and Spooner's letter to Marshall, part of which is extracted below, captures both his delight at what had been unearthed and the tantalizing possibilities that this opened up:

> It is probably part of an Asokan monastery, presumably the so-called 'Hall of Conference'; and possibly—why not? The very hall in which Asoka's Council was held. At any rate, it is a pleasure to hope that it may prove so, and I see no harm in the pleasurable hope.
>
> At all events, it was a very wonderful building, of most imposing portions. But it seems now to have been of brick, with wood freely used, probably for the roof and for beams. The absence of building blocks of stone thus becomes less puzzling. Some Mauryan brick debris, the wood afore-mentioned, and very many huge nails, are my positive evidences.
>
> I should *infer* that the extent must have been either 7 rows of 14 columns each, or if we already have the width across the columns, which is possible then 5 rows of 10 columns each, which seems more probable; but this is of course merely hypothetical. But just imagine the possibilities, in either case, with a separate Asokan stone capital for each of all these columns!
>
> It is the most thrilling work I have ever yet had the privilege of, and I am unspeakably grateful to you for having entrusted it to me.[50]

Marshall was just as enthusiastic about Spooner's discovery. But his main task now was to ensure that the euphoria of that beginning could be sustained. Along with news of the pillared hall, his superintendent had informed him of fast-exhausting departmental funds. So, enclosing a copy of Spooner's report, Marshall contacted Ratan Tata with news about the 'Hall of Ashoka' and the certainty of discovering other such remains at Pataliputra.[51] He also suggested that the work, if Tata so wished, could now be financed from the funds that he had consented to provide. Almost immediately, Tata forwarded a cheque of Rs 15,000 to Marshall. From that point on, these excavations became 'Mr Ratan Tata's Excavations at Pataliputra'.

Although the excavations had begun with departmental funds, Marshall was quite unequivocal that Spooner was to present them to the world at large as being those that, right from the beginning, were made possible by the 'princely liberality' of Tata: 'If any notices on your work are communicated by you to the Press, please take care that Mr Tata's name is kept well to the fore. The excavations must be regarded as his from the start.'[52] Over the years, more than sixty thousand rupees were to be spent on these excavations. This scale of private commitment was unprecedented for those times and apparently allowed Spooner to employ, on occasion, as many as thirteen hundred labourers in the excavations.

In November 1914, as the Archaeological Survey geared up for their winter season's work and after more than one and a half years' silence following the letters exchanged between Miles Irving and Marshall, preparations for excavation at Harappa resumed.

As before, the site reappeared in a low-key way. There are no thick bundles of correspondence of the kind generated by

Pataliputra and Sanchi, where letters and reports moved back and forth between Marshall and rich princely darbars and patrons. Just half a dozen papers tucked away in a slim file indicate Harappa's presence in the deliberations of the Survey.

But the subject of this crucial file—'Acquisition of land at Harappa for the purpose of excavation'—and the notings contained in it reveal that those who were to decide upon Harappa's future had now evolved a plan of action within a specific time frame. This plan, as before, was to conduct trial diggings there. Whereas earlier Marshall had been uncertain about when he could arrange this, now he planned to get them started in the following year. By then the young Zafar Hasan had moved up in the pecking order, in the sense that his term as an archaeological scholar had ended, as had his dabbling with things Harappan. In July that year he had been appointed as assistant to the superintendent of Muhammadan and British Monuments of the Northern Circle for the purpose of preparing a list of monuments at Delhi.[53] As we now know, the definitive volumes containing these lists eventually came to be prepared by and published under Hasan's name.[54]

Meanwhile in the Punjab Marshall had advised the superintendent of Hindu and Buddhist Monuments in the Northern Circle to visit Harappa. The fact that Marshall chose to send the top officer of the Northern Circle to visit Harappa, rather than an archaeological assistant, as earlier, indicates that he was now determined to begin work there.

The man sent was Harold Hargreaves. He had been appointed that same year as a superintendent. Unlike other officers, Hargreaves was trained neither as an architect nor as an Oriental scholar. Before serving in the archaeological establishment he had been headmaster of the Government High School at Amritsar. But he had been deeply interested in archaeology for almost a decade and had made Buddhist iconography his speciality. The archives provide no indication of how he came to do work for the Survey; it is just possible that he had been in touch with Aurel Stein, the other Archaeological Survey man who, like Hargreaves, was originally from the education department; if so, Stein may have had him co-opted into archaeological work for the Indian government. That he was first asked to officiate in the Frontier Circle during Stein's absence and deputation in England, from November 1910, seems to lead to that conclusion.[55] Hargreaves did very well when acting as superintendent of that Circle, especially in cataloguing the antiquities of the Lahore Museum and listing the monuments of the province. So, when Vogel went on leave in 1912, Hargreaves was asked to fill in for him. Subsequently, in early 1914, Vogel resigned from the archaeological department.[56]

While the education member, Sir Harcourt Butler was considering the possibility of bringing a man from England to replace Vogel, Marshall was in favour of confirming Hargreaves. This was, as he put it, because of his knowledge of the monuments of Punjab and of its languages—skills which, as Marshall pointed out, an Orientalist from Europe would take at least five or six years to acquire.[57] If at all anyone else had a greater claim to the job, it was not someone from England, but Daya Ram Sahni, who was then superintendent in Kashmir. Marshall described Sahni to Butler as 'an all round capable archaeologist'. Sahni, later the central protagonist in the story of Harappa's excavation, probably didn't get to the Northern Circle and Harappa earlier because Hargreaves was already officiating there. It was in March 1914 that Hargreaves was confirmed in Vogel's old job.

Hargreaves' main target, after his confirmation, was not visiting Harappa or beginning a dig there; that year, his concern was to get to Sarnath, the ancient scene of the Buddha's first sermon.[58] Sarnath had been excavated during Marshall's early years, in 1905, by F.O. Oertel, a United Provinces public works department man, and that had been a specially momentous dig.[59] This was because Oertel had discovered an Ashokan pillar, in fragments, and its magnificent crowning capital. It is possible that Hargreaves also hoped to muddy his hands with some equally valuable finds. But before he could proceed to Sarnath, in early September he was instructed to visit Harappa. The local authorities at Montgomery had been in touch with Marshall and appeared to be pushing plans for excavation. So, Hargreaves was asked to go there, specifically for the purpose of assessing the land to be acquired for the excavation.

Hargreaves went to Harappa in early October 1914 and stayed there a couple of days. He now prepared an 'inspection note' recording his main observations. Along with Harappa, the mound of Rajanpur, which had been referred to by Miles Irving in 1912, was visited too. In Rajanpur Hargreaves did not subscribe to Irving's assessment that this could be an important city. He pointed out that it was less than nine acres in extent and therefore not a tenth of the area of Harappa.[60]

But, before we examine what Hargreaves recorded in his note about Harappa, it is worth pointing out that another kind of recording—the first of its kind there—simultaneously took place during this site inspection. Photographs of Harappa and some of its historic artefacts were now taken.[61] Whereas earlier—for those like Marshall who had not been to Harappa—the site could only be visualized from literary descriptions and sketches (such as the ones appended to Cunningham's report), now Harappa had a clear physical presence through photography. The high rolling mounds, stretching almost endlessly into the distant horizon; the bleak, treeless environment around them; the objects that so many before Hargreaves had noticed, such as the stone rings associated with the Naogaza Pir—these are all captured in the photographs that accompanied his report (Figs 16–18). Now, when Hargreaves drew attention to undisturbed or dishevelled areas, pitted by the excavations of locals, he did so not just with words but through the power of images. His observations, much like modern research papers published

Fig. 16. Harappa's mounds, as they appeared in 1914

Fig. 17. Naogaza shrine at Harappa with pir's 'bangles/thumb-rings'

in archaeological journals, are interspersed with cross-references to the relevant photographs.

Numerous antiquities were also picked up during this visit, but only the most important ones, the seals, were photographed,

Fig. 18. Harappa seals found by Gupte in 1914

specifically two inscribed seals that had been procured by Y.R. Gupte, the assistant surveyor who accompanied the superintendent.[62] Like Hargreaves, Gupte had come to archaeology through another government department. We first hear of him in 1913, when he was registration head clerk to the collector of Nasik. But even as he performed his clerical duties he authored several short papers on ancient coins and copper plates, and escorted scholars around historic monuments near the town where he worked. One of the escorted visitors was Herman Oldenberg, Professor of Sanskrit in the University of Gottingen, who visited the Buddhist caves of Nasik under Gupte's guidance. Oldenberg was so impressed with Gupte's work and interest that he wrote him a testimonial: 'If occasion could be given to that promising young scholar to devote his whole time to archaeological and epigraphical research the result would, in all probability, prove very satisfactory.'[63] Armed with this testimonial, Gupte applied to John Marshall for a job.[64] We do not know whether it was the white sahib's recommendation or Gupte's writings which impressed Marshall, but he soon recommended him to Hargreaves, who needed an assistant.[65] And so, in the autumn of 1914, Gupte was with Hargreaves at Harappa, searching out seals, pottery, and other antiquities, while his superior inspected its mounds.

Harappa does not seem to have excited Hargreaves. This does not mean that he was unaware it was a significant city in its time. He does acknowledge in his note that 'there can be no shadow of doubt as to the former size and importance of Harappa'. Its size, for him, was suggestive of this, which, excluding certain areas closed to possible excavation, he calculated as being ninety-four acres or so. He noted that some of the walls at the site appeared to be of great thickness. He also regarded the 'countless bricks and the extensive remains of pottery' scattered all around as evidence that Harappa had been occupied for a very long time. But what Hargreaves was sceptical about was the city's antiquity. The absence of coins, of what he described as the 'pre-Muhammadan period', and especially the fact that no coins of the Indo-Greeks had been found there, as also the small size of the bricks, indicated to him that the founding of Harappa was fairly late.

Hargreaves was doubtful, too, that the devastation wrought by the railway contractors, and villagers at Harappa had left anything of great significance intact. There was only one mound which appeared to him to be relatively undisturbed. But those parts that were marked as E and D in Cunningham's plan had been subjected to continued exploitation and he thought it very improbable that anything in the way of plans of buildings could be recovered by systematic excavations of these two principal mounds. Apart from his knowledge of the lateness of the site and the depredations that it had suffered, what weighed on his mind was the large number of historical sites in his circle that still required scientific digging. There was no reason, he argued, for purchasing the mounds of a devastated city of uncertain antiquity for close to five thousand rupees 'when sites of known antiquity such as Kausambi, Kaunauj, Sankisa etc. await regular exploration.' As before, this Survey man was quite content following a familiar path rather than exploring an unknown entity.

At the same time, Hargreaves did realize that some excavation work had to take place at Harappa. This was because the zamindars who owned the mounds were only willing to enter into an agreement with the local authorities by which the latter purchased the land that they wished to protect under the Ancient Monuments Preservation Act. In view of the state of the mounds at Harappa, Hargreaves believed that such outright purchase could only be endorsed if the mounds revealed some special promise. So, his positive recommendation was that if the zamindars would not agree to anything less than purchase, an endeavour should be made to arrange with them for a temporary occupation of their lands by the Archaeological Survey for a period of two years. The areas that he suggested should be occupied in this manner were the uncultivated parts and the undisturbed mound. Trial excavations could then be carried out there which would allow the Survey to form some idea as to the desirability or otherwise of acquiring the whole site. If Hargreaves found the zamindars to be uncooperative, he also was not particularly enthusiastic about the local labour. In his note he was at pains to point out that labour in the Montgomery district was scarce and expensive. Apparently the deputy commissioner had informed him that neither diggers nor carriers could be procured for less than eight annas per day, and this was likely to go up when the new canal in that area opened up and waste land was brought under cultivation.

Surprisingly, Marshall does not seem to have been particularly concerned about the extensive brick robbing at Harappa. In a few years he would be writing about the extensive brick-built city at Harappa, but until then he seems to have considered it unlikely that the brick buildings on or near the surface belonged to the same epoch as the inscribed seals. His noting on the observations of Hargreaves stated: 'I doubt if the brick buildings on or near the surface belong to the same epoch as the interesting seals with pictographic signs which are what we want to follow up. The latter, probably, were in a lower stratum, and, in that case, it would not matter how many of the superimposed brick buildings had been removed. Indeed, the more that have gone the better, as it would facilitate our digging.'[66] Evidently, while he was convinced about the unique character of the Harappa seals and that the site would open up unknown historical vistas, he did not at this stage imagine that they could be associated with extensive brick structures.

Nor was Marshall deterred by the pessimistic tone of the superintendent's note. Instead, he went ahead and suggested to the civil authorities at Montgomery that, rather than immediately acquiring any part of the mounds, Hargreaves should carry out a trial excavation at Harappa in the winter of 1915–16. Only then would the archaeological department decide whether the land ought to be purchased. So, all indications were that the excavation of Harappa, which Marshall had first contemplated in 1906, would now finally take place in 1915–16.

There were also indications that, in 1915, Gupte planned to write an article on the seals from Harappa that he had collected, and on those which were with the Lahore Museum. This was an article which Marshall wished to vet before it was finalized: he would not be willing to endorse speculative interpretation of the seals.[67] Gupte's reply was both careful and insightful. He was almost certain that the signs or characters or letters were pictorial forms, but he admitted that all attempts made at understanding them had been unconvincing. The main interest of the seals, he told Marshall, centred 'on the curious characters and the animals sunk of them [*sic*] and probably you and all the scholars will welcome *description* of as many as come from Harappa. On comparing, after some years, all the available ones, it will be possible to solve the riddle.'[68] Marshall promised Gupte that the two or three seals that he had in his possession could also be included in his article, which he still wanted to see before deciding on its publication.

But once again, what was planned for did not happen. Gupte's article never did get written, and nor did the excavation at Harappa begin as planned. On the lack of Gupte's article there is a straightforward explanation: in 1916 Gupte chose to revert to his original post. But the postponement of Harappa's excavation appears somewhat puzzling, since the Survey and the local authorities, in this instance, had been working in tandem for the proposed dig. The probable explanation for this postponement lies elsewhere: the Great War had begun in Europe in August 1914. Although it was initially widely expected to last three or four months, it stretched on with deadly ferocity till November 1918. Great Britain entered the war in early August 1914 and the impact of its engagement was to be far-ranging. India, for instance, came under tremendous pressure in terms of both human and economic resources, and that the war years saw an eclipse in Harappa's fortunes hardly comes as a surprise.

We will return later to Harappa's ridge of ruins and the excavations there, which finally commenced in early 1921. For the moment, we have to leave it teetering on the verge of being excavated. This is because, in 1914, yet another trail becomes visible in the sands of Rajasthan—in 'Rajputana' as it was then called. This concerns the path of a scholar of languages from Italy who, around the time that Hargreaves was surveying Harappa, appears to have been spiritedly scouting around the desert state of Bikaner which lies a few hundred kilometres towards the south-east.

This very same Italian, as we shall soon see, went on to explore and excavate the Kalibangan mounds in Bikaner: mounds which, like those at Harappa, are now recognized to contain the remnants of a city of Indus antiquity.

# 6
# AN ITALIAN IN INDIA

HIS NAME WAS LUIGI PIO TESSITORI AND HE WAS born on 13 December 1887 in the small town of Udine, tucked away in the north-eastern corner of Italy. The oldest of the six children of Guido (who is said to have worked in the Foundling hospital there) and Donna Luigia Rosa Venier Romano (about whom very little is known), there was nothing either literary or Indian about his parentage.[1] Nor is there likely to have been anything 'Oriental' in the general curriculum at the Liceo Classico Jacopo Stellini, the town school where he studied before moving to the university.

But many years later, Tessitori (Fig. 19), by then a young man of twenty-three who had just completed his thesis on the *Ramacharitamanasa*, a poetic version of India's popular epic, the *Ramayana*, in a letter to a learned Jaina *acharya* (teacher, sage) called Vijaya Dharma Suri, said: 'it is since my childhood that I am fondly attached to India and I consider her as the principal object of my life.'[2] We will return later to Dharma Suri and the extraordinary relationship that Tessitori forged with him. But first let us see how this Italian's life came to be so closely linked with the subcontinent and its history.

That he was 'fondly attached to India' presupposes a degree of knowledge about it. Since his own writings do not provide

Fig. 19. Luigi Pio Tessitori

any details about how he may have acquired this, it is from other fragments of evidence that we will try and reconstruct the cultural context in which his attachment had taken shape. The trail of Tessitori's journey is labyrinthine, beginning in remote Italy, and it is through unexpected twists and chance happenings that he arrived, three decades later, to dig at the Kalibangan mounds. Kalibangan is today considered the most important Indus city in Rajasthan.

Udine is situated in the Friuli region, on a wide plain along the Tagliamento, a tributary of the Po river. It is today, as it was then, the capital of a largely agricultural province abundant in corn and wine. The town itself, though relatively small, boasted a number of things: it had a long history stretching back to the first Bronze Age settlement there, which is dated to the second millennium BC. More than a millennium later, a fortified Roman camp stood on the land where the town was to subsequently come up.[3] This is not surprising, since Udine was located at the cross-roads of north and south-east Europe, and, as Rome extended its dominion across that continent, this was usually achieved by constructing efficient long-distance roads and planting colonies of Roman citizens at strategically advantageous places.

Across the Mediterranean, as the grand *pax Romana* was consolidated—literally from the Atlantic Ocean to the Persian Gulf—it ensured that Italy became an integral part of a thriving Indian Ocean trade.[4] Although the beginnings of such trade go back to the late centuries BC, the high point was the first two hundred years of the Christian era. This is when cargo loads of Roman objects were carried across to Indian ports and markets. Beyond the wine-filled Mediterranean amphorae, ships brought gold coins, northern Adriatic olive oil, Spanish garum (fish sauce), raw and beautifully finished opaque glass, and even bronze statuettes of Cupid and Poseidon. These Roman gods, along with bronze vessels manufactured at Campania's workshops in southern Italy, became part of the repertoire of a rich household in Brahmapuri (situated in present-day Maharashtra) in the early centuries AD.[5]

The Indian artefacts that came to the Roman world were equally varied, ranging from luxury goods like spices and gemstones to more mundane items such as the cotton cloth used in making the sails of single-mast Mediterranean ships. Images of Indian deities are also known to have migrated westwards, and one of them, a Lakshmi (the Indian goddess of wealth) rendered in ivory, eventually came to be buried in the volcanic lava that destroyed the town of Pompeii in AD 79. Although Udine itself has not yielded such striking objects, it too may have forged some connection with Asia from this time onwards. Rich and powerful Roman citizens who chanced to pass through the high road on which Udine stood, after all, were a part of the elite which partook of Indian pepper and pearls. Such exotic Eastern goods were procured in large quantities and generally sold in Italy at a hundred times the original price.

Udine's appearance and character, however, was influenced less by its Roman past and more by the manner in which it developed subsequently.[6] For instance, the Castle Hill and the Piazza della Liberta around which the town is built date back to the sixteenth century. This was a century after the town and the whole of Friuli surrendered to and became part of the Venetian republic. Lying to the south of Friuli, in a lagoon near the Adriatic Sea, Venice was the centre of a maritime republic whose economic and political power radiated across the Mediterranean world. This was a link that was to influence Udine's history in many ways. The extraordinary frescoes of biblical scenes and resurrection angels that decorate its cathedral and castle were painted by the great Venetian artist Giambattista Tiepolo (1696–1770). It is in Venice that the largest group of Tiepolo's works are still displayed, but he had also come to Udine for a number of years because of the patronage of the local Patriarch, Dionisio Delfino. The city hall of Udine is a testimony to such links as well, and is rich in paintings by other celebrated Venetian masters, as is the archiepiscopal palace. Udine, in turn, sent out several sons of the soil to the centres of Renaissance art, where they came to be trained by some of the most famous artists of Italy. One of them, Giovanni da Udine, was a pupil of the great master Raphael. His paintings too decorated a number of churches in Udine.

Venice was also the hub of an expanding European trade with the East. This had been disrupted when the Roman empire collapsed, but began to revive in the medieval centuries.[7] It is likely that different parts of the Venetian republic, including the Friuli, were significantly affected by this revival. Apart from anything else, knowledge about the East must have circulated through travel accounts that are known to have been penned by merchants involved in this transoceanic trade. Of these, the most famous was the memoir of the thirteenth-century traveller and trader from Venice, Marco Polo. Born in 1254, he had left Venice with his father and uncle as a youth of eighteen and returned from his extensive travels and sojourns in China, Indonesia, Sri Lanka, Persia, and India when he was forty-four. Under circumstances which are not entirely clear but arose out of an encounter between Venetian and Genoese merchant vessels, he was taken prisoner on his return and brought to Genoa. It was during his imprisonment that he dictated the story of his wide travels in the East. Undoubtedly, Marco Polo was a merchant; but he was also a great explorer, mesmerized by the places he visited. The description of his travels remains as fascinating today as it must have been to his contemporaries.[8] He was also probably the first Western traveller to offer an essentially accurate life history of the Buddha, whose wisdom and virtue, he believed, could not be far from that of Christ.[9] It was this, more than any other account of its time, which whetted European interest in Asia's manners and institutions.

From the thirteenth century onwards, a new kind of traveller came to India: Italians with a religious bent of mind, for whom the country was both a spectacle of monstrous idols and a land whose heathens could be made Christians. From the very region that Tessitori hailed, a friar, Odoric of Pordenone, had visited several places in South India between 1316 and 1318. Among other things, his narrative vividly describes a monstrous half-man half-ox idol who demanded the blood of forty virgins.[10] Stereotypes of such dark and devilish deities continued to find a place in later accounts as well, and the seventeenth-century Roman patrician Pietro della Valle is a good example of this.

Descriptions of monstrous figures with many arms and faces, with elephant heads, and sitting upon sundry animals like tigers and rats, jostle with those of 'foolish and ignorant Indians' who related ridiculous stories about them.[11] Italian missionaries presumably came to convert such supposedly foolish and ignorant Indians. Among them, though, were some sympathetic characters, the most colourful of these being Roberto de Nobili (1577–1656), who is generally remembered as a 'Roman Catholic Brahmin'. He had always dreamt of working as a missionary, but he took on the attire of a brahmin in order to attract people to his faith in Madurai, where he arrived in the early seventeenth century. In ochre robes, with sandal paste on his shaved head, he is known to have converted a good number of Madurai folk, including Shivadharma, the Telegu brahmin who taught him Sanskrit and Hindu philosophy. Shivadharma though, continued to wear his sacred thread and hair tuft along with a cross.[12]

Travellers of such varied hues and intentions, and the descriptions that they penned, must have been known to literate, well-schooled Italians, for travel accounts enjoyed a wide circulation in Italy. Many centuries before Tessitori's time, they even formed part of the readings of country folk in the Friuli region. One of them, a sixteenth-century Friulian miller called Mennochio, who was eventually put to death because of his heretical views, was a passionate purveyor of such books. Along with the vernacular Bible and sundry chronicles and poems, an Italian translation of the *Travels of Sir John Mandeville* figures among the books that he had read, and his modern chronicler tells us that some of his heretical ideas came out of such books. Mandeville himself was a fictitious figure, and while the descriptions of the Orient contained in his *Travels* were largely imaginary, they were based on compilations of geographical texts. Apart from expanding Mennochio's mental universe from his village and region to 'India and Cathay and islands inhabited by cannibals, Pigmies, and men with the heads of dogs,'[13] this work also contained a severe judgement on the corruption of Christianity, attributed to an Eastern sultan. This text was cited by Mennochio during his inquisition trial, and it is entirely possible that it was in such narratives that the Friulian miller had found a justification for his own criticism of the church.

Many centuries later, such strange and real knowledge about the East may well have continued to circulate through the lively network of print culture in the Friuli, where Tessitori grew up and received his early education. Of course, unlike the time of Mennochio, when books were either bought or borrowed from others, by the nineteenth century there were institutional libraries open to the reading public. Udine, in Tessitori's time, had its own Academy of Letters as also a public library: the 'Vincenzo Joppi' Civic Library had been established some twelve years before Tessitori was born.[14] During its early years, Vincenzo Joppi, its librarian and subsequently its director, had successfully acquired old literary works for it, donated by various sources. One of the many valuable donations was the extensive 10,000-volume collection of Count Francesco di Toppo, which contained printed works of the fifteenth and sixteenth centuries. One can only assume that the young Tessitori's knowledge of, and attachment to, a distant Eastern land was nurtured by the accounts of India's culture and condiments that he read in the tomes that were housed in these libraries of his native town.

While Tessitori's interest in India may have been whetted by the rich mosaic of information in the accounts of travellers, traders, and missionaries, his career was formed in a specifically nineteenth-century context. After finishing his schooling he moved to the University of Florence, where he was to take his degree with honours in the Humanities. It was during his years in Florence that Tessitori developed a passion for Indian languages.

Part of this had to do with his own inclinations and remarkable talent. Although very little is known of his student life, one of his university mates remembered him as a quiet student, aloof from the boisterous elements of university life, spending all his spare time learning what he could about India. This, along with the fact that he joined Sanskrit classes on his own and without advice or persuasion, resulted in his classmates giving him an appropriate sobriquet—'Indian Louis' is what he was called. Apart from Sanskrit, he mastered Pali and Prakrit as well.[15]

What must also have helped was the tradition of Indological scholarship in Florence and the rich holdings of Indian manuscripts and literature in the national library of that city. Florence was one of the established universities in Italy, as also one of the few which had created a chair for Sanskrit.[16] This was held by Professor Paolo Emilio Pavolini. An accomplished linguist and man of literature with knowledge of ancient Indian languages, as also Polish and English literature, he wrote on various subjects ranging from Buddhism to the Indian manuscripts of the national library of Florence.

The chair itself was relatively recent (as were all Indology chairs in Europe), but it was a pointer to a new development in the nineteenth century, one that Tessitori was to fashion himself around, and which involved the academization of Indology. There were now careers open for those of the lettered world who chose to devote themselves to the scholarly pursuit of Indian texts and languages. Such chairs and careers will be discussed a little later, but what may be pointed out is that this was intrinsically connected with the European rediscovery of the East in the context of what has been described as an 'Oriental Renaissance'. This was really a verbal renaissance linked to the deciphering of different types of writings. The details of the routes by which linguistic studies began in Europe and the impact of the texts that were deciphered on its thought and literature are many and have been admirably documented in Schwab's survey of this second Renaissance.[17]

Schwab's work richly demonstrates that it was frequently the large collections of Indic manuscripts, brought back by voyagers and missionaries in the seventeenth and eighteenth centuries, which created the groundwork for the establishment of such scholarship. For instance, in 1718, more than a century before a Sanskrit chair was established in Paris, Abbe Bignon had issued a clarion call for the collection of Oriental texts.[18] As librarian to the king of France and reorganizer of the Academie des Inscriptions, he had decided to create an Oriental library in Paris, for which he asked the help of Christian missions abroad. Father Pons was one such missionary in India who responded to this call. A Jesuit father, he was a distinguished precursor of the more famous names of nineteenth-century Oriental scholarship in France. He is known to have analysed Indian books of grammar, and was the translator of *Amarkosha*, among the most famous ancient Indian dictionaries. In 1733 he sent more than a hundred and fifty manuscripts to Paris from Chandernagore. These ranged from the Upanishads to works of Indian grammar and classical literature, and they helped build the Oriental manuscript collection of the Bibliotheque de Paris. From them, in 1739, a catalogue was prepared.[19]

Again, in the second half of the eighteenth century, an Austrian Carmelist, Paulinus a Sancto Bartholomaeo, had collected various manuscripts and brought them to Rome, including a Sanskrit grammar that had been compiled by Johann Ernest Hanxleden, a Jesuit missionary who lived for more than thirty years on the Malabar coast. In fact the first Sanskrit grammars printed in Europe did not emerge from the English scholars of Calcutta's Asiatic Society of Bengal but were the work of Sancto Bartholomaeo, printed in Rome in 1790 and 1804.[20]

At the same time, it is undeniable that the full flowering of European Oriental scholarship began only from the late eighteenth century, with the British conquest of India and the arrival of English civil servants in Calcutta. These were modern conquerors who consolidated their political and administrative hold over the country through an understanding of local laws and customs. This required a working knowledge of Indian languages. It is no surprise, then, that some of the most important researches concerning Indian texts, languages, chronology, and history came out of the Asiatic Society of Bengal. As is well known, this was established in Calcutta in 1784 with the extraordinary savant William Jones as its president. Jones was a judge of the Calcutta Supreme Court, and the founder members of the society included all the judges of the Supreme Court.[21] Much of their work was published in the form of 'transactions' under the title of a series called *Asiatic Researches*. This publication had an enormous impact across Europe—mostly in England, Germany, and France; in the last country a French translation would shortly appear. Schwab captures this influential diffusion rather well when he tells us that 'Jones and the *Asiatic Researches*, whether in English or French, were to be found on the writing desks of Quinet and Michelet, of Hugo and Lamartine, of Joseph de Maistre and Lamennais.'[22]

It is against this background that the first British chair in Sanskrit was created. This was in 1833 through a generous endowment by Joseph Boden, and it was first assumed by Horace Hayman Wilson (1786–1860) at Oxford. The connection between colonial concerns and the creation of such posts comes across most forcefully in the career of H.H. Wilson.[23] Before assuming the chair at Oxford he had, during a twenty-seven-year tenure with the East India Company, combined his work in the medical service and in the mint in India with philological research that included an edition of Kalidasa's *Meghaduta* (The Cloud Messenger) as well as the first practical Sanskrit–English dictionary. But, generally speaking, England was not at the forefront of Indic linguistic scholarship; such scholarship was much more robust in France and Germany. France was to become the hub of Oriental scholarship in the first half of the nineteenth century and attracted students and researchers from all parts of Europe. In fact, the first chair in Sanskrit was established not in London or Oxbridge but in Paris, in 1814. A French Orientalist, Baron Antoine Isaac Silvestre de Sacy (1758–1838) was responsible for its establishment. A civil servant by profession, de Sacy was an acknowledged master of Semitic languages. He had a distinguished career at the University of Paris, first as Professor of Arabic, later of Persian, and finally, in 1815, as its rector. The Sanskrit chair was established at the College de France, and in 1815 de Sacy's student Leonard de Chezy became the first to occupy it.[24]

A little later, in 1821, a similar chair was instituted at the University of Berlin and its earliest occupant was Franz Bopp (1821–67). As Professor of Sanskrit and Comparative Linguistics, Bopp set out what was to become the hallmark of German Indology: the comparative linguistic approach to the study of ancient Indian texts. In Bonn, August Schlegel, Professor in the Faculty of Philosophy and History, tried to popularize Sanskrit among students and was responsible for setting up the first Sanskrit printing press in Europe. Over the century, German scholarship in Indic studies became truly formidable, and some German scholars assumed chairs in England.[25] Rosen, who was born in Hanover, became Professor of Sanskrit at London, and then there was Max Müller, who assumed the Chair of Comparative Linguistics at Oxford in 1900. It is not as if there were large numbers of students for the Indian languages, but what is significant is that these positions were nonetheless being offered and pursued in European universities from Oxford to Florence.

It was one such Sanskritist whose research came to form the foundation of the degree work of Tessitori. He was from Turin, a man of letters called Gaspare Gorresio, who held the first chair in Sanskrit to be instituted within Italy.[26] That his chair was set up in Turin was only fitting since Turin was the first capital of Italy (followed by Florence and Rome) and its university was among the oldest in Italy, having been founded in 1404. Gorresio had a degree in philology and had studied in Paris, where the Sanskrit luminary was Eugene Burnouf (1801–52), the renowned Indologist who had succeeded Chezy to the Chair of Sanskrit at the College de France. His students included Max Müller in England, Adolphe Pictet in Geneva, Rudolf Roth in Tubingen, and Gorresio in Turin. Burnouf gave Gorresio the confidence to take up the task of editing a complete edition of the *Ramayana*. Eventually, Gorresio's edition and an Italian translation of the text were published between 1846 and 1870 in twelve volumes, the first time that Valmiki's epic appeared in Europe in the Bengali or 'Gauda' version. Gorresio was thus an important point of reference for the Italian Indologists who succeeded him and devoted themselves to the *Ramayana*. Tessitori was among the first such.

Tessitori's degree work drew heavily on the Bengali version of the *Ramayana*. But its aim was far more ambitious. It involved a comparison of two versions of the hero poem. It juxtaposed Valmiki's *Ramayana* with an Awadhi (an eastern Hindi dialect) version of the same story. This was the *Ramacharitamanasa* ('Lake of the Deeds of Rama') written by the master poet of medieval North India, Goswami Tulsidasa (1532–1624). Separated from the original *Ramayana* by more than a thousand years, this is the best-loved Indian version of the Rama legend.

Tessitori's dissertation forcefully underlined that the *Ramayana* formed the main source of information for Tulsidasa but did not constitute his artistic model,[27] arguing that 'Tulasi Dasa derives from Valmiki all the particulars of the story, shortens or amplifies them as he likes, explains them according to his creed, clothes them in a new fashion, but hardly ever alters their objectiveness, their succession, their historical value.'[28] At the same time, he demonstrated that Tulsidasa's poetry was absolutely independent of Valmiki's style and expressions and, in this sense, constituted a new and original work. But more than the argument, the manner in which he arrived at this conclusion is worth noting. Tessitori did this by carefully documenting all the agreements and disagreements between the two texts through a verse-by-verse comparison. For at least two reasons, this was a work of enormous patience and labour. First, the number of verses in the two texts is formidable, going into several thousands. Second, Tessitori believed that Tulsidasa followed more than one version of the *Ramayana*. Apparently, by the time he composed his poem, the 'ur' text had undergone significant regional changes, with reciters of the various regions making their own additions and elaborations. So, in addition to the Bengal recension of Valmiki's text ('B' version), Tessitori also made a detailed comparison with the one that was widespread in North and South India ('C' version). The main text and arguments of his dissertation soon appeared, in 1911, in Italian, in a volume of the *Giornale della Societa Asiatica Italiana*.

Almost immediately, this caught the attention of those in the scholarly world of Europe who were interested in India's texts and languages. Most importantly, it was the interest that Tessitori's work aroused in a famous India-centred philologist of Irish origin, Sir George Abraham Grierson, which would prove to be providential for Tessitori's future.

Grierson (1851–1941) had joined the Indian Civil Service in 1873 and was in charge of the Linguistic Survey of India from 1898 till 1928. In the matter of Indian languages and dialects, he was among the most respected and influential men of his time. People like him also made it their business to keep up with research developments in Asian languages, and, quite naturally, Tessitori's publication came to his notice. Not only did he read it, he felt sufficiently enthused to publish a note containing his observations on it in the *Journal of the Royal Asiatic Society*. In that note, while he argued that Tessitori had paid insufficient attention to other contemporaneous Vaishnava works that dealt with Rama, he strongly recommended it to all students of vernacular literature: 'It is full of valuable comparisons and of suggestive remarks, and it must necessarily be taken into serious account in all future investigations on the connection between the two great poets of the glory of the House of Raghu.'[29] Subsequently, it was at Grierson's suggestion that Tessitori's Italian paper was translated and republished in English, in an English-language journal of Indian studies, *The Indian Antiquary*. Again, it was because of Grierson's encouragement that Tessitori would shortly apply, in 1913, for a job to the India Office in London. Apparently in that very year he also applied for the Chair of Hindustani at the Regio Instituto Orientale in Naples.[30]

But in the interregnum following the completion of his dissertation, Tessitori was not simply 'waiting' for an opening to come up in Italy or India. Rather, in those years he confidently moved on to extend his oeuvre to the Indian vernaculars, especially those that were used in the composition of non-canonical Jaina literature.[31] The literature itself was exceptionally comprehensive, ranging from epics and novels to popular narrative verses and hymns. While several such works were highly elaborate compositions, the Jainas also took great care to make their writings accessible to large numbers of people and, therefore, they were frequently composed in the vernacular languages. This is the reason why Jaina texts are so important from the point of view of the history of Indian languages.

We do not know if, to begin with, Tessitori chose to work

on such manuscripts more out of interest or sheer convenience. In later years he did engage with and showed great sympathy for Jaina doctrines and practices, but how far back we can push his interest in the religion remains a matter of speculation. That he had tried to give up eating meat is something we do know, but that was not because of his attraction to Jainism. Rather, it was a consequence of his acquaintance with two Maratha Brahmins. The circumstances of his association with them is a mystery, but it was somewhere around 1909 in Florence and, from the account that he gave many years later, the relationship seems to have been more than a passing acquaintance. During the course of their interaction, he came under their culinary influence and became convinced of their arguments in favour of vegetarian food: 'I began to be disgusted with meat and on returning to my native home I resolved to abandon meat altogether. I went thus on for about one year, but afterwards I was taken ill and became so much reduced in consequence, that my physician prescribed for my diet a large quantity of roasted meat to make me recover soon. So I took to eat meat again . . .'[32]

Rather than a personal predilection for the Jaina religion, what may have been of greater import in his decision to take up this literature was that Jaina manuscripts formed an important part of the holdings of the library that Tessitori was most familiar with. He must have come across such texts several times while he had worked on his dissertation in the Biblioteca Nazionale Centrale of Florence. These were the manuscripts, about three hundred and fifty of them, that had been purchased by an Italian Indologist, Angelo de Gubernatis, during his travels in Surat and Bombay in 1885–6.[33] This collection was further enriched by another Italian in 1903, E. Pulle, who had also begun cataloguing them. Tessitori must also have known about these works from the publications of his own supervisor, Pavolini, who had translated Jaina gnomic and didactic poetry and had also penned articles relating to famous Jaina stories.[34] Subsequently, with the possible encouragement of Grierson, who was aware of the paucity of European scholars working on neo-Indian vernaculars, Tessitori decided to take up such texts in right earnest. In fact, if we follow up footnotes and references in the papers that he published, several of the works that he examined during those years came from the holdings of Florence's national library.[35] Old West Rajasthani manuscripts of the Florence library were studied as well, and in fact became the starting point for another major work of Tessitori—on the historical grammar of that language—one that would be of some significance for the history of the development of what were called modern 'Indo-Aryan vernaculars'.[36]

From the Rama legend to the grammar of archaic Rajasthani, Tessitori had certainly changed direction. But his basic method—comparing different versions of the same story and text—continued to mark his later work. His writing on the versions of the tale of Solomon's judgement exemplifies this rather well; here he compares the two versions that he found in the Florence library with two other published accounts of the same story, and through identifying discrepancies tries to precisely determine their historical affiliations.[37]

In short, all this research gave a precise direction to Tessitori's future. His desire to work in India now became imbued with a more intense determination to devote himself to the vast manuscript literature composed in the Marwari and Dhundhari vernaculars. In 1913, when he was in the process of submitting an application to the India Office, he did this with the purpose of coming as close as possible to Rajasthan, where such literature could be located. Tessitori, in fact, seems to have been quite willing to take up work as a teacher of Latin, Greek, or Italian in a college or school, the only condition being that it should be 'the nearest possible to Rajputana'.[38] He realized there was no guarantee that such a job would be available. His second option, therefore, was to consider applying to the

Maharaja of Jaipur or some other Indian prince willing to employ him on linguistic work which, again, would ensure that he worked on the Rajasthani vernaculars. Of course, if he could not be so employed, he seemed willing to take on almost any job as long as it brought him to India: 'I am willing to assume any other appointment that may be suited to my poor abilities, in any place, provided it enables me to go over to India to study the Indian languages which I love best after my own mother tongue.'[39]

This willingness was expressed by Tessitori to an Indian religious teacher, and it brings us to an aspect of the impact that his research on Jaina literature had at a personal level—one that led him to and created a close bond with the recipient of this letter. Tessitori's letter was to an extraordinary religious personality of his time, the Jaina acharya Vijaya Dharma Suri (1868–1923). We will shortly explore the circumstances which brought Tessitori in touch with him, but first let us get a sense of the origins and antecedents of this personage.

Vijaya Dharma Suri's origins lay in a place called Mahuwa in Kathiawar, where he was born as Mula Chandra in a humble family of the Visa Shrimali clan.[40] Although his father had wanted the son to help in his shop and, consequently, had not even educated him, Mula Chandra soon disappointed him. In his teens he decided to move away from money and markets to become a monk. He was consecrated at the age of nineteen, which is when he assumed the name of Dharma Vijaya. In the next few decades he first taught himself the Jaina scriptures, then went on to preach his religion, and alongside published books, founded libraries and educational institutions, and even a *pasushala* or animal hospital. But it was his role as a preacher that brought him great respect and fame, not the least because he walked barefoot from Kathiawar to Calcutta, accompanied only by a few monks, his wooden bowl, and bundles of manuscripts. His expositions influenced both pious Jainas and orthodox Hindus. In Calcutta, for instance, he apparently had the satisfaction of seeing several babus renounce the eating of fish after his advice, an incredible achievement if we bear in mind that in Bengal the eating of fish is in itself almost a religion. Among Dharma Vijaya's powerful Hindu patrons was the Maharaja of Banaras, who was so impressed with his teachings that he became the patron of the Yasovijaya Jaina Gurukula, the college that Dharma Vijaya had set up there. Some years later, in 1908, it was in Banaras that the very same maharaja presented to Dharma Vijaya a *sammanapatra* (decree of respect) signed by more than a hundred distinguished Hindu pandits, conferring on him the title of *Sastravisarada Jainacharya* in recognition of his learning and educational activities. Since then, Dharma Vijaya's name came to be known as Vijaya Dharma (by reversing the two terms, as is often done in the case of Jaina acharyas; and the appendage Suri was added to it).

Vijaya Dharma Suri's circle of acquaintances and admirers was a large one, and European Orientalists who were directly or indirectly associated with Jaina texts were part of this circle.[41] Some of this had to do with Dharma Suri's immense knowledge of such literature and his pioneering activities in rescuing from oblivion important Jaina works pertaining to a range of subjects—such as grammar, lexicography, logic, chronology, fable, and poetry.[42] But, above all, Europeans developed a personal acquaintance with him because of the unfailing help that they received from him on Jaina texts. It is likely that one of them put Tessitori in touch with the acharya.

A regular correspondence soon developed between them which, on Tessitori's part, was suffused with a warmth and attachment developed through an active exchange of books and articles, as also ideas and views.[43] The acharya's observations on Tessitori's paper on the *Paramjyotistotra*, the manner in which he sought out the acharya when he was asked to write an entry on the Kanphata Jogis for an encyclopaedia, and so much else, shows that this was not a relationship of a subordinate native acharya and a superior European scholar.[44] Rather, it was one in which the European appears to be sitting, in a manner of speaking, at the feet of his teacher.[45] In one of his letters to Dharma Suri, written in 1913, Tessitori describes him as the most noble and generous soul that he has had the fortune to have come into contact with and expresses gratitude for all his help.[46]

This sense of gratitude must have been further enhanced when, in that same year, 1913, Dharma Suri responded to Tessitori's desperate desire to come to India. He offered him a job at Palitana in Kathiawar in the Yasovijaya Jaina Gurukula, a residential school he had set up. Tessitori, on his part, was enthusiastic about taking up this offer and hoped that he would spend his time there doing critical editions of Prakrit texts. His only fear was that the acharya may have a problem with his Christian religion.[47] So, this first job offer was tentatively accepted, with the provision that Dharma Suri clarify he was willing to accept a Christian within the Gurukula's fold. Tessitori, for his part, promised to live in a way that would not offend the Jaina residents of the Gurukula and even promised to help in the diffusion of Jainism!

While he waited for Dharma Suri's letter, hoping the latter would have no objection to an Italian Christian's existence in his school, some much-awaited confirmation from the Indian government arrived. The India Office had recommended Tessitori's appointment, which was approved by the department of education. He was to work under the aegis of the Asiatic Society of Bengal on Rajasthani manuscripts. Within a matter of weeks, Tessitori left for Naples, and from there sailed for Bombay.

Tessitori was now on the threshold of his India adventure—the culmination of a long interest first kindled in his early years in Udine.

# 7

# FROM CALCUTTA TO KALIBANGAN

TESSITORI SAILED FROM NAPLES ON 24 MARCH 1914 and reached the shores of Bombay some fifteen days later. There he was received by some old Indian friends who he had presumably first met in Italy.[1] But within a matter of days he moved on to Calcutta, arriving there on 11 April.

On that very day Tessitori presented himself before the Asiatic Society. He had been appointed editor of the 'Bardic and Historical Literature of Rajputana' and was to be formally linked to the Society because, for practically a decade, they had been involved with the task of surveying such works. As far back as 1905 the Indian government had inaugurated a scheme for the collection and publication of bardic literature, which it had entrusted to the Asiatic Society, along with a little more than two thousand rupees for a preliminary survey.[2] The first four years had gone by without any work being undertaken for the Society had not been able to find a suitable man. In 1909 Pandit Haraprasad Shastri was placed in charge of the work.

Shastri (1853–1931) was a well-known Bengali scholar who later went on to become president of the Asiatic Society. It is said that he was passionate about unpublished manuscripts and had, on behalf of the Asiatic Society, collected and bought more than 8000 manuscripts.[3] In the world of Indological scholarship his fame rested on the discovery that he had made in one such manuscript of the earliest form of writing in Bengali, in a genre of song called 'Charja Geeti' composed by Buddhist holy men. This he unearthed in a text preserved in the Royal Nepalese Library in 1907. His edition of these songs, along with three other Buddhist works, was published in a book called *Baudha Gana O Doha*.[4] It was in that book that he first introduced the concept of a code language in which the Buddhist songs were written which he called 'sandhya bhasa' or 'twilight language'.[5] Alongside discovering and editing Eastern manuscripts, Shastri had toured Rajputana and Gujarat on several occasions on behalf of the Society and submitted a report on their chronicles. This kind of work, incidentally, tied up with a larger interest within the princely states for the preservation of their old literature. Various departments of such states were in the process of cataloguing their collections. In the state of Baroda, this had been further aided by the local *diwan* (minister of finance) being a famous nationalist historian, Romesh Chunder Dutt (1848–1909), who had been actively interested in preserving 'national literature'.[6]

During the course of his tours, Shastri got copies of various bardic and historical works made and brought them over to Calcutta. So, as far as the Society was concerned, it was these copies that the newly arrived editor of bardic and historical literature was to take up for study in their office in Calcutta.[7] Tessitori, it is easy to imagine, must have been appalled at this impending anticlimax, one which threatened to thwart his long-desired ambition of going to Rajputana, the land of the bards who would form the subject of his study. But dismay turned to hope when he realized that the material with the Asiatic Society was entirely unsatisfactory. It was full of mistakes because it had been copied very hurriedly. Tessitori soon declared it absolutely worthless for any philological purposes, 'having evidently been prepared by half illiterate and careless copyists'.[8] Shortly after surveying the material, he asked permission to proceed to Rajputana for a preliminary tour, to personally get a sense of the range of its literature so that he might prepare a fresh scheme for their study and documentation. The Society, in turn, had to ask the government, and what with the delay involved in these proceedings, Tessitori ended up spending more than three months in Calcutta waiting for their consent.

Sustaining himself on macaroni, meat, and vegetables, Tessitori spent those months at a boarding house run by one of his fellow countrymen, a physician called Dr Rossa who had spent several years there.[9] In Calcutta he met up with a few of Vijaya Dharma Suri's friends as well. A Dr Satish Chandra who worked in the Sanskrit College was one of these and it was he who informed Tessitori that Pandit Rama Karna of Jodhpur, the man who would become one of Tessitori's close assistants, had made a large collection of bardic manuscripts. Tessitori continued to regularly correspond with the acharya, who advised him on all kinds of things—such as the desirability of giving up meat, as also the manner in which he should deal with Indians. While Tessitori regretted he was unable to reduce his diet to macaroni and vegetables, he does seem to have taken the advice to mix with Indians more seriously.[10] 'You know I have come here because I love India, her people, languages and literature and, therefore the more intimately I can know her, the happier I feel', wrote Tessitori, and added that he was 'not an Englishman to look down upon all that is not English or at least European. I have the highest respect and admiration for the Indian people.'[11]

Eventually, the much-awaited permission came, and on 22 July 1914 Tessitori left Calcutta, heading west for Rajputana. This was to be in the nature of an exploratory tour during which he would spend a few months visiting several of the princely states with the primary purpose of personally vetting manuscripts and texts. Jaipur was his first stop. Here he met Sir Elliot Colvin, the political agent, who gave him letters of introduction to all the various chiefs of Rajputana.[12] Within a couple of days he left for Jodhpur, and the maharaja's guest house, near the city's

Sojatia Gate, soon became his headquarters.[13] Most of the places that he visited in August were in and around Jodhpur—such as Mandor, Erinpura, Shivaganj, and Khivandi. The early part of September was spent in Nagor, while later he moved to Jaipur and then to Bikaner. Finally, he also visited Bundi, Ratlam, and Ujjain, the last two places in connection with the *Vachanika Rao Ratan Singh ji ri*, a bardic poem of the sixteenth century whose critical text and English translation he was preparing.

At Erinpura, where he halted for about a week, the Italian linguist finally met up with his Jaina mentor (Fig. 20).[14] He must have been deeply impressed by Dharma Suri because, in the course of the next few years, he visited him on three more occasions. Later Tessitori would write a short biography of him and we learn from it that their personal interaction, right from the beginning, was scholarly but also close.[15] As Tessitori put it, 'I have known him as a scholar, I have known him as an orator, I have known him as a monk, and, though, he is not permitted to yield to feelings of worldly affection, I think I can say that I have also known him as a friend.'[16] Apparently, not only did the acharya clarify the philosophical and philological difficulties that the Italian scholar had encountered in his study of Jaina vernaculars, but together they read Sanskrit inscriptions such as those engraved on the base of marble idols in Jaina temples. Tessitori also listened to Dharma Suri's eloquent sermons and got an insight through him into the monastic life of the Jainas. Among other things, during one of his sojourns, he was present at the ritual of Dharma Suri depilating (via the Jaina procedure of actually wrenching out each hair!) his chief disciple, Indra Vijaya Upadhyaya.

But coming back to the main purpose of his tour: Tessitori did get first-hand knowledge of the vast and rich literature of Rajputana, of poetical compositions in Dingala (a West Rajputana dialect) and Pingala (a kind of Brajabhasa), and of prose texts, especially genealogical narratives. Jodhpur was the richest

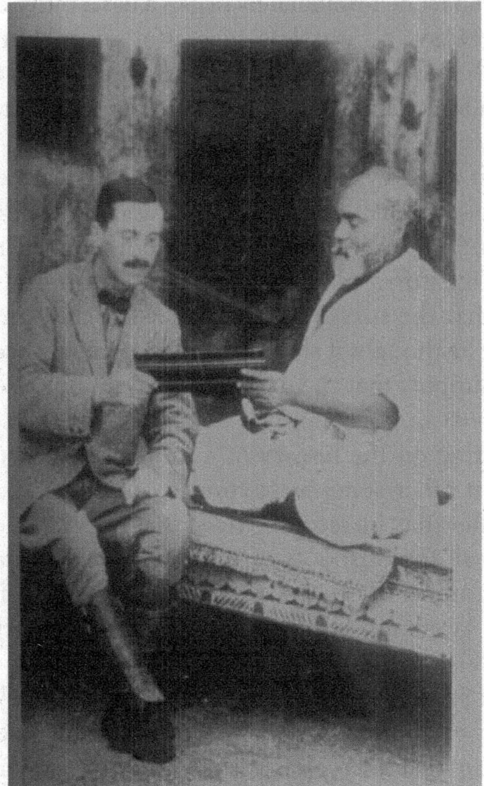

Fig. 20. Tessitori with Acharya Vijaya Dharma Suri

in bardic and historical productions and had, on its own, been spending thousands of rupees to record such work. In Bikaner, too, every facility was extended to him and he was promised a copy of the list of manuscripts in the Darbar library. But in Jaipur, Pandit Madhusudhana, the officer in charge of manuscripts, in the true tradition of a government *daftar* (office), stonewalled Tessitori's requests for several days and finally only gave him access to a few shelves of printed books. As for private bardic libraries, all those in Jodhpur were easily accessible to him, and in fact he immediately began a descriptive catalogue of them. At Nagor he was less successful; even though he was armed with a letter from the Jodhpur darbar, he was not granted access to a large Jaina Digambara Bhandar in which there were apparently about 10,000 manuscripts and books.[17]

Tessitori was now in a position to provide the detailed outline of a proposed 'Scheme for the Bardic and Historical Survey of Rajputana'.[18] This scheme aimed to be both comprehensive and accurate. Tessitori's plan to make it uniform and exhaustive required that the survey be done one state at a time. Jodhpur was where he thought it should begin, not merely because of the financial support that the darbar had given, but also because it was the most important of all the states—in the sense that it had a bearing on the history of a number of others. (Bikaner and certain other states were connected with it via blood and origin.) After that, he recommended that Bikaner, the oldest and biggest of all the offshoots of Jodhpur, be taken up, and then by turn a number of other states that had offered to assist—such as Bundi, Jaisalmer, Sirohi, Kishangarh, Pratapgarh, Dungarpur, and Banswara.

In each state, Tessitori visualized that the survey would do a number of things. First, a descriptive catalogue would be prepared so that there was a ready reference manual of the manuscripts. Then, the contents of the manuscripts would be critically examined in order to ascertain their historical value. Authentic information contained in them which deserved to be published would be used to write a connected history of the relevant province. The bardic poems would be published separately as literary texts with English translations and notes, and with introductions which would aim to examine their historical value. But since bardic manuscripts were known to be full of inaccuracies, it was necessary to obtain multiple manuscripts for the purpose of preparing a reliable edited version of each text. Also, introducing an archaeological component into the proposed survey, he underlined that the search for manuscripts and inscriptional records be carried out simultaneously.

This was not the only feature common to Tessitori's proposed scheme and archaeological surveys. Much like the work that Marshall's department undertook, Tessitori visualized a situation where he, as editor, would be based not in Calcutta but in Rajputana, where he would spend most of his time at centres of bardic activity. Some such centres were to be found within convenient distances from darbar headquarters and their resthouses. But a great source of manuscripts, Tessitori tells us, were those specialist castes, in villages and less known towns, which had preserved and transmitted the clan histories, traditions, and genealogies of the Rajputs.

These were castes like the Charanas, Bhatas, Pancholis, and the Jaina Jatis (or Yatis).[19] Some of them specialized in particular aspects of bardic tradition. For instance, the Charanas generally maintained hereditary attachments to particular Rajput families and recited biographical narratives of those families on particular occasions. On the other hand the Bhatas, also tied up in hereditary relationships of service, maintained registers (called *bahis*) that contained the genealogies and lines of descent of their patrons. Efforts were consistently made to regularly add relevant new entries into these registers since they had virtually the status of legal documents. They were resorted to in matters concerning adoption, inheritance, and even land rights. Such collections were what Tessitori proposed to examine. From the outset he was convinced that only with a direct knowledge of local conditions—especially of the bards, the languages, and the manuscripts—would the scheme work and yield results.

In this endeavour Tessitori imagined that he would have two Indian assistants: a Marwari Pandit and a Charana: the former to help him read prose chronicles, study modern Marwari, and be of help in general matters; and the latter to help in the reading of bardic poems and the interpretation of Dingala. The Charana would travel half the month in search of manuscripts. The chief travelling agent, though, would be a Bhata who would be entrusted with the search of manuscripts, as also inscriptions, copper plates, and all manner of antiquarian remains. The editor, Tessitori himself, would then visit all places rich in such materials. One more employee would be necessary: a copyist who would copy out all the manuscripts which could not be secured on a permanent basis.

Tessitori obviously saw this as the task of a lifetime. Although he had been called to India on a trial appointment for one year, in the light of such vast work as lay ahead in Rajputana he desperately wanted that his appointment be made a permanent one. 'I am only twenty-six now and am ready to spend all my life in the service of the Government of India, for a work that is a labour of love with me.'[20] 'Many years', he declared, 'have been wasted in sterile talks and fruitless attempts, and it is time to set up work in earnest and destroy the feeling which has begun to prevail in Rajputana, that the Government of India's Scheme for the publication of the Bardic literature is nothing more than a mere show and will never lead to any practical results.'[21]

The survey began in Jodhpur on New Year's day in 1915. For the first three months Tessitori was able to carry on work without serious hindrance.[22] His two assistants were Pandit Rama Karna and Carana Kisora Dana, who had been freed from their duties at the Tawarikh Mahkma (the historical records department) of Jodhpur.[23] The travelling Bhata turned out to be somewhat problematic, and eventually his services were replaced by those of another man. Notwithstanding such problems, various places were visited, impressions of inscriptions made, and bardic manuscripts studied. About a hundred bardic and historical manuscripts were collected. Out of these a few were presented to Tessitori or purchased, while almost seventy per cent of them were copied under his supervision. Around one hundred and thirty impressions of inscriptions, located in different parts of Jodhpur state, were made.

But in the beginning of April 1915 an unexpected difficulty arose. The Jodhpur darbar, which had been exceptionally helpful till then, suddenly changed its attitude and refused support to the bardic survey.[24] The reasons for this are not explained, except for a brief allusion made by Tessitori to people becoming 'afraid of lending me their books', and intimation by the Jodhpur darbar that they did not wish such researches to be made except by the Tawarikh Mahkma of the state.[25] One can only speculate about this sudden change of heart which, for all practical purposes, brought the Jodhpur survey to an abrupt halt. Whatever one knows about the functioning of the princely states in general underlines their extreme suspicion of what they perceived as a Government of India sponsored attempt at encroaching on their sphere of influence. The Begum of Bhopal, as we saw earlier, was a good example of a ruler of princely India stoutly resisting the Archaeological Survey of India's initiative to take over Sanchi. In the Jodhpur case, it is entirely possible that the state felt the editor of the bardic chronicles was playing an unnecessarily proactive role in their sphere of work, one in which they had themselves invested much money and labour.

What Tessitori encountered, in fact, was not qualitatively different to the treatment meted out in the past to some overzealous British officers in Rajputana. In the 1880s, for instance, Captain H.H. Cole, the first curator of ancient monuments, had undertaken a survey of the monuments of Rajputana and prepared many plans for their conservation. But he was firmly told by most of the princely rulers that, while they did not object to his suggestions, the actual work of conservation would only be done by their own people.[26] Eventually, all that Cole could do was offer some advice and pen some reports. Had Tessitori been aware of the extraordinary sensitivities of the Rajputana states, he may have adopted a more cautious approach. But the swift manner in which the Jodhpur state moved left him feeling 'wronged' and disappointed.

What made things even worse was that in June the Asiatic Society received a detailed reply from the Government of India on the question of supporting Tessitori's work. Possibly because of the financial problems that they faced as a consequence of the Great War, it had become impossible for them to underwrite Tessitori's venture *in toto*. Instead, they could only guarantee an expenditure of six thousand rupees which they had sanctioned as Tessitori's salary. But the scheme they had approved required a budgetary outlay of double that amount. So they now suggested that the Rajputana states be prevailed upon to assist in the undertaking to make up the shortfall.[27] The only immediate way out of the difficulty seemed to be for the Jodhpur darbar to take upon themselves the expenditure involved in the work. They were approached, but at the end of August they made it very clear that they did not wish similar researches to be made, except by their state's own office. The disappointment to Tessitori was bitter. Jodhpur was the state from which the largest help had been expected. It then became necessary to try and make arrangements with some other state. An offer was made to Udaipur, but before a reply was received the Maharaja of Bikaner, Colonel Sir Ganga Singh, offered to employ Tessitori.[28] This was to be, initially, for a period of four months, from the beginning of December 1915 to the end of March 1916. During this time, Tessitori was to examine the bardic and historical materials of Bikaner and suggest a plan for future work. Accordingly, Tessitori moved to Bikaner in the beginning of December.

The problem of finances, though, continued to cast a shadow over the future of the bardic survey. When the question of its renewal came up for 1916–17, while the government reaffirmed their commitment of an annual outlay of Rs 6000—one which they were willing to make for a period of five years—they suggested a modification in the source from which this money would come. While earlier it was the education reserve from which they had met Tessitori's salary expenses, because of other pressures they now wanted part of it to be met from the archaeological grant of John Marshall's department.[29] Fortunately for Tessitori, Marshall agreed to step in and bail him out. He knew of Tessitori's work and had met him just a few months earlier, in Simla. Recognizing him as an enthusiastic and competent scholar, he felt that 'it would be a thousand pities if Dr Tessitori's work were to be brought to a close at this stage.'[30] So, even though he recognized that the young Italian did not possess the requisite archaeological knowledge, he was sure that, guided properly, the linguist would do good work. Some months later, Marshall would instruct one of his officers to meet Tessitori and explain to him the methods to be followed in the compilation of the monument lists of Rajasthan.[31]

The financial crisis, facing Tessitori's work since 1915, was thus overcome. From December 1916, along with the bardic survey, he began to visit sites of archaeological and antiquarian interest on behalf of the Archaeological Survey. The simultaneous exploration of the state for archaeological remains and manuscripts though would be logistically a very difficult one for Tessitori. The main problem, he later said, became that of finding the time for everything: on the one side the patient desk work required in preparing critical editions of bardic texts, on the other the hardships of long excursions under extreme conditions. But, to cope with these difficulties—'I have been forced to make all my tours *longis itineribus*, and I believe that by the rapidity of my camel marches I have established a record which no archaeological explorer will ever be able to beat' (Fig. 21).[32]

Whatever the problems that Tessitori had to face, for Indian archaeology this turn of events would prove fortuitous. It led to the first systematic exploration of Bikaner, resulting in

Fig. 21. Tessitori in camp on a camel in Bikaner

a report within which a variegated and rich landscape of archaeological sites was described for the first time.

Kalibangan was one of these sites.

In all of Rajputana, the state of Bikaner, where Kalibangan is located, was perhaps the one where conditions for archaeological explorations were most difficult. The terrain was dreary and desolate, made up for the most part of miles of undulating sand hills with wind-furrowed slopes that resembled the ribbed appearance of the sea shore. The countryside was sparsely populated, the distances between villages were massive, and the vast tracts of loose sand could only be traversed by camel. The province was deficient in both water and stone. The only rocky hills deserving that name were in the south, close to the borders of Marwar and Jaipur. This also meant that Bikaner's landscape was quite different from Jodhpur's, which was extensively dotted with the ruins of stone architecture and sculpture. But this was soon compensated by the discovery of an extremely interesting archaeological field by Tessitori in the northern part of the state.[33] Here, he came upon a territory scattered with mounds. These mounds were locally called *theris* and were covered with brick bats and *thikaris*, or potsherds. These were aligned along the bank of the defunct Ghaggar river.

The Ghaggar rises on the lower slopes of the Sirmur Himalayas, and when it reaches the plains of the Punjab it is joined by the Sarasvati. As the river flows towards the west, however, it loses itself, in the sense that it becomes dry. This is around the area of Hanumangarh in Bikaner. At the same time, as geographers have so often pointed out, even though the Ghaggar was no longer a perennial stream by the time Tessitori was exploring its banks, there were many indicators that pointed to a more remote time when it was the most massive river of this zone. Its dry bed, a very substantial one, continued into Bahawalpur on the west, where the Ghaggar was called the Hakra. In parts of Bikaner this old bed could become, at points, some kilometres wide, and of a dark loamy soil, in marked contrast with the sandy soil on either of its banks.

The mounds that Tessitori found in this area apparently belonged to a time when this tract was well watered by a live river. He tells us that

> from the vestiges of antiquity which are still abundantly scattered along its bed, it is clear that the Ghaggar once bathed with its waters a florid and prosperous region. Now the bed is dry, and like an immense road of glaring whiteness, crosses a scene of desolation, which is only broken here and there by a small village built of mud, or a field of rape-seed. Otherwise the river bed is barren, a clean sheet of argil, slippery and impracticable to the camel in the rains, hard and intersected by cracks during the rest of the year, and on both its banks and sometimes even in the middle the ancient *theris* raise their heads all red with fragments of brick and pottery.[34]

During the course of his explorations, he would discover, along with mounds, dead courses which were branches of the main river, and one of these was not indicated on the map of that area. This was around Bhadara where, according to the map that he carried with him, there were no rivers. This surprised him because he did find mounds there, which in this part of Rajasthan were generally to be found around dead fluvial streams. But, he tells us,

> during the marches of the next days I discovered that there really was a river bed, now completely dry, and in most places irrecognizable, crossing the northern part of the Bikaner State from Vadopala to Bhadara, and that there were *theris* scattered all along its course. This was a branch of the Ghagghar, which detaching itself from the main stream north of Ranga Mahal and Vadopala flowed eastward and passing through Gaudheli and Nohara lost itself in the sands near the Hinar border. At Vadabirano, 18 miles to the west of Bhadara, the villagers still point out the bed of the river, which they call *bona*, and the elders remember that they saw it flooded in the year Samvat 1922.[35]

To be sure, Tessitori did have intellectual predecessors in this geographical tract. In the nineteenth century Colonel James Tod had remarked upon some mounds in the Bikaner region; Rangmahal was one that he mentioned as possessing the vestiges of a 'large town now buried in sands' and as having 'subterranean apartments still in good preservation'.[36] Tod also drew attention to the legends about such mounds. Interestingly enough, according to local legend, Alexander the Great (called by the name Sekunder Roomi) was linked with Rangmahal: 'the desert retains the tradition that the ruin called *Rungmahl*, the "painted palace," near Dandoosir, was the capital of a prince of this region punished by a visitation of the Macedonian conqueror.'[37]

Again, some years before Tessitori had begun his work, in the same desert stretch towards the west, several mounds had been visited in the Hakra tract of Bahawalpur and described in an account penned by an explorer by the name of Malik Muhammad

Din.[38] Not much is known about Malik Muhammad except that, in the first decade of the twentieth century, he was an irrigation officer of the Bahawalpur state and, like Hughes Buller in Baluchistan, also the compiler of the Bahawalpur State Gazetteer.[39] He must, in fact, have explored old mounds while collecting material for the gazetteer. But by the time he began actively corresponding with the Archaeological Survey, Malik Muhammad was not in the vicinity of Bahawalpur; he was the manager of the Mandal estates in Karnal.[40] This was in 1916.

Before that, Malik Muhammad had travelled extensively in Bahawalpur. From our perspective, his most significant traverse was made in the cold season of 1909–10.[41] That was when he explored the area opposite Ahmadpur, down to the extreme south-west corner of the state, with half a dozen desert men who knew every inch of that part of the country. His companions not only pointed out ruined mounds but also recounted traditions connected with them ('for every ruined mound they had a tradition to tell'), including one that identified a spot—some miles east of Manjgarh fort—with the place where the rapacious invader Sultan Mahmud of Ghazni had allegedly encamped on his return from Somnath. Later, Malik Muhammad sent a report on these mounds, along with coins that several of the mounds had yielded, to the Archaeological Survey in the hope that they would be identified and published. The coins were mainly medieval, although a few belonged to the very ancient Scytho-Parthians and Kushanas. But since none of them was of a rare type, it was not thought worthwhile to compile a special report on them.[42]

From the perspective of the Indus and Harappa story, however, this unpublished report is of some interest.[43] Malik Muhammad described mounds there which would be surveyed more than fifty years later, in the 1970s, by Mohammad Rafique Mughal, the premier archaeological explorer of Bahawalpur. Mughal found some of these mounds to be of chalcolithic ancestry. For example, there are two mounds in Malik Muhammad's report called 'Ratta Dahr' and 'Ratta Tibba' (also Chitta Tibba and Ratta Theh) situated about a mile apart. These were substantial structural archaeological sites: 'the height of each mound is more than a hundred feet above the ground level of the desert around. Tradition asserts that these were two flourishing towns long before the Islamic period, and were inhabited by the *Sohdas* or *Sodhas* (probably the *Sogdii* of the Greek historians) . . . The *chitta* and *ratta* mounds are very extensive and large cyclopean bricks have been unearthed from them from time to time by the people in the neighbourhood.'[44] These mounds could well be two of the three mentioned as nos. 353, 354, and 355 or Ratta-I, Ratta-II, and Ratta-III in Mughal's site list. Mughal's survey of those mounds, we know, yielded Harappan pottery.[45] Again, because of his irrigation background, Malik Muhammad was able to point out the hydrological significance of the locations of the mounds that he surveyed. In his report he noted that almost all the medieval forts in the Bahawalpur desert were built on or near the old ruined mounds, 'apparently because such localities had sweet water under the substrata of their soil—brackish and bitter water being met with in the substrata of the desert generally.'[46] This is an insightful observation, one that has not been considered by those who have tried to understand the distribution of mounds in that stretch of land.

If Malik Muhammad had surveyed the Hakra tract with desert nomads, what was the method that our linguist-turned-archaeologist followed in surveying a similar sandlocked landscape in Bikaner? His method in the field seems to have been rather like his method with manuscripts. He would first send his travelling agent to explore the villages in a determinate area with instructions to examine all the wells, tanks, temples, forts, *chattris*, *devalis*, *kirtistambhas*, and other monuments eventually found on the spot. The agent was also instructed to take impressions of all the inscriptions with dates preceding the nineteenth century. From his report and from the estampages of inscriptions brought by him, Tessitori was then able to judge if a place was important enough to deserve a visit, and if he was satisfied that it was, he would go and explore it carefully with a view to collecting material for writing a full account of it in his annual report.[47] Towards the end of the year, the director general of archaeology would lend him one of his photographers, and he would send the man off to take photographs of all the most interesting monuments that had been encountered.

Tessitori must have been enthused by the accounts that he received because he personally visited a large number of places. A sense of this can be had from the summary of his explorations which he regularly published as a part of his progress report in the Asiatic Society's journal. In 1918 he made two tours which lasted for about three months, of which the first one was from January to March while the second extended over December. He explored approximately three dozen places, including Sahivana, Bhadar, Sothi, Nohara, Pili Banga, Kalibangan, and Rangmahal. Many of these are vividly described in his unpublished report, with all kinds of detail on the memorials that he found, the antiquities that the mounds yielded on their surface, the excavations that he conducted there, and local legends surrounding them.

There was, for instance, the ubiquitous devali, this being a sati tablet that recorded the name of the Rajput chief, the exact date of his death, and sometimes the names of his wives who had immolated themselves. Many of the inscriptions here proved important in cross-checking the faulty dates of the bardic chronicles. For instance, Tessitori noted that the devalis at Udasar, a village four miles north-east of Bikaner, suggested that the murder of Rama Singha, a brother of Raja Raya Singha of Bikaner, had taken place in the early part of the seventeenth century, whereas the chronicles had inaccurately dated the event to a couple of decades after it had actually happened.[48] There are many descriptions of chattris (pillared canopied pavilions) as well, a monument more recent than the devali. But, perhaps the earliest of all the funerary monuments that he surveyed was a *govardhana* found in a tract of land to the south-east of Bikaner. This was a square pillar with four sculpted heads of the gods Siva, Vishnu, Surya, and Ganesha. Tessitori discovered cinerary vases buried all around the shaft in some instances. This practice seemed to have been discarded in the thirteenth century, when vases were substituted with the devali. Sketches of some of these memorials accompanied Tessitori's report.

Was Tessitori surveying the mounds of Bikaner because he believed that they too partook of the funeral character of the province's memorial monuments? There are occasionally thick descriptions of a variety of artefacts that were found at or in their vicinity, ranging from fine terracottas to images. But, most often, his descriptions of the mounds, the fact that he frequently referred to them as 'cinerary' theris, underline that he was primarily interested in exploring their connections with the dead and their remains. For instance, his account of Sirdargadha is dominated by the excavation of a tomb in the mound where he found as many as twenty-five cinerary vases, several of which were placed one inside the other.[49] Cinerary pottery and funerary mounds form a recurring motif in Tessitori's accounts of other sites as well.

But behind the dense and sometimes confusing details that he penned about his explorations and excavations, one can see repeatedly cropping up those bits of historical information that were relevant to contextualize them. It was these that Tessitori seized upon to try and solve the mystery of the cinerary theris and assign an approximate date to them. As an accomplished linguist with a deep knowledge of Rajasthan's written sources, he needed on the one hand to integrate their presence, within the genealogy of funerary memorials that he had observed in Bikaner, and on the other with the larger narrative of the region's past provided by its legendary and historical literature. What is surprising, though, is that while Tessitori understood that the mounds with their great number of stratifications contained within them a history of a thousand years or more, he did not describe these as remains of ancient human settlements. Rather, for him, they were necropolises containing traces of cremation practices. Today we know that many of the sites he described are, in fact, the remnants of earlier towns and villages. Unfortunately, Tessitori failed to look beyond funerary pots and bones.

Of all the mounds that he surveyed, the ones that he recognized to be qualitatively different from the time that he first set sight on them were those at Kalibangan, or Kalibanga as he called it. He first visited Kalibangan on 5 April 1917, spending two days there. He returned to explore his site more thoroughly in 1918.[50] In December that year he spent about five days there, spread over two visits.[51] We will look a little later at various clues, on the basis of which it is possible to understand Tessitori's fascination for, and his repeated visits to, this site. First, let us pause for a moment to see what he had to say about the site after his first visit there.

His exposition on Kalibangan is rather long but it has been reproduced *in extenso* below because it is the first account we have of what is now recognized to be perhaps the most important Indus city of Rajasthan. That there is nothing in the extant published literature on what he observed and found there, makes this first account even more significant.

> Kalibanga is the name of a very small village of Jatas, situated at a distance of nearly 10 miles from Vadopala, in a north north-eastern direction. The village, which is all built of mud, contains nothing of interest in itself, but I have received the information that in its neighbourhood here are two large *theris* with copious fragments of pottery, and this was the principal cause of the visit which I paid to the place on April 5, 1917; on the two *theris* nearby *I had the good fortune to discover vestiges of a very remote, if not prehistorical antiquity* [emphasis added]. The two *theris* are found about ¼ of a mile south-west of the village, and they are close to one another,

being separated only by a small depression running across between. One of the two is very large, but very irregular in shape. Much material was asportated from the spot in 1900, when the section of the Jodhpur–Bikaner railway connecting Suratgadh with Hanumangadh was being constructed, the materials being utilized as ballast on the line. Mr Warren, of the Jodhpur–Bikaner railway who superintended the work, has told me that at the *theris* dug in search of ballast, he unearthed in several places rectangular chambers of say about 5' or 6' closed by walls of large bricks, and having no entrance. He also found a considerable quantity of balls of baked clay and fragments of pottery, but no traces of moulded bricks nor of any implement, so far as he could re-collect. He did not go very deep, however, and abandoned the spot when he saw that the materials obtained were no longer paying the cost of excavation. The traces of Mr Warren's excavation are evident all over the mounds. In places one sees regular square holes, and these probably mark the spots where the chambers mentioned by Mr Warren were found. In one place, on the slope of the smaller mound, a deep trench has been cut, about three yards deep. It is evident that hardly one spot was left unexplored and wherever bricks were found within easy reach, they were ruthlessly asportated.

The balls of burnt clay, which Mr Warren found and asportated in considerable quantities, are still largely represented all over the mounds. They are small balls, or rather lumps, of an irregular round shape, the average diameter being about 2½", just the amount of clay that one can grasp in one hand and press into a ball-like form. Many of them still show deeply impressed marks of the fingers that shaped them (Photo n. 64). Mixed with the round lumps, but in scantier quantities, are found, flat lumps, 3"–4" in diameter and 1¼"–1¾" in thickness, having on the whole the form of a small modeled disk, with two slight depressions in the centre made by pressing the lump between the thumb and the index-finger. Lastly, mixed with the round and flat lumps, but in still smaller quantities, there are triangular tiles of baked clay, blunted and rounded at the three angles, from ½" to ¾' in thickness, and 3"–4" in length on each of the three sides.

The other remains which are scattered over the site, are chiefly fragments of earthen pots, brickbats, and pieces of earthen rings of various sizes and thickness. Here and there, and especially in the deep trench mentioned above, I found many fragments of bones, most of which could be easily identified as human. In one place, near the top of the larger mound, from the site of a ditch which had been probably excavated by the railway ballast-hunters, there was emerging what seemed to be the mouth of a very large vase. I had the earth dug all around and found that it really was a large earthen pot, which had been broken on one side, as well as around the orifice, but was still intact in the main body, and the inside. It was round in shape, except from some delayness in the lower part, which made the lower half of the vessel probably resemble the pointed half of an egg. The height, measured internally, was about 2'4", and the maximum diameter 2'1". The mouth, which must have been very wide, had a rim curving to the outside. The thickness of the clay was ½". I found no traces of any cover, but the vessel probably had one and it was destroyed. The pot was buried in a perpendicular position, and the orifice was about 1 foot under the surface of the ground. The vessel was filled with earth, forming a very compact mass with fragments of pottery. It took me about three hours to dig the inside, and here is a list of what I found: (a) an oblong earthen vase almost intact but for some abrasions round the mouth and the pedestal. The height was 5½", and the diameter 3¼" at the mouth, 3¾" in the middle, and only 1¼" in the pedestal. The thickness of the clay was only 1/8". The vase contained fragments of burnt bones and ashes besides a few pieces of clay. (b) Fragments of five or six other vases, whereof two or three of about the same size as the above, one very large with a mouth about 6½" in diameter, and one a diminutive size with a mouth of only 1¼" in diameter. Some of the vases were externally decorated with lines in black or white paint. (c) Three fragments of covers of the diameter of about 7½", 4½" and 1½" respectively. The form was that of a round plate or dish, raised in the middle, with a protuberance for lifting it. (d) Two earthen rings 1" in diameter, and fragments of at least another eight rings or bangles from 1" to 2" in diameter. The thickness of the clay varied from ½" in the rings of smaller dimensions, to ¼" in the rings of larger dimensions. Some were decorated with transversal lines in black paint. (e) Three round lumps of baked clay, and fragments of two or three others, and also fragments of one or two triangular tiles, (f) fragments of human bones, and traces of ashes, and small fragments of coal . . . The find leaves no doubt that the mound was a burying ground, where relics of cremated bodies were preserved, but until I explore the site more extensively, I should not venture to assign any age to the remains.

Other interesting objects which I found amongst the debris covering the mounds are: broken pieces of clay, who seemed to be tiles or part of a vase 3/8" thick, slightly curved, all riddled with holes about ¼" in diameter (Photo n. 65); a small bull of clay 1¼" high, with a thin hole made through the hump, apparently for the purpose of joining a string through; an open vessel, 4' in diameter, in the form of a flat cup, with three perforated ears attached to the rim; and a fragmentary appendage underneath looking like a broken pedestal; a few fragments of metal covered with verdigris, probably copper; broken pieces of ivory bangles; flat beads of ivory, looking like buttons with a single hole in the centre, ¼" in diameter; small sea-shells (Photo n. 65).[52]

The structures and artefacts that Tessitori had excavated out of Kalibangan are indeed impressive. And from the photographs that were taken of the site, we also get a visual impression of their range (Figs 22–24).[53] These photographs show excavated segments of the site, of the rectangular structures that he mentioned in his report, but also of some that are not mentioned—such as a brick well of the typical cylindrical form that is so quintessentially Harappan. There are also photographs of what

Fig. 22. Tessitori's excavations at Kalibangan, showing remains of a well

Fig. 23. Remains of structures and terracotta balls at Kalibangan

we would now recognize as Harappan artefacts, ranging from pottery and stone beads to bone and ivory objects.

Kalibangan soon became the point of reference for comparing artefacts that Tessitori subsequently encountered at

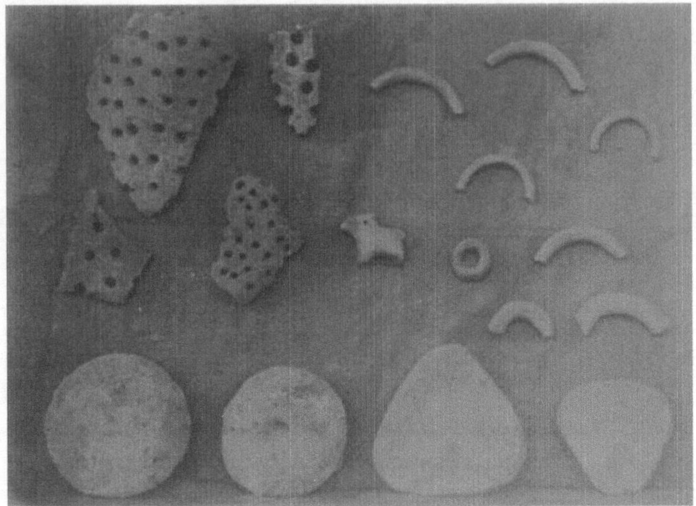

Fig. 24. Antiquities from Kalibangan discovered by Tessitori (terracotta cakes, clay animal figurine, fragments of perforated pottery and clay bangles)

other Bikaner mounds. At Uderamasara, among the pottery excavated at the base of the memorial govardhana of the village, he noticed earthen covers for vases 'round and convex in shape with a protruberance in the middle, like the fragments of covers' that he had unearthed at Kalibangan. He also remembered Kalibangan when he surveyed the two mounds on either side of the road that he travelled on from Suratgarh to Sivapuro. On one of them he recognized several fragments of riddled vases, like those which had been so richly represented in the theri of Kalibangan. Again, a mound on the road from Bugio to Rughanathapuro was strewn with typical artefacts that he had found at Kalibangan, including terracotta balls. Similar balls of burnt clay, about two inches in diameter, were also encountered by him on one of the mounds between Sirdargadha and Bhagvanasara.

The strong sense that we get from Tessitori's observations is that Kalibangan had captured his imagination, encouraging him to see its material culture as part of a larger cultural phenomenon in Bikaner.

But equally impressive is Tessitori's recognition that it had been his good fortune to have found there vestiges of a 'remote, if not pre-historical antiquity'. His use of the word 'prehistoric' here implies that he considered Kalibangan to have existed much prior to contexts in which he had found Buddhist remains, or those which had medieval associations. In fact his long report on the scores of mounds that he surveyed in Bikaner considers this the *only* one with a possible prehistoric ancestry.

But how did Tessitori feel emboldened to make this assertion?

Actually, if we examine the section of his tour report that has been reproduced above, it is not the presence of particular objects that he highlights but the absence of certain artefacts. Moulded bricks form one such category, which he had found at sites that were of later ('Buddhist') times but which he noted were absent at Kalibangan. So, it is possible that the absence of objects of historical antiquity was a reason for his assumption that this was a much older mound. Even more important is what he did not mention in this report but which he had found at the site. Kalibangan had yielded to Tessitori two very distinctive types of objects. These were long stone blades, several of them of a greyish/whitish flint, and three seals inscribed with unknown characters and pictographs which we can immediately see as being of the same genre as those at Harappa.[54] Both these categories of objects are today considered to be type fossils of the Indus civilization (Figs 25–27). So, is it possible that Tessitori thought Kalibangan to be a prehistoric site because he had found stone blades there? If so, why did his report pass over them in silence, as it did the seals?

One is tempted to resolve this quite quickly by conjecturing that, like many archaeological explorers, Tessitori was being discreetly silent about his most significant finds until he had sorted out their age and context for himself. We know that some months after his spring tour of 1917, he wrote to

Fig. 25. Flints found by Tessitori at Kalibangan on display in Ganga Golden Jubilee Museum at Bikaner

D.B. Spooner, then officiating for Marshall, asking for such books from the Archaeological Survey's library as were likely to help him understand the nature and age of some of his discoveries, especially those at Kalibangan. But the objects he mentioned to Spooner were terracottas and cinerary vases, not stone blades and seals. So there is a strong case for the possibility that, until he made himself more familiar with archaeological data from other sites which provided him with accurate equivalences, Tessitori thought it prudent to offer selective detail on his finds.

Fig. 26. Indus seals from Kalibangan found by Tessitori

Fig. 27. Sketch of Kalibangan seals

Following a lead that we get from Tessitori's itinerary during those years, one can also, though, formulate a different hypothesis. From the summary accounts of his annual archaeological explorations published in the Asiatic Society's journal, we know that, in addition to his 1917 sojourn, he visited Kalibangan in 1918. Can it be that the stone blades and seals were brought to his notice during those subsequent visits? This could explain why his report is silent about these objects. But if this is true, it still does not explain why he described Kalibangan as containing vestiges of a possibly prehistoric age. Interestingly enough, in June 1918 Tessitori had met Marshall in Simla and had handed him a long report of more than two hundred pages in which the archaeological landscape, as also the monuments and memorials of Bikaner that he had surveyed, were described.[55] It is unlikely that the blades and seals were mentioned in this report because Marshall would most certainly have noticed something of such import.[56]

Unfortunately, Tessitori left no clues about this mystery. All we can be certain of is that the juxtaposition of artefacts that he noticed there—pottery along with stone tools and Indus seals—was exactly what Cunningham had found at Harappa. In a sense, therefore, Tessitori, unknown to himself, was as much a forerunner in unearthing an Indus city in Rajasthan as Cunningham in Punjab. Perhaps much more so, because unlike Cunningham who considered Harappa to have been the locale of a Buddhist establishment during the time of Hsuan Tsang, Tessitori's first thought was to place his discovery more accurately within prehistoric parameters.

Except, of course, Cunningham was in many ways more fortunate than Tessitori. He was an institutionally powerful and well-recognized archaeologist; and he published his account of Harappa and thus made known his presence to historians with an interest in Indus cities and the story of their discovery. Tessitori's trowelling of Kalibangan, on the other hand, has long remained little known in part because, before he could put together his observations for publication, an unfortunate turn of events came to swamp his life.

It all began in early 1919 when he heard that his mother was seriously ill. On 17 April that year he left for Italy. When he arrived, she had already died. Tessitori stayed on in Italy for several months. In the summer of that year he wrote sharing his discovery of the Kalibangan seals with George Grierson, his old mentor. Even though Tessitori had never met Grierson, he always regarded him as a friend with whom he could, through letters, openly exchange thoughts and ideas. This is what he wrote about the three objects that had been found at Kalibangan (he sent a photograph as well): 'Two of them—the first one is a seal—bear an inscription in characters which I am unable to identify. I suspect it is an extremely interesting find: the mound itself on which the objects were discovered, is very interesting. I believe it is prehistorical or, at least, non-Aryan. Perhaps the inscriptions refer to a foreign race? I have not shown the finds to anybody yet, not even to Sir John Marshall, and I should like very much to have your opinion first.'[57]

Upon examining the photograph Grierson thought the inscribed seals of extraordinary interest, but he did not venture to interpret them. Instead, he referred Tessitori to some papers by Hopkins, which had appeared in recent volumes of the *Journal of the Royal Asiatic Society*, on ancient Chinese inscriptions on bone: 'some of the characters on your seals strongly resemble, in their general character, those given by Hopkins'.[58] This was not an opinion that Tessitori shared at all. A little later, possibly on Grierson's advice, he wrote to Fredrick Thomas, a well-known authority on Chinese and Tibetan sources, about his discovery:

> I enclose a photograph of two bone objects which I have unearthed from a very ancient mound near Bikaner which contain inscriptions in characters unknown. I had submitted the photograph previously to Sir George Grierson, but he was unable to explain the writing. From the fact that the mound is littered with a very large number of stone knives, and other fragments of a prehistorical character, I am inclined to assign to the bone objects a prehistorical or at any rate pre-Aryan date. The objects with the representation of the bull is a seal, therefore the characters on it are reversed.[59]

Tessitori's intuition on the age of the artefacts, we now know, was uncannily accurate. But he was unluckily expressing his notions to a scholar who had no clue about the significance of such unusual archaeological contexts, nor of the unknown script system inscribed on the objects.

In this situation Grierson counselled Tessitori that it would be a good idea to get John Marshall's permission to publish the Kalibangan seals in the Royal Asiatic Society's journal, that being widely read by Orientalists and Indologists.[60] Considering that the Harappa seals had fascinated Marshall since his youth, there is little doubt that, had the seals been brought to his notice, he would almost immediately have found the equivalence for them that Tessitori was looking for.

One imagines that Tessitori intended to follow Grierson's advice and bring the seals to Marshall's notice as soon as he returned to India. Tragically, Tessitori's return journey proved fatal. He seems to have contracted Spanish influenza on the ship. He was already unwell when he reached India on 1 November 1919, and by the time he got to Bikaner he was seriously ill. After the fever, he developed a septic throat and then pleurisy set in.[61] Tessitori died within a few days, on 22 November. As a result, Marshall never got to know what this ill-starred Italian had found. In fact, we will never know the possible trajectory that Tessitori's Kalibangan discoveries would have taken if they had not been so abruptly brought to a halt by his early and unfortunate death.

Subsequently, Tessitori's books, personal effects, and other such items were sorted. What was considered of value was sent to his father. The rest was sold at an auction.[62] Tessitori was buried at Bikaner not far from the fort of his patron and friend Maharaja Ganga Singh. His grave is marked by a cross and carries two inscriptions, in Hindi and in English. The English epitaph reads:

> To the revered memory of Dr L.P. Tessitori (Philologist) born Udine (Italy) 13.12 1887. Laid to rest Bikaner 22.11.1919.

It is said that, even now, on the anniversary of his death, scholars gather at his tomb, lay flowers there, and remember him.[63] While many who gather on that day must remember the loss that philological scholarship sustained, none perhaps really know just how close the Italian had come to things Harappan.[64]

This is because, when Tessitori was buried in Bikaner, knowledge of the Kalibangan seals was buried with him.

# 8

# EXCAVATING HARAPPA UNDER A SHADOW

EVEN BEFORE TESSITORI'S DEATH CAST ITS shadow over the discovery of an Indus city in Rajasthan, another shadow of sorts fell over Harappa, as the Great War raged on.

The theatre of that war was far removed from India, but the country's British rulers had responded swiftly to the outbreak of hostilities in Europe. In the very month (August 1914) that Great Britain entered the war, the first contingent of Indian troops sailed for France. Simultaneously, others were sent to Egypt and East Africa.[1] From that time till the end of hostilities in November 1918, the scale of India's contribution to the war effort was massive.

Staggering statistics have been assembled by scholars who have investigated the resources provided by British India.[2] Most spectacular was the manner in which the army rapidly expanded, with its Indian component growing sixfold in five years, with 877,068 combatants and 563,369 non-combatants being recruited. India sent on service overseas 285,037 British and 1,096,013 Indians, or something approaching a million and a half just by way of personnel. Such large numbers also had to be given salaries, fed, clothed and provided with ammunition and equipment. Around 168 million pound sterling was spent in marshalling stores and supplies. Additionally,

India made cash contributions to the British war expenditure to the tune of 367 million pounds. Marshalling resources on this scale resulted—if one is permitted a moment's facetiousness—in less money for Marshall.

In fact, economic stringency now became the most important priority of government. In the Archaeological Survey there came a palpable crunch in relation to manpower and money. In 1915–16 the Northern Circle of the Survey, where Harappa was located, saw a reduction of almost half a lakh of rupees in its budget for the preservation of 'Muhammadan and British Monuments'.[3] Again, even though the Survey had made all preparations and had actually begun excavating at Sarnath, the operations had to be suspended, on the orders of the local government, for want of funds.[4]

Many officers of the Survey also proceeded to Europe's western front to fight in the Indian army. J.F. Blakiston, assistant superintendent in the Eastern Circle, and Gordon Sanderson, superintendent of Muhammadan and British monuments in the Northern Circle were among these. Within a few months Sanderson died in active service, and Hargreaves, whom we left at the point when he was planning to excavate Harappa, was temporarily relocated to hold charge of Sanderson's office. This was in May 1915; by the end of 1916 he too had opted for military duty.

It was this configuration of events that brought Daya Ram Sahni to the Northern Circle and Harappa (Fig. 28). Sahni was an old Survey hand, his association with the organization and with John Marshall going back to 1903. He had been on deputation in Kashmir, serving as superintendent of archaeology in that northern princely state. His training and career, before he came to the Northern Circle, is in fact worth pausing over because it typifies the professional path through which a whole generation of educated Indians had entered the Archaeological Survey.

Fig. 28. Daya Ram Sahni

Around 1902, Curzon and Marshall, we may recall, had begun revamping the structure of the Survey. As part of that reorganization, in 1903, at Marshall's suggestion, two archaeological scholarships for Indian students were instituted.[5] Marshall's main concern had been to address the paucity of trained Indian assistants in the Survey. This was a need increasingly felt since archaeological activities, ranging from conservation to epigraphy, were being more vigorously pursued than before. Archaeological work was being supported on a reasonable scale not just in British India but also in India's princely states.

It is not as if there had been no Indians in the Survey. Marshall's first Indian assistant archaeological surveyor was Devadatta Ram Krishna Bhandarkar. Son of the famous Indologist R.G. Bhandarkar, he had earned an MA from Bombay University before being in 1904 appointed by Marshall at the recommendation of Henry Cousens, superintendent of the Western Circle of the Survey, who knew Bhandarkar personally.[6] The new appointee was a keen epigraphist, enthusiastic about archaeological studies in general, and soon contributed several articles upon such matters to the journal of the Bombay branch of the Royal Asiatic Society.[7] He had all the qualifications that made him suitable for mainstream archaeological work.

But Bhandarkar was in this respect an exception; for Indians who generally found employment in the Survey were language scholars, pandits and maulvis, who deciphered inscriptions, and who read and translated local-language texts for the archaeologists. There was, for instance, Maulvi Nur Baksh, who had served as Marshall's assistant in 1902 and translated Sir Syed Ahmed Khan's *Atharal-Sanadid* for him to facilitate the Survey's restoration of Mughal buildings in the Red Fort at Delhi.[8] Subsequently, in 1904, Nur Baksh was asked to assist W.H. Nicholls, archaeological surveyor in the United Provinces and Oudh, who was wholly unacquainted with either Persian or Arabic.

While the main qualification for the new scholarships remained proficiency in languages—one scholarship was to be held by a Sanskrit and the other by a Persian/Arabic scholar—this was not their main purpose. Rather, they were aimed at making modern archaeologists out of Indian students. The scholarship holders were to be selected by Marshall from a list of candidates nominated by the heads of the principal colleges in India and paid a monthly stipend of seventy-five rupees. Considering that archaeologists spent long spells out in the field, the memorandum to the various colleges inviting applications especially underlined that the nominated students should be 'of active habits'. After their selection, these scholars were directly attached to Marshall's office, and sent off for field training in excavation, architectural documentation, epigraphic work, and archaeological conservation. Thus, within the Survey, if there were archaeologists who could rightfully be considered Marshall's students, it was these young men, handpicked by him and apprenticed under his tutelage.

To begin with, the scholarships were awarded for one year. But as it took time for openings to materialize in the Survey, the scholarships were often extended until the archaeological scholars could be permanently absorbed. The excellent calibre of early recruits into the Survey can be gauged from their qualifications. Marshall's summary is worth quoting:

> The heads of sixty-three colleges, chosen in consultation with the Director General of Education, were invited to nominate students, and twenty seven nominations were received, 18 of them for Sanskrit and 9 for Persian and Arabic. Of the nominees nine were of MA and the remainder of BA standing. The competition, though small, was a keen one; for nearly half of the candidates had stood first in their subjects at the University examinations for their degrees, besides possessing other strong qualifications and being backed up by weighty testimonials.[9]

The first Persian and Arabic scholarship was awarded to Niaz Muhammad Khan, a student of the Oriental College at Lahore.[10] He was McLeod Arabic Reader there and had obtained the first position in Arabic and History at the Punjab BA examination in 1903. Niaz Muhammad left the Survey in July 1905, and in his place Ghulam Yazdani, also a gold medallist of the Punjab University and a student of St Stephen's College, Delhi, was appointed.[11] Yazdani too did not spend many years with the Survey, moving on to become Professor of Arabic and Persian at the Government College at Rajshahi in Bengal in 1909. Eventually, he became the first director of the archaeological department at the princely state of Hyderabad.[12]

The recipient of the Survey's first Sanskrit scholarship was Daya Ram Sahni. Like Niaz Muhammad, he came from Lahore. He was barely in his twenties and had been working as McLeod Sanskrit Reader in the Oriental College there. As a student he had obtained a medal for Sanskrit in the BA examination at the Punjab University, taken the top rank in Oriental Languages at the MA examination, and won the McLeod and Raja Harbans Singh gold medal in 1903 along with a purse of a hundred rupees. Unlike his Persian/Arabic counterparts, Sahni would have a long innings in the Survey: in fact he spent practically his entire working life there, from 1903 till 1935, when he retired as the first Indian director general of the Survey.

Among his superiors Sahni was perceived from his early years as the most promising and talented among the initial crop that the Survey had recruited. Vogel, when superintendent of the Punjab and United Provinces, described him to one of his colleagues as 'industrious, accurate and modest, three excellent qualities'.[13] Presumably because of this, even during the period of his scholarship Sahni was greatly in demand: Vogel and Marshall used to share him as assistant. Equally, both felt extremely proprietorial about him: while Sahni was assisting Vogel in the Kasia excavations of early 1905, Marshall requested that he be sent to him at Agra, where Marshall was inspecting conservation work.[14] Sahni was promptly dispatched to the director general. Vogel now sent a letter to Marshall with instructions about Sahni's training. It was in the order of things, he wrote, that

Sahni acquire a general knowledge of the various branches of archaeology as well as read some general comprehensive works on the 'pre-Muhammadan history of India'—books like those authored by Vincent Smith and Rhys Davids.[15] By this time Sahni had started reading Pali and acquired an understanding of its relationship to Sanskrit. Vogel therefore advised Marshall that Sahni devote himself to epigraphy, while warning that a Sanskrit scholar ought not to be allowed to forget his Sanskrit and be left ample time for continuing the study of Sanskrit literature.[16]

How many epigraphs and Sanskrit works Sahni managed to read while assisting Marshall in the field remains unknown. Unlike Vogel, who felt that epigraphy was much more in his line, the director general was keen that Sahni pick up the principles of architecture, and it is likely that he actively trained him in that sphere.[17] What we do know is that when Vogel wanted him back for the next season of work (when he would resume excavations at Kasia), Marshall refused on the grounds that he himself urgently needed him, in January and February 1906, to help in the field at Rajgir in Bihar.[18] When excavations commenced at Rajgir, Sahni acted as Marshall's personal assistant, supervising the workforce, assisting in the verification of plans made by the draftsmen, and helping out in many other ways.[19] In the publication that emanated from that season of work, it was Sahni who authored the report on the excavations at 'New Rajagrha'.[20]

Later that year Sahni undertook his first independent fieldwork in the districts of Gorakhpur and Saran.[21] This was in November–December when, on the suggestion of a former Survey epigraphist J.F. Fleet, he surveyed two dozen or more sites. At one of them, Sohnag, he conducted a dig which revealed a stupa. Fleet had been epigraphist to the Government of India from 1883 to 1886, but even after he returned to England, the Survey did work in order to assist his research and publications. In the case of Gorakhpur and Saran, Fleet had asked that they be surveyed in order to remove uncertainties about the location of certain places mentioned in the Buddhist chronicles. Fleet was especially interested in the location of Kusinara, where the Buddha is said to have died, and believed that this might be in the neighbourhood of the village of Pancharukkhi. So Sahni searched around there, but failed to locate any antiquities at all, Buddhist or otherwise.

He did, however—in an article that he soon published—provide a lot of useful information on the nature of the mounds that he surveyed, on the sizes of bricks, and on sculpture and inscriptions. He paid close attention to vernacular sources, to the lineages of various ruling families, and above all to local legends and myths about the historic spots and sites that he visited. No attention, however, was paid by the young scholar to pottery, the most common artefact encountered on subcontinental mounds. Potsherds must have littered many of the mounds Sahni described, but there are surprisingly no descriptions of them. Presumably, this was not his fault because there is nothing to indicate that either Marshall or Vogel had underlined how important pottery could be in assessing the date of ancient sites. The only instruction that Marshall seems to have given Sahni was reminiscent of what Cunningham would have told his assistants in the nineteenth century. Marshall instructed Sahni to carry with him the accounts of Chinese pilgrims and any other literature bearing on the subject so that he could read it as he surveyed the various spots.[22] The survey, as far as Marshall understood Fleet's instructions, was meant to examine problems concerning the identification of sites mentioned in ancient literature. It is to Sahni's credit that he decided to make his journey into Gorakhpur and Saran a more comprehensive archaeological exercise.

Alongside his field training, as Vogel had instructed, Sahni worked on inscriptions. This is evident not merely in the translations that he provided of those that he encountered in the course of his Gorakhpur–Saran survey, but also from the fact that in 1907–8, he edited an epigraph—the Banaras inscription of Pantha (the name of the builder of the shrine of Bhavani at Banaras)—in the Archaeological Survey of India's journal *Epigraphia Indica*.[23] This had been completed while Sahni was with Vogel in Chamba in the summer of 1906. While there, he went through most of the important inscriptions in the region and thus made himself acquainted with the Sarada alphabet in which they were composed.[24]

In September 1907 Sahni came to be regularly employed as Marshall's excavation assistant. Soon after, he was sent to excavate at Rampurva, the tiny village in the Champaran district of Bihar where a pillar, carrying the message of the Mauryan emperor Ashoka, had been discovered in 1877 by Cunningham's assistant A.C.L. Carlleyle. When it was discovered, the pillar was found to be lying partly in water. Consequently, impressions of the side of the pillar that could be reached were prepared, and these showed that it contained portions of Ashoka's first four edicts. However, since then, the inscribed column had sunk further. It is to Sahni's credit that this was carefully recovered, as was the lion capital that originally crowned it.[25] An estampage of the edicts inscribed on it was prepared as well. Sahni also discovered that there were two pillars, not one, as was thought, and a proposal to repair them was prepared (see Figs 29 and 30).[26]

Around this time, impressions of the Rampurva edicts were sorely needed because, under the aegis of the Archaeological Survey, a revised volume on the Ashokan inscriptions was being prepared by E. Hultzsch. An epigraphist of German origin, Hultzsch had served as the government epigraphist in Madras until 1903, when he had resigned to take up a Sanskrit professorship at Halle.[27] Even after his resignation, he had continued to assist the Archaeological Survey, on payment, in a number of ways. Apart from being given the task of producing a revised edition of the inscriptions of Ashoka, he was kept on as the editor of *Epigraphia Indica*, the official Survey journal, at an annual honorarium of a thousand rupees, till a successor was appointed.

Fig. 29. Sketch of Ashokan pillar at Rampurva, rescued by Sahni

This was in 1906 when, on Hultzsch's recommendation, Sten Konow, a linguist from Norway, became the government epigraphist.[28] Konow had a thorough knowledge of Sanskrit and a general knowledge of the Dravidian languages.[29] However, he needed to be initiated into epigraphical work, which is why, even after his appointment, the 1907–8 volume of *Epigraphia Indica* was jointly edited by Konow and Hultzsch.

Again, in the spring of 1908, along with assisting Vogel's excavations at Maheth, Sahni excavated a number of Buddhist temples and a vihara (monastery) at nearby Saheth. It was inside a cell in this vihara that Sahni made the most spectacular discovery of the excavation. He found there a copper plate, carefully packed in an earthen case, which contained an inscription that had been incised on the instructions of a twelfth-century king, Govindachandra of Kanauj, who was the scion of a dynasty called the Gahadavalas. This inscription recorded a grant of six villages to Buddhist monks residing in the *mahavihara* (chief monastery) of Jetavana, and this, in turn, helped solve the problem of identifying the Jetavana, a monastery frequently

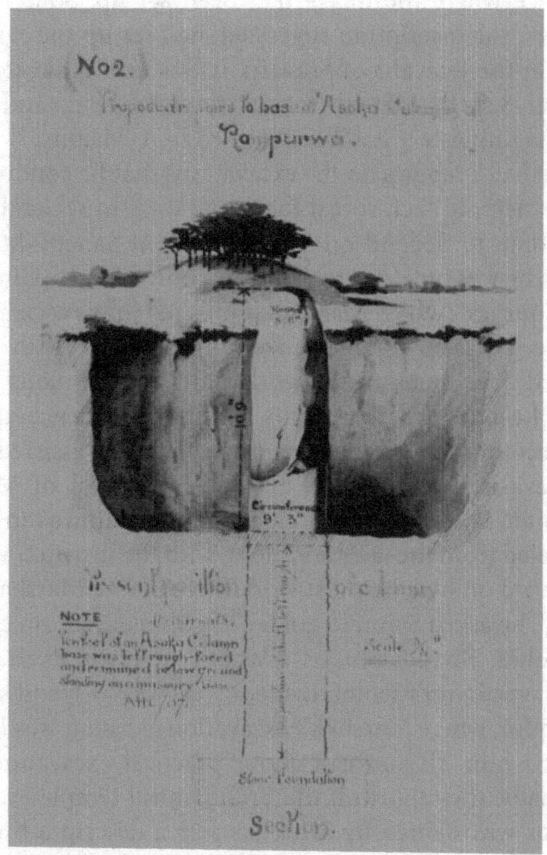


Fig. 30. Sketch of proposed restoration of the Rampurva pillar base

mentioned in Buddhist literature.[30] Sahni's discovery showed that Saheth was undoubtedly Jetavana, and therefore Maheth, where Vogel was excavating, had to be the ancient city of Sravasti.

The winter of 1908–9 saw Sahni again at Saheth–Maheth, this time assisting Marshall. Another important epigraphic discovery ensued: an inscription of the first century AD on an incomplete Bodhisattva statue. This also recorded the name of the place where the image had been set up. Some Kshatriya brothers, the inscription suggested, had set up the Bodhisattva image at the Jetavana of Sravasti. It was now quite certain that modern Saheth–Maheth was ancient Sravasti, and that the Jetavana monastery had been located in its vicinity. [31]

Marshall's reports on the excavations that he conducted with Sahni's help, in fact, reveal the many ways in which he had by then come to depend on his assistant. At Saheth–Maheth, he tells us, he was indebted to Sahni 'not only for compiling the lists of antiquities' (which Marshall published in his own article) on the site, but also for the 'unvarying diligence with which he watched over much of the work and the scrupulous care with which he recorded the results.'[32] This dependence appears to have become stronger the next year, when Sahni assisted Marshall in excavations at Mandor, the ancient capital of Marwar in Rajasthan. That Marshall thought highly of Sahni as an excavator is revealed from the fact that, along with the instructions that he sent Sahni on how he must work there before Marshall himself arrived, he asked Sahni to guide D.R. Bhandarkar on excavation techniques. Bhandarkar, as assistant surveyor in the Western Circle, was Sahni's senior. Evidently, he was to spend some days at Mandor, where Marshall's excavation assistant was instructed to teach him 'all you can about practical excavation work'.[33] Eventually, the report on the Brahmanical temple excavated at Mandor was written by Sahni, as also a description of sixteen inscribed slabs found in the course of the excavations.[34]

It therefore comes as no surprise that, when the government sanctioned the appointment to an additional post in the Survey—that of assistant superintendent—Daya Ram Sahni got the job. This was in February 1910. Sahni's appointment to a gazetted post in the Survey, rather than marking the beginning of a new phase there, actually resulted in the end of the first stage of his professional career.

This is because in the very next year, in July 1911, he was

selected to be curator of the provincial museum at Lucknow. The reasons why the United Provinces government considered Sahni the best man for the job are not stated in the relevant correspondence. So we can only surmise that they must have known about his work at Kasia and Saheth–Maheth, both situated within the United Provinces. More recently, in 1909–10, Sahni had also personally supervised the arranging and labelling of sculptures for the newly constructed museum at the Buddhist site of Sarnath.[35]

Sahni's immediate superiors were of course quite reluctant to let go of him. Vogel tried to first convince the United Provinces government that they ought to appoint another Indian, an archaeologist named Rakhaldas Banerji (the subject of the next chapter of this story), for Banerji had some experience in museum administration.[36] The government, though, was reluctant to appoint Banerji and so, eventually, after a great deal of confabulation, Vogel and Marshall came around to accepting their request to depute Sahni to the Lucknow Museum. The extract reproduced below, from Vogel's confidential note to the United Provinces government, is quite revealing inasmuch as it captures rather well why the Survey was so reluctant to release Sahni:

> Both of his scholarly attainments and personal qualities I hold a very high opinion and on that account, should not hesitate to recommend him for a responsible appointment. He is conscientious and painstaking and combines common sense with keenness in his work. His modesty is a particularly pleasing feature in his character.
>
> But just on account of these qualities, I am very doubtful whether the Department could spare his services in the field. You are aware that the number of competent Indian assistants in the archaeological department is exceedingly small and that for that reason the Government have placed us in a difficult predicament by insisting on a competent Indian being appointed to the Lucknow Curatorship.[37]

Sahni's stint with the Lucknow Museum, however, turned out to be a rather short one. Among the things that he was expected to do was to revise the manuscript of the catalogue that had been prepared by Rakhaldas Banerji in 1907–8 and add chapters on the Saheth-Maheth and Kasia finds.[38] But even as he began doing this, a major development had taken place in Kashmir. There, on the advice of the Archaeological Survey, the Darbar had decided to separate archaeology from the state department that conducted literary research.

Kashmir was one of those princely states that Marshall had had his eye on ever since the Archaeological Survey was reorganized. Around 1902 the Maharaja of Kashmir had started a state department under the name of 'Ranavira Institute' for the ostensible study of and research into all branches of ancient Oriental learning. In 1904, after Vogel made a tour in Kashmir to advise on the preservation of ancient monuments there, archaeology was added to its duties and the department had since then been called the 'Archaeological and Research Department: Jammu and Kashmir State'.[39] So, to begin with, archaeology was part of a Sanskrit research department whose main task, apparently, was to publish Sanskrit texts concerning the Kashmir School of Saivisim.[40]

Around the same time, the maharaja had also expressed his desire to the viceroy to resuscitate some of the old gardens and monuments of his state. In fact, just before leaving India, Curzon had apparently promised him that an officer of the Archaeological Survey would visit Kashmir and help in drawing up a scheme for the repair of the famous Mughal gardens near Srinagar.[41] In 1906 Marshall deputed W.H. Nicholls from the Northern Circle to do just this. The following year saw Marshall himself touring Kashmir, trying hard to organize some semblance of archaeological work there.

But for various reasons nothing substantial seems to have come out of those early endeavours. One of the reasons was that J.C. Chatterji, who was placed in charge of the department, was familiar with manuscripts but had no experience in archaeology. In 1905 he was deputed to England to take up the study of archaeology at Cambridge. He spent several years there, but most of his time was apparently devoted to philosophy and not to archaeology.[42] Part of the reason may also have been that the Darbar, while it made annual grants for the conservation of monuments, did not accept the usual procedures for repair that were prevalent in other parts of India, and in which the Survey had an important advisory role. Consequently, no work of any importance got done and the annual grants, for the most part, came to be reappropriated for different purposes.[43] As Marshall admitted to Fleet in a letter that he wrote from Srinagar, it was the most truly 'comic opera state' that he had encountered, where 'archaeology is on a par with all else. The humour of it would be supreme, were it not for the tragic note that pervades everything, and the gloomy outlook for the future.'[44] However, even at that point of time, he did think that eventually things would work out, and he looked forward 'to the time when the great tract of country will be as productive of inscriptions and other antiquities as other parts of the Himalayas already are'.

Now that time had finally come. Marshall had in mind the very man who could get archaeological matters in Kashmir on a sound footing.

Apparently, over the years, it had become obvious even to the state that the arrangement whereby archaeology was conducted within the ambit of a literary research department had not yielded satisfactory results. State officials attached to that department had concerned themselves largely with the Sanskrit texts rather than with the exploration and conservation of monuments. So, after a great deal of correspondence, in 1912 Kashmir agreed to setting up a separate archaeological department. It also decided to take advantage of the offer that Vogel had made earlier (while he was officiating for Marshall), of getting a trained officer from the Survey to take over as superintendent of archaeology there.[45] The Darbar was willing to offer a decent monthly salary (of Rs 500), with an initial contract of two years. Since they wished to appoint an Indian, Sahni was considered the most suitable man for the job. The United Provinces government had no choice but to agree to his services being deputed. With this quick promotion, Sahni joined duty in Kashmir in January 1913.

Marshall now had his own man in Kashmir. Being dead keen for archaeological work to get on there, he appears to have suggested to Sahni that the first task should be a detailed survey of and publication on the historic remains of what was then called the 'pre-Muhammadan' period in the state's history.[46] In the next few years, Sahni would do precisely this during his surveys. Numerous Buddhist monuments were dug at places like Parihasapura, where the ruins of an impressive stupa were unearthed; at Puranadishthana were revealed the remains of two early medieval stupas as well as part of a monastery courtyard; at Hushkapura excavations revealed the basement of a large stupa and a collection of terracottas of the late Kushana period.[47]

Sahni also surveyed a large number of temples. The excavations he carried out at the village of Vantipor, not far from Srinagar, proved the most interesting.[48] Vantipor is where ancient Avantipura, founded by king Avantivarman (AD 855–83), stood. Sahni's excavations, however, were largely concerned with excavating out two religious buildings that were built by Avantivarman in honour of the gods Vishnu and Siva respectively. The temple of Avantisvara, situated half a mile below the town, was the larger, but was revealed to have a relatively simple structure. The second temple near the village of Avantipura, was the smaller and more ornate and was known as Avantisvami. Sahni spent about three years, from 1913 to 1915, carefully excavating this temple. His work demonstrated—contrary to what Alexander Cunningham had presumed—that it was a shrine dedicated to Vishnu. Although the central sanctum was found to be totally destroyed, a detailed plan and excellent description of what had survived—including the gateway, colonnades, the subsidiary shrines, and the extant sculpture—was provided, as also of terracotta objects and pottery. Of these, a large jar with an inscription in the late Sarada script of Kashmir was especially important. With a date in the Vikrama era that corresponds to AD 1527, it read *Om maha sri Avantivarmaghata*. This not merely confirmed the connection of Avantivarman with the temple of Avantipura but also showed that there was worship at the temple even during what Sahni described as the 'Muhammadan period' in the history of Kashmir.

Sahni remained in Kashmir till 1916. Around that time, as we have seen, major dislocations unfolded in the Northern Circle of the Survey as the Great War continued to rage and various archaeologists enlisted. In December 1916, when H.A. Hargreaves, then superintendent of Hindu and Buddhist monuments of the Northern Circle, opted for military service only his clerk was left holding charge. This understaffed state of affairs must have made Marshall decide that it was time to end his trusted lieutenant's long deputation. In early February 1917 he brought Sahni back to Lahore as a replacement for Hargreaves.

We know that the war had put Marshall's plans for excavating Harappa on a backburner. But equally, notwithstanding the dislocations of the war, it remained uppermost in his mind. It is not fortuitous therefore that, within a week of Sahni having taken over as superintendent of the Northern Circle, Marshall sent him off to inspect Harappa.

Sahni first visited Harappa for three days from 20 to 22 February 1917, carrying with him the report of his predecessor, Hargreaves, who, it may be remembered, had suggested that since an exorbitant price was being demanded by landowners for the mounds, excavations should be made, to begin with, on only one mound—the one marked F in Cunningham's plan. This suggestion appealed to Sahni so strongly that he at once submitted a proposal for the acquisition of this mound, together with a portion of Mound AB. This last was the highest mound in Harappa, and during his visit Sahni could see an old stout wall underneath the Naogaza tomb, which raised his hopes of the existence of some important brick monument being buried there. Sahni also believed that an ancient city must have originally extended far beyond the limits of the mounds that survived on the site, for he had been able to trace the foundations of ancient buildings for considerable distances all around Harappa.[49]

But no excavation took place in the following three years, presumably because the financial crunch continued. For Sahni the only highlight of those barren years, excepting the few months he spent in the Eastern Circle, was that in March 1920 he was invited to attend a darbar held by the governor of Punjab at Rawalpindi, where he received the badge and colonial title of 'Rai Bahadur': Lala Daya Ram Sahni would now be called Rai Bahadur Daya Ram Sahni. Some years before this, in 1915, Marshall was knighted and had come to be formally addressed as Sir John Marshall.[50]

It was on Sahni's return to the Northern Circle that compensation to the landowners for the Harappa mounds came to be paid: on his recommendations, Mound F and part of Mound AB were acquired. The compensation paid for them, together with the cost of erecting boundary pillars, amounted to a little less than three thousand rupees.[51] The other mounds were not acquired but were brought under the operation of the Ancient Monuments Preservation Act. It was hoped, as a consequence of this, that the digging and carting away of old bricks would now cease.

The formalities for the proposed dig at Harappa had finally been completed, but only after almost fifteen years of

Marshall first setting in motion the process for beginning excavations there.

* * *

On 5 January 1921, Sahni commenced his first season of work at Harappa (Figs 31 and 32). It was to be a short field season by any standards, only about thirty-five days or so. The excavation was also fairly small in terms of scale—three trenches were opened up on Mounds F and AB, at a cost of Rs 4384. The money was not just spent on the excavations but also on the construction of huts. As Hargreaves had earlier predicted, local labour was scarce. Consequently, labourers from Bikaner had to be brought to work at the site and huts constructed for them.[52] Sahni was a veteran of long field sojourns and, having spent several seasons recovering temples from the ruined mounds at Avantipura, found this first phase of work at Harappa only a

Fig. 31. View of part of the mound of Harappa selected for excavation in 1921

Fig. 32. Excavations in the area west of the Naogaza tomb at Harappa

kind of a trial excavation, one aimed at gauging the character of the remains hidden beneath the ravaged mounds.

In the five weeks that he spent supervising these first diggings at Harappa, Sahni found a number of things. These will shortly be described at length, but in what must have been among his first letters to Marshall about the excavations, he appears to have been especially happy about the seals he had unearthed: 'The operation revealed two well-preserved seals with writing in the same unknown variety of the Brahmi Script, which is exhibited by the three or four seals now deposited in the British Museum.'[53] Marshall's response was immediate and sharp. Chiding Sahni for describing them thus, he wrote (the letter, as many of Marshall's letters to Sahni, begins 'My dear Daya Ram'): 'I trust . . . that you will not use the expression "unknown variety" of the Brahmi script in your official report or other public writing! No connection between the Harappa seal-characters and the Brahmi script has ever been in any measure established so far as I know and I should think was most problematic to put it mildly.'[54] Marshall also used this mild reproof to remind Sahni that he was looking forward to receiving a full report of his work at Harappa.

That report arrived several months later, in September 1921. In fact, Sahni's first impressions of the excavations and his finds are best understood by closely examining the contents of this thirteen-page typed account.[55] Later, the director general based the summary that he published in his annual report on Harappa upon Sahni's account. But, as we shall see, there are differences between the two reports. So, it is best to begin with the first write-up of the excavations, the one authored by Sahni.[56]

Sahni began by digging on Mound F, the northernmost at Harappa, and the one which, on the surface, appeared to be more or less intact. Although it was covered with potsherds and pieces of bricks, no brick foundations were discernible on the surface. This was unfortunate because such ruins would have provided a starting point for the layout of a trench, since they would have pointed to where hidden structures were likely to be found. So, Sahni chose to dig a trench there, which was 'wide and long enough' as he put it, to lay bare the general lie of any important remains that were hidden in it. This stretched from the south-east to the north-west of the mound and covered a length of 500 feet, with a 16 foot width, and was taken down to a depth of about 12 feet. Below this, there were still several strata which remained untouched by Sahni.

In spite of opening up such an extensive stretch, the structural results were somewhat disappointing. What he seems to have quickly realized was that, notwithstanding its intact outward appearance, Mound F had been robbed of its bricks—'this mound had suffered from the greed for bricks as much if not even more than the other mounds, with this difference that in this case the holes left by the entrenchments had filled up and the mound presented an appearance which led one to think as if it had never been touched.' Hardly any structures were found and the few walls that were revealed appeared to be too fragmentary to afford anything by way of a systematic plan of the buildings to which they belonged. A corner of a room, however, was found, with walls that were 2' 4" thick, and in this a seal was located. This was square in shape and was provided with a round projection on the reverse, pierced with a hole for the string by which it was suspended.

Two other fragmentary structural ruins that Sahni reported in this trench are worth mentioning. First, he found a 'covered brick drain which might have formed part of a dwelling house or of a lane.' This may be the first hint that we have of an element of city drainage at Harappa. The second was a ruined building which, according to Sahni, opened to the west and was made up of an incomplete long wall (32 feet and 4 inches long) with five partition walls. It also had an entrance that was four feet wide on the western side. It was in this ruined structure that he found another square seal (no. A.263). Sahni could not at this stage ascertain what the building was, or how far it extended, but later this was recognized to be part of the 'great granary' of Harappa.

Sahni described at length the bricks he encountered there. As the following extract shows, he recognized these to be unlike those at any other ancient site. The only analogy he could find was with a couple of bricks of the Gupta period. The Harappa specimens were

> well-burnt bricks of fine texture which have the interesting size of 11" x 5 ½" x 2 ½" to 3". This is also the size of the bricks in the building which was partly exposed in Mound A, B and, I believe, of all bricks dug out on this site. The chief interest of these bricks lies in the scientific proportion of two widths to the length, which is the essential condition of good bonding. As far as my information goes, bricks of such proportion have not so far been noticed at any other ancient site with the sole exception of a couple of Gupta

> bricks now deposited in the Sarnath Museum. These two bricks measure 14" x 7" instead of the common size of 14" x 9" to 10" of the Gupta monuments.

On the second mound (marked AB in Cunningham's plan), Sahni cut two trenches. One of them was started on the western portion of the mound but abandoned due to enormous accumulations of earth. The other measured 55 feet x 25 feet and was located to the west of the Naogaza tomb. Here he unearthed portions of a brick building and fragments of stones of various sizes, some highly polished, others rough and coarsely dressed. Most of them were identifiable as parts of undulating rings of the type that had been observed since the early nineteenth century on the tomb of the Naogaza saint. Sahni could not ascertain their precise purpose but conjectured that 'they might be bases of finials of some kind, which answered to the usually ribbed ornaments or *amalaka* of the Hindu and allied temples'. The brick building was made of the remains of two rooms, one of which seemed to be a fairly large hall.

Artefacts of various kinds were brought to the surface, of which the most interesting were earthenware objects such as pottery, figurines, balls, bangles, and crucibles (Figs 41–45, pp. 325–7). The domestic pottery was described by Sahni as being wheel-turned, unglazed ('not a single piece of glazed pottery was noticed in the excavations'), and their shapes were explained by invoking the vessel types that he knew best, those that were used in India in the early twentieth century. These included large grain or water jars (*chaties*) with broad mouths marked by stout rims but with narrow, circular bottoms; large-sized troughs ('for the use of the dyer'); *lotas* for pouring water, and a jar which resembled a 'martban for keeping pickles, of the type which is used to this day'. The first description of the fabric of Harappan pottery is also contained in this report, which Sahni classified as mainly being of a light red or brown colour, with the exception of some black specimens ('the latter colour is produced by the application of a variety of earth after it has been fired once. The pottery is put back into the kiln again and taken out when the kiln is cool'). He noted that it was generally decorated with simple black lines which were smeared on the vessels before they were baked, a few with red ochre or *geru*, and one fragment 'with a labyrinth of circles and an ornament resembling the Greek fret'.

As for the 'crucibles', in this category he seems to have included the perforated pottery that we today recognize to be a typical Harappan ceramic type. He called them 'small crucibles with pierced sides which may have been used as filters of some kind for liquids or possibly as sand-holders'. The bangles were of various sizes and found in abundance. One of these was of a high degree of excellence, made of a blue colour, while the beads were of 'exceptional length'. There was a plethora of terracotta toys, including rattles and a wheeled cart, as also representations of birds, animals (lions, dogs, humped bull), and men and women (described as 'crude caricatural representations'). The method of making these figures was thus described: 'The entire body is roughly shaped out of a lump of wet clay and features, drapery, ornaments etc. are then separately made and stuck on it in proper positions. In the more complete specimens . . . the hair is done up in a high mass on both sides in closed volutes or horns.' Sahni did not believe any of them were divine images meant either as votive offerings or for household worship.

Especially noteworthy was the near absence of metal, with the exception of a small gold hollow bead and two iron nails ('the latter might have been dropped on the site in modern times'). That the only tools found by Sahni were made of stone—small implements of a soft, dull cream-coloured kind of stone which he noticed as being similar to that excavated by Cunningham—was also something he mentioned. The significance of such stone tools he did not amplify at this stage. He was struck by the absence of coins and stone images in the excavations as well, but again he had no explanation.

On balance, most readers of this report are likely to get the feeling that Sahni's first season of excavations had turned out to be a combination of thwarted expectations and an unusual juxtaposition of artefacts. There were hardly any structural ruins in the excavated mounds which had survived intact; yet it was now clear that the enigmatic seals belonged to the time when Harappa was a brick-built city. But Harappa, unlike other cities of ancient India, had not revealed images or coins or metal technology (copper-based tools would be found later). Instead, its implements were made of stone, while its bangles, beads, and figural representations were almost entirely of clay.

Sahni did not feel sufficiently enthused, or shall we say he did not find the results of his first season's work at Harappa compelling enough to make him return there the following year. We know this perfectly well because within a month after sending his Harappa report to Marshall the question of sites to be excavated in 1921–2 in the Northern Circle came up for discussion. Sahni made it more than evident that while he had no doubt that the excavations he had begun at Harappa would require to be resumed at a later date, the funds currently available did not appear to be sufficient for further work there.[57] This was because all excavation work at Harappa was unusually expensive on account of the enormous heaps of earth left on the mounds by unscrupulous brick-diggers. Instead, Sahni suggested that the funds be used to excavate other sites, such as the mound known as Raja Karna ka Kila at Kurukshetra, which he had got protected in 1917. This, indeed, is one of the sites where Sahni would conduct excavations in 1921–2.

All the same, despite Sahni being lukewarm, Harappa was very much on Marshall's mind. He asked Sahni to bring the excavated antiquities to Lahore, where he saw them in early

December 1921. Later that month he wrote to Sahni that they were of 'somewhat exceptional interest' and wanted them to be exhibited in the Indian Museum at Calcutta before they were permanently displayed at the Lahore Museum.[58]

In the annual report of the Archaeological Survey for that year, Marshall provided a summary of Sahni's work. Describing the site as one of the most fascinating from the archaeological point of view, he outlined the difficulties that an explorer faced at the vandalized mounds of Harappa. He compared fieldwork there to 'hunting for the proverbial needle in a haystack'.[59] His account of what was found in the excavations underlined the importance of the beginning Sahni had made at this difficult site. What is most significant is that his report communicates a sense of why Marshall considered the Harappa excavation to be exceptionally interesting:

> although the results attained so far are undoubtedly meagre, they are important in that, according to Mr Sahni, they prove that the Harappa seals and their curious pictographic legends belong to the pre-Mauryan epoch; and it is to be remembered that the digging to date has pierced only the topmost levels. Fifty feet of depth remain to be explored, and it is already evident that the examination of these lower strata is likely to lead to valuable discoveries.[60]

This was both an optimistic and guarded assessment. It was also the first surmise on the possible time-frame for the brick ruins of Harappa and her seals. As we saw, Sahni's report does not provide any pointers to the broad period to which he thought the site belonged. So, what Marshall mentioned in his report—namely that Sahni considered the Harappan seals to be of pre-Mauryan antiquity—must have emerged from discussions that the two men had after Marshall saw the Harappa finds at Lahore in December 1921. The term 'pre-Mauryan' means that these were thought to belong to an epoch prior to the last quarter of the fourth century BC, when Chandragupta, founder of the Mauryan dynasty, ascended the throne of Magadha.

That, though, only provided the most general kind of datum line for Harappa. A more interesting question is: were there any pointers to how far back this datum line could be pushed? There was just one other conjecture in Marshall's report which did, implicitly, push back the time frame of the life of this site to a slightly better defined chronology. This emerges from Marshall's remarks on the character of Harappa's terracottas, which he reckoned were in the style of specimens he had himself found in the oldest strata at Bhita about a decade earlier. If we go back to Marshall's Bhita report, we find he had placed the oldest occupation at Bhita to *c.* 800 BC. The inference that can be made from this is that what Sahni had found at Harappa was considered by Marshall to be as old as these oldest remains at Bhita.

What is most important, though, is the development within Marshall of the understanding that, unlike in Bhita, at Harappa even more ancient artefacts remained to be discovered. This is because fifty feet of deposits remained unexcavated below the level that Sahni had dug in that first season. Much of value was expected to emerge from lower deposits.

For the moment, Sahni's excavations at Harappa's depleted ruins had succeeded in establishing the existence of a city older than any ancient city hitherto known to exist within the Indian subcontinent. The momentous nature of this knowledge remained, for the moment, only tentatively formed even within the minds of the people who possessed this knowledge.

Meanwhile, for John Marshall himself there were serious problems at hand, as, once again, the Archaeological Survey had come under a shadow.

The financial year 1920–1 had begun with substantial changes in the status of the Archaeological Survey as a consequence of the follow-up to the recommendations of the Montagu–Chelmsford

Report of 1918. That reform scheme, envisaged by Secretary of State Montagu and Viceroy Chelmsford, was the constitutional response of the British Raj to Indian demands for self-government. It tackled this objective by visualizing a 'dyarchy', or division of government functions, whereby some power would be transferred to provincial governments and ministers responsible to legislative assemblies, while other functions would remain with the imperial government.

Under this reform scheme the Survey, for the first time, became truly 'imperial' in the sense that now the cost of its functioning and expenditure came to be borne by the central government. Before this its situation had been somewhat anomalous, in the sense that while archaeology had been considered an imperial subject, the Survey's expenditure and control had been divided between the central and provincial governments. All this was now changed. From 1920–1 the entire cost of the Archaeological Survey and its activities was to be borne by the imperial government. With this the duties of the eight superintendents in the various circles of the Survey also came to be more specifically defined. As far as the conservation of monuments was concerned, they would now have to concentrate all their energies on the 2521 'protected' monuments, since these were accepted as a central charge by the imperial government. Also, although local governments remained formally in executive control of the Survey's provincial staff, they did so only as agents of the imperial government.

This new centralization of the Survey certainly created the theoretical grounds for a more consistent and efficient functioning. But in the real world this was not to happen in a smooth manner. This is because from 1922 onwards the spectre of harsh cutbacks came back to haunt the Survey.

Around this time, a commission was appointed, under a fellow called Lord Inchcape, whose main brief was to suggest the means by which government expenditure might be curtailed.[61]

The commission proposed bringing down spending in all departments—from the army to railways to the postal and telegraph departments to education. We may recall that this was not the first time such measures were being contemplated: shades of Elgin's time were in evidence. And Marshall knew from past experience that departments such as the one he headed would be the first to be pruned in order to effect the required economy.

By August 1922 Marshall already had a sense of the impending problem when he wrote to his old guru, Curzon, that the 'Inchcape Rock of Retrenchment is looming ahead of me and I shall have to navigate my precious little vessel with care, if I am to keep clear of danger.'[62] It soon became clear that Marshall's department, notwithstanding the bestowal of a new and high-sounding 'imperial' status on it, would have to be run on a pauper's purse—if Lord Inchcape had his way. We can in fact best illustrate the character of the drastic cuts that came to be suggested by examining the Inchcape recommendations, alongside the valiant resistance offered by Marshall and his department.

At the outset, Lord Inchcape made it amply clear that while he would be sorry to restrict Sir John Marshall's valuable work, he feared the committee would find it necessary to recommend a considerable reduction in archaeological expenditure. He seems to have visualized restricting the total expenditure of the department to five lakhs annually. This would mean a reduction of eleven lakhs, since the annual archaeological budget then was roughly sixteen lakhs. How this was to be done was not understood at all, which is not surprising, since, as the proceedings make evident, the committee hardly knew the magnitude or nature of the Survey's work in India.[63]

For one thing, the committee felt that the number of monuments being 'protected' by the Survey (2521 monuments) ought to be reduced. What they did not know, as Marshall pointed out, was that protection was only a kind of policing measure in order to prevent people from injuring or defacing monuments. Financial responsibility, Inchcape's main concern, was exercised by the Survey only with regard to 811 monuments or 32 per cent of the protected monuments, and in a country the size of India a further reduction in numbers was impossible. As it is, Marshall underlined, what the government spent in India on monuments was only a fraction of what was spent in England: 'in 1919 the number of ancient monuments which the Government was maintaining in the United Kingdom was I believe 149 and the cost of their maintenance was rather over 1,50,000 pounds ie., the average was over 1,000 pounds per monument as compared with 22 pounds per monument in India'![64]

Neither did the committee seem to know that, in a number of instances, the money being spent by the Archaeological Survey on monuments was related to the larger political considerations of the British Raj. In Delhi, for example, the bulk of the money in that year was being spent on items connected with the conversion of Delhi into the imperial capital (Rs 36,250 on 'garden improvements' and Rs 9080 on road construction for better access to monuments). In comparison, only around Rs 15,000 was spent on the repair of the fabric of the monuments themselves. In fact the only possible saving under the head of 'annual maintenance' that Marshall was willing to consider was in respect of the historic gardens that the Survey maintained. A little over Rs 173,000 was spent on gardens around monuments like the Taj in Agra and Humayun's tomb in Delhi, and Marshall was naturally reluctant to see them sacrificed (gardening being his hobby too). But he also recognized that these gardens could be revived, while if the monuments were 'sacrificed even once' their loss could never be made good.[65]

As for the money spent on field research, the committee turned a Nelson's eye to the fact that with the Great War and in its aftermath there had been a steady drop in government spending on archaeological exploration and excavation—from Rs 38,891 in 1913–14 to Rs 30,000 in 1921–2 to Rs 29,000 in 1922–3.[66] Possibly, they were more concerned about the increase in the 'special charges' under this head which had increased from Rs 38,379 in 1913–14 to Rs 61,000 in 1921–2 and Rs 66,130 in 1922–3. The bulk of this money had been provided to Aurel Stein (Rs 62,130) for his Afghanistan explorations, and for publishing the results of his Central Asian work, as also for preserving and exhibiting his finds at Delhi.

Marshall reacted to the possibility of cutting costs under this head with what can be most charitably described as barely disguised contempt. Even while he doubted that any useful purpose would be served by his discussing with the committee the scientific, historic, or artistic value of this branch of the Survey's activities, and even though it could be 'assumed for the moment that the Government is indifferent to anything but money; that it cares nothing for the past glories of India, for her history or her arts, for her religion, her languages, or for the great part she played in the development of artistic thought and that it pays no heed to the almost passionate love of Indians for these things', he was willing to put these considerations on one side and treat the matter of exploration merely as 'a business proposition—a question of pounds, shillings and pence.'[67] As far as he was concerned, he said that although he did not know the exact amount spent by the government on Stein's journeys in Central Asia, he expressed willingness to repay the government the whole cost of these journeys plus 50 per cent if they would let him have the antiquities brought by Stein. Additionally, he was willing to extend the offer to cover all the excavations that the Survey had been involved in within the frontiers of India. This was Marshall's way of telling the Inchcape-directed committee that, from the perspective of the government, they had received a very substantial return for the financial outlay that they made under this head.

On the question of field research, Marshall also pointed out that what the Indian government was spending on archaeological research throughout India and Burma was considerably less than what Sir Arthur Evans had been spending for many years out of his own pocket on the single site of Knossos: 'To talk of reducing such an allotment still further would be laughable were it not so pathetic. If India were to spend ten times that amount she would still be far behind European countries with infinitely smaller resources and infinitely smaller fields of activities.'[68]

Then there were questions concerning the museums for which the Archaeological Survey was responsible. On the suggestion regarding possible budgetary cuts in the expenditure on the archaeological section of the Indian Museum at Calcutta by reducing its permanent staff, Marshall drew attention to the fact that it was actually maintained with a much smaller staff strength than that employed by other wings—the zoological section, for instance. To the specific question of the finance secretary as to why a highly paid superintendent was necessary in that section, when a gallery assistant with a part-time arrangement with a Calcutta university professor sufficed in 1913–14, Marshall's defence was straightforward and harsh: 'The arrangement then in force was merely a makeshift which reflected little credit on the Government and which reduced the National Museum of India below the level of small provincial museums in England. Imagine a section of the British Museum (shall we say the "Graeco-Roman" or the "Oriental") being confined to the care of an assistant on 80 pounds a year with a University Professor to look in one or two days a week!'[69]

As one sifts through details of the Survey's budget under different heads, and the justification to continue them in the elaborate testimony by Marshall, what shines through is the forcefulness and cogency with which the director general argued the urgency of preventing the Survey from being skinned to the bone. His rhetorical shrewdness consisted in holding a mirror to the imperial government and demonstrating that what it would be forcing upon India if the cutbacks came into force would be unthinkable in England:[70]

> The measure of a government's efficiency is the measure of its capacity to discharge the duties demanded of it by the country, and, unless India is to adopt a standard different from that of other civilized countries, one of its obvious duties is the preservation of the national monuments and antiquities. The English government has, it is well known, been more backward than other European governments to recognize its responsibilities in this respect, but even in England no government now-a-days would dream of letting our Gothic cathedrals and abbeys, our Roman castles or our Saxon churches perish through neglect; and if the obligation is accepted in England, there is still more reason why it should be accepted in India. On the one hand there are far fewer private agencies in India than in England for discharging the task; on the other, the very existence here of an alien rule makes the people of India cling more tenaciously to their own national heritage while the moral obligation on us is all the greater to preserve that heritage.[70]

Additionally, and without restraint, Marshall showed how absurd he considered the government's priorities to be, whereby spending large sums of money on building ostentatious structures for itself in Delhi was justified, while even a fraction of that amount spent on India's historic buildings was being argued as unjustified. He was convinced that the 'monstrously pretentious structures' being planned for imperial Delhi were ones that no one in India wanted or cared for, while, as he pointed out, even though the 'ancient mosques and palaces of Delhi may seem a slight thing compared with the vast structures that are being reared at their side', they had a message and a meaning for Indians which 'our own creations, costly and pretentious as they are, will never have and the government would be wise to pay more not less regard to the sentiment attaching to them.'[71]

Even more interestingly:

> The Indian people, being subject to a Foreign government attach far more value to the maintenance of their own national traditions and their national monuments than Englishmen do. I have heard arguments that this is merely a matter of sentiment and that if their sentiment is so strong, it is up to the Indians to give practical expression to it by looking after the monuments themselves. With such an argument I have little sympathy. After all the government is for the people, and when the people demand that their sentiment in this matter should be respected and their heritage preserved to them, no Government can afford to disregard their wishes. I am well aware how little regard has been paid in the past to Indian sentiment but at the risk of appearing un-British I cannot help stating my conviction that we should have found our path in India much smoother if more attention had been paid in this and other matters to national sentiment.[72]

The director general's commitment to his department and the monuments that were in his charge was total. His defence of them was unwavering and vigorous. Many of the arguments he offered—and which have been quoted at length above for that reason—are amazingly vanguard and Forsterian, coming as they do from the executive head of an arm of the British Indian state. One encounters in such statements a monumental condemnation of the policy of the British Raj of which John Marshall himself was so distinguished a member; a clear understanding that monuments were to the subject race of Indians a symbol of their 'own' traditions; an attempt to make the sentiments of the subject people the touchstone of government policy; and a conviction that it was the disregard of such national sentiments that had created impediments and resistance against the Raj. There is absolutely no doubt that Marshall was also shrewdly deploying the threat of national resistance as his most potent reason for preventing a cut in archaeological spending.

Marshall had reason to think that policy-makers would pay heed to Indian sentiment. The British Indian government was just coming out of large-scale disorder resulting from the first non-cooperation movement (1920–2) launched by the Indian National Congress and Mahatma Gandhi. In fact, around the time that Sahni had begun excavating in Harappa, his fellow Punjabi Lala Lajpat Rai had in nearby Lahore inspired a student protest. This was only the beginning as, over the next two years, an all-India movement with various regional permutations and combinations enthused large numbers of people across the country into programmes of non-cooperation against the British. These involved economic, educational, and political protests ranging from public bonfires of imported cloth to the successful boycott of the visit of the Prince of Wales.[73] Several such protests also strained the 'non-violent' strategy that the Mahatma wished to follow; eventually, it was one such incident at Chauri Chaura near Gorakhpur which resulted in an anticlimax of sorts. Gandhi decided to unilaterally call off the movement. All the same, the British government was still reeling under the impact of that upsurge, and it was to its various ramifications that Marshall appears to have drawn attention when he accused the government that he served of ignoring Indian national sentiment.

Apart from the larger political circumstances that may help in understanding the reasons why Marshall defended his turf so passionately, it is necessary to keep in mind that he had articulated such sentiments even *before* his department's budget came to be threatened by Inchcape's recommendations. His India-centred approach had, in fact, been formulated in many earlier situations. For instance, in October 1921 he had received a letter from Stanley Clarke, curator of the Indian Section of the Victoria and Albert Museum at London, in which the latter had complained about the small and fragmentary collection of antiquities in the custody of their museum from the North West Frontier Province. He wondered whether Marshall could help them obtain a fairly representative 'gallery of Indian sculpture of all periods'.

The museum's request had to be considered because a great many complaints had apparently been made by both the London museums (the British Museum and the Victoria and Albert Museum) against the Indian government for withholding the antiquities of India from them. Marshall, however, made it immediately known, and in no uncertain terms, that he could not think of making further gifts to England unless there was a *quid pro quo* and some representative specimens of European antiquities were sent to India.[74] His letter to the London Museum's curator, who had made the request for Indian antiquities, illustrates this rather well and his tone, in the following extract, sounds more like that of a patriotic Indian than an officer of the Raj:

> Another factor to be borne in mind is that large and valuable collections of Indian antiquities have been taken to England in the past and nothing in return has ever been given to India by England. Indians naturally feel very strongly on this point and it would help me greatly in the task of supplying you with antiquities if I could be assured of some European objects in exchange of them. To me it has always seemed quite indefensible that inspite of the vast treasures taken from India this country possesses scarcely a single European antiquity—not even a British palaeolith or neolith nor one object of Celtic, or Roman, or Saxon, or of any other period from England, let alone antiquities from other European countries.[75]

Such sensitivity is evident also in Marshall's efforts to get guide books to archaeological sites written, several of these being translated into Indian languages. An Urdu translation of Marshall's guide to Taxila was prepared by M.H. Kuraishi in 1921, while a little later, on the director general's suggestion, a Bengali resident of Banaras, a Mr B. Majumdar, produced a Bengali guide to Sarnath.[76]

In pursuance of this liberal inclination, Marshall's Survey had also been working closely with Indians who were supporting and pursuing archaeology in the various parts of India. The Pataliputra excavations financed on a grand scale by a scion of the Tata family had, as we saw, been successfully executed by the Survey. Again, in 1917, excavations at Sankisa were carried out by a Survey man, Pandit Hirananda Sastri, on behalf of the Historical Society of the United Provinces.[77] Shortly after this the Varendra Research Society expressed a wish to begin excavations in Bengal. This was the most efficient private body of antiquarian scholars in India, its beginnings going back to 1910, when Sarat Kumar Ray (1876–1946), the Kumar of Dighapatiya, began the society with Akshay Kumar Maitra (1861–1930) as its director and Ramaprasad Chanda (1873–1942) as its honorary secretary. The purpose of the society was to examine ancient sites that lay scattered over Varendra, or North Bengal, and over the years it had prospered, carrying out explorations and organizing a museum in Rajshahi which had more than a local reputation.

Ray, of course, financed much of this work while Maitra guided its academic activities. A lawyer by profession, much before the formation of the Varendra Research Society, Maitra had been writing on Bengal's history. In 1899, at the instance of Rabindranath Tagore—with whom he shared a close, scholarly relationship—he had become the editor of *Aitihasik Chitra,* the first Bengali historical quarterly.[78] The purpose of this quarterly was to sensitize Bengalis to their own culture and history through their own language and by their own people. The clarion call was issued by Tagore himself: 'we shall now redeem our history from the clutches of alien hands; and we shall look at our India through our eyes independently . . . The *Aitihasik Chitra* is preparing for the holy war to free the history of our country from bondage.'[79] Although this quarterly did not last long, Maitra continued his tryst with things historical, including writing biographical sketches of various Bengali rulers and local notables. But the work for which he is remembered most fondly is connected with the Varendra Research Society. He was instrumental in getting inscriptions, coins, sculptures, and manuscripts discovered; these were deposited with the museum of the society. In 1917, in recognition of its work, the Government of Bengal had begun to give the society an annual grant of Rs 1200.

Now, the Varendra Research Society wanted to begin excavations. With this in mind, the Survey agreed in 1917 to take on deputation as a scholarship holder its secretary, Ramaprasad Chanda. Chanda was an assistant master at the Rajshahi Collegiate School and had also, through the society, published a volume in Bengali on the early history of Bengal (*Gaudarajamala*).[80] The idea was to train him thoroughly in preparation for the society's future excavations. Soon, Chanda was thought to be of such superior calibre that the manuscript of one of his articles, on an inscription from Taxila, was personally directed by Marshall to be sent to the journal of the Royal Asiatic Society in London, to be considered for publication there.[81] In fact, because he proved to be one of the best scholars that the Survey had trained under their scholarship scheme, Marshall was reluctant to transfer Chanda back to the Varendra Research Society: he wished to retain him in the Survey.[82]

Around 1919 Marshall himself had completed an extraordinary campaign of excavation and architectural restoration at Sanchi which, as we saw, was made possible because of the patronage and support of the Bhopal Darbar. Simultaneously, he was trying his best to make the collection of the Sanchi museum as complete as possible by bringing back some of its antiquities. So, for instance, the capital of a torana (gateway) pillar which had earlier been presented to the Central Museum of Lahore was returned to Sanchi.[83] The Bhopal Darbar was so impressed with these endeavours that they requested Marshall to ask for the return of the Sanchi material in the British Museum that Cunningham and Maisey had earlier excavated out of the stupas. In this case, though, while Marshall agreed that Sanchi was the rightful and appropriate place to preserve the relics, he considered it highly unlikely that the London Museum could be prevailed upon to return them.[84] However, he did succeed in getting replicas of the relics and reliquaries in the British and Victoria and Albert museums sent to Sanchi.[85]

There were many other princely states as well that were actively involved in archaeological work. In 1920, one of the most well-known initiatives came from the Nizam's government in Hyderabad, which brought over Lorenzo Cecconi, a well-known Italian expert on fresco conservation, to carry out the preservation of the famous paintings at Ajanta.[86]

All this lay at the back of his mind when Marshall took the view that Indians had a stake in deciding the future of their own heritage. He wanted his government to consider this carefully as they deliberated over the ways in which they might reduce the money allocated to archaeology.

Government policy, as we know, is seldom based on sentiment. In this case, too, despite the eloquence of Marshall's arguments, penny-pinching measures won the day. In March 1923 news that the Inchcape cuts would be implemented in the coming financial year reached Marshall. The only anodyne was that, instead of being reduced by eleven lakhs per annum, the archaeological budget was reduced by about three lakhs. This was still a substantial reduction, but less than the dreaded 'Inchcape Rock' had threatened.

The rock on which a by-now-considerable vessel, the Archaeological Survey of India, might have foundered, had been just about navigated.

# 9

# TALENT AND TROUBLE AT CALCUTTA

IN THE SPRING OF 1923, AROUND THE TIME THE Archaeological Survey learnt that its pockets would soon become significantly lighter, a sensational piece of news arrived from Sindh. One of its officers had discovered seals at a place called Mohenjodaro. These seals were the same as those that had been emerging out of Harappa's ruins.

'Three different seals', wrote the officer to Marshall,

> bearing the bull statant with a standard in front have been discovered. They are exactly similar to Cunningham's Harappa seals . . . I send impressions of these three seals to you. Two of these belong to the same period. Unfortunately the larger one is broken but in both of them the object in front of the bull is quite clear. It is really a standard. Both bulls bear a saddle on their backs and the inscriptions differ. The third seal is slightly later in date according to my opinion as the execution of the bull is not as good as in the case of the first two.[1]

An important interest within our present enquiry is to examine how this unsuspected treasure emerged from Mohenjodaro, along with the train of events that followed. So, let us look closely at the carrier of these initial tidings, who first brought Mohenjodaro's mysteries to the Survey's notice.

The bearer of this first news was Rakhaldas Banerji (1885–1930; Fig. 33). We caught a fleeting glimpse of him in 1911, when his name was recommended by J.Ph. Vogel to the United Provinces government for the curatorship of the Lucknow Museum.

Fig. 33. Rakhaldas Banerji

That job, as we know, went to Daya Ram Sahni, who moved from Lucknow to Kashmir and then to Harappa.

Banerji's professional journey, before he dug Mohenjodaro in late 1922, was both similar to and different from that of Sahni. He had come in contact with the Archaeological Survey of India in Calcutta as a university student and his career there is marked by brilliance and passion, as also by a succession of sagas, some of which seem as dramatic as what he had just experienced in Sindh.

At least two aspects of Rakhaldas Banerji's early education and training stand out. First, unlike the archaeological scholars recruited by the Survey in the first decade of the twentieth century, he was one of those who formally trained in the study of history, not languages. He spent his early years in Baharampur, in Murshidabad district, where he was schooled, and his interest in history is supposed to have first developed because of the district's many medieval monuments that were witness to the days of the nawabs of Bengal.[2] Later, he studied for his BA in History Honours at Presidency College, at Calcutta, between 1903 and 1907, then got his MA from the University of Calcutta.[3] Second, along with his formal, disciplinary training, he acquired a working knowledge of archaeological and epigraphic material in the museum of the city where he studied. The Indian Museum of Calcutta, along with its archaeological galleries, was then under the charge of Theodore Bloch, superintendent of the Eastern Circle of the Survey, and it was Bloch who initiated the young history graduate to its collection. In other words, unlike Sahni, who made the material remains of the Indian past his special concern after he was selected for an archaeological scholarship, Banerji was an archaeologist in the making even before he formally began his career with the Survey.

Banerji's fascination with things archaeological went back

to the time when he studied history at Presidency College. As today, students then were expected to submit written work on their subjects of study, and generally these were researched in closeted libraries. But the boy from Baharampur was more adventurous. Following his instincts, he journeyed westwards to see the archaeological collection in the Lucknow Museum; he wanted to examine first-hand the large number of inscribed sculptures there which pertained to the subject of an essay upon which he was about to embark. This concerned 'The Scythian Period of Indian History' and Banerji wanted to see the material evidence of that era.[4] That he could read the inscriptions on the Lucknow Museum sculptures is something that he owed to his teachers in Calcutta. The scholar Haraprasad Shastri was one such teacher, and under his tutelage Banerji trained in Sanskrit. In fact, he seems to have acquired enough mastery over languages and scripts to be able to read various kinds of ancient epigraphs.

These skills were combined with great academic ambition. As is quite common among young scholars of a similar bent, he was impatient to make his presence felt in the world of scholarship where such skills mattered. So, while studying at the university, he wrote to Sten Konow, the government epigraphist, asking if 'private persons' were allowed to contribute to *Epigraphia Indica*.[5] On hearing from Konow that he would be pleased to receive a contribution, Banerji sent off not one but two manuscript essays on inscriptions. One of these was concerned with a copper plate grant (the Patiakella grant of Maharaja Sivaraja), while the other discussed a stone epigraph (the Mundesvari inscription of the reign of Udayasena). Both essays were published in the 1907–8 volume of the journal.[6] Banerji's discussion of the various features of the grants is confident and crisp even in his first foray into the pages of India's most widely read epigraphic journal.

It may be remembered that Daya Ram Sahni's first writing on inscriptions, on the Banaras inscribed slab of Pantha, also appeared in the very same volume of the journal. His paper, like those by Banerji, was full of promise. These early writings by Banerji and Sahni reveal a close adherence to the rules of Western epigraphic discourse, inasmuch as they are marked by cross-references to various contemporaneous epigraphs, relevant authorities, and publications, following the form that was a hallmark of European scholars such as Vogel and Kielhorn.[7]

These publications not only mark Banerji's debut into the world of academic scholarship, they also reveal the chain of contacts that he had, even as a student, built up in the Survey. There was, for instance, Albert Henry Longhurst, officiating as superintendent of the Eastern Circle, who Banerji accompanied on a tour of Eastern Bengal for about two weeks, just before he sent his paper on the Orissa grant to Konow.[8] Again, around this time, he must have been in touch with Vogel, because in 1907 it was Vogel who entrusted the task of cataloguing the archaeological collection of the Lucknow Provincial Museum to Banerji.[9] Although Banerji did prepare a catalogue, it was never published because it needed many additions. This was, as we saw, one of the tasks that Daya Ram Sahni was to take up when he was appointed curator of the museum in 1910.

What Banerji's sojourn in Lucknow did result in was the discovery of several epigraphs in the museum's holdings. One of them, inscribed on the umbrella shaft of a Buddhist image from Saheth–Maheth, was studied by his archaeological mentor in Calcutta, Theodore Bloch. The bulk of newly discovered records, fourteen of them, along with a few others which he re-examined, were published by Banerji.[10] These were largely inscriptions incised on sculptural pieces and architectural elements that belonged to the time of the Kushana dynasty. They had been manufactured in the Mathura region; some of them travelled from there to other places in North India.

The inscriptions were transliterated and translated by Banerji. In the article that he wrote, the beginnings of his talent in iconography and sculpture emerge alongside his epigraphic skills.[11]

For instance, of one Jaina image he tells us that the sculptural relief on the throne on which the Jina is seated—which had women with garlands on the right of the wheel and men in a similar position on the left—is different from the majority of such bas-reliefs from Mathura, for the sculpture from Mathura showed men on the right and women to the left of the wheel. Only someone who had made it his business to compare different images of the same genre could be expected to notice such details.

If his early writings in *Epigraphia Indica* reveal the associations that Banerji had built up with European scholars in the Survey, they also throw light on his connections with the world of Bengali scholarship. The copper plate grant on which he first wrote had come to him through Nagendra Natha Vasu. The latter was honorary archaeological surveyor to the Mayurbhanj Estate in Orissa, and the inscription, which belonged to an Oriya Brahmin, had been handed over to Vasu by the Raja of Patiakella. Vasu, in turn, had given it to Banerji to decipher.[12] Vasu was also closely connected with the Bangiya Sahitya Parishad, and this brings us to Banerji's local and Indian sphere of interaction.

By the time he turned to archaeology, there were men in Bengal who had gone into the past of their region, determined that they would play a proactive role in the process of recovering it. We have, before this, drawn attention to the formation and work of the Varendra Research Society of Rajshahi and the manner in which some of the educated elite of North Bengal, ranging from the Raja of Dighapatiya to teachers and scholarly lawyers came together there. In Calcutta, such men commonly frequented and played a determining role in establishing the reputation of another society, the Bangiya Sahitya Parishad. Founded in 1894, this was among the foremost literary societies in the region, as also home to a proliferating collection of archaeological relics donated by important Bengali notables.

There were those, on the one hand, that had been contributed by 'figures like Maharaja Manindra Chandra Nandy of Kassimbazar, one of the chief purchasers of sculptures and coins being excavated in Bengal, the bulk of which he donated to the Parishad; Maharaja Jogendranath Ray of Lalgola, the donor of a special collection of enamelled and inlaid bricks from Gaur, among other artifacts, Prafullanath Tagore who contributed a rare consignment of Kushan and Gupta period coins, or Basanta Ranjan Ray, who collected *punthis* from all around the province to build up the core manuscript collection of the Society.'[13] On the other hand there were scholars like Nagendranath Vasu, as also Banerji's mentor Haraprasad Shastri; and a large number of others who regularly provided antiquarian material to the Parishad. Banerji soon became an active member and went on to have a long association with it. One of the first things he accomplished there was similar to what he did in Lucknow: he put together a descriptive list of sculptures and coins in its museum. A little later, Banerji helped organize a maiden exhibition of its collection, where, along with archaeological relics of various kinds, old Bengali manuscripts, genealogies, and natural history specimens were displayed.

Several of the antiquities and literary relics that came into the Parishad's precincts would figure in Banerji's publications. These ranged from the Tarpandighi grant of King Lakshmana Sena of Bengal, which the Parishad had purchased from the European nephew of the owner (who happened to be in Gloucestershire),[14] to the Bangarh grant of Mahi Pala (*c.* twelfth century AD), also of Bengal. The latter had been sent on loan by Vasu for the exhibition organized in the winter of 1911–12.[15] The Parishad also played a part in a major honour that was awarded to Banerji around that time. This concerned an essay on the origin of the Bengali script which he had submitted to the University of Calcutta for the Jubilee Research Prize. The essay had originally been written in Bengali, at the suggestion of Ramendra Sundara Trivedi (1864–1919), principal of Ripon College, who always lectured in Bengali and who wanted Banerji's essay for the Parishad's journal. (Trivedi is known to have twice declined the invitation of Calcutta University to give guest lectures under its auspices as he refused to comply with their rule of delivering such lectures in English.[16]) Banerji's essay never did get published in the Parishad's journal because it happened to catch the attention of Ashutosh Mukherjee, vice-chancellor of Calcutta University, who was sufficiently impressed by it to want it for his university's prize. Consequently, it was translated into English and submitted. It remains a matter of speculation whether its original sponsor, Trivedi, considered the submission of an essay in English on the Bengali script sacrilegious, but in 1913 the Jubilee Research Prize was awarded to it. Eventually, some years later, it was published as a monograph.[17]

In the years that followed Banerji would brilliantly embody the new breed of Bengali scholars who wrote in both Bengali and English.[18] In his own language he not only penned monographs on the different sources and aspects of the history of Bengal, he also composed historical novels on themes as wide-ranging as the life-history of a stone of the Bharhut stupa of Central India, to one based on the life of Sasanka, a famous king of early medieval Gauda. Simultaneously, over the same period that he was making his pioneering mark in the world of vernacular scholarship, Banerji was creating a niche for himself in the Archaeological Survey of India.

---

It is apparent from the records of the Survey that, to begin with, the young Rakhaldas was uncertain about finding a place within that organization. This was not because his talents were not appreciated. As we saw, several of the Survey's senior officers—men like Bloch and Vogel—thought much of his intelligence and abilities.

The problem was that, during the course of his work in Lucknow, Banerji seems to have done something that was viewed as an indiscretion. This related to some Lucknow Museum photographs; what exactly he did with them we do not know, but the matter was brought to Marshall's notice, who must have made evident his disapproval of Banerji's behaviour. Banerji feared that the fallout of this disapproval would be inimical to any ambitions he nursed about working in the Survey: we know this because it was alluded to by Banerji himself, a little after the incident, in correspondence concerning the death of Theodore Bloch, which happened in October 1909. (For some time before this, Bloch had been ailing with chronic stomach problems. Eventually, complications arising from those killed him.)

Bloch's death was a blow to the Survey; to Banerji, his mentor's death seemed the 'end of everything'. In an emotional note that he almost immediately wrote to Marshall, he acknowledged that Bloch had made him what he was. He implored the director general to forgive him for what had happened in Lucknow else he would abandon archaeology: 'Now I have no other hope but to study law and join the bar. I think you have not forgiven me yet for my indiscretion about the Lucknow Museum photographs and if you do not pity me my dabbling in Indian Archaeology will cease ere long.'[19]

Marshall does not seem to have held the indiscretion against Banerji. Within a few months, an opening in the Survey appeared. In early 1910, when Sahni was selected as assistant superintendent, the post of excavation assistant to the director general fell vacant. Banerji got the job.[20] Thus began his formal association with the Survey.[21]

Sahni too, as we saw, was first appointed as an excavation assistant to Marshall and, as mentioned earlier, had been sent off to excavate the remains of the sinking Ashokan pillar at Rampurva. Banerji, however, was not co-opted for excavation work. Instead, he worked at the Indian Museum, for the Indian Museum Act, which had been passed on 18 March 1910, stipulated that one of the trustees of the museum would be the director general of archaeology. This was intended to remedy the neglect from which the museum's archaeological section had suffered. It was expected that this could be partly alleviated by giving the director general a free hand in employing experts of various kinds on museum work. So, Banerji was put to work in the Indian Museum, an arrangement that continued throughout the time that Vogel officiated for Marshall and beyond.

India had, by this time, many museums. Some were provincial establishments, such as those in the cities of the various presidencies, and housed large archaeological collections.[22] The Government Museum at Madras was one such; here the range of objects extended from an enormous haul of prehistoric implements to the beautifully carved stones that belonged to the dismembered stupa of Amaravati. Then there were municipal museums like those at Mathura and Faizabad which had antiquities mainly from their respective districts. And then there were site museums at Bodh Gaya, Sarnath, and at other historic spots. Several museums had been set up by the princely states as well, for instance at Bhavnagar, Gwalior, Udaipur, and Jaipur as also some in the Himalayan hill states. The collection of the Bhuri Singh Museum of Chamba, for instance, included inscriptions on stone and metal, sculpture, pictures, wood carving, weaponry, textiles, and miscellaneous other objects.

Several of these museums had outstanding regional collections. Thus, the specimens of the Mathura School of art at Mathura or those of the Gupta School at Sarnath, were magnificent, far superior to those that had been sent from there to the Indian Museum at Calcutta. But what made the Indian Museum different was that it was *the* imperial or central museum of the country. Its inception went back to 1814 and it had been conceived of as a repository which would have *all* that was representative of the country. Its collections were organized in different sections, including natural history, geology, arts, industries, and archaeology. It may not have had the best antiquarian specimens, but it certainly had the largest archaeological collection in India. There were artefacts of all kinds from areas like Gandhara and Mathura, from Buddhist sites like Bharhut and Sarnath, and even from Burma and Java. The problem was that the museum did not have adequate space to exhibit all that it had. Its coin collection, for instance, which was then considered to be the most extensive and valuable in Asia, was mainly kept in sacks and stowed away in safes where no student could either examine or make use of it.[23]

Once the archaeological section became the responsibility of the Survey, the museum seems to have become a rather more lively place, with all kinds of scholars cataloguing its collection. Among the first things that Marshall did after assuming charge was to get different specialists to work there, classifying and arranging specimens. We know, for example, that 1913–14 was a rather busy year.[24] In early 1914 the centenary of the museum was celebrated with special exhibits, ranging from the jewellery that Marshall had recently excavated out of Taxila to sculptural scenes from the life of the Buddha. A great deal of time was also spent that year in getting the Gandhara sculpture in the museum's collection on display. Banerji himself spent a large part of 1913 in the strongroom which had been fitted up and furnished for coins, where he selected specimens for a proposed volume of the museum's coin catalogue. After examining around 6000 coins, he chose 2500 for publication. Apart from this, he examined a collection of about 3000 punch-marked coins which had been found in the bed of the Kosi river in Purnea district. In October that year he travelled to Gaya district where he was sent to copy inscriptions in the Barabar and Nagarjuni caves. He visited the Khandagiri caves in Orissa as well, again for the purpose of copying epigraphs.

Alongside all this, Banerji was writing up on the myriad antiquities and artefacts that he handled. His years in the Indian Museum saw him publish prolifically, even if not all his writings are of high quality. For instance, his discussion of three pillars of the Gupta period bearing bas-reliefs of scenes from the *Mahabharata* (acquired from Chandimau, a village in Bihar), is more concerned with textual allusions than with details of the sculptures.[25] But the extent of his oeuvre is so striking: he shows an ability to write with the same degree of confidence on the ancient sculpture from Mathura as well as the medieval coinage of the sultans of Bengal.[26]

If the images and inscriptions in the Indian Museum helped extend Banerji's oeuvre, his enthusiasm for procuring as many such artefacts as he could created all sorts of unpleasantness. People who acquired for museums were frequently on the lookout for artefacts, but the job required diplomacy, tact, and discretion, all virtues that Banerji was somewhat short of. In fact he was high-handed and intractable, and several of his antiquity-hunting expeditions ruffled feathers, with accusations being made against him and the organization to which he belonged.

An instance in point is something that transpired in Assam shortly after his appointment. During the course of a visit there, Banerji decided he wanted several inscriptions and images from that region for the Indian Museum. So he wrote to the deputy commissioner of Kamrup about what he had 'selected' and asked him to take possession of them under the Ancient Monuments Act. Nothing of the sort was done, but Banerji's demand was reported to a Colonel Gordon, who was commissioner of the Assam Valley Districts. This so enraged Gordon that he complained in writing about Banerji to the director general, pointing out that there was nothing in the act which authorized the removal of objects of historical interest in the summary manner advocated by Banerji.[27] Gordon also underlined that Banerji had completely ignored local sentiment which favoured a museum in Gauhati. 'Public opinion,' as he put it,

> would be against the removal of the ancient relics from Assam to Calcutta, where they would be far removed from view and where they would not be accessible to Assamese students of Archaeology:

> I may mention, for your information, that [the] Assamese are not frequent visitors to Calcutta and that those who take an interest in Archaeology and historical research would resent the idea of the removal of such relics from the country.[28]

Vogel, the officiating director general, was saddled with the unhappy task of calming the local government. Almost immediately, he apologized for the fact that his man, in his anxiety to enrich the Calcutta Museum, had lost sight of local interest.

None of these contretemps deterred Banerji. The very next year, Vogel found himself in the midst of another Banerji-generated controversy, relating this time to the local museum at Malda. The idea of setting up a museum there had originated with Lord Curzon but had not progressed, according to Banerji, beyond 'a sculpture shed'.[29] Banerji then used this to justify his demand, in 1911, for the prompt removal of some sculpture and inscriptions from there to the Indian Museum. As in the case of Assam, the local authorities responded swiftly and adversely. Vogel, still officiating as director general, was told that everyone from the district officer to the lieutenant governor deprecated any move to remove the local collection to Calcutta.[30] What was worse, the seniormost Survey man in the Eastern Circle, D.B. Spooner, was outraged by Banerji because, as he pointed out to Vogel, neither Banerji nor anybody else 'short of the Director General of Archaeology was empowered to go wandering about to local museums seizing on their best specimens for Calcutta.'[31] He also drew Vogel's attention to the fact that Banerji, when putting up the relevant file to Vogel, had omitted to place a letter which Spooner had written him. In that letter, Spooner had told Banerji he was not prepared to support such removal without being assured that Vogel knew and approved of the proposal. This letter, it appears, Banerji never brought to Vogel's notice. Banerji's many talents seemed to include being always able to rub people the wrong way.

All the same, Vogel appears to have been one of those who believed that Banerji's strengths as a museum man and scholar far outweighed his overzealousness as a collector. So, despite the embarrassments he had caused, within a year of his appointment as excavation assistant, Banerji was, at Vogel's recommendation, promoted to the post of an assistant superintendent. Since it had been decided that Sahni would take over as curator of the Lucknow Museum, Vogel wanted Banerji to be promoted to the vacancy that Sahni's deputation would create.[32] So, in November 1911 Banerji took over charge as assistant superintendent.[33] As before, he remained attached to the Indian Museum.

What changed, though, in a few months, was the person to whom he reported. In February 1912 Vogel ceased to be Banerji's superior because Marshall returned to India. Since the director general was also ex-officio head of the archaeological section of the Indian Museum, Marshall now oversaw Banerji's work.

Museums had always been a high priority for Marshall. He saw them as important instruments for disseminating and documenting knowledge. Quite early, he had realized that more complete series needed to be acquired for a number of museums, along with a better arrangement of the material already in their possession. Both these tasks required a close association between museum personnel and trained archaeologists. This was the background to the beginning of an active relationship between the archaeological department and museums, and from 1903 onwards, on Marshall's recommendation, superintendents of the Survey came to be officially associated with the archaeological sections of museums to facilitate improvements and enlargements in their holdings.[34] Along with this, he recommended that a small grant of three thousand rupees be made from the archaeological budget so as to enable his men to purchase antiquities for provincial museums.

Generally speaking, in the concerted effort towards building up collections for Indian museums, Marshall had himself been at the centre of all the action. He was constantly in correspondence with museum officials and his officers about possible acquisitions. So, for instance, Henry Cousens was advised on matters ranging from the price of a Chandragupta II gold coin ('Rs 22/- on the outside') to those that could be purchased from widows of dead colonial officials.[35] Marshall also insisted that the objects that were sought to be purchased be sent to him before prices were finalized. This ensured that needless expenditure was avoided and reduced the chance of forgeries of coins, intaglios (small sculpted artefacts, generally seals, in which the designs were incised into the surface), and other kinds of antiquities being passed off as originals. Of the five intaglios that were sent in 1904 by Percy Brown, curator of the Lahore Museum, Marshall rejected two as modern forgeries. For the remaining three he suggested that a sum of five rupees be paid.

Marshall also communicated directly with coin and antiquity dealers. His contacts ranged from Imre G. Schwaiger, a famous art dealer of Simla and Delhi, to a number of Rawalpindi dealers. His communications with them involved haggling, and over time the director general became quite adept at this art: a gold bangle from Charsada that was eventually purchased by him from the Rawalpindi dealers Jawahar Mal and Lakhmi Das, had originally been offered as part of a set of two, for Rs 1400. Eventually, after steady bargaining (and possibly some vigorous armtwisting), Marshall succeeded in purchasing one of them for four hundred rupees.

But in 1912, when Marshall returned to India, he was confronted with a rather unusual situation in the Indian Museum, something he had never encountered before. It all began when, about a month after his return, Banerji wrote to ask him if he might purchase a Tibetan picture representing a thousand Buddhas.[36] Marshall directed him to send the picture to Simla, specially mentioning that he never made a bid or purchased antiquities of this kind without first seeing them and satisfying himself as to their value.[37] However, unknown to Marshall, the always over-eager Banerji had already made a payment of three hundred and fifty rupees as an advance to the Buddhist lama who worked as his 'agent'. His justification, as he now put it to Marshall, was that had he not done so, the money for the purchase of antiquities would have lapsed.[38] In the circumstances stated by Banerji, Marshall agreed to its acquisition for the Indian Museum, but he made it known that he considered the price excessive. He also told Banerji to take it easy in future.[39]

Unlike Vogel, Marshall had far less patience with this assistant superintendent's aggressive functioning, in part because he had a good idea about bazaar prices, having overseen acquisitions annually made by other museums. In 1911 Pandit Radha Krishna had purchased more than forty categories of ancient objects for the Mathura Museum. In that collection, there were gold and copper coins, images of Jaina *tirthankaras*, as also those of Nagas, Vishnu, Surya, and Sarasvati, along with Kushana stone sculpture (including an early inscribed *yupa* or sacrificial pillar used by a brahmin in the early centuries AD). The entire collection had been made by him from various parts of Mathura and had cost just a little over six hundred and fifty rupees.[40] So, Marshall's insistence that purchases be made by Banerji in consultation with him was quite understandable. Yet Banerji, despite Marshall's clear instructions, seemed unabashed. The very next month, in April 1912, when the new financial year began, he suggested to Marshall that they devise a different purchasing system whereby Banerji would have to seek the latter's permission to purchase antiquities for the museum only if an item's estimated cost was more than a hundred rupees.[41] The attempt was to try and subvert the system that Marshall had put in place. Now, Banerji had to be put in place and was told that the rule which existed would remain: the director general, as before, would satisfy himself as to the value of each proposed purchase. Notwithstanding these repeated instructions,

Banerji proved incorrigible and tried to get around the rules, so that his tenure at the Indian Museum would continue to be marked by a running battle of sorts between him and Marshall.[42]

Could this propensity to subvert authority have been the reason why Banerji did not get the job of 'Government Epigraphist'? We know that in January 1913 he applied when this post fell vacant (because its previous occupant, V. Venkayya, suddenly died). As in all government departments, Banerji's application had to be sent 'through proper channels', which, in this case, meant that Marshall was expected to forward it. Evidently, while Marshall forwarded his application, he did not recommend Banerji's candidature. On the contrary, he made it clear that he did not consider Banerji suitable. In his letter to the government he acknowledged that Banerji 'had done good general work in epigraphy' and possessed great facility in the reading of ancient inscriptions. But he also pointed out Banerji's limitations. These related to his lack of experience of South Indian inscriptions, which constituted the bulk of ancient Indian epigraphs, and to the fact that, in Marshall's opinion, Banerji did not 'possess that critical and authoritative scholarship which is essential for the Government Epigraphist particularly if he is to edit the *Epigraphia Indica*.'[43]

There are different ways in which we can interpret this letter. Certainly, Marshall had reason to think Banerji underqualified for the job. For instance, we do know that Venkayya, before he was appointed government epigraphist, had worked on inscriptions for around twenty years, several of them under the close supervision and personal instruction of Hultzsch.[44] At the same time, one cannot discount the possibility that Marshall's candidness was influenced by the fact that, of all the people who worked in the Survey, Banerji was the one with whose method of functioning he had a problem. Within the structure of the organization, the director general and the government epigraphist generally worked as a team, and Marshall may have considered it unlikely that Banerji's temperament would allow for smooth functioning between them.

The other job which also did not go Banerji's way, and one that he is known to have been much more sore about, was the first chair of Ancient Indian History and Culture (called the 'Carmichael Chair') created in the University of Calcutta. The Department of Ancient Indian History and Culture had been set up some years before this, and apparently the candidature of Banerji for the first Ancient History Chair was strongly supported by Haraprasad Shastri. But instead the vice-chancellor, Ashutosh Mukherji, chose to appoint another officer of the Archaeological Survey, D.R. Bhandarkar, who, we may recall, was Marshall's first Indian officer. He was invited in March 1917 to take up the professorship for a term of three years.

While the technicalities of sending Bhandarkar on deputation from the Survey were being worked out, it appears that Banerji had been told that he himself would be transferred out of Calcutta. Banerji, it seemed, was hoping that the government would not spare the services of Bhandarkar (which would result in him being unable to take up the professorship). And he was anxious to know where he himself was headed. He wrote to Marshall, asking whether the rumours that Bhandarkar would not be released by the government were true, and if so, whether it would be necessary for Banerji to be transferred out of Calcutta; for if he had to move, 'I shall have to sell my carriage and horses, arrange for the management of my property and for the education of my sons.'[45] Soon enough he learnt that Bhandarkar would be appointed professor in July.

The fact that he had lost the job to Bhandarkar rankled Banerji, it was not easily forgiven or forgotten. For years after, the tension between the two men would be expressed in various ways by Banerji, ranging from snide remarks about Bhandarkar's archaeological observations to raising questions about his honesty in proposed publications.[46]

The only redeeming feature for Banerji was that, in filling the vacancy created when Bhandarkar moved to Calcutta, he received a promotion. He was made superintendent of the Western Circle of the Archaeological Survey. It was in this capacity that he went to Mohenjodaro, and from there wrote the sensational piece of news quoted at the beginning of this chapter.

## 10

# MAVERICK AT MOHENJODARO

THE WESTERN CIRCLE, WHEN RAKHALDAS BANERJI made his way to its head office in Poona to take charge, was an enormous one. A large chunk of it was made up of the Bombay Presidency. The Presidency was divided into four revenue divisions with as many as twenty-five districts, and there were numerous princely states within it as well. Additionally, the circle included the Native States of the Central India Agency and those of Rajputana. Given the swathe it cut, 'Western' was thus something of a misnomer for this circle.

Banerji took charge on 6 August 1917. To acquaint himself with its vast terrain and the various works relating to architectural conservation in progress there, he spent the first few months visiting sites in its diverse segments. These ranged from the monuments of Sanchi and Gwalior in Central India, to the medieval remains of Champaner in Gujarat and parts of Sindh. Mohenjodaro, too, was located in Sindh, in that part of the valley of the Indus which formed the most northerly section of the circle. Banerji's excavations here would help solve one of the great mysteries of India's ancient past.

But that was to happen only at the end of his tenure. Before that, Banerji spent some five eventful years in the Western Circle. These were eventful in more ways than one.

Banerji's years in his circle coincided with relatively prosperous times. The financial stringency which slashed spending on monument conservation because of the Great War had by this time given way to liberal budgets. In the Bombay Presidency the local government made a determined effort to provide more money for archaeology. Initially, the annual outlay was raised by half, but by 1919– 20, with the full blessings of the governor, Sir George Lloyd, the government there practically doubled their contribution for monument conservation, increasing it to eighty thousand rupees. Along with this, it made a special grant that year of fifty thousand rupees for the monuments at Bijapur.[1]

Large funds are of course never enough to ensure that work is done quickly and competently. Successful execution requires skill and energy, and to Banerji's credit his work was marked by these very qualities. In fact he appears to have tirelessly endeavoured to oversee the projects being undertaken with the new funds. Entries in his monthly diary illustrate this rather well: in 1919–20 alone more than 150 days were devoted by him to touring different parts of the Bombay Presidency, another forty days or so in Central India, and about a month in Rajputana. How hectic such touring could be comes across from details of his journeys. For instance, during the monsoon months, he tells us he paid repeated visits to Sholapur and Bijapur, apart from various places in the Dharwar district (Hubli, Dambal, Unkal and Ranebennur), Ahmedabad district (Ahmedabad, Dholka, Prantij, Ranpur, Viramgam and Sarkhej), Sind division (Tatta, Khudabad, Hyderabad and Rohri), and Kolaba (Elephanta). Frenetic touring seems to have marked the winter and spring seasons as well.[2]

Long tours formed the hallmark of archaeological work in other parts of India as well, but in the Western Circle things were especially hectic because the monuments that were repaired and conserved there in these years were double the number similarly treated in the past. In 1919–20, for instance, repairs were undertaken at six mosques in Champaner; various tombs and mosques in and around Ahmadabad ranging from the masjid of Rani Sipri to the tomb of Diwan Shah Raju; the caves at Elephanta and Bhaja; monuments inside the fort at Belgaum; and the tombs of the Kalhora Amirs at Hyderabad in Sindh.[3] The most important repairs were those at Bijapur, where the monuments had been inspected by the governor of Bombay, accompanied by Banerji. It must have been during this visit that details of the special grant for Bijapur, and how it was to be used, were decided. Much of the money was spent improving the surroundings of the monuments, with a large amount going towards renovation of the tomb of Sultan Muhammad Adil Shah—a monument known popularly as Gol Gumbaz. The compound of another domed structure, the Jod Gumbaz which was used as a residence by the district and sessions judge of Bijapur up to 1918, was also cleared, as were about twenty more monuments.

Banerji's work that year was not merely concerned with conservation. He examined numerous inscriptions and coins at the behest of various people and institutions. Since the Prince of Wales Museum building continued to be occupied as a war hospital, the trustees had decided to spend a large part of their annual income purchasing specimens. Banerji advised them on several proposed purchases. So, for instance, six copper-plate records were bought from the widow of the late Gerson de Cunha for Banerji's examination of them had shown that they included records of various early dynasties, including the earliest copper-plate grant then known of the Silahara dynasty of the Konkan.[4] Epigraphic work also took him out of the Western Circle. He was sent to Khandagiri in Orissa by the imperial government to copy the Hathigumpha inscription of Kharavela. Additionally, different kinds of coins had to be scrutinized, several of these being sent to Banerji by the Bombay branch of the Royal Asiatic Society.

Banerji's enthusiasm, energy, and talent in these years impressed a number of people and earned him accolades from the Bombay government, especially from the governor. In 1921–2, with the impending visit of the Prince of Wales to India, he was personally asked by the governor to undertake various conservation works in Bombay and Poona. The prince was supposed to visit Poona, where a reception was to be held in the Shanivar Vada, the ancient seat of the Peshwa. In the course of clearing and excavating the area surrounding the plinth of the old palace there, all kinds of structural remains ranging from fountains and cisterns to footpaths and gardens, were brought to light. The main fountain turned out to be the largest that had till then been discovered in India—and it was one with a unique form. It contained almost two hundred jets, made of pure copper, which were distributed symmetrically inside an expanded lotus of sixteen petals. As it happened, the visit of the prince to Poona did not materialize. Nevertheless, it is a measure of the faith that the government had in Banerji that they believed he should undertake the necessary repairs and arrangements.[5]

Thriving in the hustle and bustle of restoring ruins and researching antiquarian remnants, the only limiting circumstance for Banerji was a governmental prohibition on excavations. In spite of the Western Circle having such a large archaeological budget, none of it could be spent digging up ancient sites. Even though the war was over, government remained chary of expenditure on fresh excavations, so the structural remains Banerji excavated were only those that came to light during debris clearance. That is how the garden architecture of the Shanivar Vada was unearthed, and how a Chalukyan-type temple at Sholapur was exhumed from beneath the inner wall of the fort there.

Still, intrepid explorer that he was, within his hectic tours Banerji managed to make time to visit and explore monuments and sites. His tours of Central India were full of such explorations in the states of Nagod and Jaora, as also in the

Rampura-Bhanpura and Garoth districts of the dominions of Maharaja Holkar. During these tours numerous ancient monuments were brought to light.[6] These tours are relevant to our story because it was during one of them that Banerji first set eyes on Mohenjodaro (Fig. 34).

This happened during Banerji's winter tour of 1919 when, in the month of December, he came to the province of Sindh. To be sure, this was not the superintendent's first visit to Sindh. Within months of taking charge he had toured Karachi and Hyderabad, as also Sukkur and Rohri. Again, in March 1918, he had taken his assistant superintendent, V.S. Sukhthankar, with him there.[7] Sukhthankar was an accomplished scholar of literary and epigraphic material but had little experience in conservation work, and the reason Banerji had brought him to Hyderabad and Tatta in Sindh was to give him practical instruction in conservation methods. Banerji had also, in the winter of 1918–19, made it a point to visit several of the ancient stupas of Sindh. He seems to have been suitably impressed with some of these.[8] He noted with interest that several Buddhist monuments were held in veneration by various Hindus in Sindh. On particular

Fig. 34. Mohenjodaro's citadel mound crowned by a Buddhist stupa

days, it was to these shrines that Hindus brought their children to be tonsured. One of the stupas that he surveyed was Mitho Dero, located in Larkana district, the very district where Mohenjodaro is situated (in Labdarya *taluka*). This is where Banerji was again headed in late 1919.

Larkana district is made up of lowlands that lie between the western Kohisan tract or hill country and the Indus river towards the east. The tract has been described in government gazetteers as being one of the finest alluvial areas in the whole of Sindh, with a soil so productive that the district was called the 'garden of Sind'. We do not know how Banerji viewed Larkana during his tours there, but one of his predecessors, Henry Cousens, more than fifteen years earlier, had spent some time surveying monuments there, and had sarcastically remarked that it was 'an Eden one did not require to be driven out of'. Cousens said it was 'loaded with an abundance of soft impalpable dust which insinuates itself into every nook and corner.'[9] Having surveyed Larkana, he had hastened away to breathe pure air again.

Banerji must have breathed the same Larkana dust on the train which took him to Dokri, the small urban headquarters of Labdarya taluka. The railway station near Dokri was the one closest to Mohenjodaro, eight miles distant. From there, Banerji would have travelled by tonga along a stretch of unmetalled road.

On reaching the mounds of Mohenjodaro (which means 'Mound of the Dead'), Banerji was surprised and delighted because, although the ruins were well known in the immediate neighbourhood, their character and importance had not been captured in any archaeological account of Sindh. As he well knew, Mohenjodaro was not listed as an ancient site in the revised list of ancient monuments within the Bombay Presidency. This was astonishing because what he saw before him was an extensive site of multiple rolling mounds over an area of about two square miles, visible from a great distance. Most significantly, a Buddhist stupa crowned the highest part of the ruins (Fig. 35).

Fig. 35. Enlarged view of stupa showing its drum

Banerji spent just a day there, but let us look at what he says about the mounds:

> The ruins consist of vast mounds of burnt bricks surrounded by smaller ones. In the centre of this area is a very high mound about 80 or 90 feet above the level of the surrounding country. This is called Muhen-jo-daro. The top of the entire mound consists of debris and brickbats but here and there loose debris had slipped away exposing straight walls of burnt bricks. The mound is about 600 feet in length and 200 in breadth. In one place on this mound there is the drum of a stupa made of sun-dried bricks. Only the shell of the drum remains as the core has been excavated to a depth of some 30 to 40 feet by treasure seekers. The inhabitants of the surrounding village have dug out and removed bricks from this mound from time immemorial and do so even now. Some of these people who do not acknowledge to have excavated this mound for bricks within the last ten or twelve years, state that when they

> dug for bricks previously, they found the entire mound to consist of a huge platform of burnt bricks on which were built numerous round hemispherical objects of burnt as well as sun-dried bricks (?votive stupas).
>
> Close to this platform of stupas there is another high mound which is the second largest in this place. This appears to have been a temple or a monastery as the old villagers state that they found rows of small square chambers arranged around a square courtyard in this mound. Search among the ruins led to the discovery of numbers of carved bricks but no human figures or images were found. The villagers are unanimous in stating that no coins have ever been found in any of these mounds.
>
> These two mounds are surrounded by numerous small mounds which represent the ruins of the village or township which had grown around this stupa and temple in the height of their glory. The stupa at this place is much higher than the stupas at Depar Gangro or Mirpur Khas and appears to have been the largest and highest Buddhist stupa in the country of Sindh.[10]

Banerji was in fact quite filled with excitement. There were both Buddhist religious structures and the remains of a settlement which supported them. What may also have given him perverse pleasure was the thought that he would now have the satisfaction of demonstrating that Bhandarkar—his immediate predecessor, who got the Calcutta professorship that Banerji coveted—had committed an appalling oversight in his assessment of Mohenjodaro.

In 1911 Bhandarkar, then in charge of the Western Circle, had visited the site, hoping to find an impressive Buddhist stupa of the type he had seen in many parts of Sindh. He was greatly disappointed. He thought it a relatively small site ('about three-fourths of a mile') and failed to recognize the stupa there.[11] In fact he categorically—and as Banerji now realized, erroneously—concluded that it was unlikely the site ever had a structure that was either ancient or Buddhist. He believed the ruins were probably just two hundred years old because the bricks were small—of 'modern type' he noted—with not a single carved moulded brick of the sort usually found in stupa sites: 'what a contrast to the Mirpur Khas stupa, where cart loads of such bricks were found before it was excavated! The probabilities, therefore, are that Mohenjodaro does not represent the remains of a Buddhist stupa or of any ancient monument.'[12] Bhandarkar, as Banerji was quick to point out in print, was wrong on both counts. He himself, as he mentioned in his circle report of that year, had instantly recognized the brick stupa as also the fact that it was ancient.

The brick-built stupa landscape of Sindh, and Mohenjodaro in particular, appears to have left an abiding impression on Banerji. Six months later, this landscape crops up once again, now in connection with Rajputana. In May 1920, when he visited the Bikaner Museum to examine the antiquities that the late Tessitori had collected, Banerji is known to have examined some of the mounds that the Italian had explored—those at Bhatner, Hanumangarh, and Suratgarh. Seeing them, he felt 'they resembled to a very great extent the stupa mounds of Sind. These mounds are strewn over with potsherds and broken bricks but there was no evidence of stone work in any of them.'[13]

This observation by Banerji, about a general resemblance between Sindh's stupa sites—he must have had Mohenjodaro also in mind when he wrote this—and the Bikaner mounds undoubtedly suggests that he perceived a general similarity in the archaeological remains of the two areas. As is now well known, this similarity extended much beyond the world of Buddhist stupas. Some of the mounds that Banerji saw in the Bikaner tract of Rajasthan are sites that formed part of the Indus civilization. What Banerji did not know of course was that at one of them, Kalibangan, the ill-starred Tessitori had found seals of the same type as those at Harappa. Soon, as we shall see,

Banerji himself would discover seals in Sindh similar to those at Kalibangan and Harappa.

Even at this time, and again unknown to Banerji, another explorer was ferreting out a different yet related archaeological terrain in Sindh. The explorer was an ICS officer called G.E.L. Carter, who was then based in the city of Hyderabad in Sindh. Quite by coincidence, Carter was searching out sites around the same time that Banerji was exploring Sindhi stupas and tombs.

Carter was the municipal commissioner of Hyderabad. Like many exceptional colonial officials, he had made it his hobby to explore the historic spots within his jurisdiction. His correspondence reveals a curiosity about various kinds of relics and historical issues, ranging from the relationship of various races with different categories of burial mounds to the path that Alexander the Great had taken through Sindh. Carter, incidentally, published articles on the religious locations and practices of his area.[14]

Carter also discovered flint implements at a number of places that he had visited. These stone tools, he was convinced, were of prehistoric antiquity, relating to the 'Stone Age' of Sindh. Since late 1917, Carter had been in touch with John Marshall about his finds, which had so excited Marshall that he requested the governor of Bombay to put Carter on special duty with the Survey for a year or so. This would allow a more systematic exploration which would then serve as a kind of groundwork for future researches: 'The study of prehistoric antiquities', he wrote to the governor, 'is, as you know, a highly special subject and none of our own Indian Archaeologists in Western India has the requisite qualifications for taking it up.'[15]

As it turned out, Carter's deputation for archaeological work did not come through and he was unable to follow up his discoveries. By 1919, when Banerji visited Mohenjodaro, Carter was serving as assistant collector at Thane, near Bombay.[16]

In retrospect, it must be counted an omission on the part of Marshall—otherwise an archaeologist of uncommon intuition—not to have taken the slightest notice of one particular site described in Carter's correspondence. This was Tharro, which Carter had described as a 'walled Stone Age city'. Carter had here found beautiful flints on the very ground that he saw littered with potsherds: 'It is a fine red pottery painted in patterns with the common reddish-brown colour. I kept a few pieces, one because of a peculiar pattern which I thought at the time to be a variant of the swastika.'[17] Whatever Carter may have thought, in terms of what was then known about archaeological sites in north-west India, the presence of flints along with painted pottery could hardly have been regarded by Marshall or anyone else as a 'Stone Age' assemblage. The site Carter described is one which we recognize today as Harappan.

If he had given it some thought, he would have realized that this juxtaposition of artefacts had also been noticed at Harappa as far back as Cunningham in the nineteenth century. At the very least, if this had struck him, Marshall would then have asked Banerji to visit and explore Tharro. But the significance of Carter's finds at Tharro seems to have escaped him entirely, at this point of time.

The irony is of course that, some years later, once the discovery of the archetypal elements of the Indus civilization had been understood, the presence of long flint blades of the type that Carter had found at Tharro would be considered by Marshall as one of the best indicators of an Indus site.[18]

At the time Carter was writing up his observations on the 'Stone Age' sites around Tharro, a different set of events were unfolding in the Western Circle of the Survey. As we saw, Rakhaldas was proving an energetic and highly successful circle superintendent. But the erratic ebb and flow of his official dealings was causing concern, and his relationship with Marshall continued to deteriorate. The problems between them simply refused to go away. They began to crop up within a year of Banerji being brought to the Western Circle, and, as before, they connect in various ways with how Banerji perceived his work. This was his first posting as a circle superintendent and he appears to have unilaterally decided the manner in which he would run his circle.

At first glance, this appears reasonable enough. But in order to understand why there were problems, a brief explanation about the manner in which circle superintendents worked is required.

Before the Archaeological Survey became an imperial department in 1920–1, it was, as we saw, partly under the control of the Government of India and partly under the provincial governments. The director general and his staff were appointees of the imperial government while provincial officers were under the executive control of their respective provincial governments. So, for instance, a provincial superintendent like Banerji prepared plans for his own archaeological tours and got the local government to sanction them. Theoretically, it was not necessary for Marshall to approve these tours.

But in fact Marshall exercised a great deal of control over the local superintendents because he was the coordinating authority for archaeological work. It was therefore his duty to ensure that he and his small band of officers work in tandem with regard to both conservation and research. This meant that he was to be told in advance about tour programmes, so that there was no overlap of work. But with Banerji assuming charge of the Western Circle, precisely the kind of duplication that Marshall had tried to avoid began to take place.

In early 1918, for instance, Marshall journeyed to Khajuraho to assess conservation work at the temples there. Unknown to him, around that time Banerji made it a point to also visit it. This, as it transpired, proved a waste for Marshall had already done all that was required to be done there.[19] A peeved Marshall then asked the Bombay government to send Banerji's tour schedules to him in advance. Yet even this did not stop problems cropping up again and again. One such problem recurred in January 1919: even though he had been told that a member of the director general's staff would be going to Bharhut in winter that year, Banerji made plans to go there himself.[20] What made things worse was that, simultaneously, he also began to make various and apparently unusual demands on the local authorities there. He informed J.D. Colvin, political agent at Baghelkhand (under whose jurisdiction Bharhut fell), that he expected to be treated as 'the guest of the State during the entire period' and requested him to arrange with the Rewah state that he and his staff be provided accommodation and conveyance during their tour.[21] As a government man, Colvin must have found this improper. He knew that officials drew travelling allowance for their journeys, to be used towards their accommodation. Colvin took up the matter with Marshall who, in turn, forwarded his letter to the relevant department of the Bombay government.[22]

Such problems with the states of Central India constituted just one aspect of Banerji's general inability to get along with others. Within the circle itself, there was a welter of similar conflicts. For one thing, there was a high turnover of subordinate staff.[23] Problems relating to subordinate staff were, however, minor compared to the friction between Banerji and Marshall. Their longstanding disagreements grew considerably worse over the years.

A particularly ugly disagreement between them erupted in 1921. In that year, a new archaeological circle was to be created by separating Rajputana and Central India from the jurisdiction of the Western Circle. Banerji, as superintendent of the undivided circle, was unhappy with this decision in part because it would shrink his jurisdiction. He therefore tried to get the impending division postponed. To begin with, he asked that the transfer be delayed from October 1921 till April 1922 so that he could complete several works in progress there.[24] When this was not agreed to, he expressed his inability to hand over all the papers in his circle office pertaining to Rajputana and Central India. Banerji's cooperation in making the new circle viable was quite crucial, because monument conservation could not be executed without the relevant structural drawings in his custody.

Simultaneously, Banerji appears to have got the governor of the Bombay Presidency to intervene. Just weeks before the impending separation, the governor sent a communiqué asking that Marshall consider postponing the division until he had an opportunity of personally discussing the matter with him.[25] Marshall informed the governor that the matter rested with the Government of India and not with him. He requested the governor's secretary to directly telegraph the education department on the issue, if the governor wanted to pursue the matter.[26] In response, Marshall received a rap on the knuckles: 'His Excellency . . . much regrets you did not refer his request to the Government of India, if the matter, as you say, rests with them'.[27] This seems to have rattled Marshall, who immediately docketed the entire correspondence and sent it to the imperial government. He also asked if they wanted the division postponed.[28] The governor's request must have been turned down because, on 15 October 1921, the transfer did eventually take place.

Even so, at the time of transfer, Banerji merely handed over the files; he sent photo negatives and drawings only in the following year.[29] Even that finally transpired when the Bombay government *ordered* Banerji to dispatch them. Interestingly, once the local government issued written orders, within a week of receiving them Banerji seems to have sent the relevant material to Marshall. The Bombay government issued these orders in March 1922, not so long after the governor had so vociferously and openly tried to help Banerji get the departmental transfer of Rajputana and Central India scuttled. So, what happened in the interregnum to now spur the Bombay government's crack-down on the superintendent of the Survey's Western Circle?

The answer to this puzzle lies in a mass of detail contained in a Government of India file. The subject of the file is ominous: 'Disciplinary action against Mr R.D. Banerjee'. In this file are letters and orders pertaining to Banerji—some written by him, others addressed to him, still others about him.[30] This correspondence allows us to catch a glimpse of what transpired in the Western Circle.

For the Bombay government the winter of 1921–2 had been marred by endless troubles spawned by Banerji. They now realized that they were confronted with the case of an able officer with a propensity for financial messes which he could neither explain nor clear up.

The most serious of these related to the archaeological wing of the Prince of Wales Museum, then being set up. In July 1921, the board of trustees had sanctioned around a lakh and twenty-five thousand rupees so that the archaeological exhibits could be properly displayed.[31] By November that year almost the entire amount had either been advanced directly to Banerji or paid to others at his request. But later, when he was asked to submit a statement of expenditure with receipts, Banerji gave an incomplete account of the amount advanced. Equally serious was the fact that he had, in at least one instance (relating to some plate glass that had been purchased), paid a rate higher than the market rate. In other words, in March that year, around the time the Bombay government ordered Banerji to dispatch to Marshall's office what remained of the Rajputana material, there was a sense in the secretariat at Fort, Bombay, of a looming crisis over the lack of financial propriety on the part of the circle superintendent.[32]

Matters seem to have got messier as the year proceeded. Banerji was asked in May, June, and July to provide explanations regarding various items of expenditure and, presumably, for a final statement. However, instead of sending the accounts, in early September he asked for the return of all original vouchers for correction and renumbering. By this time the board of trustees had reached the limits of their patience. On 26 September it was resolved at a meeting that the original vouchers ought not to be corrected or renumbered.

What alarmed the Bombay government was that it now appeared the mess created by Banerji was only part of a larger pattern of delinquency. In 1921–2 he had apparently purchased furniture for his office in Poona out of a grant meant for excavation. When asked to explain this, his defence was that reappropriation was permissible under the rules and that this had become obligatory because of the increase in his office establishment![33] Then there were problems relating to an excess of expenditure he incurred on travel. The necessity of scrutinizing his travelling expenses had been pointed out to the Bombay government even in 1920, but they had then not considered the matter very carefully.[34] Subsequently, Banerji's travel charges ballooned. When he was questioned about them, his argument was that because of the increase in grants for conservation, his touring had considerably increased, consequently, so had his travelling allowance and contingencies. None of Banerji's explanations convinced his superiors.

By this time Banerji knew he had created a mess from which he would find it difficult to extricate himself. The best option seemed to him to get himself sent to another circle. So, in May he wrote confidentially to Marshall asking if he would help him obtain a transfer.[35] Marshall counselled caution and underlined the fact that while a transfer to the Eastern Circle was possible, given the interpretation that would be put on it in Banerji's present circumstances, it would be wise not to make such a request.[36] October 1922 saw Banerji resign his honorary curatorship of the Prince of Wales Museum. Matters, though, did not end there. Large sums of money had been spent during his tenure as curator, for which Banerji had failed to properly account. Consequently, the Government of Bombay recommended that disciplinary action be taken against him.

Such action, naturally, brought Marshall into the picture. As far as Marshall was concerned, the problem was that while Banerji represented a 'serious difficulty', he did not want to lose him.[37] So, to find a solution to this crisis, he shrewdly suggested to the Bombay government exactly what Banerji had confidentially asked him to do. In November 1922 Marshall recommended that Banerji be transferred from Poona to Calcutta.[38] This was something that the Bombay government itself subsequently pressed for. By early December the imperial government had indicated they had no objection to the transfer.

It was an astonishing comedown for Banerji. An officer of wide archaeological knowledge, one whom the governor had acknowledged for his remarkable services to the Bombay Presidency, was now on the brink of leaving the Western Circle in disgrace.

It was with his fate thus decisively sealed that Banerji proceeded to Sindh, to live out the last winter of his tenure as superintendent of the Western Circle. Some time before this, the government's prohibitions on new excavations had been lifted. It was in these circumstances that Banerji headed towards Mohenjodaro, to the ruins which had so impressed him in 1919.

The decision to excavate the site had been taken by Banerji in the previous field season, and he was now keen to start work. In the true tradition of government archaeology, to assist in the excavations he had with him several subordinate staff of the Bombay public works department. Work began in December 1922, even though the mounds were transferred to the Archaeological Survey only around early January in the following year.[39]

The first task, as is usually the case in most excavations, was to get the site surveyed. The mounds were spread across two hundred acres or more and varied in height. One of them—the one on which Banerji had sighted a stupa in December 1919—was more than seventy feet above the cultivated fields in its vicinity and towered over all that surrounded it. Other mounds, towards the east, were much lower. A survey of the dimensions and heights of all that was on the site started in right earnest. Eventually, by the end of the field season, a contour survey had been completed.[40]

Now the digging began. At first glance, this was nothing new for Banerji. He had by then been dealing with archaeology and monuments for fifteen years and more. But in fact, even though he himself never acknowledged this, he was here entering territory about which he had very little idea. This was the first time that he was conducting a full-fledged excavation. Unlike Sahni, he had not apprenticed practically as an excavator, not even when the sites in the Eastern Circle, to which he was attached till 1917, were excavated. This is because he had remained in the archaeological section of the Indian Museum. Again, in the Western Circle, he had explored a great deal, but the diggings he had supervised were, as we saw, more in the nature of debris clearances around medieval temples and gardens. Now, in the presence of vast mounds, he must certainly have recognized that this was very different from rescuing structural ruins. Unlike monuments, mounds entombed successive cultures piled on top of each other.

Before examining Banerji's methods and results, it is important to ask what exactly the protagonist of this chapter was searching for when he decided to excavate the ruins of Mohenjodaro.

The few who have read the full report that Banerji wrote of his excavations know that he presented his return to excavate Mohenjodaro in 1922 as if he already knew he was on the trail of something momentous. So, let us first carefully scrutinize this version of events. At the outset of his account, Banerji remembered his first visit, where, as we saw, he had lost no time noticing Bhandarkar's oversights. But he says he also noted that he had, at that point of time, found a flint implement there.[41] Over the next few years, as he surveyed other parts of Sindh, Banerji says he became convinced that Mohenjodaro was of a remote antiquity. This is because, on the mounds and ruins that he visited between 1919 and 1921, he found similar flints associated with bricks of a small size. These were spread across a wide stretch and included Vijnot in the Sukkur district on the one hand, and several sites (Dhamraho-daro, Mitho-daro and Ghaibo-daro) in Larkana district on the other.[42]

Ghaibo-daro in Larkana, according to Banerji, was quite crucial in confirming his intuition on the antiquity of Mohenjodaro. Apparently, his visit to it had coincided with a winter rain shower that accidentally revealed a 'brick tower'. Inside it, he found large-sized jars arranged in a row.[43] When Banerji casually put his right hand into the topmost of these, he found it poked by something sharp which apparently bled his little finger. This alarmed the local people, who suspected he had been bitten by a snake. However, when they broke the jar, instead of a serpent they found a stone scraper!

One imagines that they must have been very relieved. But for Banerji the relief was combined with delight because this was the first time he had found a stone scraper in its original context and not on the earth's surface. What was also interesting was that the pot, as also the other jars in the brick tower of Ghaibo-daro, were necropolitan in character and contained human bones. As he put it: 'this was the first discovery of neolithic or sub-neolithic stone implements underground and not on the surface. The discovery at Ghaibi-Daro proved definitely that knives or scrapers of neolithic flint was associated with pre-historic cremation burials and the specimens found by me at Reti, Alor, Mithodaro, Dhamraho, Badin and Mohenjo-Daro were not exactly chance finds.'[44] According to Banerji, it was this discovery—of a stone tool in its original context—'which prompted me to start the excavation of Mohenjo-Daro immediately as I felt sure that it was one of the oldest sites in India.'[45]

But there seems something a trifle odd in this account. For, even while Banerji insists that he had understood the antiquity of Mohenjodaro *before* he began digging there, it is odd that the unique character of this site—a culture marked by brick-built structures and flint implements—does not form the main theme of his report. Shrines on islands and brick-built stupas, quadrangles lined with rooms and Buddha images—these were the things Banerji took up and expanded on when he wrote about Mohenjodaro. In fact, after going through dozens of pages filled with thick description of the various areas that he excavated, one can hardly avoid the feeling that, even while there is here a strong awareness of the successive cultural debris of different ages, Banerji has basically not moved away from the stupa and related structures, i.e. the sorts of objects he had been looking at when he first came to Mohenjodaro, many years earlier.

Quite crucially, we must also remember that this report, which we have paused to consider, was written some years *after* Banerji had excavated Mohenjodaro. He had excavated in the winter of 1922–3, but his account had only begun to be written in 1924. It was finished and dispatched to Marshall in 1926. If we go beyond this report, and instead examine more contemporaneous accounts and correspondence, we invariably find that there are discrepancies in Banerji's presentation of facts. So, is it possible that by 1926 he was retrospectively showcasing his excavation as the culmination of a neat evolutionary unfolding of events; whereas, in fact, the trajectory of his explorations in Sindh and his subsequent dig at Mohenjodaro was far more untidy?

There seems more than a distinct possibility that Banerji was being economical with the truth in his 1926 report. For one thing, in the earlier accounts that he penned, he never once mentioned the scatter of flints and small-sized bricks across numerous mounds in Sindh. An instance in point is his 1919 account, wherein he chronicles his first visit to Mohenjodaro. Banerji does not here draw attention to the fact that he picked up a flint scraper from the surface. This is something we only learn from his 1926 report. Rather, in 1919, it is the stupa that Bhandarkar missed which Banerji seems keenest to highlight. Dhamraho, in the same account, is also described with reference to the possibility of stupas being located on its mounds. These, he noted, were 'roughly hemispherical and appear to be the remains of Buddhist stupas.'[46] Similarly, at Mitho-daro (also known as Jhukar), he was equally taken up by the ubiquitous stupa; the mound there probably marked the 'site of an ancient stupa and it, with its surrounding temples and monasteries were made of sun-dried bricks.'[47] So, if Banerji had known all along that Mohenjodaro and other sites in Sindh were of immense antiquity because they were marked by the presence of stone tools and small-sized bricks, why did he fail to mention any of this in his earlier reports?

The obvious conclusion is in fact that things did not happen in quite the way Banerji later described them. On the whole, it would be fair to say that he had found such artefacts but had not thought them significant, not even significant enough to merit mention in his descriptions. At bit like Masson, who saw signs of Alexander the Great wherever he looked, or like Alexander Cunningham, whose vision was filtered through Chinese pilgrim spectacles, Banerji had come to explore a historical landscape of Buddhist shrines and attendant structures. His plan was to excavate three 'shrines' there as also what he believed was a monastery attached to one of them. Banerji's blinkers were Buddhist.

He began by concentrating on the stupa site that dominated the ruins, which he called site No. 1.[48] One gang of labourers was put to work at clearing the large number of loose bricks on the platform upon which the stupa was built. A second gang was employed in clearing the debris just below the eastern retaining wall of the high platform. It was in the course of work of this second gang that, quite unexpectedly, seals turned up (Fig. 36). While Banerji's reports do not mention when exactly this happened, since it was in the course of clearance work on what was to be the main arena of this dig, it must have been quite early in the field season of 1922–3.

Apparently N.S. Chikte, a lower subordinate of the Bombay public works department, was in charge of the trench below

Fig. 36. Excavations at Mohenjodaro's citadel mound: find-spot of inscribed seal from the corner of retaining wall on the east (view from the east)

the platform, and it was he who made the momentous discovery.[49] He found two inscribed seals, one of which was a complete specimen, while the other was broken. There is some confusion about what was inscribed on them. Initially, Banerji thought they were inscribed with the figure of a bull statant; he subsequently said the figure was a one-horned quadruped.[50] One had been found on 'the staircase on the river side' while the other was discovered in a drain at the same place. Later, a third specimen was discovered north-east of the stupa site.[51]

This was an unexpected and amazing category of artefacts which, in fact, came to be described by Banerji as the 'most important discovery of the season'.[52] They were indeed incredible finds because, before this, such seals had only been known to have turned up at one other place in India—the site of Harappa.[53] Banerji had certainly read about them in the newly published *Cambridge History of India*, where photographs of two of the Harappa seals were published. That ruined city, as he knew, was nowhere in the vicinity of the ruins where he was. Harappa was several hundred miles to the north-east of Mohenjodaro.

Unlike at Harappa, here was a Buddhist stupa with an underbelly that contained seals with unknown pictograms. At the very least, this was an unusual archaeological juxtaposition. It must have made Banerji wonder whether the large accumulation of ruins at site No. 1 represented the debris of successive ages, especially since the superimposition of structures must have been clearly visible after the clearance. As the excavations proceeded, successive walls and buildings began to turn up with increasing rapidity. It is unlikely that they fell into a coherent pattern immediately, but by the end of the field season the necessity of making sense of them must have been urgent and obvious.

It is to Banerji's credit that he did try to date them with reference to the remains of whatever coins and inscriptions he found, even though several of his ideas have turned out incorrect. He believed that at site No. 1 there were buildings that belonged to four different periods.[54] The topmost phase, associated with Kushana coins, was made up of the crowning stupa and the latest walls of a quadrangle that surrounded the courtyard where it had been built. The quadrangle, incidentally, was constructed on 'the top of a high artificial tower of burnt bricks', which was forty feet higher than the old river bed in its vicinity.[55] The walls of the third phase were associated with uninscribed round coins, while below them were found walls of a second period, along with which thousands of thick oblong coins, of the type associated with Taxila, were found. However, it was the first or earliest period that was the most crucial. Below a thick layer of ash (over which the platform mentioned above was built), a pavement was found which was associated with four thick oblong copper pieces (called 'coins' by Banerji). These were engraved with pictograms of the same type as those on the seals. Also, the entire area of the site was apparently covered with funeral urns of various sizes and shapes.

But there are other elements about this first excavation that are less comprehensible. For one thing, if at site No. 1, Banerji had clearly detected different layers of buildings in which the bottommost one had turned up material that—as we saw at Harappa—was pre-Mauryan, a natural reaction ought to have been for Banerji to correspond with or contact Daya Ram Sahni, who had excavated there in 1921. There is nothing to show that Banerji attempted to get in touch with Sahni. In fact, as will soon be evident, he did not refer at any point to the pattern of cultural remains that had turned up in Sahni's excavations at Harappa.

Again, professional excavations generally record, with some precision, the buried ghosts of past cultures that come tumbling out during such digs. Here, what seems inexplicable is why, as a trained archaeologist, Banerji did not pay close attention to such documentation. None of his reports mention the sizes of trenches that were dug, nor the dimensions of the platforms, rooms, verandahs, cross walls, and other architectural features that had turned up. By any standards, this was sloppy documentation; and certainly, it compares poorly with Sahni's report on Harappa. The latter, as we saw, contained lists of objects, measurements of buildings, sizes of bricks, and many such details pertaining to Sahni's excavations there.

What appears equally surprising in relation to Banerji is that the portable finds are not described with reference to the four periods of occupation that he appears to have detected. So, for instance, flint scrapers, cores, and bouchers are mentioned in the same breath as pieces of small images and white marble umbrellas.[56] Similarly, in his description of the second shrine marked by ruins of a stupa and monastery, Banerji had no compunction in noting the presence of flint scrapers and cores along with coins of Vasudeva. Even if stone tools had been found with coins of the early centuries AD, this was most obviously a 'deviant' pattern that required some explanation. None was forthcoming.

In trying to grapple with Banerji's dig at Mohenjodaro we have therefore come a long way. Questions have arisen about why he failed to mention unusual artefacts such as flints and small-sized bricks. Answers to these are necessarily speculative, but they have been considered here because there is so much that is unclear about Banerji's fateful first excavation.

Yet what is clear is that Banerji had retrieved from the ruins of Mohenjodaro—even if his techniques seem amateurish and his method of recording deficient—a quite remarkable treasure. He had found and recognized inscribed seals of the Harappa type. This would later become the reason why, in the story of the discovery of the Indus civilization, he would always be considered an important protagonist.

For the moment, though, Banerji decided that it was time to

touch base with Marshall and send him word of his finds. The field season was nearing its end and so, in March 1923, he wrote from Mohenjodaro to John Marshall at Taxila the very letter with which we began our tryst with Rakhaldas Banerji. In that letter, Banerji asked Marshall for his advice regarding certain finds just made at Mohenjodaro.

In this letter Banerji first drew Marshall's attention to certain coin specimens ('personally I have not come across any similar specimens anywhere').[57] There was a round coin with a king/god seated on an altar, throwing incense on a smaller altar, with a pillar surmounted by a wheel to the right of it. The reverse showed a lion statant. Banerji thought the specimen an Indo-Greek coin. The second type, of which a large number was found, was square and cast with punch marks on it. On one side it had a fire altar. Only towards the latter part of the letter did Banerji draw Marshall's attention to the three inscribed seals that he had found. As he put it, 'At this time I should bring to your notice that three different seals bearing the bull statant with a standard in front have been discovered.'[58] These were identical, as he noted, to the Cunningham Harappa seals. Banerji mentioned that he would send impressions of the seals to Marshall and asked him to suggest any other scholar to whom the same impressions might be sent. Interestingly, there is no query about the flint implements that he had discovered, surely a surprising omission which lends added credence to the view that Banerji was retrospectively 'wise', for he later presented them as crucial clues for understanding the chronology of Mohenjodaro. Nor does Banerji's letter to Marshall reveal any sign of knowledge that Harappa had been recently excavated by one of his colleagues in the Archaeological Survey. The tone of Banerji's letter is quite tentative, even though—as we can now see—it was conveying a piece of news that was sensational.

Given the Marshall–Banerji equation, the latter may have been apprehensive but Marshall was full of warm praise and enthusiasm. This is what he said:

> I am immensely interested in your discovery of the Harappa seals at Mohenjo daro and I shall look very eagerly forward to hearing more about them when I come to Bombay. If you can establish the date and give any indication of the cultural connexion of the people who produced these seals, you will achieve a great thing. It may be that the site at Mohenjo daro is smaller and in better preservation than the one at Harappa. In any case it will be well worth while following up your excavations. What I specially want to know is whether these seals were found in association with any of the coins or in circumstances which give an indication as to their age. At Harappa Mr Daya Ram came to the conclusion that they were pre-Mauryan. I wonder if this conclusion is borne out by your finds at Mohenjo daro.[59]

As is obvious, Marshall's reply communicated to Banerji a strong sense of the importance of his discovery. The need for establishing the date of the seals and the cultural character of those who had crafted them, was crucial and would constitute a major step forward.

By what methods could Banerji's discoveries at Mohenjodaro be dated? In the 1920s, and for many years after, methods dependent on scientific systems of measurement—which provide absolute calendrical dates of the kind that we are familiar with today— simply did not exist. These were developed over World War II, when radioactive clocks, based on the principle of radioactive decay, first came to be deployed for archaeological dating—by Willard Libby, a chemist who, during that war, had formed part of a scientific team studying cosmic radiation.[60]

The means available to Marshall and his predecessors for chronologically organizing archaeological finds of the kind at Mohenjodaro were established and in vogue since the nineteenth century and involved a system of cross-dating. An example of this is discernible in the work of the legendary archaeologist Flinders Petrie at Tell el Amarna in Egypt where he discovered pottery that he recognized to be of Aegean origin. This provided Petrie with a broad chronology for his own find.[61] Similarly, if the seals of Mohenjodaro or the writing on them could be demonstrated as being present in some well-dated context in Asia, Africa, or Europe, their chronology could be fixed with a fair degree of certainty. Several of those ancient Old World contexts were also dated by other historical methods that were—and still are—fairly well accepted. Egyptian chronology, for instance, was constructed reasonably well by working backwards from the conquest of Egypt by Alexander the Great in 332 BC, with further refinement being provided, quite independently, by certain astronomical events mentioned in Egyptian sources.

A further way of ascertaining the age of the Mohenjodaro material would have been to compare them with artefacts from archaeological contexts at other Indian sites. If such an exercise demonstrated that Mohenjodaro material was singularly different from anything that was known from the ancient historical cities of India—those that the Archaeological Survey had been excavating for years—then it would become possible to argue, as in the case of Harappa, that Mohenjodaro flourished in a period prior to their establishment. This is what Marshall meant when he wrote to Banerji that the Mohenjodaro remains could be quite early, for Daya Ram Sahni who had excavated at Harappa had found similar seals there. Sahni, as we saw, had considered the site pre-Mauryan.

On the question of Harappa, it comes to us as a considerable surprise that this was the first time Banerji appears to have learnt of Sahni's excavations there. The Archaeological Survey of India did not have a very large officer cadre. Therefore it is odd if it appears they all functioned within their own orbits, without any regular knowledge sharing and intellectual interaction. Thus, the news that Sahni had found seals at Harappa in contexts that appeared to be quite early came to Banerji, most surprisingly, not from his fellow officer but through Marshall.

In a matter of days, Marshall was to proceed on long leave to England. It is a measure of the importance that he attached to Banerji's finds that he made a noting on the office copy of his reply to Banerji, instructing that this reply be shown to the officer who would officiate for him.[62] D.B. Spooner was to be officiating director general, and when he saw Marshall's letter, his response was equally enthusiastic. In the middle of April 1923 he wrote to Banerji 'to congratulate you most cordially on your magnificent finds at Mohenjo-daro. To have proved so conclusively as you have already done the occurrence of the distinctively Harappan culture at another site is in itself a big thing, and I do hope that you will be able to continue the work and reap the splendid results which these first fruits promise.'[63]

Despite Spooner's hopes that he would continue his work there, Banerji knew that he would not be returning to Mohenjodaro. The orders provisionally confirming his transfer to the Eastern Circle had been passed some months earlier, and these would have been intimated to him during his sojourn at Mohenjodaro.[64] The transfer only remained to be implemented. The imperial government had also decided to withhold Banerji's next salary increment for a year.[65] They simultaneously instructed Marshall to exercise close control, after Banerji's transfer, over his travelling expenses.[66] Banerji's most recent bills, concerning the tonga-hire charges paid by him over the three months he had spent at Mohenjodaro, came under scrutiny.[67] He was asked by the Bombay government to explain why, instead of a tonga, the cheaper alternatives of *dak* runners, or a peon on bicycle, were not engaged to bring provisions, cash, and the daily post from Dokri!

Even diehard sceptics of the notions of fate and heavenly intervention might marvel at the uncanny timeliness of good fortune at Mohenjodaro for Banerji in his dark hour of disgrace. His finds had brought him recognition of a kind that was as unexpected as it was abiding. After this, no one outside the

Survey would recall the circumstances that had led to his banishment from the Western Circle.

Instead, Rakhaldas Banerji was remembered then, and is so remembered to this day—as the man who first ferreted out the marvels of Mohenjodaro.

# 11

# STRINGING SCATTERED IDEAS

THE YEAR 1923 WAS, SOMEWHAT UNEXPECTEDLY, a relatively quiet one. It began, as we saw, in a remarkable way, but that beginning was not followed up. One would have expected a feverish flurry of confabulations among the officers of the department, or at least further visits and examinations to facilitate a better understanding of what had been unearthed at Mohenjodaro. Instead, the phlegmatic pace and pattern of work within the Archaeological Survey continued much as before.

If the dramatic discovery of Harappa-type seals at Mohenjodaro was the high point before Banerji's exit from the Western Circle, the excavations also inflicted a heavy personal toll on him. Banerji was a chronic diabetic. His condition had been diagnosed as early as 1912. In the months that he spent at Mohenjodaro in 1922–3, the piercingly cold winds, which frequently blow across the Larkana plains in winter, combined with the rigours of camp life to make his condition much worse. He developed carbuncular sores and by the middle of March he became so sick that he had to leave camp and return to Bombay. During his sojourn in Bombay he met Marshall, who was preparing to sail for England. Marshall was keen to see what the Mohenjodaro seals looked like, and after seeing casts of them both he and Banerji agreed that the script was a somewhat later development of the script on the seals from Harappa.[1]

In all likelihood, Marshall must have impressed upon Banerji the urgency of following up his amazing dig with a written record of his findings. There is a sense in Banerji's letters—those that he wrote in April and May 1923—that he was impatient to get on with writing his report, tabulating the finds, and comprehending the pattern and implications of what he had unearthed. In the middle of April he wrote to Spooner, asking for Marshall's address in England so that he could send him his report (still unwritten, of course) on the Mohenjodaro excavations.[2] Spooner, officiating for Marshall, was naturally keen to learn more about Banerji's finds. So, along with Marshall's address, he let it be known to Banerji that he would appreciate a carbon copy of what Banerji sent Marshall. Spooner was, in fact, 'most anxious to learn the details of such interesting work.'[3] But Banerji had written up nothing even till early May 1923 because of the breakdown in his health.[4] He was unable to finish his report before he left for Calcutta on medical leave. In Calcutta, he will have hoped to complete it, as also compile the list of coins he had found. These he had carried with him from Poona. The intense heat of a Calcutta summer, however, aggravated his carbuncles, and so Banerji moved in June 1923 to Darjeeling. The coins stayed in the original dispatch box in his home in Calcutta.[5] The excavated material remained carefully stacked away in the head office of the Western Circle in Poona, still within the original packing in which it had been brought from Mohenjodaro.

To those who are unfamiliar with how government departments worked, all this must appear curiously quixotic. A sensational caché had been discovered but remained in the shadows. Its discoverer was ill and away from both the site and the finds. The bulk of the excavated artefacts had been safely borne away to Poona because it was the usual practice of the

Survey to house them in the head office of the circle in whose jurisdiction the site lay. But the materials were neither studied nor even unpacked. The head of the Survey himself was far away, on long leave in England. And the man officiating in his place, even while excited about the Mohenjodaro finds, neither saw them for himself nor chose to get them compared with those that Daya Ram Sahni had dug out of Harappa in 1921. To any professional archaeologist today, this state of affairs would seem nothing short of amazing.

More than a year would elapse before the treasure from the two cities was sorted out and carefully compared. For the moment, let us first see what happened in the interregnum, especially in the mind of the officer whose excavating of Mohenjodaro had culminated in such an unexpected and exciting result.

---

Mohenjodaro may have broken Banerji's health, but during his long illness it remained very much on his mind. Some ideas about it had crystallized inside his head during the couple of months between his return from Sindh and departure for Calcutta.

To begin with, Banerji was now well aware that his discovery of the Mohenjodaro seals had proved that Harappa was not a unique site. On the contrary, these seals, it was clear, were signifiers of a culture that extended several hundred miles south-west of Montgomery district, where Harappa was located.[6] As for the seal symbols, he believed that there was 'enough evidence to prove that the characters from the seals are Hieroglyphics or Ideograms and not old Brahmi letters.'[7] By this what he meant was that the script was a kind of picture writing, the characters being pictorial representations of ideas to be conveyed. One of them, he wrote, 'was a circle with a duck in it.' We imagine that this must have been similar to what is now No. 82 in the sign list of the Indus script.[8] This, to him, indicated a lake teeming with waterfowl. He did not think that the hieroglyphs on the Harappan seals bore any resemblance or were in any way related to those of Egypt.

Alongside, very quickly, Banerji grafted on to the builders and inhabitants of this culture a racial paradigm of conquest and subjugation by one race over the other. He felt that the seals were used by 'Negroid people who were overthrown by the early Dravidians when they migrated from Mesopotamia to India.'[9] This group of Negroids, he thought, formed a highly cultured community since they also had their own system of coinage.

What was the basis of Banerji's surmise? It seems that he came to his conclusion on the basis of what he knew about the anthropology of Baluchistan, which lay to the west of Mohenjodaro. He believed, like many other scholars then, that in the barren Baluchi terrain there still survived relict pockets of ancient inhabitants who had once peopled different parts of north-west India. The Brahuis, for instance—according to Banerji—represented one such group. These, a confederacy of tribes that lived across a large part of Baluchistan, were believed by him to be the descendants of 'the Dravidian people who passed on their way to India at some remote period and whose Dravidian origin is betrayed by the sure affinity which the Brahui tongue bears to Tamil and Telegu.'[10] Marshall too, in his contribution to *The Cambridge History of India*, had mentioned some scholars surmising that Dravidian people had once dwelt in the highlands of Western Asia, who had come by way of Baluchistan to India, which was why a Dravidian language, Brahui, survived there.

Banerji had read Marshall's account closely: he would refer to it in several letters over the next few months, and he must have noticed that the ancient culture associated with the Dravidians at Baluchistan was the neolithic culture in India. But he obviously imagined that what he had found was to be connected to an even earlier people, of Negroid ancestry. Baluchistan, as he put it, had the remnants 'of a Negroid race who live mostly on dried fish as the historians of Alexander tell us. They are most probably the Icthyophagi of the Greek.'[11] His conjecture was that the seal makers of Mohenjodaro were these Negroid people.

This framework, which connected material evidence to various racial groups, had been implicit in European studies of ancient India from the very beginning of Indological research.[12] As Banerji's first forays show, Indians were not slow to take over these racial categories for the purpose of identifying cultural remains. Nor can this be regarded, on Banerji's part, as only a fleeting flirtation with this paradigm. Some of his later writings are equally preoccupied with dovetailing the early Indian past with different races. For instance, in a book that Banerji wrote (primarily for students) called *Prehistoric Ancient and Hindu India*, the Indus cities were once again refracted through the racial prism, which was, by any standards, wildly speculative, apart from being far from the truth. These cities were described by him in his chapter on 'The Races of India and their Languages'. There, though, Negroids were no longer the creators of an urban sphere or users of a hieroglyphic script. They had, instead, been demoted into being the producers of palaeolithic tools. Instead, it was now Dravidians who were credited with having created those cities: 'These cities were built by Dravidians, or proto-Dravidians.'[13] Other groups, according to Banerji, also became visible towards the end of the city period in the Indus region, such as the Alpine race with their 'round heads', and, perhaps, proto-Mongols. His opinion was that it was this Alpine 'round-headed' race which drove the Dravidians out of North India. In this, he differed with those proponents who believed that the 'long-headed' variety of Aryans were the culprits who exterminated the Indus Dravidians. In other respects, Banerji's scheme, within which racial stereotypes were imposed on historical evidence, remained much the same.

Banerji's early ideas were articulated in several letters that he exchanged with D.B. Spooner. So, one may ask: what did Spooner make of them?

First of all, Spooner was as fascinated by the script symbols on the Mohenjodaro seals as Banerji. However, he imagined that there were two different writing systems represented there rather than a unified one. The figure of a duck within a circle, for instance, which had struck Banerji, was according to Spooner different from the characters occurring on the other Mohenjodaro seals, as also on those from Harappa.[14] Again, it was Spooner who pointed out the possibility that the animals represented on the seals were not bulls but unicorns. 'But may I call your attention to one point?' Spooner wrote. 'You speak in your letter more than once of the *bull* device borne by these seals. If you reexamine them you will find, I think, firstly, that they have no hump (which is true also of the Harappa seals), and, secondly, that they have, not *two*, but only *one* horn. Would it not be better therefore to describe them as *unicorns* instead of bulls?' Today we know that the largest number of animal representations on seals from the Indus civilization are those of the so-called unicorn, and it is striking that Spooner had instantaneously recognized this representation.

The unicorn, though, represented a real species rather than a mythical type in Spooner's scheme of things. He told Banerji that if he was correct in his supposition about this being a representation of a unicorn, it was of special interest since the earliest known reference in classical literature occurred in the *Indica* of Ctesias, where a wild ass with a single horn on its forehead was mentioned as being peculiar to India. According to Spooner, Aristotle also spoke of the one-horned Indian ass, and Pliny mentioned not only the Indian ass but also a one-horned Indian ox. So, the Mohenjodaro seals might well illustrate the sources of these legends: 'If so they are likely to attract wide interest, for a good deal has been written on the subject of the unicorn whose first home seems to have been admittedly in India.'[15]

Spooner, though, was much less enthusiastic about Banerji's ascription of racial connections to the Mohenjodaro people. He drew Banerji's attention to the pitfalls of identifying race with language. In the case of the Brahui that Banerji had imagined as remnants of the Dravidian race, although their language had Dravidian affinities, the physical differences between them and the Dravidian groups were very marked. At the very least, Spooner found it difficult to imagine that they were the racial remnants of Dravidians who may have come from the Near East. Again, among other things, the fact that the Mohenjodaro people used hieroglyphics and had a 'system of coinage', according to him, militated against the possibility of their belonging to a period as remote as that of the hypothetical immigration of the Dravidians from Mesopotamia.[16] The fact that Banerji described what we today recognize to be copper tablets as 'coins', in fact, created considerable confusion. Spooner, for one, wanted to know the stratigraphic association of the coins and seals. As he put it, 'indeed if you have found a coin with the same sort of writing on it as the seals show, that fact alone seems to suggest that the culture represented by the latter is less ancient than one had hoped.'[17]

None of these ruminations appear to be pathbreaking or even particularly exciting. But, they are revealing because, more than anything else, they highlight the preconceptions that scholars bring to bear on the problems that they study. As we saw in the last chapter, Marshall had advised Banerji to see if he could establish any date or give an indication of the cultural connections of the people who produced the Mohenjodaro seals. Banerji obviously seems to have imagined that the best way of doing this was to find a place for the seal makers within the early spread of races. His archaeological investigations at

Mohenjodaro had revealed an unsuspected literate culture. Rather than considering the character of that culture in its totality, he gave priority to an exercise which involved pigeonholing it into a pre-conceived patchwork of race and language groups.

Simultaneously, as Banerji tried to make sense of Mohenjodaro, he felt with his customary panache that it was time to get some publicity. For some time now, he told Spooner, he was being pressed to give information about his discoveries but felt that he could not do this without permission. Spooner himself had no objection to this as long as the publication of details and photographs was reserved for the Archaeological Survey. Consequently, towards the end of June, the London *Times* published an article filed by their Bombay correspondent on the subject of Mohenjodaro. Interestingly, it appeared before Banerji had written up his own account of the excavations.

*The Times* article was entitled 'Ancient Cities of Sind'. It was accompanied by a map of the province with the location of Mohenjodaro clearly marked on it (Fig. 37). Its subtitle was 'Buddhist Shrine Excavated', this being its focus. This article constitutes the first publication on Mohenjodaro:

REMARKABLE FINDS

> Up to the present explorers of ancient ruins in the province of Sind have confined their attention to its delta, and none has attempted to explore the ruins in Upper Sind. The credit of being the first to excavate one of the ancient cities of Upper Sind belongs to Mr R.D. Banerji, of the Indian Archaeological Survey, details of whose explorations during the winter of 1922–3 are now made known.
>
> After examining all the different ancient sites in Upper and Lower Sind, Mr Banerji fixed upon the ruins of an ancient city, now known as Mohenji-daro, or Mohenjodhari, for excavation. These ruins lie some six miles from Dokri, a station on the Ruk–Kotri section of the North-Western Railway, and cover an area of more than two hundred acres. Mr Banerji selected the highest mound for excavation and the results have been extremely gratifying.

Fig. 37. Map of Mohenjodaro published in the London *Times* in 1923

This mound turned out to be the ruins of a Buddhist shrine. It was built on a high artificial platform on an island in an ancient bed of the river Indus. Like the architects of ancient Babylon, architects in Sind in the earlier centuries before and after Christ built their religious shrines on huge artificial platforms protected by retaining walls 40ft–50ft. in height, to save them from the ravaging effect of high floods to which the flat country of Sind was subject.

Mr Banerji excavated two more mounds containing the ruins of religious establishments or shrines built on islands in the ancient bed of the river Indus. These three mounds were built in the second century AD and consisted of high Buddhist 'stupas' or *tumuli*. In the centre of the first mound was a high stupa of sun-dried bricks built on an oblong platform of burnt bricks. Surrounding the central structure there was a series of rooms on all four sides. The structure of this mound was erected in the second century AD during the reign of the great Kushan Emperor Vasudeva I (AD 158–77), many of whose coins have been discovered separately as well as in large finds. The stupa of sun-dried bricks was hollow, and once contained a deposit of relics which has been ruthlessly destroyed by the Mahomedan zemindars of the neighbouring villages, who excavated the interior of the stupa a few decades ago with a view to find a buried treasure.

### AN ANCIENT SHRINE

This stupa was once decorated with fresco paintings in the manner of similar stupas discovered by Sir Aurel Stein at many places in Central Asia. Fragments of the fresco paintings show the use of indigenous Indian pigment which, in spite of exposure to the sun and rain of nearly seventeen centuries, have preserved their colours remarkably well. The fragments show the use of a deep blue as a background and deep indigo instead of real black. Floral decorations in white on a blue ground or in yellow on a ground of dark chocolate, and Buddhist mythological fragments showing the use of green, blue, yellow, red, white and black have been recovered from the ruins.

Under the platform of the stupa there is a layer of canes [*sic*] showing that some time in the first century AD an older shrine was burnt down most probably by the Scythian invaders of India, who ravished the North-Western Frontier for nearly two centuries about the time of the birth of Christ. This shrine of the first century AD was decorated with bas-relief in stucco, fragments of which have been recovered from sand beds in front of the shrine. One of the stucco heads represents a barbarian with a short pointed beard and a long conical cap. Large numbers of ancient coins were discovered in earthenware pots built under the pavements of the rooms which belong to the second century AD.

Some of these coins do not appear to have been discovered anywhere else in India. They represent the earliest copper currency of North-Western India and they differ from ancient copper coins discovered in other parts of India in being die-struck not punch-marked. The first group of coins also prove that in ancient Sind Buddhism flourished side by side with the ancient Persian religion, because on the coins are small images of Buddha seated or standing with a halo round his head as well as the oldest representations of a Fire-Altar in Asiatic coins. Fire-Altars have not been found in the coins of the Parthian dynasty of Persia, and their earliest appearance is on the coins of the Kushan Emperors of India. The first group of coins discovered at Mohenjodaro is much older in date than Kushan coins. The second group of coins consists of round pieces, thinner than the thick copper coins of the great Kushan Emperor. They also do not appear to have been discovered anywhere else in India up to this time. They contain the representation of the Indian god of war on one side and various deities on the other side.

## HIEROGLYPHICS OF A NEW TYPE

The third group of coins bear inscriptions in unknown characters, which have not been deciphered as yet. Mr Banerji maintains that these characters are hieroglyphics or ideograms, and not ancient Brahmi characters and he is supported by Dr D.B. Spooner, the Director-General of Archaeology in India. Three seals show the use of two different varieties of ideograms or hieroglyphics. Four or five other coins also discovered by him show the use of a variety of hieroglyphics which suggests that, unlike the ancient Egyptians, the people who used these hieroglyphics were cultured enough to possess a system of currency of their own.

This is the only recorded discovery of hieroglyphics of a new type in Asia, and as they are altogether different from Ancient Egyptian Hieroglyphics, they will form a new branch of ancient Oriental epigraphy. Another point of interest in these seals is the presence of a unicorn in their centre with a saddle on its back.

On another mound on the same island, Mr Banerji discovered another platform containing the ruins of another stupa, inside

> which were found nearly two hundred relic caskets of marble, all of which had been broken to pieces by treasure-seekers. At different places small glazed bricks neatly laid in the pavement were discovered. During these excavations no remains of the Mahomedan period were found. Even the small copper coins of the early Arab Governors of Sind which are numerous in the delta of Sind, were not to be found, proving that the ancient city, the ruins of which are now called Mohenjo-daro, was abandoned on account of the shifting of the river course about the third century AD and long before the Mahomedan conquest of Sind in the eighth century AD.[18]

The article has been reproduced in full because of its historiographic significance. It appeared a little less than three months after the end of the first season of excavations at Mohenjodaro. It captures quite tellingly for us what Banerji thought was worth highlighting in print about his discoveries. In his interactions with the press he must have waxed eloquent about the Buddhist stupa, something that he would do in his later writings as well. It is therefore not surprising that the report is dominated by the Buddhist stupa on the main mound, the subsidiary shrines on other mounds, their frescoes, and the coin series. But in spite of the press correspondent having highlighted such data, this is not what is most significant within this description of Mohenjodaro. The point that emerges quite strongly is that Banerji realized the main stupa stood on a forty to fifty foot high artificial platform with a retaining wall around it. This, as we now know, is one of the most striking architectural features of what is called the stupa mound. It certainly means that Banerji's field observations could be unusually sharp. Notwithstanding the confused character of what he subsequently wrote on Mohenjodaro, the fact that he noticed the presence of this platform reveals his skills as an archaeologist.

What is disappointing, though, is that the most important artefacts from Mohenjodaro—the seals and 'coins' in an unknown script—are hardly highlighted. They are relegated to the penultimate paragraphs. The little here written on them appears to be a combination of Banerji's and Spooner's views. The unicorn element on the seals and the possibility of two different varieties of ideograms being used had, as we saw, been pointed out by Spooner. Most amazingly, the fact that the Mohenjodaro seals were similar to those found at Harappa appears to have gone unnoticed: in fact Harappa is not mentioned at all. Again, and equally strangely, the stone tools of Mohenjodaro that Banerji had found do not figure in the article. This silence seems so odd because, subsequently, Banerji made it a point to specially mention the flints that he had found, as also the fact that they had been pivotal in making him realize the antiquity of Mohenjodaro.

It is possible that since that article was a dispatch filed by a *Times* correspondent, the reporter left out bits of information that did not interest him. But it could equally be that Banerji did not succeed in focusing correctly or forcefully on what was truly pathbreaking about his dig. Either way, Mohenjodaro's debut into the public domain was undistinguished. The report does not seem to have stirred public interest in the new discoveries, nor did it capture scholarly imagination.

What the report did result in were two letters from Marshall, apparently unhappy about what had been reported. The first letter was addressed to *The Times* and appeared four days after the original story. It pointed out various errors in that story. First, it highlighted that Mohenjodaro was not unique in having yielded inscribed seals:

> Speaking of certain inscriptions on the seals found by Mr Banerji at Mohenjodaro, your Bombay Correspondent remarks that they constitute 'the only recorded discovery of hieroglyphics of a new type in Asia.' This is incorrect. Both the seals and the pictographic legends engraved upon them are similar in character to those from

> Harappa, in the Montgomery District of the Punjab, which have been known for at least half a century, and specimens of which have been published in Sir Alexander Cunningham's *Reports* and in the new 'Cambridge History of India'.[19]

He also drew attention to the recent excavations at Harappa:

> Excavations carried out last year by Mr Daya Ram Sahni on the Harappa site showed, in his opinion, that the seals found by him there belonged to some period before the third century BC. The lettering of these seals, however, though similar in character to that on the seals from Mohenjodaro, is of a distinctively earlier type.

Finally, Marshall suggested that what the correspondent had described as a unicorn-with-saddle could be the Indian humped bull in profile.

The second letter Marshall wrote was to the man officiating for him in India, namely to Spooner. Marshall here reiterated what he had said in his letter to *The Times*. He said he thought the *Times* story incorrect in reporting hieroglyphs of a 'new' type, as also in its representation of the unicorn on the seals.[20] Spooner, though, did not 'think the published account is so incorrect as it seems.'[21] For one, he believed that there were two different types of scripts on the seals, 'one the rectangular sort of thing you get on the Harappan seals, and the other a round or cursive type that seems perhaps pictographic, and is certainly quite new.'[22] Again, on the question of the unicorn representation, Spooner informed Marshall he agreed with the surmise in the *Times* article because he himself had pointed this out to Banerji. He believed Marshall would agree with this view, once he re-examined the cast.

None of this appears to have convinced Marshall. However, as he put it, he intended to 'discuss the question again when we foregather in India'.[23]

A conclave was not destined to discuss this or even meet in the immediate future. Marshall remained on leave till the third week of October 1923. After that, he proceeded from England, for two months on a deputation, to Palestine, Syria, and Egypt, to observe the character of archaeological work in progress there.

Since joining the department in India, this was probably the first time Marshall had got in personal touch with fellow workers in other areas, discussing with them the various problems that archaeologists in the Near East and India faced. Also, reading his very brief report on this journey in the annual report of the Survey, one gathers he was moving around with a sense that the history of the country he served was linked in many ways with those of the lands he was visiting:

> Archaeology is not a science to be pursued in a watertight compartment nor within the limits of any one country, least of all if that country be India. From first to last, the cultural history of India is intimately bound up with that of other lands and every new discovery serves to emphasize this interdependence more and more. To appreciate the significance of Indian antiquities without reference to those of other countries to the East and West is as impossible as it would be, let us say, to appreciate the hieratic art of China without some knowledge of the art from which it took its source in India.[24]

As we shall see, many dimensions of Mohenjodaro and Harappa, especially those pertaining to the period when they flourished, would eventually be solved only, as Marshall pointed out, when they were seen in relation to other lands.

But that was still several months away. For the moment, when Marshall returned to India, he had to confront a less pleasant task. As he took hold of the reins of the department from Spooner, he knew it once again as an organization which was coping with a much reduced financial outlay. The Inchcape Commission recommendations had come into effect in April 1923 and, as we saw, resulted in the budget of the Survey being sheared annually by about three lakh rupees. Owing to this, the Sanskrit scholarship for training in archaeology and the scholarship for training in archaeological chemistry had to be discontinued. The budgets for conservation work were similarly affected and, as Marshall admitted, it left little margin 'for anything except the bare maintenance of the more important national monuments.'[25] Most severe, though, were cutbacks in the funds for excavation: a pittance of about Rs 14,000 was allocated to these. At Taxila, for instance, all that could be accomplished was a partial clearing of some Buddhist monasteries and a few structures at the city site of Sirkap.

A decision had earlier been taken to excavate Mohenjodaro and Harappa in the winter season. But the money was so meagre that the work there was likely to be more in the nature of trial trenching. Mohenjodaro, as we shall see, was reduced into seeing a field season of just one month.

If any irony is today apparent in this situation, however, it is not only that sites in India as old as those in the Near East—of the kind that Marshall had just visited—were about to be excavated on shoe-string budgets. It is equally ironic that even when these Indian excavations were well under way, Marshall did not visit either Mohenjodaro or Harappa. Instead, within a short while after his return, he proceeded straight to Taxila to supervise the season's work there. In this, of course, he was merely following the routine to which he had religiously adhered since he began digging at Taxila. Beginning with 1913, he had, as we noticed, spent practically every spring and autumn season slowly and laboriously uncovering its magnificent monuments. At the same time Marshall well knew that, by any standards, the field season of 1923–4 was an unusual one. For even in the spring of 1923, Marshall had been quick to recognize the value of the Harappa-type seals that had emerged from Mohenjodaro. Now it was on his instructions that the two sites were being trenched—for the first time more or less simultaneously. Why did he then not break his routine to get a first-hand glimpse of the excavations? Surely, he must have been or should have been curious about what would emerge there.

Since Marshall's writings do not throw any light on this conundrum, all that can be conjectured is that while he was aware of the links between Mohenjodaro and Harappa, rather than visit the city sites themselves he preferred to wait till the end of the field season before making a full and thought-through assessment.

But even if Marshall was reluctant to physically fathom Mohenjodaro's mounds in person, Rakhaldas Banerji at least ensured that its mysterious relics remained within his mental horizons. Banerji was still unwell and continued to be on medical leave in Calcutta. But we can assume that, by early 1924, he was in much better health than before, because, beginning in the second week of March, he started a steady correspondence with Marshall concerning Mohenjodaro. It would in fact be truer to say he virtually bombarded Marshall with queries and clarifications. These concerned some of Marshall's writings; these were also concerned with previous discoveries in Baluchistan as Banerji tried to comprehend the possible congruences between them and Mohenjodaro; and there were in addition a host of other interrelated issues. An endless, frequently chaotic, outpouring of ideas is encountered in Banerji's letters. But along with the chaos there is an interesting mixture of insight and intuition.

Since the time that he began feeling better, Banerji had been hard at work searching out cultural parallels for Mohenjodaro. He tried to do this by following up two kinds of leads. There was, on the one hand, a range of publications that he pored over, mainly those concerned with the archaeology of north-west India. These ranged from the annual reports of the Archaeological Survey to the back issues of the Royal Asiatic Society's journal. On the other hand, he went back to his original training ground, the Indian Museum in Calcutta, this time to rummage through its substantial collection of old pottery from Baluchistan. These formed part of what Major Mockler had scoured from various Baluchi *tumuli* in the late nineteenth century. By early March Banerji had formulated some specific ideas about Mohenjodaro and felt confident enough to write to Marshall about them.

'Will you kindly help me with some information about the pre-historic pottery found in some tombs in Baluchistan which you described in your Annual Report Part II for the year 1904–5', wrote Banerji to the director general, who was then in Taxila.[26] The pottery to which he alluded had been found at Nal in 1903 by an assistant of Hughes Buller, the officer who, as we noticed much earlier, was in charge of the compilation of the Baluchistan gazetteers. This pottery, Banerji felt, was of the same species as discovered by him at Mohenjodaro. He also believed that ceramics of the same genre had been found earlier by Bellasis at Brahmanabad in Sindh and by Mockler at Surag, Gati, and Gwadar in Baluchistan. He called this a 'kind of pre-historic polychrome' and wanted photographs of the entire lot from Marshall so as to make a comparative assessment and provide a connected account of this ceramic type in his projected memoir on Mohenjodaro.

As we know today, Nal did contain relics of chalcolithic pottery and a culture that contributed to the background from which Mohenjodaro and other such cities emerged. Brahmanabad and the Baluchi sites of Mockler that Banerji mentioned, though, were all part of the historical period, and thus are entirely unrelated to Mohenjodaro. But at least Banerji was on the right track, in the sense that he recognized potsherds from Baluchistan would be a crucial archaeological tool for postulating common cultural links. This certainly appears a progression from his earlier attempts, wherein he had tried to squeeze his dramatic discovery into a racial framework.

Marshall seems to have become keenly interested in the connections being considered by Banerji. From Taxila he asked the latter to send him the photographs or specimens of the pottery from Mohenjodaro, as also those that had come from sites in Baluchistan—the ones Mockler had discovered. 'If you are correct in saying that the pottery from those sites is of the same species,' he wrote, 'it ought to lead to interesting results.'[27] But even before Marshall's reply had reached him, Banerji wrote off another letter, now with a query about some structures that Hughes Buller had described in Baluchistan. Buller, as we saw, had discovered all kinds of artefacts and structures in Marshall's early years. The ones that now interested Banerji were pre-modern dams, locally called 'gabarbands', on dried-up river courses, which Buller had noticed in 1903 and about which he had published an article in the Survey's annual report for that year.[28] Apparently, at the foot of one these dams, Buller had found pottery decorated with bichrome and polychrome painting. Although these had been described as belonging to the time of the Achaemenids, Banerji suggested they were probably prehistoric, belonging to the 'copper age'.[29] In other words he was implicitly, if not explicitly, expressing his belief that they were contemporaneous with Mohenjodaro. What Banerji wanted to know from Marshall was whether the Archaeological Survey had photographs of such dams. Simultaneously, Banerji was also trying to search out parallels with cultures outside the Indian subcontinent. Among other things, he felt 'convinced that the Baluchistan Sind pottery is a development of the neolithic pottery of Anau in Western Turkestan and bears a distinct connection with Cretan pottery of the middle Minoan period.'

Let us pause a moment to make sense of the nomenclature being used by Banerji. He uses the word 'prehistoric' to describe artefacts and structures that he considered as belonging to the same period as Mohenjodaro. This generally refers to a time before writing had been invented and used for communication ('prehistory' denoting all ages before written history). In India the geologist Robert Bruce Foote, who had in the second half of the nineteenth century made the study of stone tools and their contexts from Gujarat to Madras his life work, frequently used 'prehistory' and 'prehistoric' in this sense within his publications.[30] Some of Foote's publications on prehistory had appeared in the journal and proceedings of the Asiatic Society of Bengal, a series with which Banerji was familiar. Banerji could not have used prehistoric in precisely the sense used by Foote, since Mohenjodaro obviously represented a literate culture. This brings us to the other way in which the word 'prehistoric' had been used in archaeology. In this second sense, the word was used to describe sites and civilizations that had writing systems which were undeciphered, and which lay far beyond the chronological limits of the historical period.[31] So, the reason why Banerji described literate Mohenjodaro as prehistoric was because its writing could not be read or interpreted.

Coming back to Banerji's letters: what was the reaction of the recipient to whom these enthusiastic formulations were addressed? Marshall, as we know, had some experience of prehistoric sites in the Mediterranean, and with that knowledge at the back of his mind he advised restraint. He wrote to Banerji to say he was very sceptical about the connection which Banerji proposed between the Baluchistan pottery and Cretan pottery of the middle Minoan period on the one hand, and that of Western Turkestan on the other: 'I am personally very familiar with the Cretan pottery as well as with prehistoric wares in Palestine, Syria, etc., and with a great deal of Turkestan Ceramic ware as represented in the Stein collections . . . If you were familiar with the collections of the near East and southern Europe I am sure that you would tread very lightly in this difficult field.'[32] Nor was Marshall convinced about Banerji's proposed prehistoric date for the gabarbands of Baluchistan. As things stood, he believed that it was quite possible the dams were of prehistoric antiquity, but it was equally possible that they were of the medieval period; Marshall was inclined in favour of the latter.[33] On the question of Baluchistan, he also drew Banerji's attention to what he had learnt recently at the British Museum, which he had visited in 1923. Apparently, the British Museum had some pottery identical with the Baluchistan types, and that pottery had been found in Persia during the Great War. While he himself had not had an opportunity of examining it, Marshall promised to get further information on it from the museum.

But if Marshall advised caution, Banerji grew impatient. He wanted as soon as possible to lay all the material before Marshall and solve the riddle of Mohenjodaro. He urged the director general to permit him to come to Taxila: 'My Memoir on the excavations at Mohenjodaro is complete but I am unable to write the sections on pottery and the general culture of the period without consulting you. I hope you will kindly permit me to come to Taxila just now at my cost. I shall not disturb you for more than a day or two.'[34] Knowing how impetuous Banerji could be, an alarmed Marshall wired him to say that he would not have the time to discuss pottery at Taxila.[35] He was up to his eyes in work there and moreover, considering Banerji's delicate state of health, he felt the long journey from Calcutta to Taxila would be unwise. 'We must consider the pottery later on when a more convenient opportunity offers itself,' Marshall counselled.[36]

Banerji's enthusiasm remained undiminished. He spent much of April 1924 trying to ferret out further clues about the archaeology of the north-west. He sent an urgent plea to Marshall to search out the London address of Hughes Buller so that more information on Baluchistan could be had. As it turned out, however, his efforts did not meet with much success. Hughes Buller had no idea of the whereabouts of the photographic negatives of his article on the gabarbands—he mused they may have been kept in the Quetta Museum in Baluchistan. That was also where, he informed Banerji, the painted pottery that he had discovered was likely to have been stored.

Around the time Banerji was writing to Hughes Buller, there was more news from Mohenjodaro, where a four-week season of excavations had ended. Soon after the digging had concluded, Madho Sarup Vats sent a note to the director general recounting the major findings that had been made. Vats was now the archaeologist supervising the excavations, and in a few years he would become a major figure in the archaeology of Indus cities; first as the principal excavator of Harappa, later as the first to excavate a Harappan site in Gujarat (Fig. 38).

In mid 1924, though, Vats was a junior member of the archaeological establishment. An MA from the Punjab University, he had begun his career in the Patna Museum. In 1918 he was appointed there to prepare impressions of the inscriptions in Bihar and Orissa.[37] His association with the Survey began a little later, in March 1920 when he was awarded its Sanskrit scholarship, which was regularly extended till 1923. In that year the scholarship had to be discontinued, thanks to drastic pruning of the archaeological budget. Fortunately, there was soon to be an alternative opening for him in the Survey. When Rakhaldas Banerji proceeded on medical leave in the summer of 1923, the assistant superintendent of the Western Circle, G.C. Chandra, was the man appointed to officiate for Banerji. In place of Chandra, Vats was asked in early July 1923 to officiate—as assistant superintendent. During that year, Vats is likely to have been involved in various circle activities, such as the wide-ranging conservation that was the hallmark of the Western Circle. He also deciphered several newly discovered votive inscriptions from the *chaitya* cave at Karle.[38] But the excavations with which he was entrusted in Mohenjodaro must have made the winter season truly memorable for him. It was news concerning his month-long sojourn there that he now conveyed to Marshall.

Vats had chosen a mound for his excavation which lay to the north of the modern cart track at Mohenjodaro. His letter

Fig. 38. Madho Sarup Vats at Mohenjodaro

begins with a long description of the seven Harappan seals that his dig at that mound yielded.[39] The various symbols used on them, of the 'pictographic script, the ideographic nature of which it is now too late to mistake', were outlined and compared with those that Banerji had found at Mohenjodaro, as also with the Cunningham seals from Harappa. Interestingly, Vats believed that the seals were not used for affixation but functioned as amulets. For one thing, the round projection on the reverse side of the seals was too small to be held and pressed down. The material from which they were made, according to Vats, also was too friable and 'singularly inappropriate for the preparation of seals proper'. Moreover, several of the symbols that were used on the seals such as the fish and unicorn, lent additional support to the idea that they were used as amulets. About the unicorn, Vats wrote:

> Curious ideas are associated with unicorn viz. that cups prepared from his horn are supposed to be efficacious against poison; that when the animal drinks water from a pool and dips his horn into it, the water gets purified and sweetened; and the animal is supposed to represent the softening influence of love, which is sometimes represented by his becoming so tame as to surrender himself to a virgin. This is said to be the only means by which he could be caught as he is supposed to be peculiarly fierce, and fleet of foot. His fierceness gives a mythical background to his traditional rivalry with the lion. Thus the device of the unicorn conjures up an idea of charm, mystic efficacy or symbolism . . .

In suggesting the seals were like amulets, Vats anticipated the ideas of those archaeologists who, in more recent years, have argued for this. Several features of the Indus specimens that Vats noticed, as also the fact that they are found abraded only at the edges and not on the inside, has fuelled speculation that these were not used as seals (for making impressions on clay), but functioned either as amulets or as identifying devices.

Marshall may have mulled over these insights about the Mohenjodaro seals and the symbols on them. Most of all, he must have been both startled and enthused by what was conveyed in the last paragraph of Vats's letter. There, the possibility that Mohenjodaro existed prior to the time of the Mauryan dynasty was underlined, this being a chronology in line with what Sahni had suggested for Harappa. Most importantly, Vats pointed to the fact that the similarities that existed between the two sites extended beyond synchronous dates and seals. This was something that no excavator before Vats had highlighted.

> The presence of dull creamy-coloured flint scrapers, and the blocks from which they are chipped, together with the general absence of coinage, as also the negative evidence regarding iron, of which not a single bit was found, goes to show that the site is very old. Pottery, specially tiny vases, is more general than anything else on the site, and the shapes of some of them here, as at Harappa, are similar to those of the pre-historic pottery found in the Tinnevally [*sic*] District. Further, it would go a great deal to establish the cultural affinity of Mohenjo-Daro with Harappa and their lying in one and the same zone of influence when we remember that not only the size of bricks is the same—viz 11" x 5 ½ " x 2 ½" to 2 ¾"—but the essential bond between the so-called seals from the two places—the strongest and the most valuable link—as well as the crude caricaturing of terracotta figurines, earthen bangles, balls for slings etc. are found essentially to be of a kindred kind. The cumulative evidence of the finds shows that the site is probably pre-Mauryan, though in the absence of a dateable piece, and further and fuller exploration it would be difficult to assign them a definite or even an approximately accurate date at present.

For the first time, Marshall was confronted with a range of cultural congruences between the two sites. It was not just a question of having located similar seals; there were also identical bricks used in Harappa and Mohenjodaro; and there were clay bangles that were of the same type in both places, as well as 'kindred' terracotta art. It is to Vats's credit that he could outline all this with great clarity and insight. It is therefore also somewhat surprising that such similarities had not been highlighted by experienced archaeologists such as Sahni and Banerji in their communications and reports on Harappa and Mohenjodaro.

Marshall had neither seen the sites nor the material in any depth. But, that summer, Vats's letter forced him to break routine and begin coming to grips with the enigma of Mohenjodaro and Harappa. The indications of something unique had been steadily mounting. It was crystal clear now that he would himself have to understand the significance of what had been unearthed.

## 12

# ANNOUNCING THE DISCOVERY

IN THE SUMMER OF 1924 MARSHALL WAS EAGER TO confront the riddle that the relics of Mohenjodaro and Harappa had thrown up. But it would be a while before he could set sight on their artefacts. For the antiquities, along with the archaeologists who had unearthed them, resided in widely separated regions of India.

Harappa's antiquities were stacked at Lahore, the headquarters of the Northern Circle of the Archaeological Survey. Those from Mohenjodaro, as we saw, languished in the storerooms of Poona, the Western Circle headquarters. The officers too were spread out in several directions. Sahni's base was Lahore. Madho Sarup Vats lived in Poona. Banerji was recovering his health in Calcutta (he would shortly take over as superintendent of the Eastern Circle). Marshall had moved up to the cooler climes of Simla.

Marshall naturally reckoned that the only way in which he could come to grips with the situation was by simultaneously seeing and comparing what had been excavated out of Mohenjodaro and Harappa. He also needed to understand the plans of the excavations, the configuration of structures that they had revealed, and such related matters. These, he figured, could only be explained to him by those who had seen and surveyed them. In order to do this, it was necessary that they all congregate at one place. So he quickly decided to convene a meeting. The venue he chose was neither in the Western Circle nor in the Northern Circle: the conclave of archaeologists and artefacts would assemble at Simla.

Simla was the summer capital of the government where Marshall, like most important colonials, spent nearly every hot season: the director general's office (not just in summer, but all year) had been functioning from here since 1902. It had for many years been housed in the civil secretariat, located at Gorton Castle Estate. Dominating the pine-clad hills that stretched from the Mall to Viceregal Lodge, the old Gorton Castle had, by then, given way to a huge pile of new offices.[1] The building had originally been designed by Sir Swinton Jacob but apparently underwent considerable modification during the course of construction in order to accommodate all kinds of offices. One of these was the director general's office, located on the ground floor of this building.

By May 1924 Marshall had begun a major requisitioning exercise of masses of material and a few men to his office. Over the next few weeks, consignments of various kinds would reach Simla from Poona, Lahore, and Calcutta.[2] From Poona the bulk of the Mohenjodaro antiquities excavated by Banerji in 1922–3, in as many as sixteen boxes and insured for a thousand rupees, were sent by rail. In the latter part of June, Marshall would ask for further antiquities from Poona, those that had been more recently discovered by Vats at Mohenjodaro. Representative samples from Harappa followed a little later. These were brought from Lahore in person by Daya Ram Sahni. Sahni had been asked to come to Simla for a few days in June in order to discuss the Harappa finds with reference to those of Mohenjodaro and other sites. Additionally, from Calcutta, Marshall directed that Mockler's collection of Baluchistan pottery, the ceramics that Banerji had so frequently mentioned in his letters, be sent.

That collection had been under the care of the Indian Museum. Now, however, as it came to be packed, it was evident that its custodians had been rather careless. While more than 300 pieces had been counted and catalogued in the 1880s, scarcely 137 specimens had survived. Ramaprasad Chanda, the officer who looked after the archaeological section of the museum, tried his best to explain the circumstances under which the losses were sustained: 'The losses very probably occurred after the specimens had been originally withdrawn from exhibition. They must be partly due to the shifting of the collection from one place to another and partly to the natural disintegration of the pottery.'[3] The latter reason, that the pottery had naturally crumbled, was unlikely to have passed muster because, before being brought to Calcutta, it had survived for hundreds of years in Baluchistan. However, since all this had happened before Chanda's tenure, little was likely to be achieved by fixing blame. Whatever was now in the Indian Museum cabinets, he forwarded to Simla.

Even before Chanda could arrange to send the Mockler collection, the Mohenjodaro man, Rakhaldas Banerji, arrived in Simla from Calcutta towards the end of May.[4] He had travelled to the head office in part so that the question of the accounts of the Prince of Wales Museum, still pending from the time when he was actively serving as superintendent of the Western Circle, could be finally settled. Once that problem was out of the way, he was asked by Marshall to stay on, since Daya Ram Sahni was to join them around the middle of June.

While they awaited the arrival and unpacking of its antiquities, Marshall and Banerji sat down to scrutinize the drawings of Mohenjodaro.[5] Banerji had carried with him tracings of the plans of the excavations that he had undertaken in 1922–3. As we saw, he had begun by digging into the mound marked by a massive stupa (Site No. 1) and had, after this, excavated two other mounds near it—Site No. II which stood north-west of the Buddhist stupa, and Site No. III, on the north-eastern corner of the stupa. Marshall soon realized that the drawings were uncorrected and incomplete. Instructions were immediately issued for a draftsman to rectify them and to procure a fresh tracing of the excavation plan of Site No.1. In the next few days, many more lapses became manifest. Photographs of the excavations had not been sent and had to be asked for; there were unwritten reports which would have to be quickly prepared; and some excavation material, such as specimen bricks from the first season of excavations at Mohenjodaro, still remained to be dispatched.

By the middle of June, Sahni reached Simla with his haul from Harappa. He had returned that winter to Harappa, to extend the excavations that he first began there in 1920–1. The long trench that he had dug on Site F was expanded. It yielded several walls parallel to each other, one of which was about 80 feet in length. Mound AB was also trenched, and as many as seven successive layers of buildings were exposed, underlining that Harappa had remained inhabited for a very long time. Sahni's haul of antiquities was impressive—several seals, terracottas, painted pottery, and copper objects. He appears to have personally carried these artefacts as also those that he had earlier unearthed, to Simla.

The task of comparing and correlating the bulk of the collections of the two sites could now begin. This exercise, of focusing in a concentrated way on what was before them, constitutes something akin to what laboratory researchers do. Archaeologists generally describe this as an examination of archaeological evidence.

Archaeological parlance, though, cannot quite capture what must have been, for these three men—Marshall, Sahni, and Banerji—the most exciting archaeological examination of their lives. The excitement eludes us inasmuch as none of it was put down in their own words; none of the officers who formed part of that momentous conclave put down for posterity the drama of that moment. Still, if what was spread before them was as spectacular as we imagine it to be, the significance of what had been excavated out of the earth of the Indus region must have been immediately evident, and made blood race.

Mohenjodaro and Harappa stood separated from each other by several hundred kilometres. Yet the painted and plain pottery, chert knives and flakes, the seals with pictographic symbols, the stone beads and so much else from the two sites were strikingly similar. As they sifted through this material, the Survey's men will have immediately seen these cultural congruences. Till this day, Indus artefacts, whether they originate from Sindh or Punjab, appear to be impressively similar. At that point of time, this strong similarity was hardly comprehended.

*The only person to have until now articulated the presence of an overarching archaeological identity was Vats, as we saw, in his letter to Marshall.*

Surveying such similarities for himself, though, was for Marshall different from reading about them. Marshall would later remark: 'That the finds from the two sites belonged to the same stage of culture and approximately to the same age, and that they were totally distinct from anything previously known to us in India was at once evident.'[6]

He wrote this in his annual report of that year, in a series published by the Archaeological Survey in which Marshall's prose was measured and precise, as is the remark quoted above. At the same time, Marshall, more than anyone else, understood the enormity of what had emerged. For many years, in the pages of annual reports, he had summarized the work of the Survey as it sunk spade and shovel into sites spread across the subcontinent, searching out historical cities and stupas. More than once, Marshall had pondered over the possibility of finding antiquarian remains of an earlier age than that the Survey's excavations turned up. But he had never until now found firm archaeological proof for what he intuitively suspected.

Now, unexpectedly, his officers, Banerji and Sahni, had

reclaimed one such culture. They had reclaimed it from under the alluvium of the Indus, where it had been waiting, as it were, to script a new story. On examining its artefacts, Marshall realized that he was looking at the very archaeological proof that had long eluded his department. These objects, he could foresee, would result in pushing back the Indian past into what had hitherto seemed an inconceivably early era. Banerji was to point this out, some months later, when he talked about the Simla conclave and what followed it:

> The credit of pointing out the real importance of the objects discovered by me at Mohenjo-Daro and by Rai Bahadur Pandit Daya Ram Sahni at Harappa belongs to Sir John Marshall, the present head of the Department. The objects excavated by me at Mohenjo-Daro in 1922–3 had remained locked up in the godowns of Poona during my long illness.
>
> In May 1924 I went to Simla to discuss the finds with the head of our Department. When Sir John Marshall saw these finds he was the first to recognise their importance. I was thinking that I have come across the remains of an ancient civilization which had some distant connection with the pre-historic civilization of Crete. Sir John Marshall pointed out to me that the affinity of the new finds must be sought for somewhere nearer India. After discussing the question with me patiently Sir John Marshall was of the opinion that the new finds did not belong to the Mediterranean group of culture.[7]

Having recognized that Mohenjodaro and Harappa represented a singular culture, the immediate task ahead was to draw attention to their distinctive character. The herald of this discovery saga, the man who would pen the public announcement, would be Marshall himself.

There was a good reason for this. As director general of the organization under whose aegis the excavations had been undertaken, it was entirely in the order of things that Marshall should formally announce this epochal discovery.

After all, once the Indus excavations entered the public domain, it was Marshall who would be responsible for whatever followed from the announcement. So, he had to ensure that the first public pronouncement, one that would be read by lay readers and scholars alike, was crafted with care. He needed to accurately formulate the novelty and the wide-ranging implications of this discovery. Before this, Marshall had not put mind to matter in anything like the way now required of him; nor had the discoverers individually paused to understand that the presence of writing combined with the configuration of brick buildings actually added up to a highly sophisticated kind of culture, a culture better described as a city civilization. It is this aspect that must have emerged most strongly from the confabulations of the three officers at Simla. It would also form the crux of what Marshall would vividly evoke in his first account of the discoveries in the valley of the Indus.

But first, before turning to that account, let us linger to look at a singular and unnoticed detail about Marshall's manner of functioning. As he sat down to solder a splendid account on the cities of the Indus, Marshall did not explore at first hand the archaeological arena about which he was on the verge of offering such important information. To put it another way, he focused the 'first light on a long-forgotten civilization' without visiting the ruins which had yielded the road signs to it.[8] This looks, prima facie, startling, if not absurd.

Men before him had presided over the announcement of such momentous discoveries. But unlike him, they had invariably done so after they had visited and verified the original localities. About sixty years earlier, in Marshall's own country, two English scientists, John Evans and Joseph Prestwich, had sailed to France to see for themselves the gravel pits in the Somme river valley from where prehistoric axes and arrowheads had been unearthed by a Frenchman. It was only after this physical confirmation that Evans publicly corroborated a ground-breaking discovery relating to the prehistoric presence of humans and formulated conclusions about their remote antiquity.[9]

Marshall, on the other hand, mapped out the implications of the excavations at his head office, without having seen the sites. This speaks much for his unerring professional intuition, but all the same it appears astonishing in the context of his assignment. He was on the verge of announcing a discovery of a kind—as he himself put it—that had never before 'fallen to the lot of an Archaeologist in this country'.[10] Most explorers would have immediately sallied forth to see those ancient mounds, if for nothing else, for the pleasure of setting foot on the soil that had yielded such extraordinary finds. For those of the archaeological tribe who thrive on the sheer excitement of physically taking stock of sites and discoveries, the fact that Marshall remained unmoved in the face of such a seductive prospect seems not merely odd, but quite simply incredible!

True, it is possible that Marshall's reluctance to leave Simla was a consequence of the problems that clamoured for attention in his office. Unlike other executive heads of government departments, he only spent a few months there annually. The rest of the year he devoted to examining monuments, overseeing their conservation and excavating Taxila. Consequently, he was forced to spend the summer months clearing accumulated paperwork.

Some insight into Marshall's temperament may also help in better understanding his curiously odd approach to such a dramatic discovery. Actually, his distance from the Indus sites was in keeping with his archaeological style since the time he first came to India. A sense of this can be had if we briefly retrace our steps, going as far back as 1903. It was in that year that a compiler of British gazetteers, Hughes Buller, first informed the director general about the discovery of an unusual genre of pottery at Nal in Baluchistan. The mound that yielded those finds is one that we recognize today to be even older than those at Harappa and Mohenjodaro. In 1903 itself, Marshall's instinctive reaction was to consider the finds as being of an impressive antiquity, although much younger than what they later proved to be. He had then sought out analogies for the Nal ceramics in Mediterranean types of the late Mycenaean civilization, which, he pointed out, had never before been seen in India. However, Marshall himself never ventured to visit Nal. Instead, he asked for accurate coloured paintings of its ornamental vases to be made. These he carried with him to England in 1906, where he carefully, if rather unsuccessfully, compared them with the British Museum's repertoire of Mediterranean wares. In other words, Marshall was someone who often preferred to contemplate and follow up his intuitions on artefacts without being consumed by the normal archaeologist's desire to visit the place that had yielded them. A bit like Sherlock Holmes, he liked to use the mind's eye in isolation, away from the thick of the excitement.[11]

This was in fact to become his general mode of functioning over the years. In early 1905, at Sarnath, F.O. Oertel, a United Provinces public works department man, made an especially momentous discovery. He found an Ashokan pillar in fragments, as also its magnificent, excellently preserved crowning capital (surmounted by four lions and more than seven feet high). The news of this discovery was telegraphically communicated by Oertel to Marshall. Here too, while very impressed and excited by news of the Sarnath discoveries, Marshall does not seem to have visited it, neither then nor even later that year. Similar was his reaction when, as we saw, a pillared hall was unearthed at Pataliputra, in 1913. This hall was among the most spectacular structural remains relating to the time of the Mauryan empire. Certainly, Marshall shared the enthusiasm of D.B. Spooner, who had excavated it. But for him the immediate task ahead was to push Ratan Tata, who had expressed a desire to finance an excavation, towards becoming the chief patron of Pataliputra from this point onwards. In this, he was almost immediately successful. As before, though, we don't see him instantly journeying across to Patna to share in the thrill of what was being unearthed there.

But, of course, what had now been unearthed, as Marshall realized in 1924, was not an unknown site or a magnificent piece of sculpture. It was far more dramatic—the remains of a lost civilization whose cities—Mohenjodaro and Harappa—were neither described in ancient literature nor associated with historic kings and their lineages. This was clearly a discovery that had the potential of pushing back the antiquity of India's monumental past into previously unimagined vistas. Yet, even this, it seems, was not enough to rouse Marshall from his habitual disinclination to rush off and directly imbibe the flavour of new discoveries. The Indus cities thus remained unseen by the very man who would shortly tell the story of their ancient presence.

Marshall, in fact, would finally set eyes on the central sites of his discovered civilization in early 1925.

But all that came later. Now, in June 1924, after an examination of the Mohenjodaro and Harappa collections in the company of the men who had found them, Marshall began preparing an account of what they had unearthed. He had decided that this would be published in *The Illustrated London News*.

*The Illustrated London News* was one of the earliest graphic magazines of its time. It first appeared in May 1842 and soon came to enjoy a wide circulation as a consequence of a combination of excellent reporting accompanied by a large number of pictures. It put together stories on all kinds of topical events, ranging from wars and natural disasters to accounts of recently published books and archaeological discoveries. In the case of discoveries, several pieces in it were authored by the very archaeologists who had directed the work. Marshall's mentor, David Hogarth, had written an article in January 1914 about the civilization of the Hittites of Syria, which the excavations at Carchemish had revealed. By the end of 1913, funds for these excavations had been nearly exhausted, and Hogarth hoped to attract financial support by publicizing what had been achieved there. It was his good fortune that the same anonymous benefactor who first donated several thousand pounds for the excavations now decided to send a further donation.

Like many who had written for *The Illustrated London News*, Marshall too intended to compose a richly illustrated article on the civilization of the Indus—of the kind that was the hallmark of this magazine. His article would provide an evocative and emphatic account about the significance of the excavations of Mohenjodaro and Harappa. In sum, his officers had unexpectedly unearthed a series of strata, centuries older than the storeyed sites explored and excavated by the department to which he and they belonged. The cross-section of history contained in those strata augured the end of an era within which India's historical past had generally begun with the advent of the Mauryas. This first publication of the news, Marshall knew, would become a fundamental starting point for another kind of past, one more in tune with the hoary antiquity ascribed to India. More than anything else, Marshall hoped his pen would succeed in appropriately projecting the work that had given birth to a new beginning for India's ancient past.

Marshall opened his account with flair and imagination. His words impart a strong sense of occasion:

> Not often has it been given to archaeologists, as it was given to Schliemann at Tiryns and Mycenae, or to Stein in the deserts of Turkestan, to light upon the remains of a long-forgotten civilization. It looks, however, at this moment, as if we were on the threshold of such a discovery in the plains of the Indus.

> Up to the present our knowledge of Indian antiquities has carried us back hardly further than the third century before Christ. Of the long ages before the coming of the Greeks and the rise of the Maurya dynasty; of the birth and growth of civilization in the great river basins; of the cultural development of the races who one after another poured into the peninsula from the north and west—of these and other problems relating to that dim and remote past, archaeology has given us but the faintest glimmerings; for almost the only remains of those early times that have come down to us have been rough implements of the Stone and Copper Ages, groups of prehistoric graves in the south of the peninsula, and some rude cyclopean walls at Rajagriha in Bihar. On the other hand, from the third century BC onwards, we have, on the whole, a fairly clear idea of man's handiwork in general: of his religious and domestic architecture, of his formative arts, of his weapons and utensils, of his personal ornaments and his jewellery, his coins and gems, and of the scripts which he used in his writing. And whenever it happens that new antiquities come to light—no matter to what race or religion they may belong—it is invariably possible to assign them with confidence and within relatively narrow limits to their respective age or class.
>
> Now, however, there has unexpectedly been unearthed, in the south of the Panjab and in Sind, an entirely new class of objects which have nothing in common with those previously known to us, and which are unaccompanied by any data that might have helped to establish their age and origin.[12]

Marshall's narrative then began to build up the story of the civilization. To begin with, what did the sites of this 'long-forgotten civilization' look like to a modern observer? Even though there is no hint in the article that Marshall himself had never set eyes on either Mohenjodaro or Harappa, he did offer a description of the mounds, perhaps through inputs from his officers. His description is brief but suggests vast expanses of artificial mounds, accumulating to as much as 60 feet above the surrounding plains. The mounds were similar to the *tells* of the Near East, and these, he stated, were as abundant in the Indus plains as they were in Mesopotamia and the valley of the Nile. As in those lands, here too they were 'conspicuous along the banks of the old, dried-up beds of the main stream and its tributaries, not only in Sind, but in Bahawalpur State and in the Panjab'.

That he mentioned Bahawalpur in the same breath as Sindh and Punjab is interesting because, more than a decade earlier, he had happened to read about its antiquarian ruins in a long communication from a man called Malik Muhammad Din. At that stage, as we saw, Marshall had not thought it worthwhile to get a special report compiled on the mounds that Malik Muhammad had visited. But now, he remembered their presence, not least because Bahawalpur lay adjacent to both Sindh and Punjab. As in those areas, in Bahawalpur too ancient mounds lined the extinct river channels that once flowed across its entire length and beyond, towards Kutch and Sindh. In an important sense, Bahawalpur thus lay in the same geographical zone, one which in ancient times formed part of the Indus river system and its tributaries.

Marshall then moved on to elucidate the architectural remains of Mohenjodaro. Before burrowing into the oldest layers, he described what overlay them—the Buddhist stupa, other contemporaneous structures such as monastic remains and shrines, as also artefacts relating to the time of the Kushanas. But, he was quick to point out, valuable as they were, it was what lay beneath the Buddhist monuments that was truly epochal. These were extensive brick constructions, and among the elements that he highlighted were various halls, passages, an altar of small glazed bricks, and a possible 'shrine' structure 'with walls seven or eight feet thick, pierced by several conduits.' The conduits, 'in the opinion of the excavator, served for carrying off the lustral water when the shrine or image within it was washed.' Several photographs graphically illustrated the presence of such remains; photographs of brick walls below the stupa; of a small grave to 'hold a hunched body', and of the panorama of vast rolling mounds dominating the alluvial expanses on which they stood. All these must have left little doubt in the minds of readers of *The Illustrated London News* that Banerji's spade had unearthed a singular city.

The most sumptuous of the photographs, though, concerned the smaller antiquities. According to Marshall, their significance stemmed from the general identity of their appearance; but surprisingly, those at Harappa, whose brick ruins had suffered much depredation (as Sahni's work had revealed), were better preserved. The photographs, spread across two full pages, successfully captured the range and character of the objects (Figs 39–46). More than anything else,

Fig. 39. Seals from Harappa and Mohenjodaro, as they appeared in the *Illustrated London News*

Fig. 40. Seals from Harappa and Mohenjodaro, as they appeared in the *Illustrated London News*

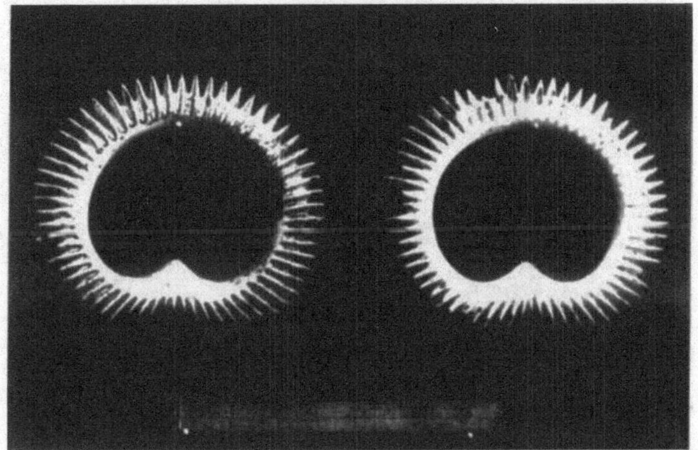

Fig. 41. Paste bangles from Harappa

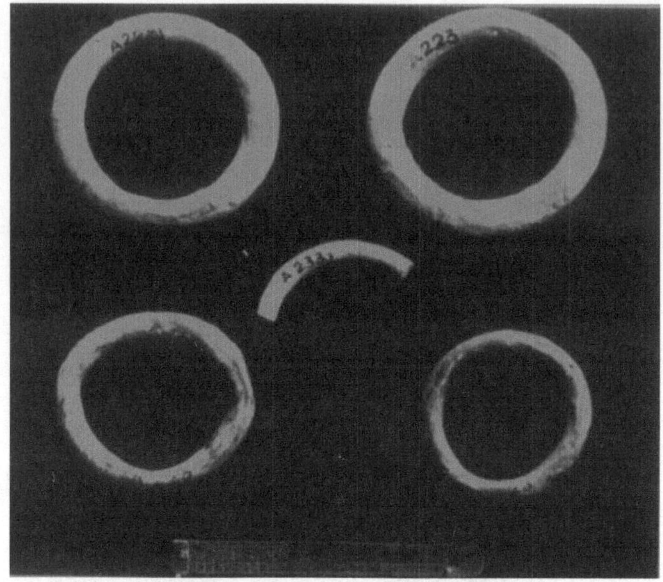

Fig. 42. Clay bangles from Harappa

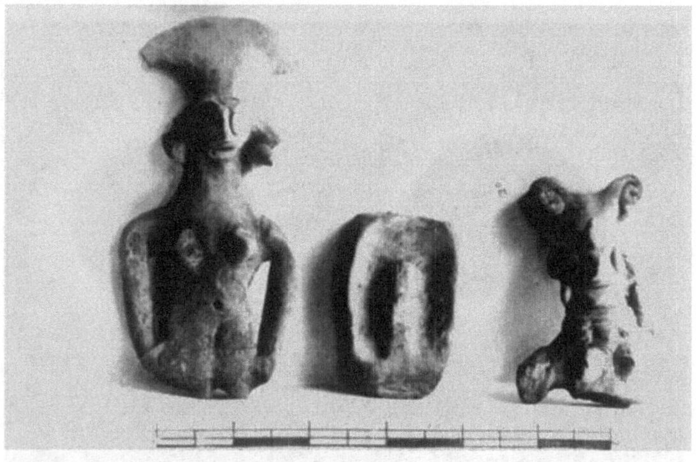

Fig. 43. Terracotta figurines from Harappa

Fig. 44. Terracotta toy carts from Harappa

Fig. 45. Pottery from Harappa

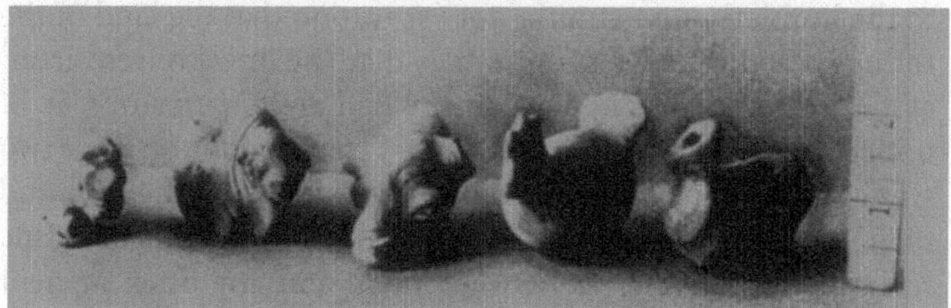

Fig. 46. Terracotta animals, birds, and other toys from Mohenjodaro

these allowed modern spectators to imagine the articles that the ancient people of the Indus used in their everyday lives; various sorts of jars, some that stored food and water, as also one that had served as a funerary urn; stone objects such as flints, several of which were used as knives; a black haematite pestle and rings; terracottas with elaborate head-dresses 'recalling the medieval fashions in Europe' and 'similar to some found at Patna, in Bihar'; an array of terracotta toy animals and birds 'made perhaps to amuse little prehistoric people'. Readers were given a glimpse of the spectacular steatite and stone seals (around nineteen of them), both square and rectangular in shape. The unicorns, the bulls, and the characters of 'an unknown form of picture-writing' glow against a dark background, beckoning those more accomplished in ancient scripts than Marshall to unravel their mystery. The editors of *The Illustrated London News* explained that, at the author's suggestion, they had published all the photographs of seals so 'that there may be a greater chance of any of our expert readers helping to elucidate the script.'

Marshall's attempt was to inject transparent clarity into what he wrote by simultaneously showcasing the discovery and articulating how partial and provisional the Survey's knowledge about it still was. The director general wisely realized that while Banerji and Sahni had stumbled upon a sensational discovery, neither they nor he had been able to unravel more than a fraction of its mysteries. So, in his account, if he drew attention to the limitless opportunities for excavation that the land of the Indus presented, he also admitted that the 'meagre resources' at the disposal of his department had only 'permitted it to undertake little more than preliminary trial-digging on these two sites'. Again, even as he offered his observations on the seals and their 'strange pictographs', he alluded to the absence of any resemblance whatsoever between them and any other ancient Indian alphabet. Possibly influenced by Banerji's opinion, Marshall noted that the seal symbols did 'bear a certain general affinity to pictographs of the Mycenaean age in the Mediterranean area'. But in the same breath he acknowledged that he could not point to 'any of the symbols as being actually identical'. The age to which the cities of the Indus belonged was equally uncertain, and, as he later put it, he hoped that 'through the medium of a widely read journal' he 'might succeed in getting some light thrown on their age and character by archaeologists in other countries'. This would happen, as we shall shortly see, almost immediately.

When Marshall penned his account, he offered no clear answer as to the age of the cities, only possibilities:

> all that can be said at present is that the period during which this culture flourished in the Indus valley must have extended over many centuries, and that it came to an end before the rise of the Maurya power in the third century BC. So much may be inferred, on the one hand, from the many successive strata of habitation, particularly on the Harappa site; on the other, from the presence of copper weapons, and the total absence of any iron on either site, as well as from the fact that none of the objects, except the bricks and a few toy terracottas, can be paralleled among the known antiquities of the Mauryan or subsequent epochs.

To put it another way, while this was a chalcolithic (using copper and stone) civilization that had collapsed before the third century BC, the era to which its beginnings could be traced remained uncertain. The caption which framed the photograph of the mounds of Mohenjodaro also underlined the absence of a firm datum. It said that Mohenjodaro's remains 'are older than anything known in India . . . dating probably between 1000 and 400 BC'.

Equally nebulous were the connections of Harappa and Mohenjodaro with other ancient cultures of the West. Marshall thought it 'possible, though unlikely, that this civilization of the Indus valley was an intrusive civilization emanating from further West.' He did not, however, forget to draw attention to the opinions of those who were more inclined to such a view. His article, for instance, indicated Banerji's preference for a connection between the culture of the Indus with the Aegean culture of the eastern Mediterranean. At the same time, he indicated he remained unconvinced about this. The resemblances that Banerji believed were present in the painted ceramic wares and the pictographic epigraphs were, according to Marshall, 'at best, problematical, and in any case, too slight and intangible to warrant any inference being drawn as to a cultural connection between the two areas.'

Marshall's account ended by offering to readers of *The Illustrated London News* what he thought was a far more likely explanation for the origin of the cities than the one which invoked either the migrations of people or the movement of Western ideas into the subcontinent. The birth and character of the civilization, he believed, was entirely indigenous, a product of the environmental conditions of the river valley:

> this forgotten civilization, of which the excavations of Harappa and Mohenjo-Daro have now given us a first glimpse, was developed in the Indus valley itself, and just as distinctive of that region as the civilization of the Pharaohs was distinctive of the Nile. In the marvellous forward progress which mankind made during the Neolithic, Copper, and Bronze Ages, the great river tracts of the then inhabited parts of the world played a most important part; for it was in these tracts that conditions were found most favourable for supporting a dense and settled population—namely, fertility of the soil, an unfailing water supply, and easy communications; and it was, of course, among such large and settled populations that civilizations had the best chance of making progress. The debt which, in the early stages of its development, the human race owed to the Nile, to the Danube, to the Tigris, and to the Euphrates, is already known. But how much it owed to the Indus and the Ganges has yet to be determined. In the case of the Indus, it is probably true

> that successive migrations from outside had a useful effect, as they did in Mesopotamia and Egypt, in promoting the development of indigenous culture; but there is no reason to assume that the culture of this region was imported from other lands, or that its character was profoundly modified by outside influences.

While in retrospect one savours the slight tinge of nationalist sentiment with which Marshall articulated such a conclusion, one also realizes that at this stage he could only have sensed the civilizational autarky of the Indus region through uncommon intuition. Nothing was actually known about the background from which the ancient civilization of the Indus had emerged. Only hindsight and the work of archaeologists who, since then, have slowly unearthed the cultural mosaic which makes up this background, permit us to say that Marshall's conclusion was indeed correct.

But, apart from its unerring accuracy, what makes Marshall's conclusion exceptional is that it was articulated in an era when it was quite the fashion to see the stimulus of all high culture in ancient India as emanating from the West. Among the (in)famous proponents of this was Vincent Smith, who remained convinced that 'the best elements in the plastic, pictorial, numismatic and dramatic arts of ancient India are of foreign, chiefly Graeco-Roman origin.'[13] The fact that many such writings emanated from the pens of colonial officials who, in various capacities, manned the administration of the British Raj, is not fortuitous. Smith himself, we may recall, was an old India hand whose writings, like those of many of his Kiplingesque countrymen, by harping on the pivotal influence of ancient Western civilization on Indian culture, were offering, at least implicitly, ideological justification for the subjugation of India by conquerors from the West. In contrast, a colonial sahib in the shape of a Forsterian liberal was now announcing that India's most ancient culture was a product of its own soil.

# 13
# AN ASTONISHING AFTERMATH

WE DO NOT KNOW WHEN JOHN MARSHALL FINISHED polishing up his piece and how he chose to dispatch it to *The Illustrated London News*. What we do know is that, following its dispatch from Simla, the parcel took time to reach its destination. Several weeks elapsed as it sailed across to England and was ultimately typeset in the style characteristic of the newsmagazine. Masses of photographs had accompanied the piece and three full pages, it was decided, would be devoted to the most important of them. Eventually, Marshall's article announcing the discoveries at Harappa and Mohenjodaro appeared in *The Illustrated London News* on 20 September 1924.[1]

In England, scholarly readers reacted instantaneously. They reacted in a way that must have astonished and delighted Marshall. In fact, as we shall see, the first responses to the news of the discovery were almost as epochal as the announcement itself.

Among those who avidly scanned the story, especially the illustrations of the Indus seals that graced page 532 of the weekly, was Archibald Henry Sayce (1845–1933). The Reverend Sayce had been an accomplished linguist in his day. He had specialized in Carian and Hittite languages, in Assyrian philology, and in other aspects of West Asian philology and archaeology as well. Ordained in 1870, he had spent a large part of his life at Oxford, as a fellow, as a lecturer, and subsequently as Professor of Assyriology. Long sabbaticals he had devoted to working in various lands of the Near East where he copied and edited all kinds of epigraphs. Now, nearly eighty, his physical frailty perhaps prevented him going into the field. But he remained mentally agile and, in any case, publications pertaining to his field of specialization were not going to escape his attention. He immediately recognized the seals of Mohenjodaro and Harappa.

These, Sayce realized, were identical to those that had been found at the ancient royal city of Susa (in present-day Iran). While their symbols remained undeciphered, the Susa seals themselves had been securely dated. Surely, this meant that those that had emerged out of the earth of the Indus cities also belonged to the same age. This, in other words, would instantly dispel uncertainty about the period when the Indus civilization had flourished, which Marshall had so frankly acknowledged in his announcement.

Putting pen to paper, Sayce dashed off a note to *The Illustrated London News* which the newsmagazine published on 27 September.[2] This is what Sayce wrote:

> remarkable discoveries in the Panjab and Sind, of which Sir John Marshall has given an account in *The Illustrated London News*, September 20, are even more remarkable and startling than he supposes. The inscribed 'seals' or plaques found at Harappa and Mohenjo-Daro are practically identical with the Proto-Elamite 'tablettes de comptabilite' discovered by De Morgan at Susa. The form and size of the plaques are the same, the 'unicorns' are the same, and the pictographs and numerals are also the same. The identity is such that the 'seals' and tablets might have come from the same hand.

He pointed out that these dated to the third millennium BC, from the time of the Babylonian King Manistusu to that of the

Third Dynasty of Ur. 'It is evident, therefore', as he put it, 'that as far back as the third millennium BC, there was intercourse between Susa and North-West of India. The discovery opens up a new historical vista, and is likely to revolutionize our ideas of the age and origin of Indian civilization.'

Importantly, Sayce also mentioned publications where the Susa tablets with characters identical to the Indus seals had appeared. Evidently, the Archaeological Survey of India had been unaware of these. We now know that Indus or Indus-type seals had also occasionally turned up in Iraq. A round seal bearing an Indus bull, as also five Indus pictographs in the Louvre collection, had originally come from Lagash and had been published much before the Indus discoveries.[3] Marshall and his officers, it seems, had not looked for leads in the right direction. Although Banerji had examined the claims of prehistoric Crete as a possible area where Indus analogies could be sought, ancient Mesopotamia was not even considered, neither by him nor by Marshall. If they had looked for suitable analogies there, inevitably, links and affinities would have turned up. The speed with which Sayce had responded certainly suggests this. Thanks to him, the dates of the Indus civilization could now be pushed back from the first to the third millennium BC.

More was to follow. A week later two other scholars, C.J. Gadd (1893–1969) and Sidney Smith (1889–1979), elaborated on the similarities that Sayce had communicated.[4] Both scholars were specialists of Old World civilizations and associated with the Department of Egyptian and Assyrian Antiquities of the British Museum. They did not merely mention the various resemblances in the signs on the seals from Harappa with those at Susa and at Babylonian sites of an early period. They went further and graphically represented them in the form of two tables (Figs 47 and 48). There, the Indus and Sumerian signs were placed next to each other, along with the approximate date of use of each of the Sumerian symbols. What their

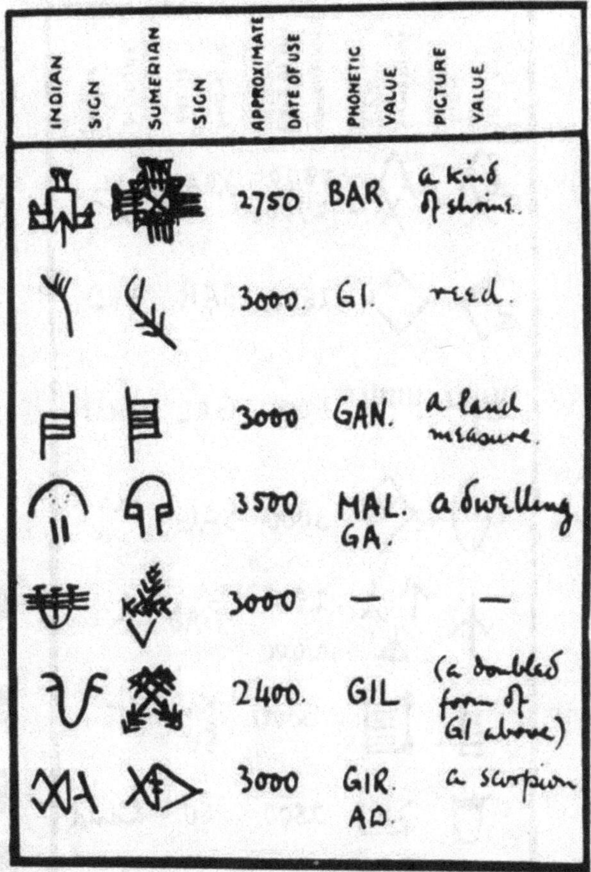

| INDIAN SIGN | SUMERIAN SIGN | APPROXIMATE DATE OF USE | PHONETIC VALUE | PICTURE VALUE |
|---|---|---|---|---|
| | | 2750 | BAR | a kind of shrine. |
| | | 3000. | GI. | reed. |
| | | 3000 | GAN. | a land measure. |
| | | 3500 | MAL. GA. | a dwelling |
| | | 3000 | — | — |
| | | 2400. | GIL | (a doubled form of GI above) |
| | | 3000 | GIR. AD. | a scorpion |

Fig. 47. Figures from Gadd and Smith's 1924 article, comparing Indus and Sumerian script signs

charts demonstrated was similar to what Sayce had suggested. The seal makers of the Indus had indeed been in close contact, over several centuries, with the Sumerians. This forms the most useful part of the Gadd and Smith communication.

The rest of it sought, with much less success, to extend the comparisons to other features of the Indus cities that Marshall

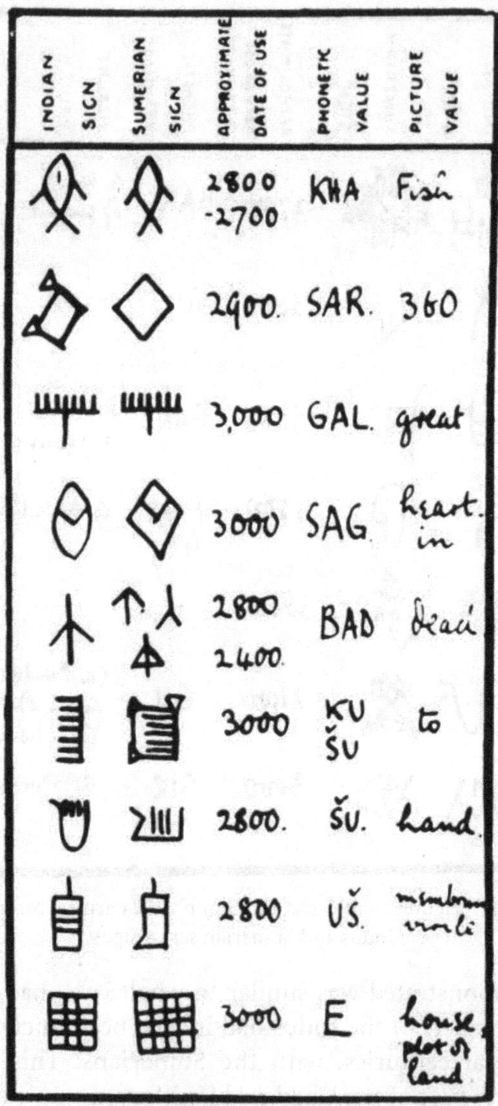


Fig. 48. Figures from Gadd and Smith's 1924 article, comparing Indus and Sumerian script signs

had described. The stone rings of Harappa, for example, came to be compared with Babylonian mace-heads which, the authors claimed, 'vary in size and weight exactly as the Indian objects are said to do, and are of exactly the same form'. Since the exact dimensions had not been specified in the announcement of 20 September, this could only be speculation. Similarly, the brick buildings, especially the one with ornamentation using glazed bricks, seemed to be very similar to the pictures of the excavations at Ur that had been previously published in *The Illustrated London News*. The miniature pottery found at Ur, too, was thought to strikingly resemble the miniature funeral wares from Mohenjodaro. It was these that Marshall must have had in mind when he described some of the analogies offered by Gadd and Smith as 'fanciful'.[5] At the same time, he also acknowledged that many of their analogies were correct: above all, the congruences in the detailed sign lists which the authors had offered. More than anything else, they confirmed that the inscribed antiquities of the Indus and, by extension, other artefacts that had been found in the same context were roughly contemporaneous with those of Mesopotamia and dated from the third or fourth millennium before Christ.

The information first provided by Sayce and later by Gadd and Smith surpassed everything that Marshall had hoped for when he announced the discoveries at Mohenjodaro and Harappa. He lost no time in drawing the attention of the Survey's officers to this turn of events. When he wrote to ask them if they had seen *The Illustrated London News* of 24 September, he also asked them to see those of 27 September and 4 October. His letter exudes a sense of wonder at how quickly all this had altered India's history. 'At one bound', he exulted, 'we have carried back the dateable antiquities of India from the third or fourth [century] BC to 3000–2500 BC and established a connexion with Sumeria and Elam which may revolutionize our knowledge of early India.'[6]

While Marshall was digesting the immensity of what had come to pass, another communication reached him—again about the presence of Indus seals in the Near East. The correspondent was E.J.H. Mackay (1880–1943). An archaeologist of some standing, Ernest John Henry Mackay had been trained by Flinders Petrie in Egypt and, since then, had excavated extensively across the Arabian Gulf and Iraq.[7] He sent a letter from Tell Ahaimir (Kish) in Iraq, where he was directing the work of an American expedition. In a few years, he would, at the initiative of Marshall, be brought over to assist in the excavations at Mohenjodaro. But now, he was writing to Marshall about a seal that the American team had found at Kish. The description that he gave of it showed it to be of the same genre as the Indus seals:

> It is made of steatite which was once glazed. It measures 30 by 30 mms and is 8 mms thick including a small boss at the back. There is a hole measuring 3 mms in diameter boxed through the boss to take a cord.
>
> The seal is incised with the figure of a long haired bull standing over what appears to be a table of offerings—or a pile of grain. Above the bull on the right are three signs, the first of which is a fish.[8]

This had been found in the foundation filling of a temple of Hammurabi's time (*c.* 1792–50 BC), but the seal itself was older than Hammurabi's reign.[9]

Mackay's letter arrived in late autumn, when Marshall was again ensconced at his favourite site, Taxila, working away as he usually did at that time of the year on the mounds of Bhir and Sirkap. By then, books on Sumerian, Elamite, and Babylonian antiquities had also reached him. These had been sent to Marshall, at his request, from the Central Archaeological Library in Simla. If he hadn't already begun, Mackay's letter must have ensured that he would now start carefully poring over them. Exploring the character of ancient Mesopotamia and its links with the Indus cities was an urgent new task, one that he knew very little about.

From Taxila Marshall poured out to colleagues and friends all kinds of observations about the 'the vista of marvels that this discovery had opened out', even as he pondered over and visualized the future course of action that he would now have to plan.[10]

In the letter that Marshall sent to his officers—to those who would oversee the next season of work—he issued instructions on how they should now proceed. Three months would be devoted to the excavations of Mohenjodaro, four months to Harappa, and three months to an exploration of Baluchistan. He asked his officers to carry out the excavations at Harappa and Mohenjodaro on as large a scale as was possible with the staff at their disposal. Equally, he impressed upon them the importance of what they were now about to undertake. 'When you have perused the articles in *The Illustrated London News*, there will be no need of further encouragement on my part to make you throw yourself zealously into this work', he predicted. 'You have an opportunity before you such as falls to the lot of few archaeologists and I am sure that you will do everything possible to take advantage of it.'[11]

This letter was also dispatched to the government epigraphist in Ootacamund, H. Krishna Sastri. Marshall had other kinds of expectations from him. He hoped that Sastri would forthwith examine the symbols on the inscribed seals and extend the conclusions of Gadd and Smith. Again, the task he set out for Sastri was combined with enthusiastic encouragement: 'I need not point out that any light that you may be able to throw on this or other problems connected with the new discovery will be of the greatest possible value to Indian archaeology.'[12]

Other letters were sent to friends and colleagues in Europe. 'Have you heard of the thrilling news of our discoveries in the Punjab (Harappa) and Sind (Mohenjodaro)?', Marshall wrote to J.Ph. Vogel in Leiden. Vogel was, as we know, his old friend and former colleague, the very man who had, on Marshall's instructions, sent Hirananda Sastri to survey Harappa in 1909. To him, Marshall expanded upon what the Survey had unearthed and about the parallels between the writing systems of Sumer and the Indus cities: 'If you or one of your co-workers in Leiden want a really fascinating subject to take up now, you might look into the possibility of a connexion between the Sumerian and proto-Dravidian languages.' Most importantly, he offered a new hypothesis about the character of the connections between the Near East and India, one which he had evidently formulated in the aftermath of his announcement: 'Taking all facts at present available into consideration it seems likely that India may prove to be the cradle of this Indo-Sumerian culture which in its turn gave birth to the culture of Babylonia and Assyria. *I cannot conceive of a discovery more likely to appeal to Indian national sentiment!*'[13] Again, one notices how characteristically uncolonial Marshall was in proclaiming that his department had unearthed a culture that was 'Indian' in its origin and character, and this at a point in time when the Gandhian national movement had gained momentum and antagonized most colonials against all things Indian.

This was a theme that Marshall would shortly enunciate in greater detail. Within a few days of writing to Vogel, he sent a press note from Taxila.[14] The purpose was to give publicity to the Indus remains. Bearing Marshall's signature, it was sent out to about twenty newspapers and newsmagazines in different parts of India: to *The Amrita Bazar Patrika* and *The Statesman* in Calcutta, *The Times of India* in Bombay, *The Leader* and *The Pioneer* in Allahabad, *The Hindu* in Madras, and *The Searchlight* in Patna. Unlike his announcement in *The Illustrated*

*London News*, this communication has remained unnoticed by those who have interested themselves in the story of the discovery of the Indus civilization. The piece, though, is worth pausing over, because through it Marshall directly addressed the Indian public. It thus provides a window into how he believed he should relate to them the new story of their past, which the Archaeological Survey of India had so recently scripted.

The opening paragraph of this piece, like the one that heralded the discovery in *The Illustrated London News*, imparts a strong sense of occasion. The contextual setting, though, is entirely different. Instead of comparing the discovery of the Indus with those that had been unearthed by explorers like Schliemann in the Mediterranean or Stein in Turkestan, Marshall chose to measure it in relation to the ideas that Indians themselves had long held about the antiquity of their civilization:

> Indians have always been justly proud of their age-old civilization and believing that this civilization was as ancient as any in Asia, they have long been hoping that archaeology would discover definite monumental evidence to justify their belief. This hope has now been fulfilled. Excluding such things as palaeolithic, Neolithic and copper age implements, the rough cyclopean walls of Rajagriha and certain other monuments, our knowledge of Indian antiquities has, upto the present taken us back no more than 2500 years. Now in a single bound we have doubled that period and found that five thousand years ago the people of Sind and Punjab were living in well made cities and were in possession of a relatively mature civilization with a high standard of art and craftsmanship and a developed system of writing.[15]

Various aspects of the architecture and material culture of the Indus civilization were then touched upon. This part of Marshall's discussion is very brief, but it does refer to brick-built houses and temples of massive proportions, well-constructed conduits covered with marble slabs, and to smaller antiquities ranging from a variety of potteries to dice, bangles of various kinds, and, above all, the engraved seals bearing inscriptions in 'an unknown pictographic script.' There was a somewhat lengthy discussion of the writing system in the latter part of the note where, among other things, the character of Sumerian pictographs and Chinese ideographs was dwelt upon, along with the uncertainty about whether the script that had just been discovered in India was used for its pictographic or phonetic value, or for a combination of the two.

Rather than offering a description of such artefacts and remains, it was their antiquity which formed the central theme of Marshall's piece. He will have reasoned that it was important to explain how uncertain he was about this question when he first wrote, and how, since then, much to his astonishment, the problem had been solved:

> Until the last few weeks the age of these remains was wrapped in obscurity. All that could be definitely established was that they were wholly unlike anything unearthed in India, and that they were anterior to the third century before Christ, since some of them were found beneath the strata of remains belonging to the Mauryan period, but how much anterior, it was impossible in the absence of synchronisms to say. One thing, however, seemed clear to me, that they represented a widespread culture which must have flourished for many centuries in the plains of the Indus. This fact I emphasized in an account of the discoveries which I published in *The Illustrated London News* of September 20 last. As a result of that article fresh and important light has now been thrown on the problem from Mesopotamia and there can be no longer any doubt that these Punjab and Sind antiquities are closely connected and approximately contemporary with Sumerian antiquities of Southern Mesopotamia dating from the 3rd or 4th millennium BC.

The question of the antiquity of the Indus discoveries also provided an entry point for discussing them in relation to what had been unearthed in Mesopotamia. Here, by juxtaposing the indigenous evolution of the Indus civilization with the intrusive character of the Sumerian, Marshall returned to the theme that he had first mentioned in his letter to Vogel. He enunciated the possibility of India being the fountainhead of Sumerian culture:

> The majority of the scholars hold that the Sumerians, who are on all hands admitted to be entirely distinct both linguistically and in other respects from all other races in the region, were an intrusive element in the population and various attempts have been made in recent years to derive them from one region or another outside and to the east of Mesopotamia. The fact that at Harappa and Mohenjo Daro, where the present materials were discovered, seals etc. of Sumerian type are found to lie near the surface of city sites covering very large areas widely separated and remote from the sea, with clear evidences of multiple strata lower down, proves that whatever the history of the Sumerians in Mesopotamia may have been, a culture closely akin to theirs must have been widely disseminated in the valley of the Indus and have undergone a development reaching back incalculable centuries on Indian soil. If therefore, these scholars are right who consider the Sumerians to have been an intrusive element in Mesopotamia, then the possibility is clearly suggested of India proving ultimately to be the cradle of their civilization which in its turn lay at the root of Babylonian, Assyrian and Western Asiatic culture generally.

Marshall did try to inject a measure of provisionality into this by stating that it was far too early at this stage to regard this as 'more than a reasonable hypothesis'. But he must have known that the mere statement of such links was likely to make Indians respond with a strong sense of pride.[16]

The last lines of Marshall's piece also aimed to elicit a popular response. Marshall expressed the hope that the explorations which had yielded such a rich archaeological harvest would be expanded: 'How desirable is the further exploration of the

Indus valley,' he declared, 'in the light of even the little that is known will be manifest to all those who are in any way interested in the origin and development of Indian civilisation or in the assessment of her full influence on the evolution of Asiatic culture.' Actually, this was Marshall's way of suggesting that popular interest could play a role in propelling field research. The government that funded his department had drastically reduced the budget of the Survey and, we may recall, Harappa and Mohenjodaro had been excavated with what can only be described as a pittance.

Marshall knew that the kind of explorations now required would not be possible without a revamp of the archaeological budget, which, in turn, was unlikely to happen if pressure was not generated. Publicizing the connection between the Indus discoveries and Indian sentiment was a useful weapon for creating such pressure. Considering the wider political situation, in which nationalist resentment was running strong, Marshall foresaw that funding would have to be found by the government to carry forward the discovery to its conclusion.

He was not disappointed. Whether any doubts about increasing the archaeological budget were expressed in the corridors of power remains unknown, but it soon became evident that a great deal would be provided by the government for archaeology. For the Archaeological Survey of India, the discovery of the Indus civilization could not have come at a more opportune moment. More than anything else, it ensured that the Survey's years in the cold would soon come to an end.

Much before the government loosened its purse strings, a strong current of interest in the discoveries had begun to spread in India. From Calcutta, Ramaprasad Chanda, the Survey archaeologist in charge of the archaeological section of the

Indian Museum (the man who had dispatched the Mockler collection to Marshall that summer), wrote to say that he was 'thrilled with delight' that 'at last Indian archaeology has been brought in line with the Archaeology of other ancient nations'. Chanda had also been handed over the Mohenjodaro collection of antiquities earlier that year so that he could arrange for their temporary display in the museum. These he exhibited in the northern part of the New Hall (the ground floor of the new wing of the Indian Museum), along with photographs that Banerji had provided of the different mounds of Mohenjodaro. The gallery soon began to attract many visitors. Prominent among them was the viceroy, Lord Lytton, who came in December to see for himself the antiquities that had created such ripples.[17] Their finer details were explained to the viceroy by none other than Banerji.

The treasures of Mohenjodaro and Harappa continued to make good press copy. Newspapers and magazines competed with each other in bringing out sequels to Marshall's note because, as one of them put it, 'Archaeological excavations in Sind and the Punjab have become a universal topic of discussion with the intelligentsia of India.'[18] Calcutta papers, undoubtedly, had the edge. The Mohenjodaro collections graced the city's museum and the Mohenjodaro man, Rakhaldas Banerji, was now the local lad made good and based in Calcutta.

So, for instance, within four days of publishing Marshall's note, *The Statesman* devoted two full pages of its Sunday edition to the Indus discoveries.[19] The article was interspersed with numerous pictures of seals while a full page was devoted to photographs of the mounds and brick structures of Mohenjodaro. Large parts of Marshall's *Illustrated London News* article and the responses to it were reproduced, as were the details of the history of exploration at Harappa. Naturally, given that this was a Calcutta paper, Mohenjodaro dominated the narrative. Several subsections were devoted to its different facets: the first excavations there, the 'island shrines' situated in old bed of the Indus river, the burial customs (of four different types), the offerings to the dead in the form of necropolitan pottery, and so much else. Both the language of the article and the details mentioned strongly indicate that Banerji made important inputs into its writing. Several of the newspaper subtitles replicate those that Banerji had earlier outlined to Marshall. It is likely that he provided a written note to the newspaper, and this became the nucleus of *The Statesman* article.

This was also the first publication to draw attention to how the potential significance of Mohenjodaro had dawned early on Banerji. He had found flint implements there, *The Statesman* wrote, which had made him realize its unique character. In fact, as we saw, Banerji had failed to draw attention to them in any communications that had emanated from his explorations. They had not figured in his letters, nor in the annual reports of the Western Circle, nor even in the article that had appeared in the London *Times.* The flint implements were discussed at length in Banerji's memoir on Mohenjodaro, a memoir which he only completed later, in 1926. So, in a sense, *The Statesman* article is important in making evident that Banerji's retrospective recognition of the significance of the flints can be dated to roughly the latter part of 1924. It is entirely possible that the significance of this class of artefacts dawned on him in the course of the Simla confabulation that summer. The 'Neolithic knives made of flint', were, he now thought, worth highlighting.

Banerji also provided other facts about his excursion in upper Sindh. Apparently, during that time, he had discovered as many as eighteen old beds of the Indus river between the Khirthar range and the present bed of the river on the east. And, there were extensive archaeological ruins as well: 'ruins of no fewer than twenty-seven large and fifty-three small towns. From the coins that can be picked up from the surface of the ruins Mr Banerji came to the conclusion that all of the cities and towns were deserted at the end of the second century AD.'

The nature of Banerji's survey and the ruins that he had seen during the course of it, incidentally, were little known. While Marshall may possibly have been generally aware of them, the discovery of dead river beds and cities was clearly unknown to the archaeologists of the Western Circle. The archaeologist Kasinath Narain Dikshit, who was now involved in overseeing the fieldwork that had just commenced at Mohenjodaro, was certainly surprised to learn about these via a newspaper report.

Dikshit had, like many of the men associated with the story of the Indus, begun his career as a Sanskrit scholar in the archaeological department more than ten years earlier (in 1912–13). Before he held the archaeological scholarship, he had studied at Deccan College, Poona, where he had won almost all the Sanskrit prizes at the university examination.[20] His first permanent appointment was in western India, when he was appointed curator of the Prince of Wales Museum, Bombay, in November 1914. In a couple of years he had moved from Bombay to Lucknow to hold charge of the Provincial Museum there, as its curator. Shortly after, his association with the Eastern Circle of the Archaeological Survey had begun when he held charge, initially temporarily (1918–19), and from 1920–1 as the officiating superintendent. In 1922–3, he was confirmed in that position but very soon, in the summer of 1924, as Banerji became superintendent of the Eastern Circle, Dikshit moved out to take charge of Banerji's old post—that of superintendent of the Western Circle. Eventually, Dikshit would go on, in 1937, to become director general of the Survey.

But in the winter of 1924 Dikshit was at Mohenjodaro, where he would spend the next few months supervising excavations. He had also been instructed by Marshall to undertake a survey of other archaeological sites in Sindh. 'There must be scores of such sites scattered along the present or old beds of the Indus', Marshall had informed Dikshit.[21] What he wanted him to do was discover sites (particularly large and important ones) where 'Sumerian' remains came near the surface, so that he could excavate them with the least possible expense. Now, for the first time, Dikshit realized that his predecessor at Mohenjodaro had undertaken some years ago a similar survey in Sindh. This was something that had evidently not been mentioned to him by Banerji, even though they had met several times in Calcutta. An irritated letter soon reached Marshall, in which Dikshit asked him to request Banerji to provide notes on the cities that he had surveyed, and this Marshall promptly did.[22] Behind the newfound fame that the Survey had just earned, old problems with the lack of information sharing, coordination, and communication among its officers remained.

*The Statesman* had provided fulsome praise and fine detail about the Indus discoveries. It soon became clear, however, that not everything that emanated from the Calcutta press was complimentary. A few weeks after *The Statesman* story, and taking its cue from it, another piece on the Archaeological Survey and the Indus cities appeared. Published on 30 December in the pages of another English daily, *The Amrita Bazar Patrika*, this took the form of a long editorial. *The Patrika* had originally started as a Bengali weekly, having been founded in 1868 as a kind of mouthpiece for popular discontent. Among the Calcutta papers, it was known for its patriotic slant. Such an undercurrent can be discerned in its editorial on the Indus discovery. Entitled 'A Word to the Archaeological Department', its purported aim was to give advice to that organization.[23] There was, undoubtedly, good counsel in the editorial—on the necessity of devoting all possible funds and energy for the systematic exploration of the Indus cities, as also about the possibility of bringing an expert Assyriologist to India to help in field operations. But in the garb of offering advice, it unleashed a scathing attack on many aspects of the Survey's manner of functioning, and principally against Marshall.

The editorial began on an innocuous note. Following Marshall's circular to the Indian media, *The Amrita Bazar Patrika* represented the Indus discoveries as furnishing monumental evidence that India was 'as ancient as any in Asia'. For this reason, it expressed full sympathy with the press campaign that had been launched to garner support for proper government funding of Indus sites:

> What Indian is there who will not feel proud that the civilisation of his country thus reaches up to the hoary age of the third or fourth millennium BC? He must therefore fully sympathise with the Archaeological Department that is now carrying on a vigorous campaign in the Press to win popular help and support for further excavations in the Indus Valley which at present seem limitless. We therefore stoutly maintain that the systematic excavation of these sites is not simply of provincial but of national importance and we strongly urge the Government of India to spare no money until the object is fully realized.

The compliments over, the *Patrika* proceeded to use the information provided in the Sunday issue of *The Statesman* to demonstrate that there was something 'rotten' in the Archaeological Survey. On the one hand it mocked the organization for triumphantly blowing its own trumpet on the discovery of the Indus civilization because, in fact, it suggested the credit for pointing out the real importance of the excavations did not belong to Survey officers but to 'antiquarians abroad'. *The Illustrated London News* article, it said, quite clearly showed the director general 'did not understand the importance of the discoveries when his article was published'. Their epochal significance was only pointed out by scholars like Sayce and later, Gadd and Smith of the British Museum. 'The finds were like pearls before the swine, and that they were pearls was first pointed out by the Assyriologist', said the *Patrika*. 'Why the Archaeological Department should therefore be so jubilant and give themselves airs when they should have been struck dumb with shame and dismay is more than we can understand.'

The editorial went on to denounce the Survey for having contributed to the destruction of Harappa.[24] As we saw, Harappa had only been brought within the purview of the Ancient Monuments Preservation Act in 1920, almost fifteen years after Marshall had first begun the process of acquisition: 'It seems that seals from Harappa were known to the Archaeological Department long before the recent excavations. But unfortunately the officers of the Department failing to grasp the real importance of these seals, allowed the neighbouring villagers and the railway contractors to destroy many priceless gems and carry away "thousands of cartloads of bricks" from the prehistoric mounds of Harappa.'

But this was only one instance of the Survey's apathy. Noting that the writer of *The Statesman* piece had alluded to the collection of Major Mockler, which had 'lain neglected for the last fifty-four years' in the Indian Museum, the *Patrika* asked—'why was no attempt made so long to understand their nature and significance'. This, the editorial believed, had been ignored because, till now, its value had not been realized. In an apparent dig at the publicity that the Survey was now seeking, it wondered what the organization would have done if they had actually understood its significance: 'Surely the Governor and the Viceroy would have been invited more than once to inspect these Baluchistan antiquities, if the Department had perceived their importance.'

On a more personal note, the change in the fortunes of Rakhaldas Banerji came in for scrutiny. It was well known that he was now in charge of the Eastern Circle of the Survey, and thus far from the excavation work at Mohenjodaro. The reasons for Banerji's transfer were not known to the *Patrika*, but the editor implied unfairness: 'Above all, those who have already done spade work on these sites should be allowed to join the party. What we find however to our great regret is that one of the officers had been transferred and there is no likelihood of his resuming the work.' In light of this unholy mess, the newspaper's advice was that, rather than push press campaigns, the Survey should put its house in order: 'If this is the condition of things prevalent in the Archaeological Department, it stands in need of speedy improvement, and we hope that they will soon show more of historical than histrionic activity and care more for the opinion of the scholarly world than for encomium from the Press.'

The *Patrika* editorial was as much an attack on Marshall as on the organization that he headed. If the archaeological department was portrayed as being in poor health, Marshall was represented as ignorant (he had not initially understood the importance of the Indus finds), mean-minded (he had removed Banerji from Mohenjodaro), and publicity-seeking (he cared more for propaganda than the proper functioning of the department he headed).

If some of the editorial's phrasing was overly harsh, some of its criticism was valid. Mounds like Harappa had been treated very tardily, as were some collections, such as the one bequeathed by Mockler to the Indian Museum. Yet it is equally legitimate for us to speculate on the possible hidden agenda of this editorial. For all its good advice, transparently intended as constructive criticism of the Survey, the intention may also have been to support the cause of Banerji who, the *Patrika* believed, had been unjustly transferred. Whichever way we look at it, there seems to have been a larger plan behind this editorial because, around the same time, similar statements appeared in the *Pausa* issue of the Bengali monthly *Prabasi*.

What Marshall's immediate reaction to the press attack on him would have been is difficult to predict, for it so happened that Rakhaldas Banerji, instead of immediately informing Marshall, decided to answer the accusers himself. That he did this is perhaps less strange than in keeping with his impetuous, extravagant, and erratic character, for he will certainly have known that no officer was permitted to write letters or communicate in any other way with the press on official matters without sanction from the government. Later, he gave two reasons for violating this code. First, he stated that his purpose was 'defending the credit of the department and controverting a number of lies' that had appeared in the *Patrika*, which were aimed at discrediting the head of his department in the eyes of the public.[25] Second, he maintained that the letter was meant to dispel any ideas that people may have had that he was the instigator of the *Patrika* article, for it attacked his transfer out of Mohenjodaro: 'This letter was written in order to remove the impression from the minds of the public that the article published in *The Amrita Bazar Patrika* of 30 December 1924 was written either by me or at my instigation because I have been purposely transferred from Poona to Calcutta so that Sir John Marshall might have all the credit of my discoveries at Mohenjo-Daro in 1922–3.'[26]

Rather than dwell on why Banerji dashed off this response, let us look at what he said. Banerji's letter tried to clarify a number of things.[27] To begin with, it said the credit for pointing out the importance of the discoveries of Harappa and Mohenjodaro belonged to Sir John Marshall. This part of his letter we mentioned earlier, and it certainly set the record straight about what had transpired at Simla. But what is more difficult to stomach about Banerji's letter is the part where he claimed that Marshall was aware of the Mesopotamian connections of the Indus discoveries even before Sayce, Gadd, and Smith had pointed them out. This, as we shall see, would soon be refuted by Marshall himself. To his credit, Banerji disabused the idea that he had been forced out of Mohenjodaro: 'I have given up the excavations of Mohenjo-Daro of my own free will and was not removed by Sir John Marshall to my present post.' We may recall that Banerji had, in the midst of the Prince of Wales accounts mess, asked for and obtained his transfer to the Eastern Circle.

Banerji's reply was followed by another letter—as a rejoinder to Banerji. Published under the name 'Fair Play', it sarcastically accused Banerji's response as representing 'a most grevious example of Boss Worship'.[28] That 'boss worship' was highly unusual in a man such as Banerji was also pointed out by this anonymous correspondent—'the slave mentality' 'does not seem quite genuine and natural to him'. The correspondent was evidently someone who had knowledge of Banerji's problems with Marshall. In all probability, 'Fair Play' was penned by someone who had close connections with the Archaeological Survey, for it said Banerji was compelled to give up the excavations of Mohenjodaro by 'some adverse circumstances of a confidential nature'.

The spat had now turned ugly. It was at this point that Marshall learnt of it. Furious with his subordinate for having kept him in the dark, he telegraphically ordered Banerji to send across all the relevant communications. Even before he set eyes on them, though, he had sent out a clarification to the letter signed 'Fair Play'. Marshall's letter tried, once and for all, to set the record straight on how the Sumerian connections were discovered:

> If Mr Banerji has credited me with having been aware of the cultural connections between the Indus Valley and Sumeria in the 3rd millennium BC, he has credited me with knowledge which I certainly did not possess. That I appreciated the surpassing value of the finds made at Mohenjodaro and Harappa need hardly be said. No Archaeologist could have failed to do so. But that was a very different matter from recognizing the direct connection between the early cultures of the Indus Valley and Mesopotamia. When I wrote my article of September 20 in *The Illustrated London News*, the riddle of our discoveries was still unsolved and it was largely in the hope of solving it with the help of archaeologists in other countries that I published that article. With the antiquities of Crete

> I was personally too familiar to believe in the Cretan affinities suggested by Mr Banerji; but just as certainly was I unaware of the affinities to be found in Mesopotamia. The information supplied by Professor Sayce and independently also by the Director of the American Expedition at Kish, surprised as much as it delighted me. It is quite true that the credit of solving this interesting riddle goes to the two archaeologists; but let it not be forgotten that it was our Indian excavators who made the discoveries at Harappa and Mohenjo Daro and it was due to their good spadework that the riddle was even propounded.[29]

Unlike Banerji, Marshall did not deploy the Indus discovery as a platform for claims which gave him more credit than he knew to be his due. The transparency of his statement and the temperate language in which it was couched seems to have brought this round of public and contentious exchanges to an end.

But the hurt that Marshall must have privately harboured remained and resurfaced time and again, every time he was requested by the government to get publicity for his work. Some six months later, he was asked to consider providing material to *The Times of India* by Sir Leslie Wilson, governor of the Bombay Presidency. Wilson had just had the pleasure of seeing some of the Mohenjodaro artefacts that Dikshit had unearthed that year. These were carried by Dikshit to the Government House in Mahabaleshwar, on Marshall's advice, since the Survey was hoping that the Bombay government would actively support their programme of work at Mohenjodaro. Wilson, in turn, had shown them to all members of his council and ministers in order to encourage them in 'giving every assistance, financial and otherwise, to Marshall in the work which was soon starting on a large scale.'[30] In this campaign of raising more money, he thought some publicity via Marshall in the *Times* would help their cause.

In his reply to the governor, Marshall wrote that while he agreed a certain measure of publicity was desirable, he said he had not found earlier responses to his efforts in that direction very encouraging: 'I contributed a couple of columns on this particular subject to the Indian press and was forthwith attacked by *The Amrita Bazar Patrika* for "trying to advertise." I was told that it would be much better to get on with the work and say less about it.'[31]

In short, reportage of the Indus discoveries in the press, within India and abroad, show that the aftermath was astonishing in more ways than one. The remains of a civilization whose existence Marshall had announced turned out to be thousands of years older than he had ever imagined. He must have expected the approval and accolades which followed the announcement. That these accolades would so quickly turn into trenchant attacks, though, was something that neither he nor anyone else could have foreseen.

# AFTERWORD: INAUGURATING A NEW ERA

THERE WAS, IN THE MEANWHILE, A FAR MORE pleasant task ahead for John Marshall. He would, in the early months of 1925, finally set sight on the Indus cities.

He went first to Harappa, then to Mohenjodaro. It was Mohenjodaro which appears to have taken his breath away. A trace of the excitement that must have seized him when he first gazed upon it is known to us in his own words. In the month of March, he replied to a letter that he had received from the widow of D.B. Spooner, his late deputy. Spooner had suddenly taken ill in early January and had passed away within a matter of weeks. Marshall must have felt his loss deeply, because he had been one of his most trusted officers, having officiated for him in all kinds of situations—when he needed to catch up with the backlog of writing that endlessly accumulated on his desk or when he was away on furlough in England. Spooner had been full of excitement at the sensational news that had reached the Survey in early 1923, when Mohenjodaro's mounds had yielded seals. To Mrs Spooner Marshall now described that 'far off spot in Sind' from where those seals had emerged. It was 'a most wonderful site far beyond my wildest expectation. There is no doubt whatever that we shall make a magnificent collection of antiquities here. East and West I have never seen any more promising spot for excavation.'[1]

The experience of seeing the Indus cities, one imagines, must for Marshall have been extraordinarily exhilarating. As he made his way across the mounds, he would have taken in a countryside that stretched to the horizon. Standing on their summits, he could not have failed to notice that the barren rolling mounds were actually higher than the 60 feet or so that he had mentioned as their height in *The Illustrated London News*. Various trenches he examined, whose digging his men were now supervising on a much larger scale than before. He had, at the start of excavations there, sent out guidelines on how to move forward. He had asked Dikshit at Mohenjodaro and Daya Ram Sahni at Harappa to carry out a network of trial trenches over the entirety of the sites. Simultaneously, he had wanted trial pits to be sunk down to virgin soil, so as to ascertain the strata that might exist far beneath the surface.[2] He will now have had a chance to assess how far the excavations were proceeding according to plan.

The diggings were actually not unfolding in quite the manner that Marshall wanted. The number of vertical pits was considerably smaller than he had hoped. The excavators, he felt, needed to go beyond the uppermost strata and 'make a definite effort to lay bare the lower levels.'[3] They did not appear to be doing this with the sense of purpose he expected. The spoil earth that was taken out of the trenches, which should have been piled well outside the limit of the sites, was apparently not being dumped with caution. On all these issues Marshall would soon send out instructions. From these directives, we can also surmise that the equipment had been inadequate for the archaeological fieldwork at hand. Marshall reminded them of the necessity of using apparatus such as dumpy levels, theodolites, levelling staves, and stands for the taking of vertical photographs. Special stress was laid on such things as the purchase of 'sufficient' knives and canvas bags in which to keep delicate pottery. Most importantly, the method of recording that was being followed in early 1925 must not have been thorough enough. What was being done we don't know, but evidently it was a system that needed far greater rigour.

So, one of the first things Marshall did was to firmly lay down the recording procedure to be followed henceforth. A daily journal of the excavation had to be maintained: 'A page of an ordinary foolscap sized diary for each day should ordinarily suffice for the purpose, but extra leaves may be inserted as occasion arises. The record in the diary should be kept in the handwriting of the Superintendent himself.' A daily photographic record, showing the progress of work, also had to be kept: 'He should not only photograph the diggings and the monuments excavated but he should also photograph each antiquity of importance as soon as possible after it has been taken out.' Finally, there was to be no more laxity in the matter of simultaneously preparing survey plans. They were to be brought up to date and countersigned by the superintendent in charge before the close of the season's work. The memory of Banerji's incomplete drawings of Mohenjodaro was still fresh in Marshall's mind; it was something that an excavation of this nature could ill afford.

This would no longer be a campaign of work where individual officers could, in whichever way they liked, organize their digs. Things were going to be different because, apart from anything else, these were excavations towards which all of India and large parts of the world were looking.

By this time Marshall had already begun initiating surveys which would help unearth new sites of the Indus civilization. Unlike any other archaeological campaign he had undertaken in India, he wanted this to be a combination of aerial and ground surveys. This was, admittedly, not the first attempt made in India to survey from the air. A Lieutenant (Later Colonel Sir) Charles Close had in the nineteenth century apparently produced indifferent pictures of Calcutta from an unmanned balloon (which probably carried a self-releasing camera). At the same time, archaeological aerial surveys with the aid of airplanes saw major advances because of the Great War of 1914–18, not surprisingly, for it was during those years that the airplane came of age. From then on, a 'bustling new frontier' for the study of sites and monuments opened up.[4]

In the Indus area, as an experiment, and because of Marshall's request to Vice Air Marshall Edward Ellington in the spring of 1925, a survey of some four hundred square miles around the old river bed of the Ravi was done by the Royal Air Force stationed at Risalpur.[5] This was apparently quite helpful in determining the location of ancient sites along the banks of the river, and Marshall hoped to extend such surveys along the banks of the Indus beds. Even before the aerial survey, Sahni had begun looking for old mounds along the old course of the Ravi. Among others, he surveyed a mound called Pal, a mile north of Harappa, which apparently stood on an island in the old river bed and which, Sahni believed, belonged to the same epoch as its famous neighbour.[6]

The old river channels of the Indus in Sindh, we may recall, were supposed to be surveyed by Dikshit. There were scores of settlement ruins, Marshall believed, along those old beds, and the idea was to discover sites where the 'Indo-Sumerian' remains came near the surface so that, as we saw, they might be excavated at the least possible expense.[7] Marshall also thought it probable that sites would be found in lower Sindh, in the district of Hyderabad. That area, for one thing, was much closer to the sea ('the nearer the sea, the richer the sites ought to be'), from where Marshall presumed contacts with the Sumerians were maintained.[8] This was one of the directions in which he wanted Dikshit to look out for sites. Following such clues, one of Dikshit's subordinates was sent out and he did find an enormous site in the south-east corner of Hyderabad district, known locally as Doadow Chinaeer. This was one of the sites that Dikshit himself planned to survey a little later in the year.[9]

Simultaneously, the Baluchistan campaign had begun with

Harold Hargreaves as the archaeologist in charge. Hargreaves is the man we met who, some years earlier, had surveyed Harappa. Since then he had moved on as superintendent of the Frontier Circle, Baluchistan now being very much part of his domain. Nal, in the Las Bela region, was where Marshall wanted him to concentrate his energies. After all, it was from Sohr Damb (the name of the mound at Nal) that, more than two decades earlier, the intrepid Hughes Buller had recovered an uncommon kind of pottery. In 1903, when Marshall had first seen photographs of the Nal pottery, he had described it as the finest that he had seen, and of a kind as yet unrepresented in the antiquities of India. But it was a clue that he had not seriously followed up. Now, after the discoveries at Mohenjodaro and Harappa, he had a sense that the mound from where those ceramics had come needed to be opened in order to ascertain its relationship with the Indus region.

Work at Nal, as Hargreaves soon learnt, could not begin in the winter of 1924 because of scarce labour. The local population was largely nomadic and did not return to the area until March. In the meanwhile, in the month of March, Hargreaves toured the Kacchi area of Baluchistan in the hope that since it was nearer the Indus basin, it would yield contemporaneous remains. Apparently the Luni mound at Sibi yielded shell beads, worked flints, and a barrel-shaped carnelian bead (suggesting it was an Indus-related site), but Hargreaves thought it too small and unimportant to carry out an excavation.[10] Before reaching Nal he would also open up Sampur Damb in the Mastung area, but there was nothing 'Indo-Sumerian' about it. Instead, it appeared to belong to the early centuries AD. It was only in the month of May that the digging of Sohr Damb at Nal would finally begin.

The results of the digging of Sohr Damb and those that emerged from successive seasons of work at Mohenjodaro and Harappa were spectacular and several. To record fully and vigorously the details of those excavations, though, would require another book. Let us, therefore, pause here and try to perceive what Marshall had attempted to get done since his *Illustrated London News* announcement in 1924. This set the stage, in a manner of speaking, for the next phase of discoveries in and around the Indus. His announcement is thus in the nature of a first indicator of how the new era would unfold.

From Punjab through Sindh to Baluchistan, it is a similar kind of field programme that we now encounter. In each of the regions it was a combination of settlement surveys aimed at locating sites and excavations of the most promising ones. Taking his cue from this, Marshall would soon develop a blueprint with a much larger canvas. He would underline the desirability of undertaking explorations and excavations of a similar kind in Bahawalpur, as also in the western states of Rajputana.[11] These, too, were areas where he expected to find sites bearing the same kind of culture as Mohenjodaro and Harappa. Equally, he believed that there could be an extension of the 'Indo-Sumerian' culture towards the east of India. So, simultaneously, he trained his eyes on an examination of neolithic and copper-age sites there, along with the earliest strata of Pataliputra because the Survey had earlier made finds that suggested 'a connection between the oldest known culture of Bihar and that of the Indus region.'[12]

Not all of this would get implemented in the way that Marshall visualized it. Neither did the antiquities unearthed always turn out to be quite as old as Marshall imagined them to be. But the blueprint shows that, from 1925 onwards, Marshall was already looking beyond the grandeur of the two monumental cities of the Indus. His idea was to understand the different ramifications of this civilization in the entire geographical stretch that lay to the east, south, and west of the Indus valley. He would also take the excavation work of Mohenjodaro personally in hand. All this, of course, would be made possible by much larger budgets. In comparison to the Rs 12,000 which the government had provided in 1923–4 for digging purposes for the whole of India and Burma, in 1924–5 an extra disbursement of Rs 80,000 was ordered. Better was to follow. In the following year, a special grant of two and a half lakh rupees would be made for exploration and excavation work.

In the entire scheme of work in and around the Indus region, Marshall's stamp would be writ large, even as the different parts of the field campaign came to be undertaken by individual officers. His academic planning formed the invariable basis along which their work would unfold. He would organize the archaeological and scientific expertise that was required for such work from outside the Survey. He would even supervise the publications that would emanate from the pens of his compatriots. No wonder then that, from now on, his name came to symbolize an entire era of Indus research. One of his collaborators later summed this up: 'to future generations he will always be the man who, archaeologically speaking, left India three thousand years older that he had found her.'[13]

Indian archaeology had now reached an exciting new phase dominated by large campaigns and lavish budgets. Far from being over, the story of the discovery of new sites and strata of the Indus civilization would continue. What had come to an end was the age when gifted men individually unearthed cities and sites of unsuspected antiquity.

The real heroes of this story of the discovery of the Indus civilization were such individuals—a discerning archaeologist like Sahni and a brilliant one like Banerji, who had within a few years of each other uncovered the relics entombed in Harappa and Mohenjodaro respectively; alongside, a debutant like Vats who first saw cultural congruences between the two cities which went beyond the enigmatic seals, and which veterans like Sahni and Banerji had failed to notice; the unfortunate linguist-turned-explorer Tessitori, who excavated seals of Harappan antiquity from the earth of Kalibangan but never lived to tell their tale;

all kinds of government officials who were also self-taught archaeologists, such as Hughes Buller in Baluchistan, Carter in Sindh, and Malik Muhammad in Bahawalpur. Men such as these on their own discovered the 'aberrations'—the evidence that was at odds with what was known about India's past. And presiding over the process was a slow-moving, cautious, academically inclined Marshall who, once he got down to grappling with the puzzle of the Indus, put together the pieces with visionary insight even if, rather strangely, without having visited the cities from where they came.

In the new era an unprecedented and sustained archaeological campaign began to reveal in more precise ways an array of unsuspected relics and contexts. The work of these men would slowly fade. Some of them would soon be forgotten. But for those privileged few, such as myself who have had a glimpse of them in the dusty files to which they came to be consigned, they live on.

They live on as the real pioneers, these men who first stumbled upon and then solved the many riddles of the long-forgotten civilization of the Indus.

# ENDNOTES

## CHAPTER 1: A RUINED CITY IN PUNJAB AND ITS FIRST EXPLORERS

1. Cunningham (1875): 107.
2. Marshall (1924b): 6 and 8.
3. See Singh (2004): 3ff.
4. Cited in Imam (1966): 18.
5. See letter of R.G. Macdonnell to Viceroy's secretary of June 1905, file no. 27, Archaeological Survey of India, New Delhi (hereafter ASI ).
6. See Hambly (1974): x.
7. Masson's account was published in 1842 in three volumes. See Masson (1842).
8. Burnes (1834).
9. Letter of Lionel Curtis of 21 July 1917, file (no file number) of 1917, ASI.
10. This is the eponymous method by which archaeological cultures are frequently named. Some of the early cultures of north-western India named in this manner are Kulli, Amri, and Kot Diji. This is only a way of remembering that this kind of culture was first discovered at the specific place after which it is named.
11. Masson (1842): 452–3, volume 1. Also see Possehl (1999): 44–9.
12. For a discussion of this, see Bosworth (1996).
13. The observations of Alexander's companions were later used by ancient historians such as Strabo, Arrian, and Plutarch. See Bosworth (1996).

14. For translations of the classical accounts, see Majumdar (1960). For an account of the invasion of Alexander, see chapter xv in Rapson (1921): 309–50.
15. Masson (1842): 453, volume 1.
16. Majumdar (1960): 49.
17. Masson (1842): 402, volume 1.
18. Ibid.: 453.
19. See Cunningham (1875): 153–5.
20. Masson (1842): 452, volume 1.
21. Masson's account talks of them as the bangles of the faqir, while Cunningham says the black stone there was regarded as the *nag* or gem of the ring, while the other two perforated stones were called the *nal* and *manka* or thumb-rings of the gigantic Naogaza.
22. See Lahiri (1996): 259–61.
23. Burnes (1834): 137, volume III.
24. Cunningham (1875): 153–5.
25. For this and other details, ibid.: 130–1.
26. Cunningham provides a great deal of such detail. See Cunningham (1882): 41, 79.
27. Burnes (1834): 137, volume III.
28. Ibid.
29. Ibid.: 58–9.
30. For an immensely readable account of the Great Game, see Hopkirk (1990).
31. Daniel (1966): 13–19. Also see Daniel (1962).
32. See Court (1836): 387ff. Court was a French general in the service of Maharaja Ranjit Singh of Punjab.
33. Histories of Indian archaeology of this phase include Imam (1966), Chakrabarti (1988), and Singh (2004).
34. Chakrabarti (1988): 115.
35. A great deal of information in this chapter on Cunningham is based on Imam's (1966) account of his life and work.
36. See Kejariwal (1988) and Nair (1999).
37. Kejariwal (1988): 199.
38. Cunningham (1875): 106.
39. Cunningham (1843): 241ff.

40. This has been pointed out, most recently by Singh (2004): 38. Her observations on Cunningham's statement about the political gains from such a project are worth quoting: 'This may look like proof of hidden political and evangelical agendas behind Cunningham's archaeological investigations, the revelations of an unguarded moment by a young man in the course of personal correspondence. But there is a more plausible explanation. At this time Sykes was an influential member of the Court of Directors of the East India Company, and the sentiments in Cunningham's letter, as also its subsequent publication, can be seen as part of an attempt to elicit backing for a project which had taken shape in Cunningham's mind, and which was never to leave him.' The member of the Court of Directors mentioned here is Colonel W.H. Sykes who, in 1842, had published a tirade against Brahmins (Singh 2004: 37): 'He gleefully sought to demonstrate that the Brahmins, who gave themselves such airs and graces, might well have been foreigners to this land; that the Pali language was older than Sanskrit; and that in the remote past Buddhism and not Brahmanism had reigned supreme in India.'
41. Cunningham (1848): 535–6.
42. Cunningham (1854): x–xi.
43. In Canning's own words, 'It is impossible to pass through that part—or indeed, so far as my experience goes any part—of the British territories in India without being struck by the neglect with which the greater portion of the architectural remains, and of the traces of bygone civilizations have been treated, though many of these, and some of which have had least notice, are full of beauty and interest.' This is quoted in Cunningham's 'Preface' to the first volume of his Report. See Cunningham (1871): i.
44. For this memorandum, see ibid.: iii.
45. Ibid.: viii.
46. Chakrabarti (1988): 57. The break in the survey that Chakrabarti mentions was because of the shifting priorities of the British Raj. In 1866, it was felt that, instead of field research, documentation of India's architectural and art remains was necessary. This was at the instance of the Lords of the Committee of the Council of Education in England who required that photographs, plaster casts, and accurate measurements of India's ancient buildings be sent to England.

This, in turn, is intimately connected with the movement for the reformation of industrial design in England which several reformist designers—Gottfried Semper, Owen Jones, and Henry Cole, among others—believed would be accelerated through inputs from traditional Indian ornamental design. The archaeological documentation undertaken in India from 1866 until 1870 was related to this concern.

47. Ibid.: 166.
48. Imam (1966): 181.
49. Daniel (1966): 60.
50. Cunningham (1875): 105–6.
51. Ibid.: 108.
52. See Cunningham (1877). Cunningham tried to read the inscription as well—he read it as 'Lachhmiya'.
53. Cunningham (1875): 108.
54. Proceedings of the Home Department (Archaeology and Conservation—hereafter PHD-AC), October 1884, nos. 21–4.
55. See Dames (1886): 1.
56. Ibid.
57. Ibid.
58. Dames (1907).

## CHAPTER 2: FROM SEALS TO A SPECIALIST

1. Dames (1886): 1.
2. This is mentioned in Fleet (1912): 699–701.
3. Grigson (no date): 11ff.
4. Ibid.: 22.
5. See Greenfield (1989): 133ff.
6. Ibid.: chapter 2.
7. Ibid.: 62.
8. See Singh (2001).
9. For medieval sculptures of Indian origin in the British Museum collection, see Chanda (1936) and Caygill (1985): 74–7.
10. See Davies (1997): 164. As Davies points out, John Chamberlain, a Baptist missionary, had met this priest and recorded the conversation that he had with him in his diary on 20 November 1817. While the brahmin's name is not mentioned by Chamberlain, apparently he

was the guardian priest of a Lakshmi idol which Stuart wanted to acquire. As the story goes, Stuart initially tried to persuade the priest to sell it, even taking him to Calcutta to see the large assemblage of images that he had collected. But the priest refused to sell his goddess. Stuart then decided to steal it (he got his people to take away 'the goddess by night'), leaving both the priest and the pilgrimage spot bereft of their object of reverence.

11. Caygill (1985): 76.
12. Letter from Marshall to Arthur Godley of 11 October 1901, Revenue and Statistics Department (hereafter R & S), no. 326 of 1901, The Oriental and India Office Collection of the British Library (hereafter OIOC), London.
13. Chakrabarti (1988): 156 cites a statement of Pandit Madho Sarup Vats, an officer of the Archaeological Survey during the Marshall era and excavator of Harappa, that clearly suggests this. According to Vats, 'even before coming to India, as far back as 1901, and again in 1906, when he went home to England, Sir John had interested himself in the British Museum seals from Harappa.' Apparently, this was something that was mentioned by Marshall to Vats.
14. By a curious coincidence, 1924 is also the year of publication of E.M. Forster's *A Passage to India*, a novel which seeks to unravel some of India's deepest mysteries. Like Marshall's announcement, this also figured in the pages of *The Illustrated London News* in 1924. It is mentioned among the events of the year in *The Illustrated London News* of that year, as summarized on the newsmagazine's website, www.iln.org.uk.
15. M. Marshall (undated) manuscript, titled 'Retirement and After'. Typed copy. This was written by Margaret Marshall, John Marshall's daughter, and provided to me by Raymond and Bridget Allchin. All the details I have gleaned about Marshall's childhood and adolescence come from this typed copy.
16. Other luminaries of Dulwich College were P.G. Wodehouse and Raymond Chandler.
17. See enclosure 1 of 30 September 1901, R & S no. 326 of 1901, OIOC.
18. See website of the British Academy, www.britac.ac.uk.
19. This has been discussed by Gill (2000): 517–26. Incidentally, this was the beginning and the end of Marshall's 'collecting' activities.

During the long years that he spent in India (1902–34), he did not collect any antiquities, either for himself or for Britain's museums.

20. For the work of Evans and Hogarth, see Huxley (2000): 15–27.
21. See Horowitz (1981). Arthur Evans was the son of John Evans, a noted scientist and businessman. John Evans made pioneering contributions to geology, anthropology, and prehistory. He also financially supported much of his son's work at Knossos in Crete.
22. Enclosure 3 of 29 November 1901, R & S no. 326 of 1901, OIOC.
23. For Marshall's fieldwork in Greece, see Gill (2000).
24. Apart from Marshall, the team included R. Douglas Wells, who was to act as surveyor. Wells held the Architectural Studentship while he surveyed sites in the Mediterranean on behalf of the British School and, like Bosanquet, he had studied at Trinity College, Cambridge.
25. Huxley (2000): 24.
26. Marshall mentioned this in a letter to Edward Maunde Thompson, Director of the British Museum, 30 September 1901, R & S no. 326 of 1901, OIOC.
27. See Marshall's 'Agreement for Service in India as Director of Archaeology', 23 December 1901, ibid.
28. The work that Marshall had undertaken in Greece remained incomplete. Gill (2000): 523 says: 'His publication of the pottery from Kato Zakro had to be abandoned, while that of his excavation at Praisos had to be completed, at Bosanquet's request, by Frederick Henry Marshall, then an Assistant in the Department of Greek and Roman Antiquities at the British Museum, and no apparent relation.'
29. I say this because, in the Archaeological Survey of India, till then, no officers with such credentials had been recruited. Rukun Advani, in a personal communication, says Marshall's selection was actually not strange at all, for 'It was colonial philosophy to recruit Oxbridge Firsts on the assumption that such training equipped them for EVERYTHING.' See Robert M. Ogilvie, *Latin and Greek: A History of the Influence of the Classics on English Life from 1600 to 1918* (London: Routledge and Kegan Paul, 1964).
30. See Lahiri (1997): 127–39. Cunningham was director general of the Survey from 1871 till 1885, while Burgess, who succeeded him, retired in 1889.
31. Gopal (1965): 157ff; also see Beloff (1969): 31 ff.

32. Finance Committee Note on the Archaeological Department of 18 December 1886, Proceedings of the Department of Revenue and Agriculture (hereafter PRAD) (Archaeology and Epigraphy—A [hereafter AE]), no. 4759 of 1887, National Archives of India, New Delhi (hereafter NAI).
33. Letter of Elgin and Council to Secretary of State for India of 16 June 1898, PRAD (AE-A), no. 31 of 1898, NAI.
34. Letter from Secretary of Asiatic Society of Bengal of 5 January 1895, PRAD (AE-A), no. 41 of 1894, NAI.
35. Article xx, PRAD (AE-A), no. 39 of 1898, NAI.
36. Letter from Elgin and Council to Secretary of State for India of 16 June 1898, PRAD (AE-A), no. 31 of 1898, NAI.
37. For Curzon's statement, see *Indian Archaeology 1899–1905*: 102.
38. Cited in Roy (1953): 26.
39. Gilmour (1994): 82. According to Uday Singh Mehta (1999), it was ironically British Conservatives (Curzon being one of them) who were more in favour of retaining things in their original form, whereas the Liberal philosophy was more to 'improve' and thereby to alter things (often for the worse).
40. Raleigh (1906): 182–94.
41. Gopal (1965): 292–3.
42. The budget was increased from Rs 61,000 to Rs 88,450.
43. *Indian Archaeology*: 4ff.
44. Telegram from George Hamilton to Curzon of 14 May 1901, PRAD (AE-A), no. 28 of 1901, NAI.
45. See Lyall's note of 29 March 1901, R & S no. 326 of 1901, OIOC.
46. Ibid.
47. Minute on the subject of Director General of Archaeology for India of 29 March 1901, ibid.
48. *Indian Archaeology*: 8.
49. Gilmour (1994): 175.
50. Memo from Vincent Smith of 11 March 1901, R & S no. 326 of 1901, OIOC.
51. Letter of J.B. Keith of 13 January 1900 in *Indian Archaeology*: 97.
52. Telegram from Viceroy to Secretary of State of May 1901, PRAD (AE-A), no. 22 of 1901, NAI.

53. Minute on the subject of appointment of a Director General of Archaeology of 29 May 1901, R & S no. 326 of 1901, OIOC.
54. Letter of Maunde Thompson to Arthur Godley of 30 September 1901, ibid.

## CHAPTER 3: JOHN MARSHALL'S EARLY YEARS IN INDIA

1. Lahiri (1998): 2ff.
2. Note of Marshall of 28 July 1903, no. 47 of April 1903, ASI.
3. Marshall (1939): 26.
4. Ronaldshay (1928) II: 209–11.
5. Curzon's letter to Hamilton of 17 April 1902, *Indian Archaeology*: 197.
6. Letter from Curzon's private secretary to Marshall of 17 March 1904, *Indian Archaeology*: 54.
7. Letter from Curzon's private secretary to Marshall of 25 March 1904, *Indian Archaeology*: 56.
8. Stephen (1876): 240–1.
9. See Lahiri (2003) for the manner in which this happened in Delhi.
10. Curzon's letter to W.M. Young of 15 January 1900, *Indian Archaeology*: 421.
11. Cited in Gopal (1965): 224.
12. Despatch from Curzon to Hamilton of 20 December 1900, *Indian Archaeology*: 5.
13. Burgess's letter to Hamilton of 5 April 1900, PRAD (AE-A), no. 7 of August 1902, NAI.
14. Letter from F.C. Lascelles, Ambassador to Berlin to Secretary of State for Foreign Affairs of 30 July 1900, PRAD (AE-A), no. 3 of December 1900, NAI.
15. Despatch from Curzon and Council to George Hamilton of 18 September 1902, PRAD (AE-A), no. 61 of 1902, NAI.
16. Gilmour (1994): 180.
17. Extract from the Notes of the Viceroy of November 1902, no. 40 (22) of 1902, ASI.
18. Marshall (1903–4): 1–12.
19. Curzon's (undated) note on Mandu, Southern States of Central India and Malwa Agency Records, no. 4/21/1903 (II), NAI.

20. Marshall's letter to Captain Ernest Barnes of 17 February 1903, ibid.
21. See 'Notes' section, Curzon's note dated 29 October 1902, PRAD (AE-A) nos. 32 and 33 of June 1904, NAI.
22. Letter from Marshall to Secretary to Government of Punjab (PW Department) of 18 January 1904, no. 2 (1–3) of January 1904, ASI. A great deal of information on repairs at Moti Masjid and the other monuments of Delhi mentioned in this section is based on this communication.
23. Marshall's review is contained in no. 291 (1) of 1915, ASI.
24. Marshall (1939): 23.
25. For a brief discussion of the literary legends, see Marshall and Vogel (1902–3): 143.
26. Vogel's letter to Marshall of 15 March 1903, no. 86 of May 1902, ASI.
27. Keith (1922): 70.
28. Marshall (1924a): 428.
29. Hirananda's letter to Marshall of 21 March 1903, no. 206 of June 1903, ASI.
30. Marshall's letter to Secretary, Revenue and Agriculture Department of 21 March 1903, no. 55 of September 1903, ASI.
31. Hirananda's letter to Marshall of 29 January 1904, no. 206 of June 1903, ASI.
32. See 'Routine Notes' in PRAD (AE-B), no. 6 of April 1903, NAI.
33. Mockler (1877).
34. The archaeological details here as also those in the next paragraph come from the letters of Hughes Buller to Marshall of 5 May 1903, 31 July 1903, 7 September 1903, 22 October 1903; also see letter of Burkitt to Marshall of 25 September 1903. All these are in no. 104 of July 1903, ASI.
35. Letter from Buller to the Director of the British Museum, of 15 July 1902 and letter from the Director, British Museum to Buller of 12 September 1902, no. 104 of July 1903, ASI.
36. Letter from Bloch to Buller of 15 May 1903, ibid.
37. Letter from Buller to Marshall of 12 October 1903, ibid.
38. Letter from unnamed assistant of Minchin to John Marshall of 10 January 1907, no. 71 (1–4) of May 1905, ASI.
39. Letter from Buller to Marshall of 12 October 1903, no. 104 of July 1903, ASI.

40. Letter from Marshall to Buller (date not stated), October 1903, ibid.
41. Letter from Marshall to Buller of 30 July 1904, ibid.
42. Stein's letter to Marshall of 30 September 1904, no. 157 of October 1904, ASI.
43. Note of Marshall of 26 September 1904, PRAD (AE-B), no. 1 of October 1904, NAI.
44. 'Notes', no. 119 of September 1904, ASI.
45. Marshall's letter to Secretary, Department of Agriculture of 28 September 1904, PRAD (AE-B) nos. 4 and 5 of October 1904, NAI.
46. Marshall's letter to Messers Herman & Co., contractors, of 4 January 1905, no. 119 of September 1904, ASI.
47. For details, see Chakrabarti (1990): 13ff.
48. See Curzon's note of 30 December 1904 in 'Foreign Department Notes', Proceedings of the Foreign Department (hereafter PFD) (External—B), nos. 173–81 of March 1905, NAI.
49. Marshall's letter to P.Z. Cox of 21 January 1905, no. 119 of September 1904, ASI.

## CHAPTER 4: HARAPPA MAKES A FLEETING REAPPEARANCE

1. See Gilmour (1994): 318 ff.
2. Rea's letter to Marshall of 2 November 1905, no. 204 of December 1905, ASI.
3. See his despatch to Secretary of State (Finance no. 373) of 9 November 1905 in *Indian Archaeology*: 42–7.
4. Marshall's letter to Curzon of 19 March 1906, no. 234 of 1905, ASI.
5. Statement of the case of Mr. J.H. Marshall by G.T. Birdwood, Civil Surgeon Agra. PHD (AE-A), nos. 13–35 of June 1906, NAI.
6. Marshall's letter to Secretary, Home Department of 2 April 1906. He wrote: "The second subject which I propose to investigate concerns certain antiquities which were acquired last year from Baluchistan and which appear to be closely related to certain Cypro-Phoenician wares of the eastern Mediterranean. The problem is one which merits investigation not only for the sake of elucidating this particular chapter in the prehistoric civilisation of Baluchistan, but also by reasons of its bearing on the early civilisation of the Persian Gulf and particularly of the island of Bahrein . . .'. See ibid.

7. These were later described in detail by H.A. Hargreaves. See his 'Inspection Note on Harappa, Montgomery District, Punjab', no. 40 of 1914, ASI.
8. Marshall (1951): xv, volume 1.
9. Correspondence with these dealers can be seen in no. 46 of 1904 (Parts 1 to 8), ASI.
10. Extract from Punjab Government Gazette, Notification no. 529 (Revenue) of 12 September 1911, no. 321 of 1911, ASI.
11. Letter of W.C. Renouf, Deputy Commissioner of Rawalpindi district to Superintendent, Northern Circle of 18 February 1913, no. 398 of 1912, ASI.
12. Letter of Marshall to Renouf of 11 July 1913, no. 323 of 1913, ASI.
13. This is mentioned in Hargreaves' note of 1914. See endnote 7 above.
14. Longhurst (1909): 5.
15. Vogel (1907–8).
16. Marshall's letter to the Resident at Gwalior of 31 July 1909, no. 246 of 1909, ASI.
17. Marshall's letter to H. Lake of 18 February 1910, ibid. For a detailed account of Bhita, see Marshall (1911–12).
18. See Vogel (1908–9): 127.
19. See Vogel (1909–10): 63.
20. Letter from Vogel to Marshall of 2 November 1908, no. 10 of 1908, ASI. The makara ('half man half makara') referred to in this letter is a mythical crocodile, frequently represented in early Indian sculpture.
21. See Vogel (1911–12).
22. Sastri (1944): 17–18.
23. This was mentioned in the 1914 note of Hargreaves. See endnote 7 above.
24. Hardinge (1948): 5.
25. Gilmour (1994): 404.
26. Despatch from Hardinge and his Council to Secretary of State for India of 11 August 1911, Proceedings of the Education Department (PED hereafter) (AE-A), nos. 20–3 of 1912, NAI.
27. This section is based on the discussion on decentralization in Wolpert (1967): 201ff.
28. These were the Sanitary Commissioner with the Government of India, Inspecting Officer of Cantonments, Inspector General of

Forests, Inspector General of Agriculture, Inspector General of Civil Veterinary Departments and the Inspector General of Excise and Salt and Director General of Archaeology. See despatch from Lord Hardinge and his Council to Marquis of Crewe, Secretary of State for India of 11 August 1911. This section is based on PED (AE-A), nos. 20–3 of 1912, NAI.

29. Marshall (1908–9): 7.
30. Despatch from Hardinge and his Council to Secretary of State of 11 August 1911, PED (AE-A), nos. 20–3 of 1912, NAI.
31. Note by Denison Ross of July 1911, no. 210 of 1911 (Part 2), ASI.
32. Note of Cousens of 19 September 1906, no. 121 of October 1906, ASI.
33. Remarks by R.G. Bhandarkar on Dr. Ross's Note, no. 290 of 1911 (Part 2), ASI.
34. See proceedings of the second day, 13 July 1911, ibid.
35. Harcourt Butler's Note of 31 July 1911, ibid.
36. L.C. Porter's note on the 'Archaeological Department' of 23 September 1911, ibid.
37. The details of this scheme are outlined in ASI no. 291 of 1911. See H. Sharp's note on 'Oriental Research Institute' of 15 September 1911.
38. The second paragraph of the abovementioned note states: 'For Indians it will offer instruction in Western methods of research; training for posts in the Archaeological Department, and for professorships in Colleges; and practical courses in numismatics, in the preparation of *catalogues raisonnes* and in Epigraphy.'
39. Vogel's comments to Secretary, Department of Education, of 7 October 1911, no. 290 of 1911, ASI.
40. Vogel's letter to all gazetted archaeological officers etc. of 22 September 1911, ibid.
41. Taw Sein Ko's letter to Vogel of 30 September 1911, ibid.
42. Ibid.
43. Rea's letter to Vogel of 28 September 1911, ibid.
44. Banerji's letter to Vogel of 25 September 1911, ibid.
45. Hardinge (1948): 15.
46. Extract from a despatch from the Secretary of State of 8 December 1911, PED (AE-A) nos. 20-23 of March 1912.
47. Gilmour (1994): 404.

48. Extract from a despatch from the Secretary of State of 8 December 1911, PED (AE-A), nos. 20–3 of March 1912, NAI.
49. This was in May 1912. See *Cambridge University Reporter* (1912): 1121.
50. Letter from Marshall to Curzon of 10 July 1912, Curzon Collection, IOR MSS EUR F112/644, OIOC.
51. Letter from Marshall to Curzon of 13 June 1912, ibid.

## CHAPTER 5: AMONG CITIES AND STUPAS

1. For a discussion of Sanchi's modern history, see Lahiri (2004): 99–114.
2. Spilsbury (1835): XVII.
3. Begum (1867).
4. Cunningham (1854).
5. For an overview of techniques and methods, see Daniel (1975).
6. Ibid.: 165.
7. Ibid.: 173.
8. Griffin's Note of 2 October 1882, PHD (ACM-A), nos. 7–10 of 1882, NAI.
9. For details, see Lahiri (2004).
10. Some of these concerned the crevices on the outer surface of Stupa 1 and the urgency of filling them up. Others pointed out the loose sculpted and inscribed stones around the site which were to be collected and arranged. Curzon's note of 8 May 1905, PHD (AE-A), nos. 6–8 of July 1905, NAI.
11. Ibid.
12. Marshall's note of 24 November 1905, PFD (Internal-B), nos. 378–9 of May 1906, NAI.
13. See Khan (2000): 155.
14. For details, see Lahiri (1999).
15. Ibid.: 35. The Hinglaj shrine in Baluchistan is another example of this. It was dedicated to a goddess known as Bibi Nani by Muslims, and Parbati or Kali by Hindus. Most importantly, in the late nineteenth century, the proprietress of Hinglaj was a Muslim woman. This also unambiguously shows that there was nothing unique about the fact that the legal proprietor of Mahabodhi was not a Buddhist.
16. Note by Marshall of 12 December 1906, PFD (Internal—B), nos. 378–9 of May 1906, NAI.

17. Begum (1922 and 1927): 233ff & 272 (volume II), 203 (volume III).
18. Marshall's letter to Colonel Spence, Political Agent at Bhopal of 23 May 1912, Central India Agency no. 221 of 1912, NAI.
19. See letters of Sultan Jahan Begum to W.S. Davis, Political Agent in Bhopal of 16 July and 23 September 1912, ibid.
20. B.R. Beck's testimonial of 7 July 1908, no. 101 of 1908, ASI.
21. Irving (1910).
22. Irving's letter to Marshall of 22 October 1912, no. 371 (1–2) of December 1912, ASI.
23. I have not seen any reference to this note in the publications on Harappa.
24. Zafar Hasan's report of 5 September 1912, no. 350 ( nos. 1–20) of 1915, ASI.
25. Ibid.
26. Marshall's letter to Miles Irving of 15 November 1912, no. 371 (nos. 1–2) of December 1912, ASI.
27. Eventually, the Sanchi volumes were published in 1940. See Marshall and Foucher (1940), three volumes.
28. Marshall's letter to the private Secretary of the Begum of Bhopal of 10 January 1913, no. 27 (part 3) of January 1913, ASI.
29. Marshall and Foucher (1940), I: preface.
30. Marshall (1951), I: xv.
31. Ibid.
32. For a comparison of the work of Cunningham and Marshall at Taxila, see Abbi (2000), especially chapter 2.
33. See Marshall (1912–13).
34. Ibid., part 2: 9.
35. These details are from no. 44 of 1913, ASI.
36. Ibid.
37. See the website relating to the Tatas, www.tata.com.
38. Letter of L. Porter of Department of Education to Vogel of 4 January 1912, no. I (1–2) of 1912, ASI.
39. Cousens' report to Marshall, no. 26 (1–11) of May 1905, ASI. In the same file, also see report of Major Tilley dated 12 June 1905.
40. For a detailed discussion of archaeological conservation in Kashmir in the early decades of the twentieth century, especially with regard to

the complex intersections of state politics and religious differences in this project, see Rai (2004): chapter 4.

41. Marshall (1915–16), I: 8.
42. *Indian Archaeology*: 420.
43. See letter of Jivanji Jamshedji Modi to Marshall of February 1920, no. 406, 1920–2, ASI. Modi pleaded with Marshall to excavate those ruins because, as he put it: 'Your department has done a good deal of good work in the matter of the Ancient History of other communities—the Hindus, Buddhists and Mahomedans, but nothing has been done in the matter of our community.'
44. Letter of Stein to Marshall of 28 March 1912, no. I (1–2) of 1912, ASI.
45. See Allchin (1995): 200–94.
46. See note of Marshall of 14 July 1912, no. I (1–2) of 1912, ASI.
47. See letter of L.C. Porter to Chief Secretary, Government of Bihar and Orissa, of 14 October 1912, no. 300 (part I) of October 1912, ASI.
48. Spooner (1912–13): 55.
49. Ibid.: 55.
50. Letter of Spooner to Marshall of 10 February 1913, no. 300 (I) of October 1912, ASI.
51. Letter of Marshall to Tata of 12 February 1913, ibid.
52. Letter of Marshall to Spooner of 16 February 1913, ibid.
53. Letter of L.C. Porter, Secretary to Government of India, to Chief Commissioner at Delhi of 7 June 1913, no. 205 of 1913, ASI.
54. Hasan (1916).
55. See Note of J.Ph. Vogel of 28 April 1911, no. 169 (nos. 1–9) of June 1911, ASI.
56. Vogel was appointed a professor at Leiden University in Holland.
57. Letter of Marshall to Harcourt Butler of 9 March 1914, no. 23 (1–10) of February 1914, ASI.
58. Hargreaves (1914–15).
59. Oertel (1904–5).
60. Hargreaves' note on 'Rajanpur', no. 400 (no. 1) of 1914, ASI.
61. Photographs of historic monuments in India go back to the middle of the nineteenth century, but, generally speaking, in the nineteenth century mounds were photographed if there were architecturally significant remains in their vicinity, as for example in Sanchi. For a history of photography in India, see Thomas (1981). This book (p. 16)

mentions that Cunningham's assistant, J.D. Beglar, was an excellent photographer who produced around four hundred photographs for the Archaeological Survey before his retirement.

62. Hargreaves' 'Inspection Note on Harappa, Montgomery District, Punjab', no. 400 (1) of 1914.
63. Testimonial of Hermann Oldenberg of 27 March 1913, no. 200 (1–14) of 1913, ASI.
64. Gupte's letter to Marshall of 19 April 1914, ibid.
65. Marshall's letter to Hargreaves of 3 May 1913, ibid.
66. Marshall's note of 19 November 1914, no. 400 (1) of 1914, ASI.
67. Marshall's letter to Gupte of 31 August 1915, no. 352 (nos. 1–48) part 3 of 1915, ASI.
68. Gupte's letter to Marshall of 9 September 1915, ibid.

## CHAPTER 6: AN ITALIAN IN INDIA

1. For family details, see 'All About Tessitory' by Anna Brosolo in File no. 22 of the Tessitori Collection of the Rajasthan State Archives, Bikaner (hereafter RSA). Some details on the Tessitori family are also contained in a file of Hazarimal Banthia in the same collection of RSA. I have not been able to consult the correspondence exchanged between Tessitori and Grierson which is at the Oriental and India Office Collection of the British Library, London. These, however, have been used by Fasana (1999).
2. Tessitori's letter to Vijaya Dharma Suri of 23 July 1913, Tessitori Correspondence with Vijaya Dharma Suri, Tessitori Collection, RSA.
3. For Udine, see reference in note 6.
4. There is a vast literature on Indo-Roman trade, a great deal of which is cited in Begley and de Puma (1991). Also see Rajan (2002) and Chakrabarti (2003): 44ff.
5. See Ghosh (1989): 84, volume 2. A hoard of these objects was excavated from a house of the early centuries AD at the site of Brahmapuri (in the western part of Kolhapur town) in Maharashtra.
6. See 'Archdiocese of Udine' on the website of *Catholic Encyclopedia* (www.newadvent.org/cathen). Also see 'Udine—An Italian City Empty of Tourists', http //info.jpost.com/C001/Supplements/Fiuli/ udine.html; 'Udine, the City of Tiepolo', www.iniitaly.com/regions/

friuli/udine.html; and 'Liceo Classico "J. Stellini"—Udine', http// progetti.webscuola.tin.it/multilab/udin02/citta-ind-en.html.

7. See Fromichi (1950).
8. Latham (1958).
9. Tucci (1954).
10. Mitter (1977): 11.
11. Ibid.: 29.
12. See 'Roberto De Nobili (1577–1656) Roman Catholic Brahmin', in Kamat's Potpourri, http //www.kamat.com/kalranga/people/pioneers/nobili.html.
13. Ginzburg (1980): 44.
14. The details about this library are from http: //www.commune.udine.it/biblio/e_v_5.html.
15. See Anna Brosolo's 'All About Tessitory', File no. 22 of Tessitori Collection, RSA.
16. Florence University was set up in the middle of the fourteenth century, when Pope Clement VI gave the city a bull permitting the establishment of a university with all faculties. See Thomson (1963): 95.
17. Schwab (1984).
18. Ibid.: 29.
19. Ibid.: 32.
20. Ibid.
21. See Singh (2004): 8.
22. Schwab (1984): 56.
23. Ibid.: 38–9.
24. Ibid.: 78.
25. This was discussed by Indra Sen Gupta in a paper entitled 'Shishyas of Another Order: Students of Indology at Berlin, Bonn and Tubingen in the Nineteenth Century', at a conference hosted by the University of California, Los Angeles, in April 2000, on 'The History of Indology and Comparative Philology 1750–1958'. The abstract of Sen Gupta's paper can be seen on www.sscnet.ucla.edu.
26. Botto (1954).
27. See Tessitori (1912 and 1913a).
28. Ibid.
29. Grierson (1912): 798.

30. The *Memoria* that he prepared for the public competition for the chair has been mentioned by Freschi (1999): 199. At the beginning of the twentieth century, Italy was a nation afflicted with a surplus of intellectual labour in relation to demand. Consequently, unemployed Italian intellectuals frequently moved out of Italy in search of jobs. See Barbagli (1982).
31. For an overview of Italian scholars of Jainism, see Vallauri (1952).
32. Tessitori's letter to Vijaya Dharma Suri of 16 October 1913, Tessitori Collection, RSA.
33. See Caillat (1999): 8. Angelo de Gubernatis was active in Florence in the late nineteenth century but later moved to Rome. He himself wrote on a variety of subjects, ranging from animals in comparative mythology to the Zoroastrian community of Bombay.
34. See Vallauri (1952): 109. Also see Balbir (1999).
35. Tessitori (1913b) and (1913c).
36. Tessitori (1914a and 1916a). Old Western Rajasthani was the offspring of the Saurasena Apabhramsa and the common parent of both Gujarati and Marwari.
37. For a recent assessment of Tessitori's investigation of this theme, see Balbir (1999).
38. See Tessitori's letter to Dharma Suri of 23 July 1913, Tessitori Collection, RSA.
39. Ibid.
40. Details about the life of Dharma Suri are mainly from Tessitori (1917).
41. Ibid.: 2. The European scholars in this circle included F.W. Thomas, H. Jacobi, J. Hertel, A. Guerinot.
42. Ibid. Also see Winternitz (1988 reprint), volume II: 570.
43. See Tessitori's letter to Dharma Suri dated 23 July 1913 in Nahata (1986): 21. Also see his letter to Dharma Suri dated 7 August 1913, in ibid.
44. Tessitori's letter to Dharma Suri dated 16 October 1913, in ibid.
45. Whereas in his first letters Tessitori addressed Dharma Suri as 'Mahodaya', from August 1913 onwards his manner of address was 'Guru Maharaj', and later 'Gurudev'.
46. Ibid.
47. Tessitori's letter to Dharma Suri of 23 July 1913, Tessitori Collection, RSA.

## CHAPTER 7: FROM CALCUTTA TO KALIBANGAN

1. The one whose name we know is S.R. Harananhalli, to whose address he asked Vijaya Dharma Suri to send a letter. See Tessitori's letter to Dharma Suri of 23 July 1913 in Tessitori Correspondence with Vijaya Dharma Suri, Tessitori Collection, RSA.
2. Tessitori (1914b): 373.
3. Poddar (1977): 226.
4. Shastri (1916).
5. Sandhya bhasa, as Shastri explained, is a *bhasa* (language) of light and darkness; some parts can be understood while others cannot.
6. See Fasana (1999): 31–3.
7. Tessitori (1914b): 373.
8. Ibid.: 374.
9. See letter of Tessitori to Vijaya Dharma Suri of 19 April 1914, Tessitori Correspondence with Vijaya Dharma Suri, Tessitori Collection, RSA.
10. Ibid. In that letter Tessitori writes: 'There is one thing which makes me very sorry and it is that I have not yet been able to leave flesh-eating all together.'
11. Tessitori's letter to Dharma Suri of 10 May 1914, Tessitori Correspondence with Vijaya Dharma Suri, Tessitori Collection, RSA.
12. Tessitori's letter to Dharma Suri of 11 July 1914, ibid.
13. Tessitori's letter to Dharma Suri of 28 July 1914, ibid. Tessitori seems to have liked Jodhpur immensely, and in his usual emotional style, he declared to Dharma Suri in this letter that he would like to spend the rest of his life there.
14. See 'Da. L. P. Tessitori ka Bharat Bhraman', in file on itinerary of Tessitori, Tessitori Collection, RSA.
15. Tessitori (1917): 3.
16. Ibid. Tessitori made a distinction between the relationship that Dharma Suri had with other European scholars and himself: 'I am so far the only European who has had the opportunities to know him intimately in his own surroundings.'
17. Tessitori's letter to Muniraja Maharaja of 13 September 1914, Tessitori Correspondence with Vijaya Dharma Suri, Tessitori Collection, RSA.
18. This entire scheme is spelt out in depth in Tessitori (1914b), on which

I have depended for this and the next few paragraphs, where the scheme is outlined.

19. For a discussion of the genealogist castes and historical chronicles of Rajasthan, see Zeigler (1976).
20. Ibid.: 388.
21. Ibid.: 373.
22. Annual Report for 1915 (1916): xxi.
23. For details of this tour, see Tessitori (1916b).
24. Ibid.
25. See Tessitori (1916b): 59.
26. Cole's work, including his Rajputana experience, has been discussed at length by Kashyap (2001) and Singh (2004): 199ff.
27. Annual Report for 1915 (1916): xxi.
28. Ibid.
29. See Note of E.D. Maclagan of 5 July 1916, no. 435 (sl. nos. 1–14), December 1916, ASI.
30. See Marshall's note of 24 July 1916, ibid.
31. Marshall's letter to D.R. Bhandarkar of 9 January 1917, ibid.
32. Tessitori (1919): 7.
33. A typed copy of his report describes the archaeology of Bikaner in great detail. See L.P. Tessitori, 'A Report on Tours in Search of Archaeological Remains in Bikaner State During the years 1916–17 and 1917–18', File no. 8 of Tessitori Collection, RSA. Hereafter 'A Report'.
34. Ibid.: 35.
35. Ibid.: 57–8.
36. Tod (1832): 166, volume II.
37. Ibid.: 144.
38. Marshall was only informed of this in 1915. See no. 283 (nos. 1–3) of 1915, ASI. The account is entitled 'A List of the Ruined Mounds in Bahawalpur State from which Ancient Coins were Discovered between 1903 and 1909'. Hereafter 'Ruined Mounds'.
39. Din (1908).
40. The letter to Malik Muhammad from the director general's office of 17 August 1916 bears his designation and address.
41. Malik Muhammad's undated letter to Mir Asad Ullah, Overseer, Imperial Subdivision, no. 283 (1–3) of 1915, ASI.

42. Director General of Archaeology's letter to Malik Muhammad Din of 17 August 1916, ibid.
43. 'Ruined Mounds'.
44. Ibid.
45. Mughal (1982): 87–90.
46. 'Ruined Mounds'.
47. For details see Tessitori, 'A Report', pp. 2–3.
48. Ibid.: 33.
49. Ibid.: 36–7.
50. The first visit is mentioned in Tessitori (1919): 9.
51. In 1918 Tessitori was at Kalibangan from 23 to 24 December and again from 29 to 31 December. See Tessitori (1920): 255.
52. The extracted portions are from Tessitori's 'A Report', pp. 107–10.
53. This report suggests that photographs were taken during Tessitori's first visit. Some of the photographs in this book come from the Rajputana Album (volume 8) of 1917–19 in the photographic library of the Archaeological Survey of India. We do not know, though, whether it was a photographer from the Survey who recorded Kalibangan. This is because there is a letter by Tessitori dated 28 July 1918 to D.B. Spooner, then officiating for Marshall, asking him if the government's sanction for a photographer had come: 'Sir John had asked Government to sanction a post for a draftsman-photographer under myself. Would you kindly inform me as soon as the Government's decision is known. Naturally, I am very anxious to know that the post has been sanctioned for a draftsman-photographer will be a great help to me.' No. 300 of 1918, ASI.
54. Those seals are now in Italy, but photographs of them can be seen at the Ganga Golden Jubilee Museum at Bikaner, where the stone blades discovered by Tessitori are displayed as well.
55. See Marshall's note dated 10 June 1918, no. 300 of 1918, ASI. A brief resumé of the results of Tessitori's survey, based on this report, was published in the annual report of the Survey. See Spooner (1917–18): 21–3.
56. In the official correspondence and the publications of Marshall relating to the Indus civilization, there is no mention of Kalibangan as being of pre-historic significance.
57. This letter, dated 9 June 1919, has been reproduced in Freschi (1999): 219, footnote 79.

58. Grierson' s letter to Tessitori of 18 June 1919, Tessitori Collection, RSA.
59. Tessitori's letter is dated 21 July 1919 and has been reproduced in Freschi (1999): 219, footnote 79.
60. Grierson's letter to Tessitori of 6 August 1919, Tessitori Collection, RSA.
61. The details of his illness and his last days were poignantly described by G.D. Rudkin, Revenue Member of the Bikaner State Council, in a letter to Tessitori's father of 26 November 1919: 'he passed away on Saturday, Nov. 22nd. A Mr & Mrs James here took him into their house when he became seriously ill, and he had every care and attention possible. The doctor telegraphed for trained nurses but unfortunately they could not be obtained in time. The priest from Ajmer could not arrive till Sunday morning, and he held the burial service in the evening. I can assure you, you have the deepest sympathy of all of us here in your sad loss; he was very much liked by everyone and I know that his work was of the highest value. He did not seem so well as usual when he came up from Bombay at the beginning of the month and the voyage had perhaps been up down so that he was somewhat weak to face the illness that attacked him. He refused to think he was going to die and left no instructions about his affairs; I am told just before the end he called father and mother (in Italian) but said little else.' See Tessitori Collection, RSA.
62. The Unpublished Documents page in www.tessitori.org/p_unpdoc.htm.
63. See 'All About Tessitory' by Anna Brosolo in File no. 22 of Tessitori Collection, RSA.
64. One of the only writings where the seals that Tessitori discovered are discussed is Banthia (1989). The author of that article, Sri Hazarimal Banthia, himself played a stellar role in rekindling interest in Tessitori (see the preface to the present book). Banthia's interest in Tessitori goes back to the 1950s, when he began looking for his grave, which he found and had repaired. See Banthia (1999).

## CHAPTER 8: EXCAVATING HARAPPA UNDER A SHADOW

1. See Saini (1988). Also *India's Contribution to the Great War* (1923).
2. The details in this paragraph are from Saini (1988).
3. Marshall (1915–16): 2.

4. Hargreaves (1916): 1.
5. Letter of Secretary, Government of India to Marshall of 6 November 1903, PRAD (AE-A), no. 3 of November 1903, NAI.
6. Letter of Sladen, Acting Secretary to the Government of Bombay, to Secretary to the Government of India of 5 April 1904, PRAD (AE-A), nos. 2–3 of May 1904. In April 1914, Bhandarkar was confirmed in the appointment of Superintendent, Archaeological Survey, Western Circle, with effect from 17 October 1913. See notification dated 9 April 1914 in no. 56 of 1914, ASI.
7. Bhandarkar (1902a and 1902b, 1904a and 1904b).
8. See Marshall's report entitled 'Restoration of the Palace Garden Hayat Bakhsh (Life-Giver) in the Delhi Fort', no. 129 of 1902, ASI.
9. Letter of Marshall to Secretary, Revenue and Agriculture Department of 10 August 1904, no. 133 (I) of 1903, ASI.
10. Ibid.
11. No. 107 (nos. 1–43) of 1905, ASI. This file contains the testimonial (dated 2 September 1905) that was given by Reverend G. Hibbert Ware (Principal, St Stephen's College) to Yazdani. Part of it reads: 'I have the honour to recommend Ghulam Yazdani a graduate of ths college for the Arabic & Persian Scholarship.

    Ghulam Yazdani passed the Intermediate examination from the Panjab University in 1903, securing the first place in the province in Persian. He passed the B.A. of the Panjab University in 1905, taking Persian and Arabic as two of his subjects, and securing the first place in the province in Arabic. His age is twenty years and six months. He belongs to a good family and bears a good character. He is at present reading in the M.A. English class of this college, while also studying Arabic for the Arabic M.A. He is a student of decidedly scholarly tastes, and has developed very rapidly during the last two and a half years. I believe that he is capable of considerably further developing his talents. He is of good physique, and plays both football and cricket for the college with credit.'
12. Yazdani published extensively on the archaeology of the Deccan. See Yazdani (1930–55, 1947, 1966).
13. Letter from Vogel to Cousens of 21 August 1906, no. 13 (1–11) of 1906, ASI.
14. Letter from Marshall to Vogel of 21 January 1905, no. 55 of 1905, ASI.

15. Letter from Vogel to Marshall of 5 February 1905, ibid.
16. Ibid.
17. Letter of Vogel to Cousens of 21 August 1906, no. 13 of 1906, ASI. In that letter Vogel expressed his misgivings about Marshall's views on Daya Ram's training: 'After all, it is better that he should become a good epigraphist than a bad architect.'
18. Marshall's undated note, no. 55 of 1905, ASI.
19. This is evident from Marshall's report on the Rajagriha. See Marshall (1905–6): 86.
20. Ibid.: 101–2. 'New Rajagrha' was the new capital that was believed to have been built *c.* 600 BC outside the hill-girt valley, which was the site of the first city or 'Old Rajagrha'.
21. Sahni (1906–7): 193–205.
22. Extract from letter of Marshall (date and name of recipient not mentioned), no. 345 (1–22) of 1907, ASI.
23. Sahni (1907–8a): 59–62.
24. Letter of Vogel to Cousens of 29 September 1906, no. 13 of 1906, ASI.
25. Sahni (1907–8b): 181–8.
26. See A.H. Longhurst's 'Conservation Notes on the Champaran district' sent to Secretary, Government of Bengal of 16 April 1907, no. 73 (1–7) of May 1907, ASI. A.H. Longhurst was appointed as superintendent of the Eastern Circle of the Survey in the autumn of 1907 and he happened to be Marshall's brother-in-law (the brother of Marshall's wife, Florence).
27. The file concerns Hultzsch's resignation and acceptance by him of a Sanskrit professorship at Halle. See no. 53 of 1902, ASI.
28. Letter from Under Secretary, Government of India to Chief Secretary, Government of Bombay of 5/8 October 1906, no. 31 of 1906, ASI.
29. Letter of Hultzsch to Marshall of 28 February 1905, no. 31 of 1906, ASI.
30. Sahni (1907–8c): 117–30. Also see Sahni (1911–12): 20–6.
31. Sahni (1908–9): 133–8.
32. Marshall (1910–11): 1.
33. Marshall's letter to Sahni of 10 February 1909, no. 337 (1–34) of 1908, ASI.
34. Marshall and Sahni (1909–10): 93–103. In this, see footnote 1.
35. He also, simultaneously, prepared a catalogue of the exhibits which was published in 1914. See Sahni and Vogel (1914).

36. Vogel's confidential letter to Marshall of 11 May 1911, no. 109 (1–11) of 1911, ASI.
37. Vogel's note to R. Burn, Secretary to the Government, United Provinces of 11 May 1911, no. 109 (1–11) of 1911, ASI.
38. Letter from Sahni to Marshall of 17 October 1912, no. 109 (1–11) of 1911, ASI.
39. Letter from J.C. Chatterji, Director of the Archaeological and Research Department of Kashmir to Marshall of 18 June 1905, no. 123 of 1905, ASI.
40. See Kak (1939): 279–88.
41. Letter from Marshall to Resident, Kashmir, of 7 April 1906, no. 40 of 1906, ASI.
42. Note of Marshall (undated) of 1908 on Archaeological Work in Kashmir, ibid.
43. Ibid.
44. Letter from Marshall to Fleet of 27 August 1907, no. 200 of 1906, ASI.
45. Letter from S.H. Fraser, British Resident at Kashmir to Marshall of 16 March 1912, no. 182 (1–19) of 1912, ASI.
46. This period is supposed to have ended in AD 1339 when the widow of the last 'Hindu' ruler of Kashmir, Queen Kota, was murdered by Shah Mir.
47. Sahni (1915–16): 49–78.
48. Sahni (1913–14): 40–62.
49. Sahni (1917): 7.
50. *The Morning Post* (1915).
51. See Daya Ram Sahni's typed report 'Excavations at Harappa'. The exact amount was Rs 2,771/9/5. See no. 548 of 1920, ASI.
52. Ibid. This is an undated report but reached Marshall's office by 30 September 1921. All details about Sahni's excavation and the quotations as well, unless otherwise stated, are from this report. See no. 367 of 1922, ASI.
53. Letter from Sahni to Marshall of 14 April, 1921. No. 549 (1) of 1920, ASI.
54. Letter from Marshall to Sahni of 21/26th April 1921, ibid.
55. Letter of Sahni to Marshall (undated), received at the latter's office on 30 September 1921, no. 548 of 1920, ASI.

56. The subsequent section is written entirely on the basis of Sahni's undated report 'Excavations at Harappa', ibid.
57. Sahni's letter to Marshall of 27/28 October 1921, no. 375 (III) of 1920–2, ASI.
58. Marshall's letter to Sahni of 27 December 1921, ibid.
59. Marshall (1920–1): 16.
60. Ibid.: 17.
61. Hennessy (1925): 495.
62. Letter from Marshall to Curzon of 10 August 1922, no. 604 of 1921, ASI. I thank Rukun Advani for drawing my attention to the literary allusion in this letter. 'The Inchcape Rock' is a narrative poem by Robert Southey about the shipwreck of a pirate vessel which is dashed against the notorious Inchcape rock. It was much anthologized and taught to schoolchildren, from at least Marshall's time down to the 1970s in India. In using this expression, Marshall was satirizing Lord Inchcape, via Southey's poem.
63. Practically all the details and quotations, unless otherwise stated, are from this file, which contains papers regarding the Inchcape Committee, no. 367 of 1922, ASI.
64. Typewritten and handwritten undated note, ibid.: 10.
65. Ibid.: 12.
66. This was without taking into account the amount that had been provided for Aurel Stein, namely Rs 24,000 for exploration in Afghanistan and Rs 36,130 for publishing the results of his Central Asian work and for preserving and exhibiting his finds to the public at Delhi.
67. Typewritten and handwritten undated note, no. 367 of 1922, p. 13, ASI.
68. Ibid.
69. Ibid. This portion is handwritten and does not bear a page number.
70. Ibid.
71. Ibid.
72. Ibid.
73. Sarkar (1983): 204ff.
74. Marshall's letter to H. Sharp, Secretary, Education Department, Delhi, of 30 January 1922, no. 520 of 1921, ASI.
75. Marshall's letter to C. Stanley Clarke of 18 May 1922, ibid.
76. Forwarding note of Superintendent, Government Printing, to Director

General of Archaeology of 18 June 1924, no. 553 of 1924, ASI. For Sarnath, Sahni's letter to Spooner of 17 May 1923, no. 498/16 of 1921–4 (II).

77. Noting on the Sankisa excavations, no. 74 of 1919, ASI.
78. The biographical details about Maitra come from the *Journal of the Varendra Research Museum 1981–82* (7) which was devoted to A.K. Maitra. It contains twenty-one papers which were presented at a seminar organized in February 1982 at Rajshahi on 'A.K. Maitra and Archaeological Studies in Bengal'. See Rahman (1981–2).
79. Cited in Islam (1981–2): 35.
80. D.B. Spooner's letter (officiating Director General of the Survey) to W.W. Hornell (Director of Public Instruction, Bengal) of 10 March 1919, no. 249 (1–15) of 1919, ASI.
81. Spooner's letter to Secretary, Royal Asiatic Society of 29 November 1919, no. 434 of 1919, ASI.
82. Spooner's note of 29 April 1919, no. 491 of 1919, ASI.
83. Sahni's letter to Marshall of 25 February 1921, no. 72 of 1921–4, ASI.
84. Marshall's letter to Political Secretary to the ruler of Bhopal of 5 February 1920, Central India Agency, no. 251 of 1913, NAI.
85. Letter of T.A. Joyce, Department of Ceramics and Ethnography, British Museum to Marshall of 8 June 1922 and extract from letter of Victoria and Albert Museum (sender's name not mentioned) to Marshall of 30 April 1923, no. 72 of 1921–4, ASI.
86. No. 479 (part II) of 1919, ASI. This file contains a large amount of correspondence pertaining to the preservation of the Ajanta frescoes.

## CHAPTER 9: TALENT AND TROUBLE AT CALCUTTA

1. Banerji's letter to Marshall of 13/28 March 1923. This letter is from 'Camp Mohenjodaro' and was sent to Taxila. See no. 839/III, General, volume I of 1920, ASI.
2. For an account of Banerji's life, see Bhattacharya (1999). Apparently, Banerji's father was a very successful district lawyer and the son of a rich Brahmin landed family: 'Rakhaldas was proud to mention that his ancestors enjoyed a zamindari received from the Mughal emperor Aurangzeb; and that, as one of his forefathers fought the British, they were forced out of their ancestral estate.'

3. Many of the details about Banerji's education and training are based on chapter 4 of Tapati Guha-Thakurta (2004). I am very grateful to her for sending me a draft of the chapter even before her book was published.
4. See Banerji (1909–10a): 106.
5. Letter from Banerji to Sten Konow of 20 August 1907, no. 268 of 1907, ASI.
6. Banerji (1907–8a and b).
7. F. Kielhorn was a well-known epigraphist and professor at Gottingen in Germany. He was among the most regular contributors to *Epigraphia Indica* and some volumes of that journal contained as many as ten articles written by him. Several inscriptions he edited and published were sent to him by other epigraphists, European and British, such as E. Hultzsch and G.H. Ojha.
8. Letter from Banerji to Konow of September (undated) 1907, no. 268 of 1907, ASI.
9. Banerji (1909–10a): 106.
10. Ibid.
11. In another article, written a little later, Banerji described and analysed three sculptures from the Lucknow Museum, where again both iconography and epigraphy were explored. See Banerji (1909–10b).
12. Banerji (1907–8b): 285.
13. Guha-Thakurta (2004).
14. Banerji (1913–14a): 6–10.
15. Banerji (1917–18): 324–30.
16. See Mukhopadhyay (1979): 174. It was only when the university eventually relaxed its rules and allowed him to lecture in Bengali that Ramendrasundar gave his guest lectures.
17. Banerji (1919a).
18. For details, see Guha-Thakurta (2004).
19. Banerji's letter to Marshall of 23 October 1909, no. 344 (1–22), part I of 1909, ASI.
20. See Vogel (1909–10b): 10.
21. The Lucknow Museum authorities, on the other hand, remembered his indiscretion rather longer. In 1910 itself, Vogel tried to get Banerji appointed to the newly created post of curator of the Museum. He was firmly told that the Lucknow Museum Committee was unwilling

because, in 1907–8, the latter had not made a favourable impression on them.

22. A list of museums with details about their sections, outlays, and personnel can be found in 'Information Regarding Museums in India' of July 1911, no. 210 of 1911, ASI.
23. Note of Marshall to Honorary Secretary to the Trustees of the Indian Museum of 20 January 1920, no. 396 of 1920, ASI.
24. Marshall (1913–14): 46–8. This paragraph and the next are based on this report.
25. Banerji (1911–12): 161–6.
26. See Banerji (1913–14b): 248–61.
27. Letter of Colonel P.A.J. Gordon to Director General of Archaeology of 9 May 1910, no. 71 of 1910, ASI.
28. Ibid.
29. Note of Banerji of 8 April 1911, no. 218 of 1911, ASI.
30. Letter of J.F. Gruning, Secretary to Government, Eastern Bengal and Assam, to Director General of Archaeology of 23 June 1911, ibid.
31. Letter from Spooner to Vogel of 9 May 1911, ibid.
32. Vogel's letter to Marshall of 11 May 1911, no. 109 of 1909, ASI. There he wrote: 'As regards further appointments, I should suggest to promote Banerji to an assistant superintendentship. He has actually been doing the work for which Daya Ram was appointed and he has tried his best for the Indian Museum (to which he is really devoted) under most adverse circumstances.'
33. Vogel's letter to Natesan Iyer, Archaeological Assistant in the Nagpur Museum of 12 October 1911. Natesan Iyer, Vogel suggested, should be appointed as excavation assistant in place of Banerji, no. 295 of 1911, ASI.
34. See J.O. Miller's letter to Marshall of 15 June 1903, no. 55 of 1903, ASI.
35. For details of transactions in this paragraph, see Lahiri (2000): 96–7.
36. Noting about Banerji's letter of 23 March 1912, no. 76 of 1912, ASI.
37. Marshall's letter to Banerji of 26 March 1912, ibid.
38. Banerji's letter to Marshall of 29 March 1912, ibid.
39. Marshall's letter to Banerji of 30 April 1912, ibid.
40. See list of Acquisitions, Mathura Museum 1910–11, no. 123 of 1911, ASI.

41. Banerji's letter to Marshall of 11 April 1912, no. 76 of 1912, ASI. These problems also seem to have become common knowledge in the corridors of government. Many years later, a deputy secretary in the imperial government (J.M. Mitra), while making his noting on a question regarding the future administration of the archaeological section of the Indian Museum, commented that it was a well-known fact that when Rakhaldas Banerji had held the post of assistant superintendent in charge of the archaeological section, he had indulged in various 'pranks against the Archaeological Department which made it difficult for Sir John Marshall to control the working of the section'.
42. Ibid. This file, in fact, is full of such notings.
43. Marshall's letter to Secretary, Department of Education of 1 February 1913, no. 41 of 1913, ASI.
44. See Marshall's letter to Home Department of 5 August 1908, no. 295 of 1908, ASI.
45. Banerji's horse-drawn carriage for his personal use is just one example of his prodigal nature. Stories of his extravagance were legion and, among other things, he was known to have tipped ten rupees to a coolie at a railway station at a time when one maund of rice could be bought for less than a rupee. Bhattacharya (1999:13) tells us that this was because of his wealthy landed background and his character: 'Rakhaldas was habituated in a way of life that would have better suited a prince of the days of the Nawabs. . . . He was a man of corpulent figure with a matching heart.' Banerji had two sons, Asim and Adris. His older son, Asim, died in 1923.
46. Note of Marshall of 18 May 1919, no. 233 of 1919, ASI. In that note, Marshall mentioned to the Government of Bombay that Banerji had sent for publication to the journal of the Bihar and Orissa Research Society an article on certain inscriptions from Andhau in the Bombay Presidency, in which he had impugned the honesty of his predecessor. He even sent to the journal a photographed copy of certain correspondence which Bhandarkar had had with Luders and which Banerji had abstracted from the office file. This would possibly have rendered Banerji liable to penalties under the Official Secrets Act, and on Marshall's directions the Bombay government got the paper withdrawn.

## CHAPTER 10: MAVERICK AT MOHENJODARO

1. The imperial government contributed a little over Rs 18,500 that year.
2. Banerji (1921): 2.
3. Ibid. These and the details on Banerji's work in that year come from the same report.
4. Marshall (1919–20): 35.
5. Banerji (1922).
6. Banerji (1921): 2.
7. Banerji (1919b): 3.
8. Banerji (1920): 57ff.
9. Cousens (1897): 5.
10. Banerji (1921): 80.
11. Bhandarkar (1912): 4–5.
12. Ibid.
13. Banerji (1922): 113.
14. The details on Carter's archaeological activities comes from the correspondence that is contained in no. 425 of 1918, ASI. For his published articles, see Carter (1917) and (1918).
15. Marshall's letter to Governor of Bombay of 8 May 1918, no. 425 of 1918, ASI.
16. See letter of D.B. Spooner, Officiating Director General of Archaeology to Carter of 20 March 1919, ibid. The letter mentions Carter's designation as Assistant Collector, Thane.
17. Letter of Carter to Marshall of 18 June 1918, ibid.
18. On 28 November 1924, for instance, in a letter to K.N. Dikshit, who was readying himself for excavations at Mohenjodaro in particular and the exploration of Sindh in general, Marshall asked him to look out for sites where flint implements, cut marble or painted pottery were found. He must also have remembered Carter's earlier work because he said Carter had 'made a fine collection of flints at Tharro near Gujo between Garo and Thathah'. See Marshall's letter to Dikshit of 28th November 1924 in no. 839, General of 1924, ASI.
19. Letter of Marshall to Banerji of 18 May 1918, no. 388 of 1918, ASI.
20. Marshall mentioned this in his letter to the Chief Secretary, Bombay Government of 14 January 1919, ibid.
21. Banerji's letter of 3 January 1919 to Colvin, quoted by Colvin in his letter to Marshall of 18 January 1919, ibid.

22. In his letter of 3 January 1919, Colvin suggested that Banerji had asked him to ensure he had a clean room wherever he went. Colvin was obviously displeased: 'the reference to a "clean room" is liable to give offence and generally I take exception to the tone of the letter.'
23. Letter of Secretary of 4 December 1922 to the Government of Bombay to Secretary, Department of Education and Health, Proceedings of the Department of Education, Health and Lands (PEDHL hereafter) (AE-B), nos. 1–4 of February 1923, NAI. Apparently, because of the increased pressure of conservation work, the Bombay government had sanctioned eleven sub-overseers to be placed at Banerji's disposal by the public works department. But none of them seemed to stick around for long. In fact, in 1921, six out of them had either resigned or had reverted to their original posts.
24. Banerji's letter to Marshall of 3 April 1921, no. 492 of 1920–2, ASI.
25. Letter from C.G. Adam to Marshall of 12 September 1921, ibid.
26. Letter from Marshall to Adam of 17 September 1921, ibid.
27. Letter from Adam to Marshall of 22 September 1921, ibid.
28. Letter from Marshall to H. Sharp, Education Secretary, Government of India of 29 September 1921, ibid.
29. See correspondence between Marshall and Banerji in ibid.
30. PEDHL (AE-B), nos. 1–4 of February 1923, NAI.
31. Letter of Chairman of 12 October 1922 to the Board of Trustees, Prince of Wales Museum, to Secretary to Government, General Department, ibid.
32. The details of some of these irregularities were spelt out by the Chairman to the Board of Trustees of the Prince of Wales Museum, ibid. These related to giving incomplete accounts of the amount advanced and of discrepancies in relation to the estimates that Banerji had given. According to them, 'the total amount of Rs 1,21,892-6-9 advanced has thus not yet been accounted for by him satisfactorily.'
33. Banerji's letter to Secretary, Department of Education and Health of 2 November 1922, ibid.
34. Note of Marshall of 12 March 1920. Marshall's comment is interesting: 'Mr Banerji, as I know from past experience, has lordly ideas about spending Government money, and if he is given all he asks for, he will spend without stint. On the other hand, if his requests are refused, he will promptly say that his work is at a stand still.' No. 73 (I) of 1920, ASI.

35. Banerji refers to this letter in another confidential letter to Marshall of 26 July 1922, no. 25/II of 1921–2, ASI.
36. Marshall's letter reads:

    I do not think there is much likelihood of Government agreeing to your transfer at present, but nevertheless I should be glad to hear from you as to whether you would care for transfer to the Eastern (ie., Bengal) Circle. That is the only Circle where transfer might be at all possible at the present time.

    I am bound to say, though, that I do not think you will be at all well advised to desire transfer in the existing circumstances. The interpretation which would be put upon any such desire on your part, would not be in your interests for reasons too obvious to need explanation.

    'Confidential' letter of Marshall to Banerji of 9 August 1922, ibid.
37. Note of M.S. D. Butler of 22 December 1922, PEDHL (AE-B), nos. 1–4 of February 1923, NAI.
38. Marshall's letter to M.S.D. Butler, marked 'Confidential' of 23 November 1922, ibid.
39. A large part of this section is based on Banerji (1984): 26. Banerji's memoir on Mohenjodaro was submitted to Marshall in 1926. Marshall originally intended publishing it in his volumes on Mohenjodaro. However, in 1929 Marshall asked Hargreaves, who had taken over as director general of archaeology to inform Banerji that he would be unable to do so. He suggested that Banerji be given permission to publish the memoir if he so wished. Marshall was unwilling to include Banerji's in his projected work because, as he put it

    after an exhaustive examination of it I have decided that it is altogether too diffuse and contains too many mistakes, and irrelevancies for me to do more than quote extracts from it. Knowing Mr Banerji, however, as I do, I think it is not unlikely that he may charge the authors of the Mohenjodaro volume with making use of his material without acknowledging their debt to him, and for this reason I think it would be well if you return this transcript to him and give him permission to publish if he so wishes. At the same time you might tell him that owing to its many errors, I am unable to publish his contribution. I am endeavouring to give him the fullest credit for his share in the work of Mohenjodaro, and for this purpose

> am making such use of what he has written as is possible. Personally, both Mr Mackay and myself would prefer Mr Banerji's article to be published before the Mohenjodaro volumes come out, as there can be then no loophole for misunderstanding the precise extent of the debt due to him. It would be unkind, however, not to warn him that many of his theories are quite untenable and many of his statements incorrect.

See Marshall's letter to Hargreaves of 30 September 1929, no. 839 of 1920–35, ASI. It has been necessary to extract this letter because it has frequently been said (most recently by Guha-Thakurta 2004) that Banerji was somehow shortchanged by Marshall. Banerji's returned memoir was discovered after his death by his son, in his late father's photographic collection.

40. Banerji (1984).
41. Ibid.: 2.
42. Ibid.: 2ff.
43. Ibid.: 16–17.
44. Ibid.: 17.
45. Ibid.
46. Banerji (1921): 78.
47. Banerji (1919b): 58.
48. The account of his excavations there is based on R.D. Banerji's summary of his excavations in *Annual Report of the Archaeological Survey of India 1922–23*. See Banerji (1922–3). Also, read this along with Banerji (1984).
49. Ibid.: 29.
50. His view that it was the figure of a bull is mentioned in his first letter to Marshall, while in the *Annual Report of the Archaeological Survey of India 1922–23*, he mentioned that the figure was a one-horned quadruped which had been identified by D.B. Spooner as a unicorn. See Banerji (1922–3): 103.
51. Ibid.
52. Ibid.
53. They had, as we saw, turned up at Kalibangan, but the Survey men were not aware of Tessitori's discovery.
54. Ibid.
55. Ibid.: 102.

56. Ibid.: 103–4.
57. Banerji's letter to Marshall of 13/28 March 1923, no. 839/III of 1920, ASI.
58. Ibid.
59. Marshall's letter to Banerji of 3 April 1923, ibid.
60. Libby also published the first radiocarbon dates.
61. For this, and other methods of dating, see Renfrew and Bahn (1991).
62. Marshall's noting of 2 April 1923 says: 'Dr Spooner will like to see this letter and the seals and coins as well as my interim reply to Banerji.' No. 839/III of 1920, ASI.
63. Spooner's letter to Banerji of 13/17 April 1923, ibid.
64. They would finally be executed only in the middle of 1924, once Banerji had cleared the matter concerning the accounts of the Prince of Wales Museum. He was unable to do anything before this because he was on long medical leave.
65. M.S.L. Butler's letter (marked 'Confidential') to Secretary, Bombay Government of 25 January 1923, PEDHL (AE-B), nos. 1–4 of February 1923, NAI.
66. Maharaj Singh's letter to Marshall of February (exact date unclear) 1923, ibid.
67. Letter of G.C. Chandra, Officiating Superintendent, Western Circle to Director General of Archaeology of 19 September 1923, ibid.

## CHAPTER 11: STRINGING SCATTERED IDEAS

1. Marshall's letter to Spooner of 14 August 1923, no. 838 (III) General, volume I of 1920, ASI.
2. Banerji's letter to Spooner of 16 April 1923, ibid.
3. Spooner's letter to Banerji of 23 April 1923, ibid.
4. Banerji's letter to Spooner of 5 May 1923, ibid.
5. Banerji's letter to G.C. Chandra of 20 June 1923, ibid.
6. Letter of Banerji to Spooner of 26 April 1923, ibid.
7. Ibid.
8. The number refers to the entry in Mahadevan (1977): 32.
9. Letter of Banerji to Spooner of 26 April 1923, no. 839 (III) General, volume I of 1920, ASI.
10. Letter of Banerji to Spooner of 26 April 1923, ibid.

11. Ibid.
12. For a discussion of this aspect, see Chakrabarti (1997).
13. Banerji (1934): 13. This was published posthumously by Banerji's son, A.C. Banerji.
14. Spooner's letter to Banerji of 7 May 1923, no. 839 (III) General, volume I, of 1920, ASI.
15. Spooner's letter to Banerji of 13 April 1923, ibid.
16. Spooner's letter to Banerji of 7 May 1923, ibid.
17. Ibid.
18. *The Times* (1923a).
19. *The Times* (1923b).
20. See Spooner's letter to Marshall of 23 July 1923, no. 839 (III) General, volume I of 1920, ASI.
21. Ibid.
22. Ibid.
23. Extract from a letter of Marshall to Spooner of 14 August 1923, ibid.
24. Marshall (1923–4a): 142–3.
25. Marshall (1923–4b): 61.
26. Banerji's letter to Marshall of 13 March 1924, no. 839 (III) General, volume I of 1920, ASI.
27. Marshall's letter to Banerji of 18 March 1924, ibid.
28. Buller (1903–4).
29. Banerji's letter to Marshall of 22 March 1924, no. 839 (III) General, volume 1 of 1920, ASI.
30. See Chakrabarti (1988): 193ff.
31. This, for instance, is how Arthur Evans described the Minoan civilization that he discovered in Crete in 1900.
32. Marshall's letter to Banerji of 28 March 1924, no. 839/III, General, volume 1 of 1920, volume 1, ASI.
33. Marshall's letter to Banerji of 28 March 1924, ibid.
34. Banerji's letter to Marshall of 31 March 1924, ibid.
35. Telegram from Marshall to Banerji of 1 April 1924, ibid.
36. Letter of Marshall to Banerji of 3 April 1924, ibid.
37. Letter from Chief Secretary to Government of Bihar and Orissa to President of the Managing Committee of the Patna Museum, no. 267 (nos. 1–2) of 1918, ASI.

38. Vats (1925–6).
39. Letter of Vats to Marshall of 29 April 1924, no. 839/III, General, volume 1 of 1920, ASI. What follows in the next few paragraphs is also based on this.

## CHAPTER 12: ANNOUNCING THE DISCOVERY

1. Buck (1989): 109–10.
2. The correspondence which is referred to in this and the next few paragraphs, in the form of copies of telegrams and letters that were exchanged between Marshall and the various Survey circles, comes from no. 839/III, General, volume I of 1920, ASI.
3. Chanda's letter to Marshall of 6 June 1924, ibid.
4. Banerji's letter to Marshall of 21 May 1924, no. 803 of 1923, ASI.
5. See Marshall's letter to G.C. Chandra of 10 June 1924 which says that 'Mr Banerji has shown me the tracings of the plans of the Mohen-jo-daro excavations'. There is also a letter of 25 June from Marshall to Chandra asking him to despatch certain antiquities—bricks, skeleton and skull, shrine relics, and fragments of large burial jars—at an early date to Simla. He says in that letter that, 'Mr Banerji tells me that they were left in the charge of Mr V.M. Karandekar, Upper Subordinate, attached to your office.' Ibid.
6. Marshall (1923–4c): 48.
7. Banerji's letter of 6 January 1925 to *Amrita Bazar Patrika*, no. 839 of 1925, General, ASI.
8. This forms the title of Marshall's announcement of the discovery of the civilization of the Indus in *The Illustrated London News*. See Marshall (1924a).
9. The Frenchman was a customs inspector called Jacques Boucher de Perthes. See Daniel (1962): 44ff.
10. Marshall (1923–4c): 47.
11. I owe this analogy to Rukun Advani, who suggests that the work of detection and piecing together puzzles seems often to be performed by intellectuals who find isolation more conducive than fieldwork.
12. This and all other quotations that follow come from Marshall (1924a).
13. Smith (1889).

## CHAPTER 13: AN ASTONISHING AFTERMATH

1. Marshall (1924a): 528–32 and 548.
2. Sayce (1924): 526.
3. It had first been published by Ernest de Sarzec and Leon Heuzey and republished in 1920 by Louis Delaporte. This has been discussed in Chakrabarti (1990): 21.
4. Gadd and Smith (1924): 614–16.
5. Marshall (1923–4): 48.
6. Circular letter to Northology, Westology and Frontology of 3 November 1924, no. 839 of 1924–5, ASI.
7. See Possehl (1999): 77.
8. Mackay's letter to Marshall is dated 20 October 1924. It reached Taxila on 10 November, no. 839 of 1924–5, ASI.
9. This is the date that is now accepted for Hammurabi's reign. Mackay's letter, though, mentioned *c.* 2200 BC as the date.
10. These are Marshall's own words. See note to Daya Ram Sahni (undated) attached to circular letter of 3 November 1924, ibid.
11. Circular letter to Northology, Westology, Frontology of 3 November 1924, ibid.
12. Note to H.Krishna Sastri (undated) attached to circular letter of 3 November 1924, ibid.
13. Emphasis added. See Marshall's letter to Vogel of 10 November 1924, ibid. In a great deal of correspondence on the Indus sites in 1924, the culture was described as 'Indo-Sumerian'. It was only following Dikshit's excavations at Mohenjodaro and Sahni's dig at Harappa in 1925 that this term was dropped. Dikshit, for example, wrote to Marshall that 'a careful comparison of the products of early Indian civilization with those of the Sumerian will probably bring out more points of difference than similarity.' See Dikshit's letter to Marshall of 11 June 1925, no. 839, 1920–35, ASI.
14. The note is dated 14 November 1924.
15. This and other quotations that follow come from Marshall (1924b): 6 & 8.
16. Marshall returned to the question of such links in his concluding paragraph. There, he affirmed that Sahni and Banerji had established 'once for all the existence on Indian soil in the third millennium BC

of a civilization as highly developed and seemingly as widespread as the Sumerian culture of Mesopotamia, with conclusive evidence of a close contact between the two.'

17. *The Statesman* (1924b): 12.
18. *The Amrita Bazar Patrika* (1924): 3.
19. *The Statesman* (1924a): 19. The article was published on 23 November and is entitled 'Forgotten Civilization Discovered in India'.
20. See the recommendation of V.S. Ghate, Professor of Sanskrit at Deccan College of 17 July 1912, no. 343 (serial nos. 1–15), December 1912, ASI.
21. Marshall's letter to Dikshit of 28 November 1924, no. 839 of 1924–5, ASI.
22. Dikshit's letter to Marshall of 14 December 1924. Also see Marshall's letter to Banerji of 24 December 1924, ibid.
23. *The Amrita Bazar Patrika* (1924): 3. All the quotations that follow are from this editorial.
24. See chapter 8.
25. Letter from Banerji to Marshall of 28 April 1925, no. 839/General, ASI.
26. Ibid.
27. Banerji (1925).
28. Fair Play (1925).
29. Marshall's letter to the editor of 17 January 1925, no. 839/General of 1925, ASI.
30. Wilson's letter to Marshall of 23 May 1925, ibid.
31. Marshall's letter to Wilson of 1 June 1925, ibid.

## AFTERWORD: INAUGURATING A NEW ERA

1. Letter to Mrs Spooner of 12 March 1925, no. 839 of 1924–5, ASI. Spooner died in January 1925.
2. Marshall's letters to Dikshit and Sahni of 28 November 1924, ibid.
3. Marshall's note of 12 March 1925, no. 839/General of 1925, Notes for parts i and ii, ASI. All the instructions to his assistants are from this note.
4. This is the phrase of Leo Deuel (1969): xvi.
5. Marshall's note of 12 May 1925, no. 839 of 1924–5, ASI.
6. Sahni's letter to Marshall of 6 January 1925, no. 839/ii General of 1924, ASI.

7. Marshall's letter to Dikshit of 28 November 1925, no. 839 of 1924–5, ASI.
8. The quotations in brackets are from Marshall's note to Dikshit of 30 December 1924, no. 839 of 1924–5, ASI.
9. Dikshit's letter to Marshall of 11 May 1925, no. 839/General of 1925, ASI.
10. Hargreaves's letter to Marshall of 11 March 1925, no. 853 (i) of 1925, ASI.
11. This was outlined by Marshall in detail in the autumn of 1925. See Marshall's undated note in no. 877 of 1925–6, ASI. The notes that precede and follow it suggest that this one was penned either in the last week of September or early October 1925.
12. This may be because of the letter that he had received from Babu Manoranjan Ghosh, curator of the Patna Museum, in 1924. In that letter, Ghosh suggested a link between the pottery he had found at Bulandibagh in Patna and the Sindh material. He wrote: 'Last March when I was at Calcutta on duty I went to see Mr R.D. Banerjee and read his draft memoir on the excavation at Sind and saw some of the antiquities found by him. He spoke of his polished pottery. I informed him of polished potteries found by me at Bulandibagh. He said that he would like to see them. On his way to Simla, he saw them and *at once* he said that he had found such similar polished potteries in his Sind Excavation.' See Ghosh's letter to Marshall of 3 September 1924, no. 851 of 1924, ASI.
13. Foucher (1939): 355.

# REFERENCES

## ARCHIVAL SOURCES

Files of the Office of the Director General of Archaeology in India in the Archaeological Survey of India, New Delhi.

Proceedings of the Revenue and Statistics Department of 1901, Curzon Collection (IOR MSS EUR F112/644) in the Oriental and India Office Collection of the British Library, London.

Proceedings of the Revenue and Agriculture Department, Foreign Department, Home Department and Education Department. Also files of Southern States of Central India and Malwa Agency, Central India Agency, National Archives of India, New Delhi.

Files and Correspondence in the Tessitori Collection of the Rajasthan State Archives, Bikaner.

## PUBLISHED SOURCES


Allchin, F.R. 1995. The Mauryan State and Empire in F.R. Allchin, ed. *The Archaeology of Early Historic South Asia*. Cambridge: Cambridge University Press, pp. 187–221.

Annual Report for 1915. 1916. *Journal and Proceedings of the Asiatic Society of Bengal* New Series XII (1–6): iii–xxii.

Balbir, N. 1999. The Story of Solomon's Judgment Revisted, in D. Dolcini and F. Freschi, eds. *Tessitori and Rajasthan*. Proceedings of the International Conference, Bikaner, 21–23 February 1996. Udine: Societa Indologica, pp. 65–90.

Banerji, R.D. 1907–8a. Patiakella Grant of Maharaja Sivaraja; [Gupta-] Samvat, 283. *Epigraphia Indica* IX: 285–8.

———. 1907–8b. Mundesvari Inscription of Udayasena the [Harsha] Year 30. *Epigraphia Indica* IX: 289–90.

———. 1909–10a. New Brahmi Inscriptions of the Scythian Period. *Epigraphia Indica* X: 106–21.

———. 1909–10b. Three Sculptures in the Lucknow Museum. *Annual Report of the Archaeological Survey of India 1909–10*: 146–9.

———. 1911–12. Four Sculptures from Chandimau. *Annual Report of the Archaeological Survey of India 1911–12*: 161–6.

———. 1913–14a. The Tarpandighi Grant of Lakshmana Sena. *Epigraphia Indica* XII: 6–10.

———. 1913–14b. Notes on Indian Numismatics. *Annual Report of the Archaeological Survey of India 1913–14*: 248–61.

———. 1917–18. The Bangarh Grant of Mahi-Pala I: The 9th Year. *Epigraphia Indica* XIV: 324–30.

———. 1919a. Reprint 1973. *The Origin of the Bengali Script*. Calcutta: Nababharat Publishers.

———. 1919b. *Progress Report of the Archaeological Survey of India Western Circle for the Year Ending 31st March 1918*. Bombay: Government Central Press.

———. 1920. *Progress Report of the Archaeological Survey of India Western Circle for the Year Ending 31st March 1919*. Bombay: Government Central Press.

———. 1921. *Progress Report of the Archaeological Survey of India Western Circle for the Year Ending 31st March 1920*. Calcutta: Baptist Mission Press.

———. 1922. *Progress Report of the Archaeological Survey of India Western Circle for the Year Ending 31st March 1921*. Bombay: Government Central Press.

———. 1922–3. Mohen-jo-daro. *Annual Report of the Archaeological Survey of India 1922–23*: 102–4.

———. 1925. Mohenjodaro Discoveries, An Explanation, to the Editor. *The Amrita Bazar Patrika*, 6 January.

———. 1934. Reprint 1950. *Prehistoric Ancient and Hindu India*. Bombay, Calcutta, Madras: Blackie & Son.

———. 1984. *Mohenjodaro, A Forgotten Report*. Varanasi: Prithvi Prakashan.

Banthia, H.M. 1989. Reprint 1995. Dr L.P. Tessitory: The First Discoverer of Kalibanga (originally printed in *Jain Journal Quarterly* XXIII [4] April), in R.C. Sharma and G.K. Agrawal, eds. *Sri Hazarimal Banthia Abhinandan Granth*. Aligarh: Sri Hazarimal Banthia Samman Samaroh, p. 48. (See section entitled Sri Hazarimal Banthia Rachit Sahitya Da. L.P. Tessitori.)

———. 1999. A Tribute to Dr Luigi Pio Tessitori, in D. Dolcini and F. Freschi, eds. *Tessitori and Rajasthan*. Proceedings of the International Conference, Bikaner, 21–23 February 1996. Udine: Societa Indologica, pp. 3–6.

Barbagli, M. (translated by R.H. Ross). 1982. *Educating for Unemployment*. New York: Columbia University Press.

Begley, V. and de Puma, R. 1991. Reprint 1992. *Rome and India: The Ancient Sea Trade*. Delhi: Oxford University Press.

Begum, S. 1867. *The History of Bhopal*, translated by H.C. Barstow. Calcutta: Thacker, Spink & Co.

Begum, Nawab Sultan Jahan. 1922 & 1927. *An Account of My Life*, volumes II and III. Bombay: The Times Press.

Bhandarkar, D.R. 1902a. The Nausari Copper-plate Charter of the Gujarat Rashtrakuta Prince Karkka I, Dated Saka 738. *The Journal of the Bombay Branch of the Royal Asiatic Society* XX: 131–49.

———. 1902b. A Kushana Stone-inscription and the Question about the Origin of the Saka Era. *The Journal of the Bombay Branch of the Royal Asiatic Society* XX: 269–302.

———. 1904a. Epigraphic Notes and Questions. *The Journal of the Bombay Branch of the Royal Asiatic Society* XXI: 392–412.

———. 1904b. Gurjaras. *The Journal of the Bombay Branch of the Royal Asiatic Society* XXI: 413–33.

———. 1912. Mohenjodaro. *Progress Report of the Archaeological Survey of India Western Circle for the Year Ending 31st March 1912*. Bombay: General Department.

Bhattacharya, A.K. 1999. *Rakhaldas Bandhopadhyay*. Delhi: Sahitya Akademi.

Beloff, M. 1969. *Britain's Liberal Empire 1897–1921*, volume I. London: Methuen & Co.

Botto. O. 1954. Gaspare Gorresio. *East and West.* Year V, no. 1 (April): 35–7.

Bosworth, A.B. 1996. *Alexander and the East, The Tragedy of Triumph.* Oxford: Clarendon Press.

Buck, E.J. 1904. Reprint 1989. *Simla Past and Present.* Shimla: Minerva Book House.

Buller, E.H. 1903–4. Gabarbands in Baluchistan. *Annual Report of the Archaeological Survey of India 1903–4*: 194–201.

Burnes, A. 1834. Reprint 1973. *Travels into Bokhara Together with a Narrative of a Voyage on the Indus*, three volumes. Karachi: Oxford University Press.

Caillat, C. 1999. Luigi Pio Tessitori and International Cooperation in the 19th–20th Century, in D. Dolcini and F. Freschi, ed. *Tessitori and Rajasthan.* Proceedings of the International Conference, Bikaner, 21–23 February 1996. Udine: Societa Indologica, pp. 7–27.

*Cambridge University Reporter.* 1912. Approved for the Degree of Litt.D. (June 4): 1121.

Carter, G.E.L. 1917. Notes on Sind. *Indian Antiquary* XLVI: 133.

———. 1918. Religion in Sind. *Indian Antiquary* XLVII: 197–208.

Caygill, M. 1985. *Treasures of the British Museum.* London: British Museum.

Chakrabarti, D.K. 1988. *A History of Indian Archaeology, from the Beginning to 1947.* New Delhi: Munshiram Manoharlal Publishers Pvt. Ltd.

———. 1990. *The External Trade of the Indus Civilization.* New Delhi: Munshiram Manoharlal Publishers Pvt. Ltd.

———. 1997. *Colonial Indology: Sociopolitics of the Ancient Indian Past.* New Delhi: Munshiram Mahoharlal Publishers Pvt. Ltd.

———. 2003. *The Archaeology of European Expansion in India.* New Delhi: Aryan Books International.

Chanda, R.P. 1936. Reprint 1972. *Medieval Indian Sculptures in the British Museum.* Varanasi: Indological Book House.

Court, C.A. 1836. Conjectures on the March of Alexander. *Journal of the Asiatic Society of Bengal 1836*: 359–96.

Cousens, H. 1897. *Progress Report of the Archaeological Survey of Western India for the Year Ending 30th June 1897.* Bombay: General Department.

Cunningham, A. 1843. An Account of the Discovery of the Ruins of the Buddhist City of Samkassa. *Journal of the Royal Asiatic Society of Great Britain and Ireland 7*: 241–7.

———. 1848. Proposed Archaeological Investigation. *Journal of the Asiatic Society of Bengal 17*: 535–6.

———. 1854. Reprint 1997. *The Bhilsa Topes*. New Delhi: Munshiram Manoharlal Publishers Pvt. Ltd.

———. 1871. Reprint 2000. *Four Reports Made during the Years 1862–63–64–65. Archaeological Survey Report I.* New Delhi: Archaeological Survey of India.

———. 1875. Reprint 2000. *Report for the Year 1871–72. Archaeological Survey Report V.* New Delhi: Archaeological Survey of India.

———. 1877. Reprint 2000. *Inscriptions of Asoka. Corpus Inscriptionum Indicarum* I. New Delhi: Archaeological Survey of India.

———. 1882. Reprint 1966. *Report of a Tour in the Punjab 1878–9, Archaeological Survey Report 14.* Varanasi: Indological Book House.

Dames, M.L. 1886. Old Seals Found at Harappa. *The Indian Antiquary* XV: 1.

———. 1907. *Popular Poetry of the Baloches*. London: Folklore Society.

Daniel, G. 1962. Reprint 1971. *The Idea of Prehistory*. Harmondsworth: Penguin Books Ltd.

———. 1966. *Man Discovers His Past*. London: Gerald Duckworth and Co. Ltd.

———. 1975. *A Hundred and Fifty Years of Archaeology*. London: Gerald Duckworth and Co.

Davis, R. 1997. *Lives of Indian Images*. Princeton: Princeton University Press.

Deuel, L. 1969. *Flights into Yesterday: The Story of Aerial Archaeology*. New York: St. Martin's Press.

Din. M.M. 1908. *Bahawalpur State Punjab State Gazetteers*, volume XXXVI A. Lahore: Civil and Military Gazette Press.

Fair Play. 1925. Archaeological Department Rejoinder to Rakhal Das's letter, Letter to the Editor. *The Amrita Bazar Patrika*. 10 January.

Fasana, E. 1999. Luigi Pio Tessitori: His Historical Research and the Rajasthan of His Time, in D. Dolcini and F. Freschi, eds. *Tessitori and Rajasthan.* Proceedings of the International Conference, Bikaner, 21–23 February 1996. Udine: Societa Indologica, pp. 29–64.

Fleet, J. 1912. Seals from Harappa. *Journal of the Royal Asiatic Society of Great Britain and Ireland:* 699–701.

Foucher, A. 1939. Translation of the Foreword in J. Cummings, ed. *Revealing India's Past.* London: The India Society, pp. 352–6.

Freschi, F. 1999. Luigi Pio Tessitori's Unpublished Works in the Archivo Peano, in D. Dolcini and F. Freschi, eds *Tessitori and Rajasthan.* Proceedings of the International Conference, Bikaner, 21–23 February 1996. Udine: Societa Indologica, pp. 197–219.

Fromichi, C. 1950. Cultural Relations between Italy and India during the Middle Ages and the Renaissance. *East and West* Year 1, no. 2 (July): 82–5.

Gadd, C.J. and S. Smith. 1924. The New Links between Indian and Babylonian Civilizations. *The Illustrated London News.* 4 October: 614–16.

Ghosh, A., ed. 1989. *An Encyclopaedia of Indian Archaeology,* volume 2. New Delhi: Munshiram Manoharlal Publishers Pvt. Ltd.

Gill, D.W.J. 2000. Collecting for Cambridge: John Hubert Marshall on Crete. *Annual of the British School at Athens* 95: 517–26.

Gilmour, D. 1994. Reprint 1995. *Curzon.* London and Basingstoke: Papermac.

Ginzburg, C. 1980. *The Cheese and the Worms: The Cosmos of a Sixteenth-century Miller.* London and Henley: Routledge and Kegan Paul.

Gopal, S. 1965. *British Policy in India 1885–1905.* Cambridge: Cambridge University Press.

Greenfield, J. 1989. *The Return of Cultural Treasures.* Cambridge: Cambridge University Press.

Grigson, G. No date. *Art Treasures of the British Museum.* New York: Harry N. Abrams.

Grierson, G.A. 1912. Notices of Books. *Journal of the Royal Asiatic Society of Great Britain and Ireland*: 794–8.

Guha-Thakurta, T. 2004. *Monuments, Objects, Histories: Institutions of Art in Colonial and Postcolonial India.* New Delhi: Permanent Black.

Hambly, G. 1974. 'Introduction' to Charles Masson's (1842) *Narrative of Various Journeys in Balochistan*, volume I. Karachi: Oxford University Press, pp. vii–xxvii.

Hardinge, C. 1948. *My Indian Years 1910–1916: The Reminiscences of Lord Hardinge of Penhurst.* London: John Murray.

Hargreaves, H.A. 1914–15. Excavations at Sarnath. *Annual Report of the Archaeological Survey of India 1914–15*: 97–131.

———. 1916. *Annual Report Hindu and Buddhist Monuments of the Northern Circle 1915–18.* Simla: Superintendent, Government Printing.

Hasan, Z. 1916. Reprint 1997. *Monuments of Delhi: Lasting Splendour of the Great Mughals and Others*, 3 volumes. New Delhi: Aryan Books International.

Hennessy, H.E. 1925. *A History of India with Notes on Administration 1526–1925.* Bombay: The Examiner Press.

Hopkirk, P. 1990. Reprint 1991. *The Great Game: On Secret Service in High Asia.* Oxford: Oxford University Press.

Horowitz, S.L. 1981. *The Find of a Lifetime—Sir Arthur Evans and the Discovery of Knossos.* London: Weidenfeld and Nicolson.

Huxley, D. 2000. *Cretan Quests: British Explorers, Excavators and Historians.* London: The British School at Athens.

Imam, A. 1966. *Sir Alexander Cunningham and the Beginnings of Indian Archaeology.* Dacca: Asiatic Society of Pakistan.

*Indian Archaeology 1899–1905.* Printed Copy in the Curzon Collection. London: Oriental and India Office Collection of the British Library.

*India's Contribution to the Great War.* 1923. Calcutta: Government of India.

Irving, M. 1910. *A List of Inscriptions on Christian Tombs or Monuments in the Punjab, North-West Frontier Province, Kashmir and Afghanistan Possessing Historical or Archaeological Interest.* Lahore: Punjab Government Press.

Islam, R. 1981–2. History of Bengal and A.K. Maitra. *Journal of the Varendra Research Museum* (7): 33–6.

Kak, R.C. 1939. Jammu and Kashmir, in J. Cummings, ed. *Revealing India's Past.* London: The India Society, pp. 279–88.

Keith, A.B. 1922. Reprint 1955. The Age of the Rigveda, in E.J. Rapson, ed. *The Cambridge History of India Volume I: Ancient India.* Delhi: S. Chand & Co., pp. 60–101.

Kejariwal, O.P. 1988. *The Asiatic Society of Bengal and the Discovery of India's Past.* New Delhi: Oxford University Press.

Khan, S.M. 2000. *The Begums of Bhopal: A Dynasty of Women Rulers in Raj India.* London and New York: I.B. Tauris Publishers.

Lahiri, N. 1996. Archaeological Landscapes and Textual Images: A Study of the Sacred Geography of Medieval Ballabgarh. *World Archaeology* 28 (2): 259–61.

———. 1997. John Marshall's Appointment as Director-General of the Archaeological Survey of India: A Survey of the Papers Pertaining to his Selection. *South Asian Studies* 13: 127–39.

———. 1998. Coming to Grips with the Indian Past: John Marshall's Early Years as Lord Curzon's Director-General of Archaeology in India—Part I. *South Asian Studies* 14: 1–23.

———. 1999. Bodh-Gaya: An Ancient Buddhist Shrine and its Modern History (1891–1904), in T. Insoll, ed. *Case Studies in Archaeology and World Religion.* Oxford: Archaeopress, pp. 33–47.

———. 2000. Coming to Grips with India's Past and Her 'Living Present': John Marshall's Early Years (1902–6)—Part II. *South Asian Studies* 16: 89–107.

———. 2003. Commemorating and Remembering 1857: The Revolt in Delhi and its Afterlife. *World Archaeology* 35(1): 35–60.

———. 2004. From Ruin to Restoration: The Modern History of Sanchi, in T. Insoll, ed. *Belief in the Past. The Proceedings of the 2002 Manchester Conference on Archaeology and Religion.* Oxford: Archaeopress, pp. 99–114.

Latham, R. 1926. Reprint 1958. *The Travels of Marco Polo.* London: Penguin Books.

Longhurst, A.H. 1909. *Annual Progress Report of the Superintendent of the Archaeological Survey, Northern Circle for the year ending 31st March 1909*: 5.

Mahadevan, I. 1977. *The Indus Script: Texts, Concordances and Tables.* New Delhi: Archaeological Survey of India.

Majumdar, R.C. 1960. *The Classical Accounts of India.* Calcutta: Firma K.L. Mukhopadhyay.

Marshall, J. 1903–4. Conservation. *Annual Report of the Director General of Archaeology for the Year 1902–3*: 3–8.

———. 1905–6. Rajagrha and its Remains. *Annual Report of the Archaeological Survey of India 1905–6*: 86–106.

———. 1908–9. Annual Report of the Director-General of Archaeology for the Year 1908–9, Part I—Administrative. *Annual Report of the Archaeological Survey of India 1908–9*: 1–8.

———. 1910–11. Excavations at Saheth–Maheth. *Annual Report of the Archaeological Survey of India 1910–11*: 1–24.

———. 1911–12. Excavations at Bhita. *Annual Report of the Archaeological Survey of India 1911–12*: 29–94.

———. 1912–13. Excavations at Taxila. *Annual Report of the Archaeological Survey of India 1912–13*: 1–52.

———. 1913–14. Annual Report of the Director-General of Archaeology for the Year 1913–14, Part I. *Annual Report of the Archaeological Survey of India 1913–14*: 1–48.

———. 1915–16. Annual Report of the Director-General of Archaeology for the Year 1915–16, Part I. *Annual Report of the Archaeological Survey of India 1915–16*: 1–29.

———. 1919–20. Annual Report of the Director-General of Archaeology in India, 1919–20. *Annual Report of the Archaeological Survey of India 1919–20*: 1–46.

———. 1920–1. Annual Report of the Director-General of Archaeology in India, 1920–1. *Annual Report of the Archaeological Survey of India 1920–21*: 1–43.

———. 1923–4a. Departmental Routine Notes. *Annual Report of the Archaeological Survey of India 1923–24*: 136–44.

———. 1923–4b. Exploration and Research. *Annual Report of the Archaeological Survey of India 1923–24*: 1–87.

———. 1923–4c. Harappa and Mohenjodaro Introductory. *Annual Report of the Archaeological Survey of India 1923–24*: 47–51.

———. 1924a. First Light on a Long-Forgotten Civilization: New Discoveries of an Unknown Prehistoric Past in India. *The Illustrated London News*, 20 September, pp. 428–32 and 548.

———. 1924b. History Revised: New Light on Ancient India, *The Statesman*, 19 November, pp. 6 and 8.

———. 1939. The Story of the Archaeological Department in India, in J. Cummings, ed. *Revealing India's Past.* London: The India Society, pp. 1–33.

———. 1951. Reprint 1975. *Taxila: An Illustrated Account of Archaeological Excavations carried out at Taxila under the Orders of the Government of India between the Years 1913 and 1914*, three volumes. Delhi: Motilal Banarsidass.

———. and A. Foucher, 1940. Reprint 1983. *Sanchi,* three volumes. Delhi: Swati Publications.

———. and D.R. Sahni, 1909–10. Excavations at Mandor. *Annual Report of the Archaeological Survey of India 1909–10*: 93–103.

———. and J.Ph. Vogel, 1902–3. Excavations at Charsada in the Frontier Provinces. *Annual Report of the Archaeological Survey of India 1902–3*: 141–84.

Masson, C. 1842. Reprint 1974. *Narrative of Various Journeys in Balochistan, Afghanistan and the Punjab*, three volumes. Karachi: Oxford University Press.

Mehta, U.S. 1999. *Liberalism and Empire: A Study in Nineteenth Century British Liberal Thought*. Chicago: University of Chicago Press.

Mitter, P. 1977. *Much Maligned Monsters.* Oxford: Clarendon Press.

Mockler, E. 1877. On Ruins in Makran. *Journal of the Royal Asiatic Society* 9: 121–34.

Mughal, M.R. 1982. Recent Archaeological Research in the Cholistan Desert, in G.L. Possehl, ed. *Harappan Civilization: A Contemporary Perspective*. New Delhi: Oxford & IBH Publishing Co., pp. 85–95.

Mukhopadhyay, A.K. 1979. Ramendrasundar Tribedi, in A.K. Mukhopadhyay, ed. *The Bengali Intellectual Tradition from Rammohun Roy to Dhirendranath Sen.* Calcutta: K.P. Bagchi & Company, pp. 174–97.

Nair, P.T. 1999. *James Prinsep: Life and Work.* Calcutta: Firma KLM Private Ltd.

Nahata, B.L. 1986. Da. Lui P.Tessitori ka patra Sahitya, in *Sanyukta Rajasthan Da. L.P. Tessitori Shradhanjali Anka* (November): 20–46.

Oertel, F.O. 1904–5. Excavations at Sarnath. *Annual Report of the Archaeological Survey of India 1904–5*: 59–104.

Possehl, G. 1999. *Indus Age The Beginnings.* New Delhi: Oxford & IBH Publishing Co. Pvt. Ltd.

Poddar, A. 1977. *Renaissance in Bengal: Search for Identity*. Simla: Indian Institute of Advanced Study.

Rahman, M., ed. 1981–2. A.K. Maitra Number. *Journal of the Varendra Research Museum* 1981–2.

Rai, M. 2004. *Hindu Rulers, Muslim Subjects: Islam, Rights and the History of Kashmir*. New Delhi: Permanent Black.

Raleigh, T., ed. 1906. *Lord Curzon in India: Being a Selection of His Speeches as Viceroy and Governor-General of India 1898–1905*, volume 2. London: Macmillan & Co. Ltd.

Rapson, E.J., ed., 1921. Reprint 1951. *The Cambridge History of India Volume I: Ancient India*. Delhi: S. Chand & Co.

Rajan, K. 2002. Maritime Trade in Early Historic Tamil Nadu. *Man and Environment* XXVII (1): 83–98.

Renfrew, C. and P. Bahn. 1991. *Archaeology: Theories Methods and Practice*. London: Thames and Hudson.

Roy, S. 1953. Indian Archaeology from Jones to Marshall (1784–1902). *Ancient India* 9: 4–28.

Ronaldshay, Earl of. 1928. *The Life of Lord Curzon*, two volumes. London: Ernest Benn Ltd.

Sarkar, S. 1983. Reprint 1999. *Modern India 1885–1947*. Delhi: Macmillan India Ltd.

Sastri, H. 1944. *Archaeology and Ancient History*. Baroda: Gujarat Vernacular Society.

Shastri, H.P. 1916. *Baudha Gana O Doha*. Calcutta: Vangiya Sahitya Parishat series.

Sahni, D.R. 1906–7. Notes in the Gorakhpur and Saran Districts. *Annual Report of the Archaeological Survey of India 1906–7*: 193–205.

———. 1907–8a. Benares Inscription of Pantha. *Epigraphia Indica* IX: 59–62.

———. 1907–8b. Excavations at Rampurva. *Annual Report of the Archaeological Survey of India 1907–8*: 181–8.

———. 1907–8c. Saheth. *Annual Report of the Archaeological Survey of India 1907–8*: 17–30.

———. 1908–9. A Buddhist Image Inscription from Sravasti. *Annual Report of the Archaeological Survey of India 1908–9*: 133–8.

———. 1911–12. Saheth–Maheth Plate of Govindachandra. *Epigraphia Indica* XI: 20–6.

———. 1913–14. Excavations at Avantipura. *Annual Report of the Archaeological Survey of India 1913–14*: 40–62.

———. 1915–16. Pre-Muhammadan Monuments of Kashmir. *Annual Report of the Archaeological Survey of India 1915–16*: 49–78.

———. 1917. *Annual Progress Report of the Superintendent, Hindu and Buddhist Monuments, Northern Circle for the Year ending 31st March 1917*. Lahore: Superintendent, Government Printing.

———. and J.Ph. Vogel, 1914. *Catalogue of the Museum of Archaeology at Sarnath*. Calcutta: Superintendent, Government Printing.

Saini, K.G. 1988. The Economic Aspect of India's Participation in the First World War, in D.C. Ellinwood and S.D. Pradhan, eds. *India and World War I*. New Delhi: Manohar, pp. 141–76.

Sayce, A.H. 1924. Remarkable Discoveries in India. *The Illustrated London News*, 27 September: 525.

Schwab. R. 1984. *The Oriental Renaissance: Europe's Rediscovery of India and the East 1680–1880*. New York: Columbia University Press.

Singh, U. 2001. Amaravati: The Dismembering of the Mahacaitya (1797–1886). *South Asian Studies* 17: 19–40.

———. 2004. *The Discovery of Ancient India: Early Archaeologists and the Beginnings of Archaeology*. New Delhi: Permanent Black.

Smith,V.A. 1889. Graeco-Roman Influence on the Civilization of India. *Journal of the Asiatic Society of Bengal* 58: 107–98.

Spilsbury, Dr 1835. Note Regarding the Bhilsa Monument. *Journal of the Asiatic Society of Bengal IV*: XVII.

Spooner, D.B. 1912–13. Mr Ratan Tata's Excavations at Pataliputra. *Annual Report of the Archaeological Survey of India 1912–13*: 53–86.

———. 1917–18. Annual Report of the Director-General of Archaeology for the Year 1917–18. *Annual Report of the Archaeological Survey of India 1917–18*: 1–39.

Stephen, C. 1876. Reprint undated. *The Archaeology and Monumental Remains of Delhi*. New Delhi: Ashish Publishing House.

Tessitori, L.P. 1912. The Ramacharitamanas and the Ramayana. *The Indian Antiquary* XLI: 273–86.

———. 1913a. The Ramacharitamanasa and the Ramayana. *The Indian Antiquary* XLII: 1–18.

———. 1913b. Paramajotistotra: An Old Braja Metrical Version of Siddha-senadivakara's Kalyanamandirastotra. *Indian Antiquary* XLII: 42–6.

———. 1913c. Two Jaina Versions of the Story of Solomon's Judgment in Gujarati and Jaipuri. *Indian Antiquary* XLII: 148–52.

———. 1914a. Notes on the Grammar of the Old Western Rajasthani with Special Reference to Apabhramca and to Gujarati and Marvari. *Indian Antiquary* XLIII: 21–6, 55–64, 84–91, 181–6, 213–16, 225–8, 245–52.

———. 1914b. A Scheme for the Bardic and Historical Survey of Rajputana. *Journal and Proceedings of the Asiatic Society of Bengal*, New Series X: 373–410.

———. 1916a. Notes on the Grammar of the Old Western Rajasthani with Special Reference to Apabhramca and to Gujarati and Marvari Part II. *Indian Antiquary* XLV: 6–7, 93–9.

———. 1916b. A Progress Report on the Preliminary Work done during the Year 1915 in Connection with the Proposed Bardic and Historical Survey of Rajputana. *Journal and Proceedings of the Asiatic Society of Bengal*, New Series XII (1–6): 57–116.

———. 1917. *Vijaya Dharma Suri: A Jain Acharya of the Present Day*. Bhavnagar: Shri Vriddhichandraji Jain Sabha.

———. 1919. A Progress Report on the Work done during the Year 1917 in Connection with the Bardic and Historical Survey of Rajputana. *Journal and Proceedings of the Asiatic Society of Bengal*, New Series XV (1): 5–79.

———. 1920. A Progress Report on the Work done during the Year 1918 in Connection with the Bardic and Historical Survey of Rajputana. *Journal and Proceedings of the Asiatic Society of Bengal*, New Series XVI: 251– 79.

Tod, J. 1832. Reprint 1957. *Annals and Antiquities of Rajasthan or, the Central and Western Rajpoot States of India*, volume II. London: Routledge and Kegan Paul Ltd.

*The Amrita Bazar Patrika.* 1924. A Word to the Archaeological Department: 3.

*The Morning Post.* 1915. Knighthoods. 1 January.

*The Statesman* 1924a. Forgotten Civilization Discovered in India, 23 November: 19 and & 23.

———. 1924b. Sind Antiquities Lord Lytton's Inspection at Indian Museum, 14 December: 12.

*The Times.* 1923a. Ancient Cities of Sind. 25 June.

*The Times.* 1923b. To the Editor of the Times. 29 June.

Thomas, G. 1981. *History of Photography: India 1840–1980.* Pondicherry: Andhra Pradesh State Akademi of Photography.

Thomson, S.H. 1963. *Europe in Renaissance and Reformation.* London: Rupert Hart-Davis.

Tucci, G. 1954. Marco Polo. *East and West*, Year v, no. 1 (April): 5–14.

Vallauri, M. 1952. Jain Studies in Italy. *East and West*, Year III, no. 2 (July): 108–11.

Vats, M.S. 1925–6. Unpublished Votive Inscriptions in the Chaitya Cave at Karle. *Epigraphia Indica 18*: 325–9.

Vogel, J.Ph. 1907–8. Excavations at Saheth–Maheth. *Annual Report of the Archaeological Survey of India 1907–8*: 81–131.

———. 1908–9. The Garuda Pillar of Besnagar. *Annual Report of the Archaeological Survey of India 1908–9*: 126–9.

———. 1909–10a. The Mathura School of Sculpture. *Annual Report of the Archaeological Survey of India 1909–10*: 63–79.

———. 1909–10b. Annual Report of the Director-General of Archaeology for the Year 1909–10, Part I. *Annual Report of the Archaeological Survey of India 1909–10*: 1–10.

———. 1911–12. Explorations at Mathura. *Annual Report of the Archaeological Survey of India 1911–12*: 120–33.

———. 1913–14. Report on the Archaeological Section of the Indian Museum (Part I). *Annual Report of the Archaeological Survey of India 1913–14:* 46–8.

Winternitz M. 1988. *A History of Indian Literature*, volume II. Delhi: Motilal Banarsidass.

Wolpert, S. 1967. *Morley and India 1906–1910.* Berkeley and Los Angeles: University of California Press.

Yazdani, G. 1930–55. *Ajanta*, four volumes. Oxford: Oxford University Press.

———. 1947. *Bidar: Its History and Monuments*. Oxford: Oxford University Press.

———. 1966. *Early History of the Deccan*. Oxford: Oxford University Press.

Zeigler, N.P. 1976. Marvari Historical Chronicles: Sources for the Social and Cultural History of Rajasthan. *Indian Economic and Social History Review* 13 (2): 219–50.

## DISSERTATIONS

Abbi, V. 2000. The Evolution of the Cities and Shrines of Taxila: An Archaeological Perspective. M.Phil. dissertation of the Department of History, University of Delhi.

Kashyap, J. 2001. Archaeological Conservation 1861–88. M.Phil. dissertation of the Department of History, University of Delhi.

## UNPUBLISHED MANUSCRIPT

Marshall, M. Undated manuscript. Retirement and After. Typed copy.

# AFTERWORD TO THE NEW CENTENARY EDITION, 2024

It is now nearly twenty years since this book on the discovery of the Indus Civilization appeared. Looking back, what do I see in the text of it as first published in 2005? What has been my own journey of enquiry around the history of Indus research since then? This Afterword traces some of the issues that have figured in my work on India's first cities since that time, extending as well as modifying perspectives that featured in the 2005 edition.

Re-reading the book now, I am relieved to see a broad accuracy in the original telling of my story of how India's first cities were discovered – which can be said to have begun nearly two centuries ago, from 1831 when Charles Masson first chanced upon the brick ruins of Harappa, to the announcement in 1924 of a 'long-forgotten civilization' on the plains of the Indus. Told over thirteen chapters, the book's narrative was written around a range of characters – British archaeologists like Alexander Cunningham and John Marshall; Indian archaeologists such as Daya Ram Sahni and Rakhaldas Banerji; and an Italian linguist-turned-archaeologist, Luigi Pio Tessitori. It was a story with unexpected loops and twirls that had till then remained untold, inchoate and consigned in the oblivion of a vast and unearthed archive – mainly the files of the Archaeological Survey of India

(ASI). None of the protagonists in this story had published memoirs that could be mined, though luckily for me they had all survived suffocation in the files of the ASI and other archaeological institutions, in government offices, and in correspondence of all kinds. (It would not have been stretching things to title my book *Finding Forgotten Files.*)

Having got the main story across, I see now that what I also could have transmitted but had not were ideas which had fascinated me – and still do – about the relationship of personality to history. I had not, for example, placed the little known saga of how the Indus cities were unearthed into a broader perspective encompassing other watershed moments of discovery. If, for instance, we pause to examine some of the insights that have emerged from innovations in science and technology, qualities specific to the Indus discovery become more clearly apparent.

## ARE ARCHAEOLOGICAL DISCOVERIES LIKE SCIENTIFIC DISCOVERIES?

How do great discoveries take place and what can we learn by juxtaposing the 1924 discovery of the Indus civilization with them? I became interested in the process of scientific discoveries and practices in order to understand if an archaeological tale of discovery shares features with other such histories. One common element that struck me was the idea of 'the slow hunch', vividly captured in Steven Johnson's bestseller, *Where Good Ideas Come From*. The pathways through which fuzzy intuitions can develop into big ideas are well described in this work.[1] Among its case studies is one that focuses on Joseph Priestley who, in deciding to seal a sprig of mint in glass (to prove that plants create oxygen), was building upon an insight that went back to his boyhood. The young Priestley had apparently trapped spiders in glass jars in the

[1] Johnson (2010).

belief that 'there was something that was interesting in the way that organisms perished when you sealed them in closed vessels, something that pointed to the larger truth.'[2] He kept this macabre hunch alive at the back of his mind and his remorseless persecution of spiders eventually yielded fruit – some two decades after he began pondering the fate of creepy crawlies in sealed containers.

Priestley's slow-burn build-up around an early inkling appears to me strongly reminiscent of John Marshall's sense of the possibility of pushing back the antiquity of India – an idea that incubated in his mind some twenty-two years. He came to India as Director General of the Archaeological Survey of India in 1902. His preparations for work in India included an examination of many objects of Indian origin in England, including three British Museum seals from Harappa inscribed in an unknown script.[3] These seals took nearly a quarter of a century to flower as the discovery of an entire civilization – a classic case of the slow hunch being worth nursing. Here was an archaeologist who had since the early 1900s intuited an unknown archaeological canvas preceding what was then thought of as the subcontinent's historical past, a 'precognition' that spurred him into a team-building exercise that eventually yielded an immense harvest. Some of this is discussed in my chapter on Marshall's early years in India (Chapter 3).

But there was more to it. An instance of Marshall's need to follow up on his sixth sense about the archaeological remnants of an undiscovered past is evident, for example, in work that he deputed to Hirananda Sastri in 1903. Sastri was the 'Pundit in charge' of the ASI's office in Punjab. He was sent to survey three sites in the Ganga–Yamuna Doab which had yielded copper objects in the form of hoards. Marshall saw the copper hoard objects found there as possibly belonging to an age of bronze; and information about an Indian 'Bronze Age' could, he believed, be correlated

[2] Ibid.: 78.
[3] See p. 42 of this book.

with what was at the time termed the Early Vedic Age. Today, such copper hoards are considered roughly contemporary with Harappan times; a century ago their age was a mystery. It continued so because nothing was unearthed by Sastri that allowed Marshall to specifically suggest archaeological scaffolding for a very ancient cultural phenomenon.

Yet it is obvious that, as early as 1903, the prism through which Marshall viewed the Indian past was one that accommodated such a notion. When I first wrote about the field work done on Marshall's orders, I had not expanded the canvas to reveal how gradual clarity – in this case about a literate 'Bronze Age' – was also the hallmark of several scientific breakthroughs and innovations. At the same time, in this case the slow pace was partly a consequence of the constraints within which field research was done in British India, where non-commercial departments worked on very small budgets. Marshall himself was keen to excavate Harappa as early as 1907, but the price for acquiring the mounds was beyond the budget of the ASI.[4] Soon after, in fact, the Indian government, to cut down spending, recommended abolishing a number of posts, including that of the Director General of Archaeology.[5] Marshall's job was eventually saved after an active campaign in England spearheaded by two former Indian viceroys, Lord Curzon and the fourth Earl of Minto. Marshall returned to India, and to his old job, in 1912. His hunch about Harappa and its intriguing seals had been waylaid by something as mundane and frustrating as budgetary constraints.

Circumstances unrelated to archaeology that put Harappa's excavation on a back burner are also discernible in other directions. In 1914 a senior officer of the ASI, Harold Hargreaves, prepared a report on Harappa in which, though unimpressed by its mounds, he still recommended that they be excavated.[6] Following this

[4] Ibid.: 94ff.

[5] This is discussed in detail from 100ff., ibid.

[6] Ibid.: 141–7 and 197–8.

report Marshall asked the civil authorities in Montgomery District, where Harappa was located, to arrange with the landowners for a temporary occupation of their fields so that excavations could begin in the subsequent year. But they could not begin: now, it was the start of the Great War that resulted in a moratorium on new excavations, the financial crunch being exacerbated by manpower shortages.

Thus, in reflecting on the discovery of the Indus Civilization in relation to the trajectory of scientific breakthroughs, and exploring whether it was similar or different, the answer would be that it was a little of both. Like some major scientific discoveries, the Indus discovery was long in the making in Marshall's mind, but the dilatory follow-up was also a consequence of unavoidable material circumstances specific to the discovery.

Moving on to the years when Harappa and Mohenjodaro first came to be excavated, my book revealed that the clues which eventually led to the knowledge that these represented India's first civilization were neither discovered by a single solitary scholar nor were found all at once. Kuhn's 1962 classic *The Structure of Scientific Revolutions* and his paper of the same year on the historical structure of scientific discovery have long established the idea of a paradigm shift and demolished the earlier notion of discoveries as unitary occurrences that can be isolated and attributed to a particular person, place, and event.[7] As he put it, 'There is no single moment or day which the historian, however, complete his data, can identify as the point at which the discovery was made. Often, when several individuals are involved, it is even impossible unequivocally to identify any of them as the discoverer.' This insight helps us understand Marshall's long suspicion of Harappa's early antiquity. The suspicion worked as a baton – it was handed over to Daya Ram Sahni, the archaeologist who actually found the evidence for an early culture at Harappa in

[7] See Kuhn (1962a) and Kuhn (1962b): 761.

a dig he conducted there in 1921. It also needs to be appreciated that an analogous process unfolded in Mohenjodaro, on which there was neither a slow hunch nor any kind of precognition that an excavation which began there in December 1922 would yield dramatic evidence. Mohenjodaro's unearthing, unlike the Harappa excavations, had nothing to do with Marshall's planning. For many years Rakhaldas Banerji, who headed the Western Circle of the ASI, had been keen to excavate it, believing it an important Buddhist site; when he went off to dig it up in the winter of 1922 he conceived of the emergence of a Buddhist Mohenjodaro.[8] Naturally, he began concentrating on the stupa site that dominated the ruins and it was there that his assistant, N.S. Chikte, made the momentous discovery of two inscribed seals. Banerji realized immediately that these were inscribed with characters similar to those on the Harappa seals. Mohenjodaro, though, was several hundred kilometres to the south-west of Harappa, which meant that Harappa was not a unique or autonomous site; and this then, by extension, meant that what was being revealed was an entire distinctive culture spread over a considerable region. It was for this reason that Banerji, who found and recognized in Mohenjodaro seals of the Harappan type, would always be considered an important protagonist in the story of the Indus discovery.

In the world of science it is fairly commonplace to speak of the initial discovery as more or less synonymous with a chance finding or unexpected occurrence. This is certainly true of Banerji's discovery at Mohenjodaro. But a lot depends on the discoverer's capacity for following up on an unexpected revelation. This necessary follow-up process has been well documented by Kevin Dunbar in his description of scientists involved in experimental work. He shows them initially building experiments which frequently capture unknown and unexpected processes. They then attend to the results, to giving explanations, and to supporting

[8] Described in ch. 10 of this book, 'Maverick at Mohenjodaro'.

them with analogies of very similar results obtained in other experiments. Then, if unexpected results continue despite changes in methodology, they form new models and theories. This is always done after passing a threshold in unexpected findings.[9]

If this kind of process is juxtaposed with matters as they unfolded after the discovery of the Mohenjodaro seals, it is evident that Banerji was hesitant to visualize a new framework on the basis of what had emerged. His search for its cultural connections eventually boiled down to finding a place for the seal makers within the early spread of races. This approach had much in common with the views of British historians working on India who constantly used a paradigm in which India's ancient past was marked by races and civilizations coming into India.[10] It was also one that was unlikely to lead to a better understanding of the significance of Mohenjodaro.

Beyond individuals, there is an important institutional lacuna in the Archaeological Survey worth pointing out. The organisation had no space for discussing ongoing research. This differs from the situation that normally prevails among experimental scientists, where laboratory meetings are common and thought extremely essential. Dunbar stresses the importance of such interactions since they constitute the arena where data are presented, where scientists suggest new experiments, and where they reason with each other about their findings. One of the consequences of this is that it leads from the particular to the general, allowing researchers frequently to persuade each other to consider alternative representations and explanations for data that is being examined or a theory being opposed.

By contrast, the colonial ASI shows no institutional space for brainstorming, no "common room" for archaeologists to discuss their digs and share information about each other's field work.

[9] Dunbar (1999); also Klahr and Simon (2001).

[10] See 288–9 of this book.

It is unlikely, for instance, that Sahni and Banerji ever visited Harappa and Mohenjodaro together, or that they discussed their findings. Mostly, what seems to have been common to them was the intermediary figure of Marshall, to whom they addressed their letters and queries. As for Marshall himself, even after learning about the discovery of the Mohenjodaro seals in March 1923, he took his time coming to grips with the new evidence. In April that year he left for England on a long-planned furlough. When he returned to India he visited neither Mohenjodaro nor Harappa and instead proceeded to Taxila, the city he had excavated for over two decades. In this he was following a routine to which he had religiously adhered since he began digging there. At the same time, Marshall knew that, by any standards, the field season of 1923–4 was an unusual one: it was on his instructions that Harappa and Mohenjodaro were being trenched in quick succession. It seems nearly incomprehensible, then, for him not to have broken his routine in order to obtain a first-hand glimpse of the digs he had ordered. Perhaps this has to be seen as being perfectly in character since he tended to be resolutely focused on tasks that needed to be finished, but the fact remains that had he been less rigidly disciplined about his own priorities the discovery of the Indus Civilization would have unfolded sooner than the autumn of 1924.

Since Marshall had not seen the sites for himself and his subordinates had no forum for discussions that could have led to a fresh perspective on the newly discovered evidence, what exactly alerted Marshall to their singularity? The answer lies in a letter that a junior officer, Madho Sarup Vats, wrote to him: the letter seems to have pushed him to get to grips with the enigma of Mohenjodaro and Harappa. In April 1924 Vats had just completed a four-week season of excavation at Mohenjodaro. In his letter to Marshall he pointed out similarities between the two cities. The resemblance in the seals apart, Vats pointed to likenesses in flint scrapers, terracotta figurines, sling balls, earthen bangles, and even in the size of bricks. Upon receiving this letter Marshall assembled his archaeologists and the excavated material in his Simla head office: it was the first formal occasion for those involved in the discoveries to meet.

That the free flow of ideas and opinions is an imperative in discovery contexts was borne out by what followed Marshall's announcement on the Indus Civilization. Several scholarly British readers of the *Illustrated London News* on 20 September 1924 reacted instantaneously.[11] Among these was a linguist, Archibald Henry Sayce, who dashed off a note which appeared in the news magazine on 27 September, suggesting that the Indus finds were even more remarkable and startling than Marshall had supposed. This was because Marshall's dating, though provisional, had not envisaged a historicity extending beyond the first millennium BCE, whereas Sayce pointed out that seals of the Indus type had been discovered at Susa (in present-day Iran) in a context dated to the third millennium BCE. 'It is evident,' said Sayce, 'that as far back as the third millennium BCE, there was intercourse between Susa and [the] North-West of India.' The discovery, he argued, 'opens up a new historical vista, and is likely to revolutionize our ideas of the age and origin of the Indian civilization.' The reception of new knowledge in London on Indus materials, having circulated among scholars with experience of ancient scripts and sites in Asia, confirms the importance of making information accessible to all who might add nuance or new dimensions to it.[12]

## DISCOVERIES AND DISAGREEMENTS AT MOHENJODARO AND HARAPPA

*Finding Forgotten Cities* (2005) ended with the beginning of the first phase of work that was followed by the announcement of the discovery in the *Illustrated London News* of 20 September 1924.

[11] Sayce (1924): 525.

[12] I am here repeating my basic argument in Lahiri (2017).

Consequently, the first edition did not encompass the large-scale excavations of the ensuing years, the findings of which were later incorporated into excavation reports on the two city sites. The first set of volumes on Mohenjodaro appeared in 1931 while the Harappa excavation report was published in 1940. In both instances the results published were distilled accounts, though much archaeological and architectural data also appears there: chapters on the site and its excavated localities, on antiquities and artefacts, and on the scientific analysis of objects. There are narrative descriptions accompanied by a large number of photographs and line drawings of buildings and streets, bones and beads, pottery and metal objects, remnants of food practices, seals and amulets, and a great deal more. These are publications that continue to be used by scholars interested in India's antiquity because they provide a fascinating window into the splendid character of those ancient cities across a substantial chunk of time. You could be forgiven for thinking that everything that needs to be known about those digs is contained in these volumes.

*Almost* everything worth knowing would be more accurate. This is because there are little-known facts hidden in the archives relating to the 1920s digs that offer information qualitatively different from what is available in the published tomes. Unlike the publications, file notes and correspondence relating to the early excavations were generated as the work progressed. These capture the flavour of the digs and the character of the personalities involved. Also, since the nature and uses of newly unearthed objects and structures were still being unravelled, the assumptions in these sources are more tentative and provisional than in the publications. A few such archival nuggets that I came upon in the course of research, which highlight the character of the excavations, seem worth outlining.

After the 1924 announcement Marshall delayed playing a role in the field; in fact, as we saw, he first visited the sites only in early 1925 and, most oddly, his detailed instructions on how the digging there should proceed were issued even before he visited the sites. He explained to K.N. Dikshit at Mohenjodaro and Daya Ram Sahni at Harappa how trenching should be done. They were asked to

> carry out a network of trial trenches at say 50 or 75 yards apart over the whole site, some running north and south and some east and west. Simultaneously, you should sink trial pits and trenches at various points down to the virgin soil so as to ascertain what strata exist beneath the surface. When this is done, you will be in a better position to decide how to prosecute your works further.[13]

The idea of sinking trenches right down to virgin soil was to get a clear idea of the stratification. As the trench went down, pottery specimens for every two feet were to be put in separate bags.[14]

Sahni and Dikshit, for their part, had begun questioning Marshall's use of the term 'Indo-Sumerian'. Sahni constantly asked Marshall about possible Sumerian parallels for designs and objects found at his site – for the terracotta coiled snake at Harappa, and for the pipal tree engraved on a seal found by Dikshit at Mohenjodaro. On finding a large shell spoon at Harappa, Sahni informed Marshall of the use of something similar in Hindu rituals: 'In Sanskrit this is called Argha and is used to this day by orthodox Hindus in their morning and evening worship for pouring out water in honour of gods and for the purification of the manes. Gifts of land, gold, etc. to Brahmans are also marked by such libations. This is a very ancient institution with the Hindus and is frequently referred to in Sanskrit literature and inscriptions.'[15] Sahni also says that while libations in scenes of

[13] Marshall's letters to Sahni and Dikshit, dated 28 November 1924, no. 839 (General) of 1924–5. Unless otherwise specified, files mentioned hereafter in the footnotes are from the Archaeological Survey of India file room (these have since been transferred, I am told, to the National Archives of India).

[14] Marshall's letter to Sahni, dated 30 December 1924, no. 839 (General) of 1924–5.

[15] Sahni's letter to Marshall dated January 1925, no. 839 of 1920–35. In

worship were engraved on Sumerian tablets, spouted jars were in evidence but not the Indian argha. Dikshit broadly echoed Sahni's sentiments and, among other things, saw an essential difference in the way in which the earliest Sumerian writing was arranged – with pictographs in perpendicular columns, whereas the Indian seals showed linear writing going left to right. From his perspective, the idea of the Indus and Sumerian sites being organically related needed more thought because 'a careful comparison of the products of early Indian civilization with those of the Sumerian will probably bring out more points of difference than similarity.'[16]

Marshall agreed with Dikshit's observation and eventually the term 'Indo-Sumerian' was dropped.[17] In a note for a small exhibition organized by the Archaeological Department in 1927, Marshall wrote that owing

> to its close connection with the Sumerian civilization of Mesopotamia, this prehistoric civilization of Sind and the Punjab has hitherto been designated by the name 'Indo-Sumerian'. With the progress of exploration, however, it has become evident that this connection was due not to actual identity of culture, but to intimate commercial or other intercourse between two countries. For this reason the term Indo-Sumerian has now been discarded, and the single word 'Indus' adopted in its place.[18]

By this time Marshall had also seen for himself certain features at both Mohenjodaro and Harappa which were uniquely Indian. In the same note, he spoke of various rings and phallus-like objects

---

fact, Hindu elements in Indus contexts were later pointed out by others. Images of 'Pasupati' thrilled Stein, who identified 'Shiva's bull' in the terracotta figures from sites in Baluchistan. Stein's letter to Mackay, dated 15 July 1929, MSS Eur. D526, File No. 10l/P/K/26, Oriental and India Office Collections (OIOC), British Library (BL).

[16] Dikshit's letter to Marshall, dated 11 June 1925, no. 839 of 1920–35.

[17] Marshall's letter to Dikshit, dated 18 June 1925, no. 839 of 1920–35.

[18] Marshall's note of 1926–7 in no. 738 of 1929.

that had been found in various sizes within the Indus cities – some of these objects were no more than an inch in diameter, while others were so 'large that two men can scarcely lift them'. He added in his description that it was a plausible hypothesis

> but nothing more than a hypothesis at present – that the rings are symbolical of the yoni and the chessmen-like objects of the linga – the worship of which goes back to a very remote age in India; but whatever their symbolism, it seems clear from their ubiquitousness at Harappa and Mohenjo-daro, that the cult was a very popular one.[19]

This subcontinental distinctiveness of the Indus phenomenon subsequently showcased in the publications was, as these letters and note reveal, a consequence of insights offered by Sahni and Dikshit.

A few months after the discovery of the Indus Civilization was announced, Marshall made up his mind to assume charge of the Mohenjodaro excavations. He assumed correctly that, unlike the depredations that the Harappa mounds had suffered, Mohenjodaro was fairly intact. His assessment was based entirely on photographs of the Archaeological Survey that he had seen, as much as on what the sites had yielded. Having still not visited them, he asked the government to put him on special duty there and explained his reasons for wanting to concentrate in particular on the ruins in Sindh:

> Assuming that for the next five years the funds available for this excavation did not exceed a lakh per annum and that I am not permitted to enlist outside help from other countries, the most that I can hope to do is to lay bare the principal public buildings and domestic architecture and antiquities of the city of Mohenjo Daro and at the same time to make a superficial examination of some other city sites. By concentrating our energies on Mohenjo Daro, I consider that I shall be serving the cause of archaeology better than by dividing our

[19] Ibid.

forces up over three or four sites, since I shall be able to restore from it a fairly complete picture of the social life of the Indo-Sumerian people 5000 years ago which I may say parenthetically appears to have attained a far higher degree of luxury and comfort than was enjoyed by the peoples of Egypt or Mesopotamia of the same age.[20]

Before starting his campaign at Mohenjodaro, though, Marshall wanted to proceed abroad. As he conceived it, the tour would involve visits across continents – to Mesopotamia for a study of the sites being excavated there; to Greece for whether analogies could be traced between the Aegean and the 'Indo-Sumerian culture'; to France, England, and America to study the Sumerian collections there.[21] Greece was certainly in his sights because his archaeological career had begun there with Mediterranean civilizational remains, and it was logical for him to refresh his memories of them now that he was presiding over the discovery of even earlier remains in India. He admitted as much to the anthropologist A.M. Hocart: 'I have long missed the pre-historic work on which I first started out in the Mediterranean region, and it will be quite thrilling now to be dealing with a civilization as old as that of Babylonia and Egypt.'[22] The issue of Near Eastern parallels with the Indus cities was of course equally crucial and needed to be understood; and Marshall, more than anyone else, realized that India's archaeologists – himself included – were unfamiliar with that world. He felt hampered by not having a first-hand feel of Near Eastern collections and sites and so suggested that he be put on an enabling deputation.[23] He pointed to the fact that the campaign of exploration in Sindh, Baluchistan, and Punjab

[20] Marshall's letter to Secretary to the Government of India, Department of Education, Health and Lands, no. 864, 1920–35.

[21] Marshall's letter to Secretary, Department of E.H. and Lands, dated 11 November 1924, no. 609 of 1920–5.

[22] Marshall's letter to A.M. Hocart, dated 18 December 1924, no. 656 of 1923.

[23] Marshall's letter, dated 23 March, to Secretary, Department of E.H. and Lands, no. 839 of 1920–35.

required not only wide 'experience of Indian conditions but an intimate familiarity with the earliest cultures of neighbouring countries to the West, particularly of Mesopotamia and Persia.'

As it happened, Marshall was denied permission to leave in the spring of 1925 – he could go only in the following year. He then decided to proceed to Mohenjodaro with the purpose of taking over the reins there. It was the only season of work that he directed at this Indus city, and he conducted it on a grand scale. Unlike earlier seasons, when officers had had to be under canvas, the field camp at Mohenjodaro offered the comfort of a bungalow and other buildings. At its busiest time, between 1000 and 1200 labourers were employed there – men, women, and children. It was an enormous force, much larger than had been employed at Harappa in early 1925.[24] Sahni had had only 250 coolies on a daily basis when engaged in Harappan excavations in January 1925.[25] There was, however, no excavation at Harappa in the field season of 1925–6 – which ran from April 1925 to March 1926 – since all hands were required for the Mohenjodaro work.

Local labour at Mohenjodaro was supplemented by workers brought in from elsewhere. The rates of pay depended upon domicile, gender, and age. Child labour was common; local labourers were paid at a per day rate of 11 annas for adults, and 8 annas for women and children. For those who came from Karachi, the men were paid at 14 annas, the women 11 annas, and children 8 annas.[26] Many of the labourers were from the north-west region. *The Times of India* described this workforce:

> At its head is the Director-General of Archaeology, as its members it has a cosmopolitan family of Sindhis, Balochis, and Pathans; and

[24] Some Rs 20,000 was spent in the first three seasons of work. Sahni's note, dated 14 January 1930, no. 877-G of 1928–30.

[25] Sahni's letter to Marshall, dated 8 January 1925, no. 839 of 1920–35.

[26] Marshall's letter to Cadell (Commissioner in Sind), dated 10 December 1925, no. 839 of 1925.

> for its territory it boasts a thousand acres of rolling mounds and prickly scrub. All day long, from early morn to the set of sun, the thousand inhabitants of this strange settlement spend their time digging with picks and spades and shovels and knives. Yet, though they are diggers, they are neither gardeners nor farmers – they are in actuality makers of history or perhaps it would be more accurate to say that they are discoverers of history. For this happy family of diggers are making these lonely monotonous sands of Sind tell the tale of their past, reveal what civilisations they once sustained, and disclose what manner of people once trod their dusty ways.[27]

Empathetic accounts of labouring life are not to be found in archaeological publications, so it is nice to get a newspaper's report vividly capturing what visitors would have encountered in this remote and sandy space.

The team that oversaw the excavation was also unprecedented in its size because of archaeologists, scholar-supervisors, and ordinary supervisors all working together. There were actually four teams at Mohenjodaro. Alongside Marshall there were K.N. Puri, J.K. Ray, N.G. Majumdar, and B.L. Dhama. Three others were a draftsman, a photographer, and a librarian, Q.M. Moneer. A second team was led by Hargreaves, who had a photographer, overseer, and draftsman, along with Philip C.R. Jayasuriya from Ceylon. With Vats in the third team was another scholar from Ceylon, N. Paranavitane, who like Jayasuriya was at Mohenjodaro as an Indian Scholarship holder. Paranavitane was, at this point in time, a teacher in the Education Department; he later became the most distinguished archaeologist and epigraphist of his generation in his country. Vats was joined, additionally, by a draftsman, a pandit, a photographer, and a draftsman-photographer. Finally, there was K.N. Dikshit with a team that included two draftsmen, a photographer, and a PWD overseer. Dikshit, though, could not complete the full season there. On 26 February 1926 he suddenly left camp, being on the point of collapse. Reaching Poona he

[27] *The Times of India* (1926): 7.

was diagnosed as suffering from diabetes. Mohenjodaro had an enervating effect on others as well. Marshall himself, in the last ten days of the season, was asked by the Civil Surgeon to rest for several days at Lahore or risk hospitalization. Unsurprisingly, Marshall described the place as infernal.[28]

Very soon, the scale of the excavations made some in Sindh suspect that precious treasures were being unearthed and salted out of the country. The *Larkana Gazette* of 18 January 1926 speaks of the costly and beautiful articles found there being sent to London, and added: 'We cannot say how far this report is correct, but in view of the rumours afloat, we would request the authorities to enlighten the public as regards their intentions in the matter.'[29] It asked that a list of all articles discovered be prepared and published with a press note 'so that people may derive pleasure from reading an account of the past history of the land of their birth.' At the request of the Commissioner in Sindh, Marshall had an explanatory note inserted in the *Times of India* to remove misconceptions.[30] The Director General was quoted saying that 'all the antiquities which India wants from Mohenjo Daro will be retained in this country. If any are eventually presented to the British Museum they will only be in the nature of duplicates.' The correspondent who wrote the article had just visited the ancient city and vouched for the existence of enough duplicates – pottery, seals, and various trinkets – to serve as specimens in a dozen museums.

On site, even as rare objects and antiquities were being unearthed, officers and scholars overseeing the excavations disagreed on their dates, and sometimes even about what they were.

[28] The infernal character of the place and the health issues facing his staff are from Marshall's letter to Blakiston, dated 4 March 1926, no. 864 of 1920–35.

[29] Translation of the Larkana Gazette article, dated 18 January 1927, in no. 839, vol. IV of 1925.

[30] Marshall's letter to Cadell, dated 13 February 1926, no. 839, vol. IV of 1925.

One class of such objects, described now as 'bearded male sculptures', has become part of a small body of statuary. Hargreaves and the young Ceylonese scholar Jayasuriya, for instance, differed in their understanding of one of these statues found in the 'HR' area.[31] Jayasuriya believed the head was decidedly that of a woman:

> . . . the low receding forehead and the general shape of the face and head suggests a feminine appearance. The hair, too, is differently dressed to those of the other male figures (HR & DK) found during the seasons and is tied in a low knot at the back of the head . . . The outline of the chin is well-marked and very feminine-like, in spite of the fact that it is hidden by a beard. As a matter of fact, if the beard of this head is covered up, there is not a single feature which will give it a masculine character.[32]

In a footnote to his typed report he noted that the 'showing of the beard may be purely conventional or ornamental; the custom of wearing mock-beards by women on certain occasions was an ancient custom in Egypt and Assyria. Perhaps the same custom prevailed here.' On the other hand, this same figure was concluded by Hargreaves to be the head of a man, which is how it has since been described.[33]

Identifications immediately offered in the first flush of excavations could be way off the mark – including Marshall's. His interpretation of what is now known as the 'Great Bath' is an example of impulsive notions proven wrong after a period of reflection. In an article that appeared in March 1926 Marshall was reported as having described the structure as a '5,000 year old

[31] 'HR' refers to the principal excavator of one area, Harold Hargreaves; 'DK', mentioned later, refers to the principal excavator Dikshit, who supervised another part of the site.

[32] Jayasuriya's report on the archaeological excavations at Mohenjo-Daro, Site HR, Season December 1925–February 1926, no. 136 of 1935.

[33] Mackay (1931): 359.

palace'.[34] The palace perhaps included, said the article, a swimming pool:

> Among the many discoveries which are being made by the Archaeological Department at Mohenjodaro there is one of uncommon interest. In one of the more important buildings – probably a palace – which Sir John Marshall is excavating, is a hall measuring 40 feet by 24 feet and sunk about 8 feet below the level of the surrounding galleries and apartments . . . double walls of burnt brick . . . finished chiselled bricks . . . lining of asphalt . . . What the sunk hall was used for, has not been determined. Conceivably it was a swimming bath.[35]

The large structures and the palace that Marshall had found in historic Taxila seem to have been swimming in his head.[36] Later, he perceived that the Mohenjodaro buildings were rooms around a considerable bath, and that it was not a private but a public bathing site. Excavations, by their very nature, tend to reveal the past slowly, after the range of material exposed has been carefully digested and understood.

There were also major disagreements over the human remains unearthed in the city. Marshall did not agree with the dating of a series of skeletons that Hargreaves had dug out in his area: he had found fourteen skeletons in a single room (Room 74 of House V) and was of the view that they belonged to a period that followed

[34] Marshall's article, dated 2nd March 1926 sent to the editors, *The Times of India*, Bombay, *The Statesman*, Calcutta, and *The Pioneer*, Allahabad, no. 839, vol. IV of 1925.

[35] *The Times of India* (1926): 7.

[36] Marshall (1915–16): 15. This is from the Annual Report of the ASI. Marshall noted that 'my trial trenches are bringing to light the remains of another substantially built and apparently very extensive structure, which to judge by the proportions of the walls and courts so far exposed, will probably be found to vie in size with the complex of buildings on the other side of the street, which I have tentatively designated the palace.'

the abandonment of the city. Marshall, however, did not think this was a proven fact and thought it quite likely that they belonged to the interval between the Intermediate I and Late III periods – these being the strata largely within the range of the civilisational phase. Their two varying interpretations continue into the published report on the excavation, though by the time of its publication. Marshall seems to have been willing to consider the possibility of the skeletons belonging to a period when the city was under strain.

The need to requisition the services of professionals other than archaeologists in the field dawned on the excavation team rather slowly. No such specialists were present during the 1925–6 season and their absence had an adverse impact on the results. The skeletal remains excavated in the HR area, for instance, were not studied on the spot by a Physical Anthropology specialist. This led to problems of all kinds. When the first skeleton (No. 1) was found, Hargreaves was not at the site and his instructions were not being followed:

> On arrival at the site early in the morning of 18th December 1925, I discovered some human bones in a basket and learnt these came from behind the wall north of the two flights of steps. These bones were femur 2, tibia 2, fibula 2, bones of the foot 12, vertebra 1. The removal of these bones was directly contrary to orders but this had been done by the workmen of one of the three gangs employed for the first time the day before and was due to insufficient supervision.[37]

The sloppiness of the work is clear from the fact that a missing upper part of the skeleton was chanced upon subsequently in the very area where its lower segments had earlier been unearthed.

[37] Typed copy of Hargreaves' Report entitled 'Description of the Buildings Excavated on Site HR, Mohenjodaro 1925–26', no. 136 of 1935.

The HR area skeletons were also measured in a rather laughably odd way. Apparently the archaeologists had no measuring instruments with which to correctly measure bones. So it was left to a young Indian Camp Medical Officer to measure them as best he could using an ordinary tape measure. These measurements were eventually published in the Mohenjodaro Report, in a chapter on the city's human remains contributed by R.B.S. Sewell (Director General of the Zoological Survey of India) and B.S. Guha (later the first Director of the Anthropological Survey of India). No wonder, then, that Hargreaves was of the view that there ought to have been an anthropologist on the spot to deal with the human remains as each was found, especially as he foresaw his team finding many more skeletons.[38]

All the bones were sent for analysis from Mohenjodaro to the Zoological Survey of India's head office in Calcutta. By the time these fragile goods reached their destination they were in a pathetic state. A combination of inadequate packing, faulty railway handling, and poor pre-packing treatment had degraded them considerably. A letter by Sewell captures their state and his rage.[39] He says the skulls were covered with so much paraffin wax that a single specimen required a fortnight's scraping before it was in a fit state to be examined. Other bones came in untreated. Long bones, such as of thighs, had merely been wrapped in newspaper and packed along with many others and put in a box. These had consequently splintered into such small fragments that they could not be reassembled. Sewell's fury may have hit home because later, in early 1927, when another series of skeletons were excavated at Mohenjodaro, a telegram was immediately sent to him asking him to arrive. It took Sewell some weeks to obey the summons since he was by this time far removed from the

[38] Hargreaves' letter to Marshall, dated 9 July 1926, no. 136 of 1935.

[39] Sewell's letter to Superintendent, Frontier Circle, dated 4 May 1926, no. 839 (General) of 1920.

excavations.[40] By the time he reached the bones had crumbled badly.

While the 1925–6 season was marked by large-scale excavations at Mohenjodaro, it ended with the realization that such work could not be sustained in the long run by requisitioning the services of Survey staff from other Circles, or by getting just the Survey librarian to help out: it was essential that more staff be hired. So Marshall asked for additional assistant superintendents, three excavation assistants, a photographer, and a draftsman. Additionally, he requested that the services of a Sumerian expert be sought – someone familiar with antiquities from south Mesopotamia who would recognize such objects if they happened to be found in Mohenjodaro. By the end of the season Marshall had also come to the realize that he himself could not continue personally in charge of such a sustained excavation exercise. As the head of a large institution, his services could not be restricted to a single field for such a long period of time.

The archaeologist E.J.H. Mackay was Marshall's chosen sucessor for the Mohenjodaro excavations. Mackay had experience in the Near East: forty-six years of age, he came with some twenty-five years of digging experience in Mesopotamia, Egypt, and Palestine. The renowned Flinders Petrie himself had trained Mackay in Egypt, and during the First World War Mackay had served as Custodian of Antiquities in Palestine while serving in the army.[41] Later, Mackay was field director of the Field Museum–Oxford University Archaeological Expedition to Mesopotamia, where he excavated Jamdat Nasr and the Sumerian site of Kish.

On 18 November 1926 Mackay was appointed to the post of Assistant Superintendent. The formal designation was overriden by his experience and age: his salary was far above what was usually paid to officers at that level. He received Rs 1000 per month

[40] Telegram, dated 5 February 1927, to Major Sewell, no. 839 (General) 1920–35.

[41] This paragraph is based on Possehl 1999: 77.

as well as an overseas pay of £ 30 per month.[42] His appointment resulted in a barrage of questions in the monsoon session of the Legislative Assembly in 1927. One Indian political luminary, Kumar Ganganand Sinha, wanted to know if the post had been advertised and applications received from Indians. The reply to his query stated that the post had not been advertised because 'For the conduct of excavations at Mohenjo Daro a practical excavator with an intimate knowledge of Mesopotamian antiquities was required' and no Indian archaeologist possessed such qualifications.[43] Other legislators wanted more information: Hari Singh Gaur wondered how the government had come to the conclusion that there was no qualified Indian when they had not, in the first instance, advertised the post.[44] There were also questions about how, in the entire world outside India theoretically open to applicants, Mackay had been assessed as best qualified for the job. Marshall stated the reasons for Mackay's appointment in a long and admirably sensible note which I have reproduced in full below:

> The discovery of Mohenjo-daro and Harappa six years ago opened up an entirely new field of research for Indian archaeology. We found ourselves in the presence of a vast and unsuspected civilization – a branch, as we believed, of the great chalcolithic civilization of Asia, Egypt and Eastern Europe, but a branch of which we knew literally nothing. The chalcolithic civilization of the East had been explored and studied by archaeologists in many other countries: in Mesopotamia, Persia, Syria, Transcaspia, Egypt, etc., but Indian archaeolo-

[42] The reasoning was explained in a telegram from the Secretary of State for India, dated 19th August 1926, Education Proceedings Nos 27–40 of February 1927.This also stated that the recommendation was made 'on the understanding that he will be appointed substantively after a year's satisfactory service as if he had been in the 17th year of service on the term scale.'

[43] For the question and reply, 1 September 1927, *Legislative Assembly Debates*, 1927 (IV), First Session of the Third Legislative Assembly, 3806.

[44] Replies to Assembly and Council questions in no. 609 of 1927–8.

gists had no practical experience of it. In my own Department, I was the only man who had studied any branch of it at close quarters, and that was nearly thirty years ago in Greece and Crete. Since the excavations at Mohenjo-daro were started four of my best Indian officers have been engaged on them. In very case the result has been the same. The actual work of digging they have done as well as could be wished; but their observation has been defective; their inferences unscientific; and their reports not worth the paper they were written on. Had I allowed them to be published, they would have brought the greatest discredit on us all.

In 1925 I determined to take personal charge of the operations, and set about initiating as many of my officers as I could into the new sphere of exploration, but by the end of the season, I realized that it would be impracticable for me to find time to continue in personal charge of the work, and that if it was to be done efficiently, I must get a qualified expert from the Nearer East. It was not essential that he should come from Mesopotamia, but it was essential that he should be expert in the chalcolithic culture of the East, and if someone could be found familiar with Sumerian antiquities. The appointment of Mr Mackay (of whom I had heard much in Egypt and Syria, but with whom I was not previously acquainted) has more than justified itself. He is streets ahead of any of us in this particular branch of archaeology, but if anyone can establish it on a sound scientific basis in this country he can. To talk of Indians being found outside my Department to do Mr Mackay's job, is sheer nonsense. There is no one who knows anything about the subject. And to talk of sending students to learn the job in Europe and elsewhere, is equally fatuous. If it were a new industry – say, the manufacture of artificial silk – in this country, the first thing we should do is to get an expert out from home to set the industry going. That is precisely what we have done in this case; and it is the only sensible course. For surely it is better to bring an expert and let him train up his staff on the spot than to spend our money in sending the staff abroad for five years or more, and in the time keep our operations here indefinitely suspended. I say five years as a minimum period; as a fact it would take any of my officers twenty years to acquire Mr Mackay's experience.[45]

It would likely have been difficult for even the most cussedly bureaucratic legislator to counter the persuasive logic of Marshall's reasoning.

## DEPARTURE OF THE MOHENJODARO MAN

In the field seasons across Punjab, Sindh, and Baluchistan that followed the discovery of the Indus Civilization, the man who came to be known as "Mohenjodaro Man", Rakhaldas Banerji, was entirely missing from the archaeological scene of action. This was a somewhat stark instance of absence since Banerji was such a key person in the whole scenario – it was he who had dug through the mounds and first penetrated the heart of an Indus city in Sindh in the winter of 1922–3.

In trying to understand his absence, I felt initially that it was perhaps because Banerji was superintendent of the Eastern Circle of the Survey, far removed from the north-west Indus area. He had been transferred there in 1923 at his own request, not long after he had created a financial mess during the setting up of the archaeological wing of the Prince of Wales Museum in Bombay.[46] In the year that the big excavations at Mohenjodaro began he had worked on the ruins of Paharpur in the Rajshahi District (now in Bangladesh). In October that year he went off to the Central Circle of the Archaeological Survey in the vicinity of Jabalpur. While correcting the proofs of his forthcoming work on the Haihaya rulers of Tripuri, he needed to cross-check epigraphs and images and had been granted permission by Marshall to visit Bhedaghat, not far from Jabalpur. This was where the Chausath Yogini/Jogini Temple, which contained many idols and epigraphs, was located; Banerji revisited it in October 1925.

[45] Marshall's note in no. 609 of 1927–8.

[46] Lahiri (2005): 268–71.

The temple Banerji went to was a famous Hindu shrine known for its female idols, primarily those of yoginis, alongside others – such as an image (more properly stone idol) of the Buddhist goddess Tara. I now know that it was this Tara image, and what happened with it, that cut short Banerji's career in the Archaeological Survey of India. For during his visit to the temple in 1925 the Tara image was taken out and made to disappear. Banerji came to be implicated in what was seen as akin to, or a development out of, colonial temple looting.[47]

Papers relevant to the case are contained in a printed confidential file of 1927 with the subject line showing 'Removal from service of Mr R.D. Banerji, Superintendent of Archaeological Survey, Eastern Circle, in connection with the theft of a stone image belonging to the Chausat Jogni temple at Bheraghat in the Central Provinces.'[48] From these papers we learn what happened to Banerji in 1925–6 and the extraordinary circumstances under which he subsequently departed from the ASI.[49] To make sense of the train of events culminating in his dismissal involves much going back and forth, but the timeline – from the removal of the image to Banerji's sacking – can be extracted from the letters and notings, court orders and police reports, available in the case files.

It all began on 18 October 1925 when Rakhaldas Banerji, accompanied by two office peons, Basu Deo and Madhav Das, along with two local labourers, Alfoo and Mankia Dhimar, arrived at the temple. In the presence that afternoon of the temple priest, Bala Prashad, the Tara image was carried down by Mankia Dhimar to the Bhedaghat Circuit House that Banerji was using, with Banerji's peon escorting the object. The *pujari* raised no objec-

[47] For a fine new account of temple looting in colonial India, see Sutton (2024).

[48] This is an Education File of the Department of Education, Health and lands (A) in the National Archives of India, Nos 1–42.

[49] This has also been discussed in Pande (2016): 36–47. Pande's assessment is that Banerji's punishment in this case was undeserved.

tion to the idol's removal since it was done on the orders of the archaeological staff.[50] He did not even inform his own superior, the temple's *mahant*, Jagjiwanpuri, of the extraction. The *mahant* only discovered the fact several days later, when an official – a *tahsildar* from Jabalpur – arrived at Bhedaghat to enquire if the *mahant* had any objection to the Tara image from the Chausath Yogini Temple being sent to the Nagpur Museum. It was at this point that the *pujari* informed the *mahant* of the image having been taken away a few days earlier.

The *pujari* later explained to the police the circumstances in which the idol was removed: it had happened in his presence.[51] On 18 October 1925, at about 8.30 a.m., when Bala Prashad was worshipping the 'God Gourishankar' (the temple's central deity), 'Mankia Dhimar, Alfoo s/o Sheikh Gafoor Mohammad the servant of Fagoo Baboo at the Soap stone quarry, and one Indian Sahib with English dress and hat on arrived at the Gourishankar Temple with one peon. That Indian Sahib began to look at the temple here and there.' The Indian Sahib was Banerji, the peon was Basu Deo. After the *pujari* had finished his worship, he asked Alfoo how long Banerji and his party expected to remain. He was told they would be around for more than half the day, till about 2.30 in the afternoon. The priest then 'handed over the keys of the temple to Alfoo' and went off to the Panchamatha Temple for worship – that being a part of his priestly duties as well. When he returned in the afternoon he found five men present, four of whom he had met that morning, and the fifth, a photographer, Sailendra Mohan Ghosh, taking photographs of the images. What the priest then noted is crucial:

[50] This paragraph is based on the order of H.A.R. Dewey, 1st Class Magistrate, that was decided on 2 September 1926, Department of Education, Health and Lands (A), nos 1–42.

[51] Statement of Bala Prasad, along with other statements was attached to the memorandum, dated 12 March 1926, from the Deputy Commissioner, Jabalpur, to the Commissioner, Jabalpur Division.

> The Sahib talked something in English with his camp clerk and returned to the Bungalow. Afterwards the camp clerk carried the image of 'Tara Debi' (Goddess Tara) on the head of Manik Dhimar to Upper Dak Bungalow. At the time of carrying the image, I, Manik, Alfoo and the camp clerk in all 4 men were there. I came with the image up to the house of the Mahant and then I went to the Bakhri (the house of the Mahant). All the 3 went to the Upper Dak Bungalow.

His decision not to inform the *mahant* had to do with what had transpired less than a week earlier when

> one Hindustani Sahib had come. He slept on top of the Gourishankar temple. I had stopped him from sleeping there. Upon this the Mahant had directed me not to interfere with the officers. Therefore I did not tell the Mahant at the same time about the carrying of the image. I thought that on some legal authority they have carried the image from there.

Since the Chausath Yogini Temple was a protected monument under the guardianship of the ASI, the *mahant* thought it necessary to treat government personnel with discretion and not risk annoying them with questions.

After the idol's removal from the temple by the staff associated with Banerji, it was brought to the Bhedaghat bungalow from where it was soon transferred to the car in which Banerji travelled to Jabalpur. Thereafter, eventually, the Bhedaghat Tara reached Calcutta.

In Jabalpur, soon after Banerji's departure, once the disappearance of the deity had been discovered, the *mahant* made an application on 29 October to the Deputy Commissioner of Jabalpur, asking that it be returned. The assumption at this point seems to have been that a government officer had removed the image, probably for purposes to do with his own work, and should now be asked to return what he had taken. A letter was therefore dispatched to Banerji on 5 November asking if he had indeed taken away the image, and to return it if he had. Banerji wrote back on 17 November to say no image had been taken away from Bhedaghat by him or by any member of his staff.[52]

It was at this point that the *mahant* insisted on further enquiry; consequently, police investigations began. Witnesses – from the labourers to the cook at the bungalow to the car driver – were examined and their statements recorded. The police submitted a report to the Deputy Commissioner of Jabalpur several months later. This official, after examining the papers, was of the opinion that the witness statements left 'no doubt that Mr Banerji did remove the image.'[53] Criminal proceedings were ordered, a case of theft registered, and a formal enquiry begun on 12 May 1926.

Banerji himself was now in Darjeeling, but at some point soon after his absence from office the missing image appeared in Calcutta where it was said to have been found by Manas (alias Manesh) Kumar Mukherji, a nephew of Banerji's wife. This nephew also happened to serve as the officiating head clerk in the Survey office of his uncle-in-law Rakhaldas.

The files also contain information on how the mystery of the missing image was 'solved'. After the formal criminal investigation began, Banerji was asked to travel to Jabalpur along with those who had accompanied him on his fateful work trip. This was to enable the police to question them and have Banerji identified by witnesses who had seen him during his visit to Bhedaghat in October 1925. Banerji was formally intimated of the urgency of reaching Jabalpur by J.F. Blakiston, officiating as

[52] Detailed report on Police case at Jabalpur by Banerji, dated 12 July 1926. In it Banerji noted that 'The Deputy Commissioner, Jubbulpore, wrote to me in the middle of November asking me to return the image. I had no knowledge of the fact that any image had been brought away and therefore I wrote to him on the 17th November that no image had been brought away by me or any of my staff.'

[53] Copy of the memorandum from the Deputy Commissioner to the Commissioner, dated 12 March 1926.

director general in place of Marshall. Upon receiving Blakiston's order, Banerji immediately started out from Darjeeling – and on reaching Calcutta found that the idol had been brought to his house.[54]

How the idol arrived at Banerji's residence was, as he put it, a consequence of a request that he had earlier made to his nephew. Apparently, in March 1926 Banerji had been told that a case of theft was being instituted against him at Jabalpur. It was then that he had asked his nephew to employ 'agents' to search out the image.[55] Banerji left for Darjeeling at the end of April 1926, and before long, *voila*, his nephew informed him an old idol answering to the description he had sent had been spotted in Calcutta. In Banerji's account, this was a red stone image found by one of Manas Mukherji's agents

> near the temple of Sitaladevi in Northern Calcutta. It was being worshipped there for the last 3 or 4 months by an Oriya Brahmin whose description closely resembles that of Basudev Panda but the man had vanished after seeing Manas Kumar. I wrote to Manas Kumar immediately to purchase or to get hold of this image by any means.[56]

Before he could receive a reply from the nephew, Blakiston's orders reached Banerji, and he departed Darjeeling for Calcutta. This, in sum, is Banerji's version of the events that transpired in the first half of 1926.

Naturally, the matter could not simply end with Banerji re-

[54] Detailed report on Police Case at Jabalpur by Banerji, dated 12 July 1926. As he put it, on 5 June he found 'that one female image of red stone exactly similar to the red stone of the Kaimur range had been brought to my house. The 5th was a gazetted holiday and therefore I could not inform anybody and so I started the same evening for Jubbulpor with the image.'

[55] Detailed report on Police Case at Jabalpur by Banerji, dated 12 July 1926.

[56] Ibid.

turning the Tara idol to the police in Jabalpur: he was now the subject of a criminal investigation. A police team was sent to Calcutta in early July 1926 to examine the witnesses Banerji had mentioned in his statement, and to trace the peon who was said to have packed the image and placed it in Banerji's car. Basu Deo, the peon, was no longer in service and could not be traced, but Banerji's wife's nephew was questioned by Mohammad Mujtaba Khan, the sub-inspector from Jabalpur, who also interrogated several other witnesses and submitted a detailed report.[57]

The sub-inspector's assessment was that several of the witnesses had been 'engineered' by Banerji's wife's nephew – by which he probably meant they had been tutored. The place where the idol was said to have been found was a busy one with a lot of human traffic around it. When Khan questioned people who lived in the neighbourhood, 'none of them stated that there was any image at the place pointed out by Manesh and his witnesses', nor had they seen anyone keeping it for the purpose of worship.

Banerji was suspended from service on 16 August 1926. When the case came up in court, however, the magistrate said he had no jurisdiction to try it because the local government had not given him the required sanction to proceed. His order did, however, record an inference from the facts before him – that the 'accused stole the idol from the temple and is punishable under Section 379 of the Indian Penal Code.'

The government then decided to hold a departmental inquiry into the allegations, and in March 1927 a commission was set up consisting of the Director General of Archaeology, John Marshall, and the Deputy Commissioner of Jabalpur, A. McDonald. Charges against Banerji were framed and a litany of witnesses examined. Banerji was present during the inquiry and was permitted to be represented by two counsels – one A.K. Basu, Government Pleader, Calcutta, and a Mr Pasley, Bar-at-Law.

[57] The report is dated 14 July 1926 and is under the title 'Result'.

The inquiry's report said it was difficult to believe that the removal of Tara had been carried out entirely without Mr Banerji's knowledge. There were strong circumstantial grounds for such a surmise: the image had been removed from the temple in the middle of the day and carried down to the dak bungalow; it had been kept unwrapped on the front verandah of the dak bungalow at Bhedaghat

> for at least an hour, probably more, and Mr Banerji was in a room opening on to this verandah. Again, the image was packed by the peon in the back of the car where Mr Banerji sat on his return journey to Jubbulpore. It is difficult to believe that the peon Vasu Deo would have had the boldness to act in this way, if Mr Banerji had no knowledge of the image being removed.[58]

Moreover, the 'image' was a large stone idol some 22″ × 11″ in size, and as such could scarcely have been invisible to Banerji in either the verandah or the car. It was thus more than reasonable to assert that Banerji could not but have been aware of its several movements.

As if this were insufficient humiliation, a further charge was laid against Banerji. This was that he had

> surrendered or caused to be surrendered the said idol or image with an explanation to the effect that the image was probably taken away without his knowledge by a certain peon serving under him, which explanation he either knew or believed to be false or did not believe to be true.

With regard to the image having been found by Banerji's wife's nephew and thereafter carried back by Banerji to Jabalpur,

[58] Letter from John Marshall, dated 8 March 1927, to the Education Department, submitting the report of the board appointed to enquire into the conduct of R.D. Banerji (together with a written statement by the defence, evidence of witnesses, and other papers).

the board said they were unconvinced by the statements that the missing image had been seen at Panchudhovani Galli near Sitla Tala in north Calcutta in March and again in May, where it was said to have been in the charge of an 'Uria' (Oriya). The suggestion of the defence team – that this Oriya Brahmin was the peon Basu Deo – was doubtful because 'the evidence on this point' was 'very vague' and had in any case little bearing on the issue.

A point raised by Banerji's legal team concerned their client's innocence on the grounds that he had himself found the image: 'It was argued by the counsel for Mr Banerji that the production of the image by Mr Banerji was not necessary for his defence, in other words, that if he had guilty knowledge, he would rather have got rid of the image than have produced it.' The commission was not 'impressed by this theory, since it is equally arguable . . . that finding so much importance was attached to the image, he hoped that, when it was produced by him, further proceedings would be dropped.' All the same, in a criminal case the threshold of proof required is very high: it is absolute proof alone that clinches matters, so that when looking at the chain of circumstantial evidence the commission's report had little option but to conclude that 'while there is little doubt that Mr Banerji knew of the removal of the image from Bheraghat, the evidence brought before us does not amount to absolute proof.'

The matter then moved from the stage of inquiry to the disciplinary action to be taken against Banerji. This entailed a body called the Public Service Commission having to examine the matter. After reviewing the circumstances of the case and the charges against Banerji, it appears that this exalted commission was not satisfied with the departmental inquiry's report – except that its lack of satisfaction was with the pusillanimity of the report rather than anything in it that tended to absolve Banerji. Stating that it would 'rather go further than the Commission of Enquiry' with regard to the charges, this next level of investigation provided a detailed reasoning for its assessment, reproduced below in full:

> The image was removed quite openly by the peon Basudev. There is evidence that it lay for some time uncovered in the verandah of the bungalow in which Mr Banerji was staying, and it was conveyed from Bheraghat in the motor car in which Mr Banerji travelled. The circumstances raise a strong presumption that Mr Banerji was aware of the removal of the image, since it is difficult to believe either that he did not see the image at one of these stages in its removal or that the peon would have dared to proceed in this open manner if he had not been acting with Mr Banerji's knowledge. The evidence recorded by the Police regarding the subsequent recovery of the image is equally significant. Mr Banerji ultimately restored the image himself, and it is clear that the burden of proving how it came into his possession lay upon him. This burden, the Public Service Commission consider, he entirely failed to discharge. His story was that the image was found in a frequented part of Calcutta by his nephew, Mr M.K. Mukerji. Four persons were produced before the police, two of whom were related to each other, and none of whom were of any standing, who stated that they had seen the image of Panchu dhawani Galli in Calcutta. Against their evidence is the fact that 18 persons resident in the locality had never seen it, one of whom lived in the shop to which the image was alleged to have been removed for safe keeping. In brief, the whole story of the recovery of the image is so improbable that the Commission have no hesitation in rejecting it. They conclude therefore that the second and third charges against Mr Banerji are clearly proved.[59]

If Banerji was culpable, his possible motives in robbing the temple had to be considered to determine the disciplinary action against him. The image itself, the commission believed, did not

[59] Letter, dated 15 June 1927, from J.H. Wise, Secretary, Public Service Commission.

have much intrinsic value, although it was of archaeological interest; therefore Banerji was not likely to have made off with it for pecuniary interest. A more charitable theory which it considered was that since the image had archaeological interest, Banerji was zealously securing it for the Archaeological Department and 'ordered its removal without considering fully the irregularity of the course he was pursuing.' A third theory – which the commission described as more probable – was that the peon Basu Deo, who was also a *panda* (priest), may have wanted to 'derive some profit from it; and asked Banerji to allow him to remove it', and Banerji consented without attaching much importance to the matter. Without pronouncing with any finality on Banerji's motive, the commission said it seemed clear that 'when enquiries from Jubbulpore regarding the removal of the image' were made,

> Mr Banerji realized that he had done wrong in allowing it to be taken away, and afraid of getting into trouble, thought it best to deny all knowledge of its removal. At a later stage, when it was obvious that he was about to be prosecuted for theft, he became thoroughly frightened and thought the wisest course was to return the image, hoping that, if it were restored to the temple, the proceedings would be dropped. He consequently fabricated a story to account for its recovery.

The commission thus had no hesitation in disbelieving the defence's argument about Banerji's actions.[60]

The motive, though, had still to be decided on to arrive at a decision on the disciplinary punishment. At this point the commission decided to take a view about Banerji's actions which, as they put it, was the most favourable possible for him. They ruled that he was not prompted by dishonest intention: 'His original action in allowing the image to be removed, while it was

[60] Ibid.

wholly irregular, did not necessarily involve moral turpitude, and his offence only assumed grave proportions when he sought to mislead his superior officers by a false account of the transaction.' They were also aware that Banerji had often suffered ill health, so when considering his dismissal a compassionate allowance was proposed. His pension, on the assumption that he had been retired for medical reasons, was halved; later, this was raised to two-thirds of the sum to which he would normally have been entitled. The raise was allowed when the case for Banerji's dismissal reached the office of the Secretary of State at the India Office in London. It was pointed out there that two-thirds of the normal pension had been granted to many offending officers whose crimes, though of a different nature, were no less serious than Banerji's.[61]

The circumstances of Mohenjodaro Man's departure were subsequently relegated to the archives. I have reconstructed what transpired through my discovery of the relevant files. The episode of Banerji's dismissal reminds us that his enormous talent could be marred by his astonishing proclivity to ignore the possible consequences of impulsive actions. Certainly, Banerji would have felt the dishonour of dismissal from the organization he had served for seventeen years hard to bear.

Luckily for him, the odium of his departure from the ASI did not adversely affect his career. Very quickly after, in 1928, he came to occupy a named chair – the Manindra Chandra Nandy professorship of Ancient Indian History and Culture at Banaras Hindu University. But the serious ill health that had dogged him cut short his tenure. He had to go on leave to get treatment in Calcutta, where he died on 23 May 1930, just forty-five years old. It was an unexpected end to a brilliant and controversial life.

[61] Confidential letter from the Secretary, Services and General Department, India Office, London, dated 25 August 1927.

Over the last couple of decades I have been able to engage with the themes outlined above because of my good luck in chancing upon new material on Indus sites in the archives. It is not, as I now see it, simply a matter of adding new data to old ideas. I have found my own views changed since I first wrote *Finding Forgotten Cities*. The world of scientific breakthroughs has made me recalibrate my understanding of how major advances unfold; consequently, I have come to place much value on situating archaeological discoveries within the world of technological leaps and innovations. This Afterword should I think be seen as both about what I did not know and what I had not sufficiently thought through when this book was first put together.

## REFERENCES

Dunbar, K. 1999. How Scientists Build Models: Invivo Science as a Model on the Scientific Mind, in L. Magnani, N. Nersessian, and P. Thagad ed. *Modelling Based Reasoning in Scientific Discovery*, pp. 89–98. New York: Plenum Press.

Johnson, S. 2010. *Where Good Ideas Come from – the Seven Patterns of Innovation*. London: Penguin Books.

Klahr, D. and H.A. Simson. 2001. What have psychologists (and others) discovered about the process of scientific discovery? *Current Directions in Psychological Science* 10 (3): 75–9.

Kuhn, T.S. 1962a (2012 edition). *The Structure of Scientific Revolutions*. Chicago: The University of Chicago Press.

———. 1962b. Historical Structure of Scientific Discovery. *Science, New Series* 136 (3518): 760–4.

Lahiri, N. 2005 (2015 edition). *Finding Forgotten Cities – How the Indus Civilization was Discovered*. Ranikhet: Permanent Black.

Marshall, J. 1931. *Mohenjo-Daro and the Indus Civilization*. Three volumes. London: Arthur Probsthain.

Pande, Y. 2016. *The Life and Works of Rakhaldas Banerji*. New Delhi: Rajesh Publications.

Possehl. G. 1999. *Indus Age – The Beginnings*. New Delhi: Oxford & IBH Publishing Co. Pvt. Ltd.

Sayce, A.H. 1924. Remarkable Discoveries in India. *The Illustrated London News,* 27 September: 525.

Sutton, Deborah. 2024. *Ruling Devotion: The Hindu Temple in the Colonial Imagination*. Ranikhet: Permanent Black.

*The Times of India*. 1926 (9 March). 5,000 year old palace, 7.

# INDEX